CITIZENSHIP AND NATIONHOOD
IN FRANCE AND GERMANY

CITIZENSHIP AND NATIONHOOD IN FRANCE AND GERMANY

Rogers Brubaker

HARVARD UNIVERSITY PRESS
CAMBRIDGE, MASSACHUSETTS
LONDON, ENGLAND

Library of Congress Cataloging in Publication Data

Brubaker, Rogers.
  Citizenship and nationhood in France and Germany / Rogers Brubaker.
    p. cm.
  Includes bibliographical references (p.) and index.
  ISBN 0-674-13177-0 (alk. paper) (cloth)
  ISBN 0-674-13178-9 (pbk.)
  1. Citizenship—France. 2. Naturalization—France. 3. Nationalism—France—History.
  4. Citizenship—Germany. 5. Naturalization—Germany. 6. Nationalism—
  Germany—History.
  I. Title.
JN2919.B78 1992
323.6′0944—dc20
91-42897
CIP

For Allan Silver

Contents

Preface

The state, wrote Aristotle in the *Politics*, is "a compound made up of citizens; and this compels us to consider who should properly be called a citizen and what a citizen really is. The nature of citizenship, like that of the state, is a question which is often disputed: there is no general agreement on a single definition: the man who is a citizen in a democracy is often not one in an oligarchy." Citizenship of the modern nation-state of course differs fundamentally from citizenship of the ancient Greek city-state. Yet Aristotle's observation has lost none of its pertinence today. We live in a world of bounded and exclusive citizenries. Every modern state identifies a particular set of persons as its citizens and defines all others as noncitizens, as aliens. Today this boundary between citizens and aliens is more important than ever. In a world united by dense networks of transportation and communication, but divided by widening economic, political, and demographic disparities, hundreds of millions of people would seek work, welfare, or security in prosperous and peaceful countries if they were free to do so. Yet because they are not citizens of such countries, they can be routinely and legitimately excluded.

Needless to say, this does not mean that noncitizens have no access to prosperous and peaceful countries. Various economic and political forces lead such countries to admit noncitizens—sometimes in large numbers—to their territories. Western Europe and North America have experienced a great surge in immigration in the last quarter-century. But this influx, large as it is, remains small in relation to the enormous global flows that would occur in a world without bounded citizenries. In a truly cosmopolitan world, as Henry Sidgwick noted a century ago in *Elements of Politics*, a state might "maintain order over [a] particular territory," but it would neither "determine who is to inhabit this territory" nor "restrict the enjoyment of its . . . advantages to any particular portion of the human race." In such a world, migration would assume unprecedented proportions.

In global perspective, citizenship is a powerful instrument of social closure, shielding prosperous states from the migrant poor. Citizenship is also an instrument of closure within states. Every state establishes a conceptual, legal, and ideological boundary between citizens and foreigners. Every state discriminates between citizens and resident foreigners, reserving certain rights and benefits, as well as certain obligations, for citizens. Every state claims to be the state of, and for, a particular, bounded citizenry, usually conceived as a nation. The modern nation-state is in this sense inherently nationalistic. Its legitimacy depends on its furthering, or seeming to further, the interests of a particular, bounded citizenry.

Yet if citizenship is necessarily bounded, the manner in which it is bounded varies widely from state to state. This book examines the bounds of citizenship in the two core nation-states of continental Europe. Vis-á-vis immigrants, the French citizenry is defined expansively, as a territorial community, the German citizenry—except in the special case of ethnic German immigrants—restrictively, as a community of descent. Birth and residence in France automatically transform second-generation immigrants into citizens; birth in the Federal Republic of Germany has no bearing on German citizenship. Naturalization policies, moreover, are more liberal in France than in Germany, and naturalization rates are four to five times higher. The overall rate of civic incorporation for immigrants is ten times higher in France than in Germany. The gap is even greater for second- and third-generation immigrants. A generation of young Franco-Portuguese, Franco-Algerians, and Franco-Moroccans is emerging, claiming and exercising the rights of French citizenship. In Germany, by contrast, more than one and a half million Turks—including more than 400,000 who were born in Germany—remain outside the community of citizens. Yet at the same time, newly arrived ethnic German immigrants from Eastern Europe and the Soviet Union—over a million in 1988–1991—are legally defined as Germans and automatically granted full civic and political rights.

This book seeks to explain this striking and consequential difference in forms of civic self-definition and patterns of civic incorporation. My approach is historical. Tracing the genesis and development of the institution of citizenship in France and Germany, I show how differing definitions of citizenship have been shaped and sustained by distinctive

and deeply rooted understandings of nationhood. French understandings of nationhood have been state-centered and assimilationist, German
understandings ethnocultural and "differentialist." I explain how these
distinctive national self-understandings were deeply rooted in political
and cultural geography; how they crystallized in the late nineteenth and
early twentieth century; and how they came to be embodied and expressed in sharply opposed definitions of citizenship.

More generally, the book seeks to illuminate the origins and workings
of national citizenship—that distinctively modern institution through
which every state constitutes and perpetually reconstitutes itself as an
association of citizens, publicly identifies a set of persons as its members,
and residually classifies everyone else in the world as a noncitizen, an
alien. The boundaries that divide the world's population into mutually
exclusive citizenries, unlike those that divide the earth's surface into
mutually exclusive state territories, have received little scholarly attention. Political sociology has treated the state as a territorial organization,
neglecting the fact that it is also a membership organization, an association of citizens. My book seeks to redress this territorial bias in the
study of the state through a sustained analysis of the genesis and
workings of the institution of citizenship.

Research for this study was generously supported by the Graduate
School of Arts and Sciences of Columbia University; the French Government's Bourse Chateaubriand; the Institute for the Study of World Politics, with funds provided by the Compton Foundation; and the Joint
Committee on Western Europe of the American Council of Learned
Societies and the Social Science Research Council, with funds provided
by the Ford Foundation, the William and Flora Hewlett Foundation, and
the French-American Foundation. The book was written at the Society
of Fellows of Harvard University, which provided a splendid gift of time
and the ideal setting for informal discussions of work-in-progress.

Numerous scholars here and abroad have been kind enough to provide suggestions and to comment on preliminary papers and individual
chapters. In France, I want to thank Vida Azimi, Pierre Bourdieu, Christian Bruschi, Jacqueline Costa-Lascoux, Riva Kastoryano, Jean Leca,
Remy Leveau, Antonio Perotti, Jean-Louis Schlegel, Jeanne Singer-Kerel,
Rudolf von Thadden, Patrick Weil, and Catherine de Wenden. Special
thanks are due François and Nicole Lajeunesse for their extended hospitality in Versailles, and Pablo Caravia and Catherine Morel for theirs
in Paris. I would also like to thank G. Oleknovitch, J. M. Bayle, A. C.

Decouflé, and Alain de Fleurieu of the Sous-Direction des Natural-isations of the Ministère des Affaires Sociales, and Suzel Anstett and Jocelyn Front of the Centre de Documentation of the Direction de la Population et des Migrations of the same ministry.

My research in Germany was greatly helped by Dietrich Thränhardt, who made available his extensive personal collection of materials on *Ausländerpolitik* as well as the facilities of the Institut für Politik-wissenschaft at the University of Münster. He and Amrei Thränhardt kindly offered extended hospitality in their Münster home, as did Reinhild Schulze-Temming in Berlin. Bernhard Schmidt, head of the staff of the Beauftragte der Bundesregierung für Ausländerfragen, was very helpful in providing material and arranging contacts in Bonn. I would also like to thank Uwe Anderson, Klaus Bade, Knuth Dohse, Jürgen Fijalkowski, Rolf Grawert, Klaus-Martin Groth, Jürgen Haberland, Kay Hailbronner, Lutz Hoffmann, Jürgen Kocka, Jürgen Puskeppeleit, and Peter Zimmerman.

In this country I am especially indebted to Mark Miller, who has supported this study from its earliest stages, generously sharing his own rich collection of French and German materials and suggesting Euro-pean contacts. Aristide Zolberg, whose work has given historical depth and global breadth to the study of international migrations, has also encouraged the project from its early stages. Loïc Wacquant provided exceptionally helpful detailed comments on the entire manuscript. At Harvard University Press, the book benefited from the expert advice of Lindsay Waters and Ann Louise McLaughlin. I would also like to thank Omer Bartov, Steve Brint, Craig Calhoun, Carlos Forment, Gary Free-man, Herbert Gans, Moshe Halbertal, Bill Heffernan, Barbara Schmitter Heisler, James Hollifield, Chip Kestnbaum, John Kleinig, Friedrich Kratochwil, László Neményi, Robert Paxton, Michael Pollak, Rosemarie Rogers, Guenther Roth, Joseph Rothschild, Peter Sahlins, Theda Skocpol, Fritz Stern, Myron Weiner, and Harrison White.

My greatest intellectual debt is to Allan Silver, whose detailed com-ments on successive versions of the manuscript occasioned much sub-stantive enrichment and innumerable stylistic improvements; my only regret is that too many of his suggestions remain unrealized.

Finally, I thank Zsuzsa Berend for her thoughtful criticisms of the manuscript, for her forbearance toward the author's overinvolvement in it, and, most of all, for joining him, at the midpoint of this project, in another, more important one.

CITIZENSHIP AND NATIONHOOD
IN FRANCE AND GERMANY

Introduction

Traditions of Nationhood in France and Germany

For two centuries, locked together in a fateful position at the center of state- and nation-building in Europe, France and Germany have been constructing, elaborating, and furnishing to other states distinctive, even antagonistic models of nationhood and national self-understanding. In the French tradition, the nation has been conceived in relation to the institutional and territorial frame of the state. Revolutionary and Republican definitions of nationhood and citizenship—unitarist, universalist, and secular—reinforced what was already in the ancien régime an essentially political understanding of nationhood. Yet while French nationhood is constituted by political unity, it is centrally expressed in the striving for cultural unity. Political inclusion has entailed cultural assimilation, for regional cultural minorities and immigrants alike.

If the French understanding of nationhood has been state-centered and assimilationist, the German understanding has been *Volk*-centered and differentialist. Since national feeling developed before the nation-state, the German idea of the nation was not originally political, nor was it linked to the abstract idea of citizenship. This prepolitical German nation, this nation in search of a state, was conceived not as the bearer of universal political values, but as an organic cultural, linguistic, or racial community—as an irreducibly particular *Volksgemeinschaft*. On this understanding, nationhood is an ethnocultural, not a political fact.

Comparisons between German and French understandings of nationhood go back, in their basic lines, to the early nineteenth century. They were first formulated by German intellectuals, who sought to distance themselves from the allegedly shallow rationalism and cosmopolitanism of the Enlightenment and the French Revolution through an historicist celebration of cultural particularism. Mid-nineteenth-century French intellectuals reversed the evaluative signs but preserved the substance of

1

the comparison, celebrating the crusading universalism of the French national tradition. Thus Michelet apostrophized France as a "glorious mother who is not ours alone and who must deliver every nation to liberty!"[1] New and more sharply antagonistic formulations were elicited by the Franco-Prussian War, particularly by the question of Alsace-Lorraine. While German scholars advanced an objectivist, ethnocultural claim to Alsace-Lorraine, based on the facts of language (in Treitschke's extreme version, the facts of "nature"), French intellectuals countered with a subjectivist, political argument emphasizing the will of the inhabitants. The French view found sublimated expression in the celebrated lecture of Ernest Renan, "Qu'est-ce qu'une nation?," the German view in Friedrich Meinecke's magisterial *Weltbürgertum und National-staat*. More detached comparative formulations have been provided by Hans Kohn, Theodor Schieder, Jenö Szücs, Anthony Smith, and others.[2]

In recent years, however, bipolar contrasts involving Germany, especially those pointing to a German "Sonderweg" (special road) to the modern world, have been much criticized. Such accounts, it is argued, measure German developments, minutely scrutinized for faults (in the geological and the moral sense) that might help explain the catastrophe of 1933–45, against an idealized version of "Western," that is, British, French, or American developments.[3] Only through the doubly distorting lens of such culpabilization on the one hand and idealization on the other, the argument continues, does the nineteenth-century German bourgeoisie appear "supine" next to its "heroic" French counterpart, the German party system deeply flawed by English standards, the "German conception of freedom" dangerously illiberal by comparison with the Anglo-American, German political culture fatally authoritarian in comparison with that of the "West" in general.

Comparisons of German and French conceptions of nationhood and forms of nationalism have not escaped indictment on this count.[4] The indictment is not without foundation. The temptation to treat differences of degree as differences of kind, differences of contextual expression as differences of inner principle, is endemic to bipolar comparison; it is heightened when the field of comparison is as historically and ideologically charged as it is here. To characterize French and German traditions of citizenship and nationhood in terms of such ready-made conceptual pairs as universalism and particularism, cosmopolitanism and ethnocentrism, Enlightenment rationalism and Romantic irrationalism, is to pass from characterization to caricature.

Yet if formulated in more nuanced fashion, the opposition between the French and German understandings of nationhood and forms of nationalism remains indispensable. I aim here to recover the analytical and explanatory potency of this distinction, by rescuing it from the status of the routine and complacent formula, ripe for criticism, that it had become. For the distinctive and deeply rooted French and German understandings of nationhood have remained surprisingly robust. Nowhere is this more striking than in the policies and politics of citizenship vis-à-vis immigrants. Even as Western Europe moves toward closer economic union, and perhaps towards political union, citizenship remains a bastion of national sovereignty. Even as the European Community, anticipating great migratory waves from the south and the east, seeks to establish a common immigration policy, definitions of citizenship continue to reflect deeply rooted understandings of nationhood. The state-centered, assimilationist understanding of nationhood in France is embodied and expressed in an expansive definition of citizenship, one that automatically transforms second-generation immigrants into citizens, assimilating them—legally—to other French men and women. The ethnocultural, differentialist understanding of nationhood in Germany is embodied and expressed in a definition of citizenship that is remarkably open to ethnic German immigrants from Eastern Europe and the Soviet Union, but remarkably closed to non-German immigrants.

State-Building and the Geography of Nationhood

The French nation-state was the product of centuries of state-building, and of the gradual development of national consciousness within the spatial and institutional frame of the developing territorial state.[5] The nation-state forged by Bismarck was also heir to long traditions of state-building and national consciousness, but the two traditions—one Prussian, one German—were radically distinct in territorial frame, social base, and political inspiration. The Prussian state tradition was not only subnational and, after the partitions of Poland, supranational, it was also in principle antinational; while German national consciousness developed outside and—when national consciousness became politicized—against the territorial and institutional frame of existing German states.

This is not to say that national consciousness had no political or institutional mooring in Germany. The medieval and early modern Empire—the Holy Roman Empire of the German Nation, as it came to be called, not without ambiguity, in the sixteenth century—was the institutional incubator of German national consciousness, analogous in this respect to the Capetian monarchy in France. But while nation and kingdom were conceptually fused in France, nation and supranational Empire were sharply distinct in Germany. And while the early consolidation and progressively increasing "stateness" of the French monarchy gradually formed and strengthened national consciousness, the Holy Roman Empire lost the attributes of statehood in the thirteenth century. Although it survived, with its increasingly rickety institutions, into the nineteenth century, it lacked the integrative power of a centralizing bureaucratic administration and failed to shape a firmly state-anchored national consciousness. German national consciousness was never purely cultural, purely apolitical; yet while it was linked to the memory and to the anticipation of effective political organization, it was for six centuries divorced from the reality. In France, then, a bureaucratic monarchy engendered a political and territorial conception of nationhood; while in Germany, the disparity in scale between supranational Empire and the subnational profusion of sovereign and semisovereign political units fostered the development of an ethnocultural understanding of nationhood.

The wider reach of territorial state-building in France than in Germany in turn reflects a deep difference in economic, cultural, and political geography between what Stein Rokkan and Derek Urwin have called monocephalic and polycephalic zones of Europe. Polycephalic Europe, a legacy of medieval overland trade patterns, consists of the broad north-south belt of closely spaced cities stretching from Italy to the North Sea and the Baltic, and running through the heart of western Germany. Here the density of cities and ecclesiastical principalities inhibited the early consolidation and expansion of territorial states. Large territorial states developed earlier on the fringes of this city belt, where contending centers (such as the Ile de France) faced less competition and enjoyed more room for expansion.[6]

The scale of political authority in early modern Central Europe, then, made it impossible to identify the German nation with the institutional and territorial frame of a state. In Germany the "conceived order" or "imagined community" of nationhood and the institutional realities of statehood were sharply distinct; in France they were fused.[7] In Germany nationhood was an ethnocultural fact; in France it was a political fact.

I am not suggesting that the sense of membership or "identity" was primarily ethnocultural in medieval or early modern Germany. To the extent that anachronistic talk of "identity" makes sense at all, the subjective "identity" of the vast majority of the population throughout Europe was no doubt largely local on the one hand and religious on the other until at least the end of the eighteenth century. For most inhabitants local and regional identities continued to be more salient than national identity until late in the nineteenth century.[8] The point is a structural, not a social-psychological one. The political and cultural geography of Central Europe made it possible to conceive of an ethnocultural Germany coinciding neither with the supranational pretensions of the Empire nor with the subnational reach of effective political authority. It was much more difficult to distinguish nation and state, and therefore to imagine a specifically ethnocultural nation, in France.

A second, closely related difference in patterns of national self-understanding is also rooted in political and cultural geography. The French understanding of nationhood has been assimilationist, the German understanding "differentialist." The gradual formation of the nation-state around a single political and cultural center in France was the historical matrix for an assimilationist self-understanding, while the conglomerative pattern of state-building in polycentric, biconfessional,[9] even (in Prussia) binational Germany was the historical matrix for a more differentialist self-understanding.[10] The vehicle for the concentric, assimilative expansion of nationhood in France was the gradually increasing penetration into the periphery of the instruments and networks of the central state (school, army, administration, and networks of transportation and communication).[11] In Germany, Prussia most closely approximates this model of the assimilationist state-nation. Yet it was the geopolitical fate of Prussia to become, in the late eighteenth century, a binational state; and Prussia failed to assimilate its large Polish population.[12] The French state did not fully assimilate Bretons, Basques, Corsicans, and Alsatians, but its failure was neither so complete, so evident by the turn of the century, nor so consequential for national self-understanding.

The ethnocultural frontier between Germans and Slavs, not only in eastern Prussia but throughout the zone of mixed settlement in East Central Europe, has been basic to German self-understanding. This frontier has no parallel in the French case.[13] Massive eastward migration of Germans in the high middle ages and again in the early modern period had created numerous pockets of German settlement in Slavic lands. Much assimilation in both directions occurred in these borderlands over the centuries. Yet the decisive fact for national self-understanding was the assimilation that did not occur.[14] The preservation of

German language, culture, and national identity over centuries in enclaves and outposts in the Slavic east and the preservation of Polish language, culture, and national identity in eastern Prussia furnished to the German elite a differentialist, bounded model of nationhood, a feeling for the tenacious maintenance of distinctive ethnonational identities in zones of ethnoculturally mixed populations. Germany defined itself as a frontier state, with reference to the German-Slav borderlands, in a way that has no parallel in France.

The Revolutionary Crystallization

The opposition between French and German understandings of nationhood, while rooted in political and cultural geography, was fixed decisively by the French Revolution and its aftermath. The idea of nationhood was first given self-conscious theoretical elaboration in the second half of the eighteenth century. In France reformist philosophes and the urban public opposed the nation to the privileged orders and corporations of the ancien régime, giving the concept of nationhood a critical edge and a new, dynamic political significance. The *cahiers de doléance,* moreover, suggest that a high political charge was attached to the idea of the nation by the population at large in the immediately pre-Revolutionary period.[15] Coinciding with the politicization of nationhood in pre-Revolutionary France, however, was its unprecedented depoliticization in late-eighteenth-century Germany. In the writings of the flourishing *Bildungsbürgertum*[16] of the epoch the German nation was conceived less and less frequently in the traditional political context of the Empire and more and more frequently as an apolitical, ethnocultural entity—an "inward Empire," as Schiller put it in 1801, when the old Empire had entered its final phase of disintegration, or a *Kulturnation,* in the later formulation of Friedrich Meinecke.[17] If this *bildungsbürgerlich* understanding of nationhood was never exclusively cultural, its political dimension was nonetheless in deep recess during the late eighteenth and the first years of the nineteenth century.[18] Elaboration of the idea of nationhood in the second half of the eighteenth century in France and Germany, then, was the work of a broad bourgeois stratum in France and of a narrower, purely literary stratum in Germany. More important, it was oriented to the reform of an existing nationwide state in France but was identified with a purely cultural, indeed a specifically literary national spirit *(Nationalgeist)* in Germany.

When reform failed in France, the radicalized Third Estate constituted itself as the National Assembly and proclaimed the sovereignty of the nation.[19] Membership of this sovereign nation was conceived in political, not ethnocultural terms. Thus Sieyès: "What is a nation? A body of associates living under a common law and represented by the same legislature."[20] The dominance of citizenship over nationality, of political over ethnocultural conceptions of nationhood, is perhaps best expressed in Tallien's remark of the spring of 1795: "the only foreigners in France are the bad citizens."[21] Qualifications for membership were much disputed during the revolutionary epoch, but such disputes turned on a political rather than an ethnocultural axis.

So too did the question of the territorial boundaries of the new nation-state. The principle of self-determination, pregnant with immense disruptive potential for a dynastically organized and ethnoculturally intermixed Europe, was invoked to justify the territorial gains of 1791–1793, and even to reinterpret retrospectively the terms of the accession of Alsace to France in the seventeenth century.[22] But the collective "self" entitled by revolutionary doctrine to self-determination was conceived in the cosmopolitan, rationalistic terms characteristic of the eighteenth, not in the Romantic terms characteristic of the nineteenth century.[23] The point of self-determination as understood by the revolutionaries was to give expression to the universal desire for liberty and thus—how could it be otherwise?—for incorporation into France. It was emphatically not to permit the projection of ethnocultural identity onto the political plane.

Even the briefly if radically assimilationist linguistic politics of the Revolution was determined by political considerations rather than by a conception of the nation as an ethnolinguistic entity. Linguistic variety was denounced as conducive to reaction, linguistic unity advocated as indispensable to Republican citizenship. Thus Barère's report to the Committee of Public Safety in January 1794: "Federalism and superstition speak low Breton; emigration and hatred of the Republic speak German; the counterrevolution speaks Italian, and fanaticism speaks Basque." Only when all citizens speak the same language, according to Abbé Grégoire's "Rapport sur la nécessité et les moyens d'anéantir les patois et d'universaliser l'usage de la langue française," can all citizens "communicate their thoughts without hindrance" and enjoy equal access to state offices.[24] This short-lived assimilationist politics was not of great consequence. Such linguistic unification as occurred during the Revolutionary and Napoleonic period was the result of the indirectly assimilationist workings of the army, the schools, and the Napoleonic administrative machine.[25] Yet the ideological and practical importance of assimilation in the French tradition and the bad name that assimilation has acquired among progressives inclined to celebrate "difference" justify a more general observation. Assimilation—a deliberate policy of making similar—is incompatible with all consistently "organic" conceptions of membership, according to which "natural" ethnolinguistic boundaries are prior to and determinative of national and (ideally) state boundaries. It is one thing to want to make all citizens of Utopia speak Utopian, and quite another to want to make all Utopiphones citizens of Utopia. Crudely put, the former represents the French, the latter the German model of nationhood. Whether juridical (as in naturalization) or cultural, assimilation presupposes a political conception of membership and the belief, which France took over from the Roman tradition, that the state can turn strangers into citizens, peasants—or immigrant workers—into Frenchmen.[26]

If the French nation-state was invented in 1789, French nationalism was a product of war. On September 20, 1792, at Valmy, under fire from the Prussian infantry, the best-trained troops in Europe, the ragtag French army held its ground to the cry of "Vive la Nation!" Valmy itself was of no great military significance, but thanks to the celebrated phrase of Goethe, who was present at the battle—"this date and place mark a new epoch in world history"—the episode has come to symbolize the transformation of war through the appeal to the nation in arms.[27] Before the outbreak of war, nationalism existed neither as a "blind and exclusive preference for all that belongs to the nation" nor as a "demand in favor of subject nationalities."[28] Only from 1792 on, when the new order felt itself besieged by enemies within and enemies without, did there develop, superseding the ostentatious fraternal cosmopolitanism and pacifism of 1789–1791 and justified by the doctrine of the *"patrie en danger,"* elements of a xenophobic nationalism at home and an expansive, aggressive, nationalism abroad, originally missionary and crusading, later imperialist and triumphalist.[29] The character of this emergent internal and external nationalism was political-ideological, not ethnocultural. But it contributed to the later emergence, during the Napoleonic period, of a German counternationalism in which ethnocultural motifs came to play an important role. Revolutionary expansion, itself driven by political nationalism, thus engendered ethnocultural nationalism; the "crusade for liberty" elicited in response the myth, if not the reality, of a "holy war" of ethnonational resistance.

Romanticism and Reform in Germany

The German tradition of nationhood was formed crucially during the Revolutionary era by the Romantic movement on the one hand and the Prussian reform movement on the other, both occurring in the shadow of the French occupation of Germany.[30] The Romantic movement, though not itself centrally concerned with nationhood, supplied patterns of thought and appraisal for the consolidation, celebration, and eventual repoliticization of the ethnocultural understanding of nationhood. The Prussian reformers, appealing to a radically different conception of nationhood, aimed to "nationalize" the Prussian state from above and thus to regenerate the state after the catastrophic defeat of 1806.

The aesthetic and sociohistorical idiom of German Romanticism was perfectly suited to the elaboration of the ethnocultural conception of nationhood. The celebration of individuality as *Einzigkeit*, uniqueness, as over against *Einzelheit*, mere oneness; of depth and inwardness as over against surface polish; of feeling as over against desiccated rationality; of unconscious, organic growth as over against conscious, artificial construction; of the vitality and integrity of traditional, rooted folk cultures as over against the soullessness and artificiality of cosmopolitan culture—all these themes were easily transposed from the domain of aesthetics and cultural criticism to that of social philosophy. In the social and political thought of Romanticism, as in the larger and more enduring body of social and political thought permeated by its fundamental categories and values, nations are conceived as historically rooted, organically developed individualities, united by a distinctive *Volksgeist* and by its infinitely ramifying expression in language, custom, law, culture, and the state. Despite the emphasis placed on the state, the Romantic understanding of nationhood is fundamentally ethnocultural. The *Volksgeist* is constitutive, the state merely expressive, of nationhood. The exaltation of the state found in Romantic political thought—Adam Müller's claim, for example, that "man cannot be imagined outside the state . . . The state is the totality of all human concerns"—reflects on the one hand an amorphous, globalizing conception of the state and on the other the teleological notion that the *Volksgeist* can reach its final and perfect expression only in the state.[31]

The social and political thought of Romanticism was completely divorced from the realities of practical politics. The Prussian reformers, conversely, were untouched by the incipient ethnocultural nationalism of the period. Awed by the French triumph and the Prussian collapse, they wished to create a Prussian nation to regenerate the Prussian state. Hardenberg wrote to Friedrich Wilhelm III in 1807: "We must do from above what the French have done from below."[32] Romantics and reformers understood the relation between nation and state in completely different terms: the former in quasi-aesthetic terms, with the state as the expression of the nation and of its constitutive *Volksgeist*; the latter in strictly political terms, with the nation—the mobilized and united *Staatsvolk*—as the deliberate and artificial creation of the state.

Thus was engendered the characteristic dualism and tension between ethnonational and state-national ideologies and programs—a dualism that has haunted German politics ever since. This suggests a way of reformulating the rough contrast that supplied the point of departure for these reflections: the contrast between the French political and the German ethnocultural conception of nationhood. In fact, traditions of nationhood have political and cultural components in both countries. These components have been closely integrated in France, where political unity has been understood as constitutive, cultural unity as expressive of nationhood. In the German tradition, in contrast, political and ethnocultural aspects of nationhood have stood in tension with one another, serving as the basis for competing conceptions of nationhood. One such conception is sharply opposed to the French conception: according to this view, ethnocultural unity is constitutive, political unity expressive, of nationhood. While this ethnocultural understanding of nationhood has never had the field to itself, it took root in early-nineteenth-century Germany and has remained widely available for political exploitation ever since. No such essentially ethnocultural conception of nationhood has taken root in France, where cultural nationhood has been conceived as an ingredient, not a competitor, of political nationhood.

Nationhood and Nationalism in the Nineteenth Century

The nineteenth century saw the consolidation of the French and the construction of a German nation-state.[33] By the end of the century there were noticeable similarities in the social structure and political style of the two nation-states.[34] Nonetheless, the deeply rooted differences in the political and cultural construction of nationhood that I have sketched remained significant, and were in certain respects reinforced. The political, assimilationist understanding of nationhood in France was reinforced in the late nineteenth century by the internal *mission civilisatrice* carried out by the Third Republic's army of schoolteachers—the *instituteurs*, whose mission was to *institute* the nation.[35] And the ethnocultural strand in German self-understanding was reinforced by the intensifying nationality struggle between Germans and Poles—both groups citizens of the German state—in the Prussian east.

Chronic regime instability did not impede the consolidation of the French nation-state in the nineteenth century. If the Bourbon regime of 1815–1830, like the general European settlement imposed by the Congress of Vienna, was antinational, the July Monarchy of 1830–1848 was based implicitly, and all subsequent regimes explicitly, on the principle, if not the reality, of the sovereignty of the nation. More important than this formal constitutional development was the consolidation of national memory effected in the works of historians such as Augustin Thierry, Jules Michelet, and Ernest Lavisse; the pedagogic consolidation carried out by the schools of the Third Republic; the linguistic consolidation furthered by school and army; and the sociogeographic consolidation effected by the development of communication and transportation networks.[36]

Nationalism, a contradictory mix of chauvinism and messianic universalism, heir to the tradition of Revolutionary and Napoleonic expansion and to the principle of national self-determination, was located on the left for most of the century. After the defeat of 1870–71 it migrated to the right, with the Boulangist crisis of 1889 serving as a crucial pivot and the Dreyfus Affair marking its definitive arrival.[37] More precisely, continental nationalism migrated to the right, while the left under Jules Ferry discovered in the 1880s a new field for the projection and reconstruction of national grandeur—a revitalized and expanded overseas empire.[38] Ideologically and institutionally, this overseas imperialism was heir to the continental imperialism of the Revolutionary and Napoleonic periods and, more remotely, to the Roman imperial tradition. Ideologically it was conceived as a *mission libératrice et civilisatrice*; institutionally it went much further than its British or German counterparts in the legal and political assimilation of metropolitan and overseas regimes, aiming at the construction of *"la plus grande France."*[39] French Republicans pursued an assimilationist, civilizing, nationalizing mission inside France as well. In the 1880s this assimilationist internal nationalism, linked to reforms of primary education and military conscription, formed the backdrop to an expansive, assimilationist reform of citizenship law whose central provisions have endured to this day.[40]

The newly nationalist right, despite its antiparliamentarism, shared with the old nationalist left (and with the new imperialist left) the sense of a privileged mission or vocation for France, a concern for national "grandeur," and a reverence for the army as the incarnation and instrument of this grandeur.[41] Despite the rise of anti-Semitism toward the end of the century, the new nationalism did not abandon the traditional, essentially political conception of nationhood for an ethnocultural conception. Indeed the question of Alsace-Lorraine led to the ideological accentuation of the French political as against the German ethnocultural understanding of nationhood. Thus Fustel de Coulanges, in his letter of October 27, 1870 to the German historian Mommsen: "It is possible that Alsace is German by race and by language, but it is French by nationality and by its sense of fatherland."[42] A similar theme was developed by Renan in his polemical letters to Strauss.[43]

The German ethnocultural conception of nationhood was a product of the distinctive political and cultural geography of Central Europe. Yet that same geography—the inextricable intermixture of Germans and other nationalities—made it impossible to found a German state precisely on the ethnocultural nation.[44] None of the proposed solutions to the problem of national unification—including the "classical" Prussian-kleindeutsch and Austrian-großdeutsch solutions—could bring into being a "perfect" nation-state: either Germans would be excluded, or non-Germans included, or both. Political considerations were dominant both in the programs of 1848 and in the later practice of Bismarck.

Unification under Bismarck, while conditioned, was not inspired by nationalism, still less by ethnocultural nationalism.[45] Nor was the constitutional structure of the unified Reich that of a nation-state. The Constitution did not invoke popular sovereignty, and the Imperial crown was offered to William I in Versailles by the princes, not by representatives of the people. There was no unified German citizenship: Reichsangehörigkeit (citizenship of the Empire) derived from Landesangehörigkeit (citizenship of the individual constituent states), and its limited political significance reflected the limited political significance of the Reichstag. The French nation-state had been constructed in polemical opposition not only to dynastic sovereignty but also to corporate and provincial privilege.[46] The German quasi-nation state challenged neither principle, even incorporating particular rights—Reservatrechte—into the treaties of accession of the South German states.

The Reich was nonetheless understood as a nation-state, both by those who welcomed and by those who feared it.[47] As a nation-state, however, it was imperfect not only in its internal constitution but in its external boundaries—indeed doubly imperfect. As a *kleindeutsches Reich*, it was underinclusive, excluding above all millions of Austrian Germans. At the same time it was overinclusive, including French in Alsace-Lorraine, Danes in North Schleswig, and Poles in eastern Prussia. These were not simply linguistic but rather, especially in the last case, self-conscious national minorities. And the intensifying conflict between Germans and Poles in eastern Prussia reinforced the ethnocultural, differentialist strand in the German understanding of nationhood.

The Reich did make significant progress toward consolidated nation-statehood between 1871 and 1914—chiefly through the development of new nationwide institutions and processes and through the integrative working of the state on national consciousness. At the outbreak of war Germany was no longer the conspicuously *unvollendete* (unfinished or incomplete) nation-state of 1871.[48] To a considerable extent the Reich had succeeded in integrating the differing, even antagonistic traditions of Prussian statehood and German nationhood. Yet the old dualism survived, the old tension between statist and ethnocultural components in the German tradition of nationhood. In the context of this persisting dualism, two generations were not sufficient to create a consolidated, *"selbstverständlich,"* taken-for-granted national consciousness, within the frame of the new state. *Reichsnational* did not completely displace *volksnational* consciousness in Imperial Germany. The ethnocultural conception of nationhood, though in recess immediately after the *Reichsgründung*, remained available for subsequent political exploitation. This is shown by the important ethnonational component in Prussian and German *Polenpolitik;* by the pan-Germanist agitation around the turn of the century, by the widespread assumption that union with Austria would and should follow the breakup of the Habsburg empire, and by the development of *völkisch* thought and of a *Deutschtum*-oriented politics during the Weimar Republic—to say nothing of the subsequent exploitation of *völkisch* thought by Nazi propagandists.[49]

Understandings of Nationhood and Definitions of Citizenship

French and German understandings of nationhood have not been fixed and immutable. They have been more fluid, plastic, and internally contested than I have suggested. At the time of the Dreyfus Affair, during the Vichy regime, and again in recent years, the prevailing French idiom of nationhood—state-centered and assimilationist—has been challenged by a more ethnocultural counteridiom, represented today by Jean-Marie Le Pen. And in Germany the ethnocultural idiom of nationhood has represented only one strand of a more complex national self-understanding.

For several centuries, nonetheless, the prevailing French and German idioms of nationhood have differed markedly; and they continue to differ today. These distinctive understandings of nationhood are embodied and expressed in sharply differing definitions of citizenship. The expansive, assimilationist citizenship law of France, which automatically transforms second-generation immigrants into citizens, reflects the state-centered, assimilationist self-understanding of the French. And the German definition of the citizenry as a community of descent, restrictive toward non-German immigrants yet remarkably expansive toward ethnic Germans from Eastern Europe and the Soviet Union, reflects the pronounced ethnocultural inflection in German self-understanding.

The sharply differing ways of defining the citizenry in France and Germany crystallized in the decades before the First World War, in 1889 and 1913 respectively. The German population during these decades was larger than the French and growing much more rapidly. One might think that differing demographic and military interests led the French and German states to adopt differing definitions of citizenship. I do not accept this instrumentalist explanation. It is true that the French were increasingly concerned about demographic stagnation after the Franco-Prussian War. Yet in the 1880s the state did not need new citizens as soldiers. Now that conscription was defined as a universal obligation of citizenship, the state disposed of too many, not too few, potential soldiers. Since military budgets did not permit the training of all fit and eligible French citizens, there was no military interest in enlarging further the pool of citizens by redefining second-generation immigrants as citizens.

There was, however, a *political* interest in an expansive definition of citizenship. Republican civic ideology, which emphasized universal and equal military service, made the exemption of second-generation immigrants from military service ideologically scandalous and politically intolerable—especially since second-generation immigrants were not considered true foreigners, but rather persons who were French in fact though not in law. One legislator denounced them, significantly, as *prétendus étrangers*, "would-be foreigners." The prevailing characterization of second-generation immigrants as socially and culturally French was made possible by an assimilationist understanding of nationhood. Deeply rooted in political and cultural geography, this assimilationist self-understanding was powerfully reinforced during the 1880s by Republican reforms of school and army. Primary education, under Jules Ferry, was made free, compulsory, secular, and intensely nationalistic, and primary schools became great engines of assimilation, welding France for the first time into a unified nation. The army too, reorganized on the basis of universal conscription and conceived as the "school of the nation," was an agent of assimilation. If schools and army turned peasants into Frenchmen, as Eugen Weber has shown, they made second-generation immigrants into Frenchmen in the same way. The interest of the French state in an expansive definition of citizenship, then, was not immediately given by demographic or military imperatives. Rather, this interest was mediated—indeed constituted—by a certain way of thinking and talking about membership of the French nation-state.

Nor can the distinctiveness of the German definition of citizenship—restrictive toward non-Germans, yet expansive toward ethnic German immigrants—be interpreted in instrumental terms. In Wilhelmine Germany as in Republican France, understandings of nationhood shaped appraisals of state interests. Yet while the French understanding of nationhood—state-centered and robustly assimilationist—engendered an interest in the civic incorporation of second-generation immigrants, the German understanding of nationhood engendered an interest in their civic exclusion.

Migrant labor was economically indispensable in eastern Prussia in the Wilhelmine era. Yet immigrants—ethnic Poles from Russia and Austria—were not wanted as citizens, for no one believed that they could be made into Germans. In part this was the legacy of a traditionally less assimilationist, more ethnocultural understanding of nationhood. Yet just as the French assimilationist self-understanding was powerfully reinforced in the 1880s, so too the German ethnocultural, differentialist self-understanding was powerfully reinforced in the Wilhelmine era by the increasingly evident failure of attempts to assimilate indigenous Poles in the Prussian east. Having failed to secure the political loyalty of Poles to the German state, and having failed to assimilate them to German language and culture, Prussian and German policy toward the indigenous Poles became increasingly "dissimilationist." The state openly discriminated by ethnic nationality, treating ethnic Germans and ethnic Poles differently in an effort to "strengthen Germandom" in frontier districts. Since the state had failed to assimilate indigenous Poles in the Prussian east, there was no reason to believe that it would succeed in assimilating immigrant Poles. An ethnocultural, differentialist way of thinking and talking about membership of the German nation-state thus supported an interest in a restrictive definition of citizenship. An expansive citizenship law like that of France, automatically transforming second-generation immigrants into citizens, presupposed confidence in their effective assimilation. The French elite possessed that confidence; the German elite did not.

In rejecting an instrumentalist account of French and German citizenship policies and practices, I do not replace it with a naively culturalist account. Instead, I show how particular cultural idioms—ways of thinking and talking about nationhood that have been state-centered and assimilationist in France, and more ethnocultural and differentialist in Germany—were reinforced and activated in specific historical and institutional settings; and how, once reinforced and activated, these cultural idioms framed and shaped judgments of what was politically imperative, of what was in the interest of the state. Understandings of nationhood and interests of state are not antithetical categories. State interests in an expansive or restrictive citizenry are not immediately given by economic, demographic, or military considerations. Rather, judgments of what is in the interest of the state are mediated by self-understandings, by cultural idioms, by ways of thinking and talking about nationhood.

The more general analytical point is that cultural idioms are not neutral vehicles for the expression of preexisting interests: cultural idioms *constitute* interests as much as they express them. These culturally mediated and thereby culturally constituted interests are not prior to, or independent of, the cultural idioms in which they are expressed. As Gareth Stedman Jones has argued, "We cannot . . . decode political language to reach a primal and material expression of interest since it is the discursive structure of political language which conceives and defines interest in the first place. What we must therefore do is to study the production of interest, identification, grievance and aspiration within political languages themselves."[50]

I do not subscribe to Stedman Jones's purely culturalist perspective. Idioms of nationhood, as I have suggested, are ultimately rooted in political and cultural geography; and they are proximately rooted in, and reinforced by, experiences and practices that, while linguistically mediated, are not reducible to speech acts. If it is necessary to "study the production of interest . . . within political languages," it is also necessary to study the social production and reproduction of political languages themselves. Yet Stedman Jones provides a powerful argument for attending to the way in which cultural idioms constitute rather than merely express interests.

"Not ideas," wrote Max Weber, "but interests—material and ideal—directly govern men's conduct. Yet very frequently the 'world images' that have been created by 'ideas' have, like switchmen, determined the tracks along which action has been pushed by the dynamic of interest."[51] Differences in citizenship policies and practices are not produced exclusively or immediately by differing understandings of nationhood. Of course definitions of citizenship are conditioned by state interests. But conceptions of nationhood, to adopt the terms of Weber's metaphor, have determined the tracks along which the politics of citizenship has been driven by the dynamic of interests. Part II of this study seeks to demonstrate this in detail, focusing on pivotal moments in the shaping and reshaping of citizenship law in France and Germany. Part I, laying the groundwork for these discussions, provides a more general account of the origins and workings of the modern institution of citizenship.

I · THE INSTITUTION
OF CITIZENSHIP

1 ◆ Citizenship as Social Closure

Citizenship is a universal and distinctive feature of the modern political landscape. Every modern state formally defines its citizenry, publically identifying a set of persons as its members and residually designating all others as noncitizens, or aliens. Every state attaches certain rights and obligations to the status of citizenship. These rights and obligations define a region of legal equality—what T. H. Marshall called the "basic human equality associated with . . . full membership of a community."[1]

The citizenry of every modern state is internally inclusive. Defined to coincide roughly with the permanent resident population of the state, the modern citizenry excludes only foreigners, that is, persons who belong to other states.[2] Yet citizenship is not a mere reflex of residence; it is an enduring personal status that is not generated by passing or extended residence alone and does not lapse with temporary or prolonged absence. In this respect the modern state is not simply a territorial organization but a membership organization, an association of citizens.

Although citizenship is internally inclusive, it is externally exclusive. There is a conceptually clear, legally consequential, and ideologically charged distinction between citizens and foreigners. The state claims to be the state of, and for, a particular, bounded citizenry; it claims legitimacy by claiming to express the will and further the interests of that citizenry. This bounded citizenry is usually conceived as a nation—as something more cohesive than a mere aggregate of persons who happen legally to belong to the state.

Although political sociology has been centrally concerned with the rights and obligations of citizenship and with patterns of civic participation, it has been curiously unconcerned with the institution of formal citizenship.[3] In part this reflects the antiformalism of postwar social

21

science. Sociology has been especially committed to going behind formal, official structures and institutions in order to discover the real working of things. A similar antiformalism has characterized postwar political science, dominated by behavioralist and functionalist approaches. Despite the "new institutionalism" and the revival of interest in the state in the last two decades, the institution of formal citizenship has received no more attention in political science than it has in sociology. From an antiformalist point of view, citizenship is *prima facie* uninteresting precisely because it is formal and official. But this neglects the fact that formalization and codification are themselves social phenomena, with sociologically interesting effects.[4]

A further reason for the sociological neglect of formal citizenship is the endogenous bias of the discipline. As Anthony Giddens and others have pointed out, sociology has tended to take the existence of a bounded national "society" for granted and to focus on institutions and processes internal to that society.[5] There is an emerging research tradition of world-system analysis, but this has tended to focus on political economy, neglecting specifically social and political structures. Significantly, the only explicitly global section of the American Sociological Association is the section on "political economy of the world system." But even analyses of global social and political structures have neglected formal citizenship.

A final reason for the neglect of formal citizenship is the territorial bias in the study of the state. The state is conceived as a territorial organization, not as a membership organization.[6] The focus on territoriality is understandable. The sociology of the state developed by analyzing the transition from the medieval polity, essentially a network of persons, to the modern state.[7] This transition did centrally involve the territorialization of rule.[8] Yet the historical focus on this transition and the conceptual emphasis on territoriality have obscured another aspect of the development of the modern state and state system: the division of the world's population into a set of bounded and mutually exclusive citizenries. This has paralleled and reinforced the division of the earth's surface into a set of bounded and mutually exclusive territorial jurisdictions. Territory and membership are closely related. Indeed political territory as we know it today—bounded territory to which access is controlled by the state—*presupposes* membership. It presupposes some way of distinguishing those who have free access to the territory from those who do not, those who belong to the state from those who do not. The modern state is simultaneously a territorial organization and a personal association. With its analytical focus on territorial rule, political sociology has much to say about the former but little about the latter.

The neglect of formal citizenship is unfortunate. For citizenship is not simply a legal formula; it is an increasingly salient social and cultural fact. As a powerful instrument of social closure, citizenship occupies a central place in the administrative structure and political culture of the modern nation-state and state system. The notion of social closure finds its classical exposition in the opening pages of *Economy and Society*, where Max Weber distinguishes between open and closed social relationships.[9] Social interaction may be open to all comers, or it may be closed, in the sense that it excludes or restricts the participation of certain outsiders. A pick-up softball game, for example, may be open, while a game played by teams belonging to an organized league may be restricted to team members, and in this sense closed. Retail commerce is usually open to all buyers, though less often, unconditionally, to all sellers. Worship, conversation, fights, neighborhoods, countries—all may be open or more or less closed.

Although closure is most easily visualized in everyday interaction, the notion of closure illuminates large-scale structures and patterns of interaction as well. The nation-state is architect and guarantor of a number of distinctively modern forms of closure. These are embodied in such institutions and practices as the territorial border, universal suffrage, universal military service, and naturalization. Closure pivots in each of these cases on the legal institution of citizenship. Only citizens have an unqualified right to enter (and remain in) the territory of a state. The suffrage and military service are normally restricted to citizens. And naturalization, which governs access to the status of citizen, is itself closed, restricted to the qualified. Citizenship is thus both an instrument and an object of closure.[10]

The Territorial State and Closure

In general, closure may occur on the threshold of interaction or "inside" interaction. In the former case initial participation is restricted through barriers to entry or selective admission; in the latter continued participation is controlled through institutions such as probation or performance review. Closure against noncitizens is exercised mainly on the threshold of interaction. This is the case when noncitizens are prevented from entering the territory, or when they are excluded from forms of action reserved for citizens (such as voting or serving in the army). In one important respect, however, closure occurs inside interaction. Citizens alone enjoy an unconditional right to remain and reside in the territory of a state, including the right to reenter should they leave for any reason. The territory of the state is their territory, and they can plan their lives accordingly. Noncitizens' entry and residence rights, in contrast, are never unconditional. Some noncitizens—clandestine entrants, for example, or persons at the end of a legally limited period of residence—have no such rights. But even privileged noncitizens—those formally accepted as immigrants or settlers—remain "probationary" residents, subject to exclusion or deportation in certain circumstances.

Territorial closure occupies a controlling position in the web of interaction. A person excluded from the territory is excluded from all interaction inside the territory, and from all associated goods and opportunities. These include such basic goods as public order and security and access to a promising labor market. For one fleeing poverty or civil strife, access to the territory of a prosperous or peaceful state may decisively shape life chances. That such access is closed vis-à-vis noncitizens does not mean that it is absolutely or unconditionally closed. States need not, and often do not, exercise their power to exclude noncitizens; and when they do exercise this power, they usually do so selectively, not indiscriminately. Yet in global perspective, the widely ramifying secondary consequences of even selective territorial closure against noncitizens give citizenship a crucial bearing on the basic goods and opportunities that shape life chances.

From the point of view of the noncitizen, then, territorial closure has a decisive bearing on life chances. From the point of view of the state, territorial closure is equally important. The modern state has a fundamental interest in territorial closure. More precisely, it has a basic interest in the principle of territorial closure—that noncitizens may be excluded or expelled from the territory—and in the administrative capacity to bar the entry or continued residence of noncitizens. This does not mean that the state has a basic interest in actually excluding noncitizens. Depending on circumstances, the state may opt for perfect openness, for absolute closure, or (most likely) for partial and selective exclusion. But while the practice of closure varies across demographic, economic, political, and cultural contexts, the principle and the administrative apparatus of closure are essential to the modern state and its project of territorial rule.[11]

Committed to spreading its authority evenly throughout a territory, to "filling up" a bounded space with its authoritative presence, the modern state makes spatially comprehensive claims to rule.[12] The order it enforces is binding not only on "members" but, to a great extent, on all persons temporarily or permanently present in the territory.[13] Mere presence in the territory makes a person an object of administration by, a provider of resources for, and a subject of claims on the state, while absence from the territory may undo these relations. For this reason the state cannot view with indifference the numbers or characteristics of persons entering, residing in, or leaving its territory.[14] Movement across the boundaries of the space it administers necessarily engages its vital interests.

By contrast, migration did not engage so directly the vital interests of ancient or medieval personal polities, since rule in these settings was exercised over particular sets of persons, not over territories: mere presence did not entail political, administrative, or legal inclusion. Space was not politically neutral or insignificant in such polities, and I do not want to suggest that they were indifferent to migration. But since jurisdiction depended on the personal status of the agent rather than the spatial coordinates of the action, migration was less consequential. Because jurisdictional closure buffered such polities against the consequences of migration, territorial closure was less urgent.

The territorial state, then, has a basic and distinctive interest in being able to control the flow of persons across its borders—in being able to compel, induce, discourage, or forbid the entry or exit of particular categories of persons. The capacity to exclude noncitizens serves this interest, permitting states to compel the exit and forbid the entry of a particular class of persons. But why is it only noncitizens who may be excluded or expelled? The modern state does not have the right, although it does have the capacity, to compel the exit or prevent the entry of its own citizens. The state's right to expel is thus severely restricted, for expellables—noncitizens—usually comprise only a small fraction of the population. Its right to prevent entry is not so severely restricted, for excludables—again noncitizens—comprise the great majority of potential entrants. Yet even this right remains significantly limited: the state may not deny entry to its own citizens.

The territorial state's interest in controlling entry and exit is a general one. Why is territorial closure directed against noncitizens alone? It would seem to be in the state's interest to be able to expel or exclude persons regardless of their status. Why may it not do so? Why are citizens exempted? In practice, illiberal states do sometimes expel and exclude their own citizens. But this violates generally accepted principles of international law. Moreover, this practice is increasingly difficult to sustain, especially when it involves large numbers of persons or occurs in world regions that are "filled up" with relatively strong states.

Unimpeded, the territorial state might seek to externalize the material and ideal costs associated with unruly, unemployed, unfit, unassimilated, or otherwise undesired residents, whatever their status, by excluding or expelling them. But the territorial state is not unimpeded. With the disappearance of "nonstate, semistate or pseudostate areas of the world,"[15] every state is embedded in a system of coordinate territorial states, each with the same vital interest in controlling migration. Jointly, these territorial jurisdictions exhaust the inhabitable surface of the earth. In such a world a person cannot be expelled from one territory without being expelled into another, cannot be denied entry into one territory without having to remain in another. The one exception is that pathetic and characteristically modern form of limbo in which the unwanted may find themselves, shuttled back and forth between states unwilling to admit them.[16] Occasional instances of complementarity aside, exclusion and expulsion become zero-sum games.[17] One state's gain is another's loss: the costs successfully externalized by one must be borne by another. To permit states to exclude or expel persons at will, under these zero-sum background conditions, would multiply occasions for interstate conflict. States into whose territories undesirables had been expelled would threaten or engage in retaliatory "dumping." A state would hesitate to admit any outsider, for fear that it might be stuck with him if his state of origin denied him reentry. Basic conditions for the orderly interstate movement of persons would not exist.

The limitation of states' powers of expulsion and exclusion to noncitizens thus responds to the imperatives of the modern state-system.[18] This limitation, though, presupposes the institution of citizenship, with its internationally recognized rules for allocating persons to states. Yet this allocative institution, this social technique for consistently assigning each individual to one and only one state, had to be invented. The modern system of territorial states engendered not just territorial closure against noncitizens but, more fundamentally, the institution of citizenship as such.

The emergence of clearly defined and sharply bounded citizenries in response to the imperatives of the modern state-system can be seen clearly in early-nineteenth-century Germany. After 1815 there were thirty-nine sovereign German states, linked in a loose confederation and sharing an increasingly integrated economy and a relatively homogeneous culture. Given the large number of small states, migration within Germany, even over relatively short distances, often crossed state boundaries. And rural overpopulation, together with the breakup of the *ständisch* social order and its restrictions on freedom of movement, engendered large-scale migration among the poor and destitute. Having assumed formal responsibility for poor relief, states tried to protect themselves against the migrant poor by expelling them. But expulsion was a zero-sum game. A state could expel its unwanted migrants only into the territory of a neighboring state, where the migrants were equally unwanted. Increasingly, states sought to coordinate and rationalize their expulsion practices, following two basic principles: a state could expel into the territory of another state only a person belonging to that state; and a state was obliged to admit to its territory its own members. This made it urgent to specify who belonged to the state. Explicit membership rules, specifying who was to count as a member of the state, were spelled out for the first time in the bilateral and multilateral treaties enacted to coordinate and regulate expulsion practices. Thus the need to coordinate admission and expulsion rules among states in a compact and economically integrated state-system led directly to the codification of the rules governing citizenship.[19]

The Nation-State and Closure

Territorial closure against noncitizens serves vital and tangible state interests; it is essential to the modern territorial state and state-system. The same cannot be said for other modes of membership closure. If noncitizens are regularly excluded from the suffrage and from positions in public service, and if they are exempted from military service, this cannot generally be attributed to any overriding tangible state (or group) interest. The interests sustaining domestic closure against noncitizens are often intangible.[20]

The modern state is not only a territorial state, embedded in a system of coordinate territorial states; it is also a nation-state. The concept of the nation-state, to be sure, is much more ambiguous than that of the territorial state, and its appropriateness for the analysis of late twentieth century states is disputed. For some observers the general lack of fit between political and ethnocultural boundaries vitiates the concept of the nation-state.[21] Others, emphasizing states' universal nation-making aspirations and immense nation-making powers, defend its continued analytical usefulness.[22] There is no need, however, to engage these disputes here, for in one uncontested sense almost all modern states are (or claim to be) nation-states. Almost all subscribe to the legitimating doctrine of national or popular sovereignty. Almost all claim to derive state power from and exercise it for (and not simply over) a nation, a people.[23] A state is a nation-state in this minimal sense insofar as it claims (and is understood) to be a nation's state: the state "of" and "for" a particular, distinctive, bounded nation. For present purposes, the manner of distinctiveness is immaterial, the fact of distinctiveness alone essential. *How* the state-bearing and state-justifying nation is culturally and legally bounded is irrelevant; *that* it is bounded is what matters here.

Domestic closure against noncitizens rests on this understanding and self-understanding of modern states as bounded nation-states—states whose telos it is to express the will and further the interests of distinctive and bounded nations, and whose legitimacy depends on their doing so, or at least seeming to do so. The routine exclusion of noncitizens from modern systems of "universal" suffrage is exemplary in this respect. Suffrage has always and everywhere been closed, but the post-French Revolution nationalization of politics occasioned a gradual shift in the axis and rationale of closure, with complex "functional" systems based on *ständisch* and capacitarian criteria yielding to simple "plebiscitarian" systems based on citizenship.[24] That the exclusion of noncitizens from the franchise for national elections has nowhere been seriously challenged, even in the many European states with sizable populations of long-term resident noncitizens,[25] testifies to the force—indeed the axiomatic status—of nationalism in modern states. This is not the exacerbated, aggressive, passionate nationalism that is the "starkest political shame of the twentieth century," but the routine, ordinary, taken-forgranted nationalism that is the "common idiom of contemporary political feeling," the "natural political sentiment for modern states."[26] The closure of suffrage (and other institutions) to noncitizens, based on the axiom that the nation-state may, in fact must, discriminate between members and nonmembers, is one expression of this "normal," "legitimate," "rational" nationalism.

Domestic closure may serve material interests as well. These may include security interests of state elites in excluding noncitizens, viewed as politically unreliable, from the suffrage, from military service, or from positions in public administration; fiscal interests in limiting noncitizens' participation in costly social programs; or occupational group interests in restricting competition. Where noncitizens comprise a substantial fraction of the population, these material interests might be compelling.

Where they are a small minority, though, closure is sustained mainly by the ideal interest, inscribed in the characteristic legitimation claims of modern states, in maintaining a conceptual, legal, and political boundary between members and nonmembers of the nation-state. Domestic closure against noncitizens is essential to the modern state qua nation-state, just as territorial closure against noncitizens is essential to the modern state qua territorial state.

Insiders and Outsiders

All forms of closure presuppose some way of defining and identifying outsiders or ineligibles. Outsiders may be defined and identified residually, as nonmembers, or directly, as bearers of some disqualifying attribute. If insiders are defined positively—as members of a family, clan, association, organization, or state—outsiders are defined negatively and residually. They are excluded not because of what they are but because of what they are not—because they are not recognized or acknowledged as insiders. On the other hand, outsiders may be defined directly, and insiders residually. Shunning, blacklisting, and quarantining are directed against directly defined outsiders. Ethnocultural closure may be structured either way: it may be exercised against ethnic or religious outsiders defined residually (non-European, nonwhite, non-Christian, non-Anglophone), or directly (Asian, Black, Jew, Spanish-speaking). The noncitizen is a residually defined outsider. Every modern state defines its citizens positively, in accordance with explicit, formally articulated criteria, and its noncitizens residually.

Insider-outsider groupings may have a narrower or a wider interactional and temporal span. At one extreme they may be ad hoc and ephemeral, linked to a particular and fleeting interaction; at the other, they may crystallize into a structured "group," persisting over time and spanning a variety of interactional settings. In the first case definitions of insider and outsider are narrowly context-bound: outsiderhood in one context has no connection with or implications for outsiderhood in another. In the second case they are relatively independent of context: insiderhood and outsiderhood become general qualifying or disqualifying statuses, entailing inclusion in or exclusion from a variety of interactional contexts. Citizenries are insider groupings of the second kind. To be defined as a citizen is not to qualify as an insider for a particular instance or type of interaction; it is to be defined in a general, abstract, enduring, and context-independent way as a member of the state.

Insiders and outsiders may be defined formally or informally. Formal techniques include the elaboration of explicit and unambiguous criteria of insiderhood or outsiderhood (such as criteria for inclusion in Medicaid or Food Stamp programs or criteria for exclusion on medical grounds from the armed forces); exhaustive enumerations of individual insiders or outsiders (guest lists, registers, rosters, membership rolls, blacklists); and formally administered identification routines in which a particular person is identified as an insider or outsider through the application of general criteria or through matching against enumerative lists. On the other hand, insiders and outsiders may be defined and identified informally through the use of tacit, uncodified, internalized classificatory schemes, the practical mastery of which is distributed among participants in an interaction rather than monopolized by specialized administrators.

Closure based on citizenship is regulated by formally articulated norms and enforced by specialized agents employing formal identification routines. Territorial closure, for example, is regulated by immigration law and corresponding administrative regulations. It is enforced by specialized agents such as border patrol officers and officials at points of entry who employ formal identification routines based on specialized instruments such as passports, visas, and computerized files. Closure against noncitizens is necessarily formal, for the legal quality of citizenship is invisible in ordinary interaction and visible only under the special lens of administrative scrutiny. Thus the development of citizenship proceeds *pari passu* with that of an administrative apparatus of classification and surveillance (in the broadest sense) and a corresponding body of administrative knowledge.[27]

Citizenship is an abstract, formal construct. In principle it has nothing to do with ethnocultural nationality or with any other immediately interpretable markers and identifiers of everyday life.[28] Yet formal closure against legal noncitizens may overlap in practice with informal closure against ethnocultural nonnationals. Enforcement of closure against the former may be biased against the latter. This happens when formal administrative scrutiny is not uniform, but is "triggered" by informal ethnocultural markers—when identity checks, for example, carried out as part of a campaign to detect and expel undocumented noncitizens, are systematically geared to informally defined ethnocultural outsiders.[29]

Closure against noncitizens is enforced for the most part directly, by front-line gatekeepers who deny or limit their access to the territory, the labor market, voting booths, social benefits, and so on. Direct exclusion may be supplemented by legal sanctions. Territorial closure, for example, is enforced primarily by directly barring entry or compelling exit. If such direct enforcement is viewed as too weak a deterrent of illicit entry or residence, it can be supplemented by sanctions such as fines, imprisonment, or future exclusion from the territory.[30] Sanctions play a more central role in enforcing the closure of the labor market. Here, front-line gatekeepers are not agents of the state, but employers whose economic interest in hiring noncitizens runs counter to their duty, in certain cases, not to do so. Because the front-line gatekeepers have an incentive to grant (illicit) access, exclusion can be enforced only with sanctions.

Access to Citizenship

Citizenship is not only an instrument of closure, a prerequisite for the enjoyment of certain rights, or for participation in certain types of interaction. It is also an object of closure, a status to which access is restricted. From a global perspective, to be sure, citizenship is virtually universal. In this perspective, citizenship is an international filing system, a mechanism for allocating persons to states. The citizens of a given state comprise the fraction of the world population that "belongs" to that state, rather than to some other state. In a world divided among exhaustive and mutually exclusive jurisdictions of sovereign states, it is axiomatic that every person ought to have a citizenship, that everyone ought to belong to one state or another.[31] And this principle is largely realized in practice. The vast majority of persons possess the citizenship of at least one state. Modern state citizenship differs sharply in this respect from citizenship in the ancient Greek polis or in medieval towns. There it was axiomatic that some persons ought *not* to be citizens of any city. Persons lacking citizenship were not placeless; their status was not anomalous. Rather, they did not form part of the self-governing or otherwise privileged civic corporation.

Although globally inclusive, citizenship is locally exclusive. Every state limits access to its citizenship. It limits the circle of persons to whom it ascribes its citizenship at birth, and it specifies the terms and conditions on which it will permit others to acquire its citizenship.

Ascription.[32] Every state ascribes its citizenship to certain persons at birth. The vast majority of persons acquire their citizenship in this way. The ascription of citizenship at birth represents a striking exception to the secular trend away from ascribed statuses. And it is difficult to reconcile with a central claim—perhaps the central claim—of liberal political theory: the idea that political membership ought to be founded on individual consent.[33] Why is citizenship typically ascribed at birth?

Administrative convenience is part of the reason. Unlike residence, assimilation, loyalty, and other concepts appearing in naturalization law, birth is an unambiguous event about which states maintain relatively clear administrative records. Attributing citizenship at birth, moreover, makes possible a clear and unambiguous assignment of individuals to states without a period of uncertainty. Some individuals will be assigned incorrectly, in the sense that their formal citizenship does not correspond to their actual ties and attachments. But such mismatches can be corrected later. And in any event they are a small price to pay for the clarity and convenience of assigning persons to states at birth. The alternative— a system of voluntary or contractual citizenship that would leave individuals unassigned until their actual social attachments and individual preferences became clear—would be an administrative nightmare. It would also be politically unacceptable. All states regard their citizens as bound to them by obligations of loyalty and service—even when they do not routinely demand service or invoke loyalty. These core obligations of citizenship are too important to the state to permit individuals to opt into or out of them at will.[34] Despite the concern of liberal political theory to found political obligation on the voluntary consent of individuals, the state is not and cannot be a voluntary association. For the great majority of persons, citizenship cannot but be an imposed, ascribed status. This is not to deny that many persons at least implicitly consent to this ascription later in life. But this does not alter the basically ascriptive character of citizenship assigned at birth.

The ascription of citizenship at birth is based on a presumption of membership. This presumption reflects the fact that at birth certain persons have a high probability of developing the close attachments and loyalties to a particular society and state that are supposed to underlie citizenship. Rules of ascription vary among states, but most use birthplace or parental citizenship or both as indicators of membership. The presumption of membership is strongest in the case of persons born on the territory of the state to a parent or parents possessing the citizenship of the state. Reflecting the strength of this presumption, almost all states ascribe citizenship to such persons. At the other extreme, there is no presumption of membership in the case of persons born outside the territory of a state to parents not possessing its citizenship. And no state attributes its citizenship to such persons.

The presumption of membership is ambiguous for persons born abroad to citizen parents and for persons born in the territory to non-citizen parents. It is this ambiguity that allows for variation in states' ascription rules. Variation with respect to the first of these categories is limited and need not concern us. Variation with respect to the second, however, is quite marked, and returns us to the theme of closure.

Traditional countries of immigration—including the United States, Canada, and most Latin American countries—generally ascribe citizenship to all persons born on their territory. Surprisingly, France too ascribes its citizenship, though only at the age of majority, to most persons born on its territory and continuing to reside there. At the other extreme, some countries, including Germany and Switzerland, make no special provision for conferring citizenship on second- or even third-generation immigrants. Their exclusively descent-based citizenship law takes no cognizance of birth in the territory, not even of birth in the territory over two or more generations.[35] In conjunction with restrictive naturalization policies, the ascription of citizenship on the basis of descent alone effectively excludes second- and third-generation immigrants from citizenship.

Naturalization. Persons to whom the citizenship of a state is not ascribed at birth may be able to acquire it later in life through naturalization. Rules governing the acquisition of citizenship, like those governing its ascription, can be more or less restrictive. At one pole, naturalization is a purely discretionary decision of the state. The candidate must fulfill certain conditions; but even if these are fulfilled, the state must judge whether or not the grant of citizenship is in its own interest. A negative decision need not be justified and cannot be appealed. Naturalization is anomalous and infrequent, a privilege bestowed by the state on certain deserving individuals. The procedure is long and complex; each case is carefully scrutinized. The state does not promote naturalization and may impose a dissuasively high fee. At the other pole, all candidates meeting certain clearly specified conditions are naturalized. In this system naturalization is expected of immigrants; the failure to naturalize is anomalous. Naturalization is actively promoted by the state. The procedure is simple, scrutiny of most applications perfunctory, and the fees low.[36]

The systems of naturalization in place in the United States and especially in Canada, but also in Sweden, approach the latter pole; those in Switzerland, and especially in Germany, approach the former. This is shown by their results. Taking Germany as a base, foreign residents naturalize at a rate four times higher in France, ten times higher in the United States, fifteen times higher in Sweden, and over twenty times higher in Canada.[37] Yet even in countries of immigration, naturalization remains closed in an important sense. Naturalization may be open to, and expected of, all persons meeting certain conditions, but the opportunity to satisfy these conditions is itself closed. Naturalization may be limited, as in the United States, to persons who have been formally accepted as immigrants; it is almost always limited to persons who have resided legally in the territory for a certain length of time. By restricting immigration, states indirectly restrict access to naturalization.

Citizenship is both an instrument and an object of closure. Closure against noncitizens occurs in two stages. Free access to the territory and to certain benefits and activities within it is reserved to citizens; and access to citizenship is reserved to persons meeting certain qualifying conditions. Since the qualifying conditions usually include residence in the territory, there is a circular quality to closure based on citizenship. Only citizens enjoy free access to the territory, yet only residents have access to citizenship. This circularity permits nation-states to remain, albeit in considerably differing degrees, relatively closed and self-perpetuating communities, reproducing their membership in a largely endogenous fashion, open only at the margins to the exogenous recruitment of new members.[38]

2 · The French Revolution and the Invention of National Citizenship

Modern national citizenship was an invention of the French Revolution.[1] The formal delimitation of the citizenry; the establishment of civil equality, entailing shared rights and shared obligations; the institutionalization of political rights; the legal rationalization and ideological accentuation of the distinction between citizens and foreigners; the articulation of the doctrine of national sovereignty and of the link between citizenship and nationhood; the substitution of immediate, direct relations between the citizen and the state for the mediated, indirect relations characteristic of the ancien régime—the Revolution brought all these developments together on a national level for the first time. This model of national citizenship, as Marx said of English industrial development, showed the rest of the world "the image of its own future."[2]

The Revolution, in short, invented both the nation-state and the modern institution and ideology of national citizenship. Neither, of course, was invented *ex nihilo*. Just as the invention of the nation-state presupposed centuries of state-building and the slow growth of national consciousness within the frame of the developing territorial state, so the invention of the modern institution of national citizenship built on the theory and practice of state-membership in the ancien régime.

State-Membership in the Ancien Régime

Ancien-régime society, in France as elsewhere on the Continent, was essentially inegalitarian. It was a society honeycombed with privilege, with "distinctions, whether useful or honorific . . . enjoyed by certain [persons] and denied to others."[3] Legal inequality, not simply factual inequality, was the basis of the social order. The privileged included, naturally, members of the two privileged orders or estates, the nobility and clergy. The French nobility, unlike the British aristocracy, was a legal category rather than a social class. Noblemen monopolized the officer corps of the army and the highest posts in church and government; they alone had the honorific right to carry a sword; and they were exempted from the *taille*, the principal direct tax.[4]

Sieyès' famous 1789 broadside, "What is the Third Estate?" although regarded as an attack on privilege as such, in fact attacked only the privileged orders, ignoring the many other bases of privilege. These were above all territorial and functional: there were privileged villages, towns, and provinces; there were privileged guilds, companies, associations, and corporations of every kind. And there were other bases of privilege as well. Catholics were privileged vis-à-vis Protestants and Jews. Men were privileged vis-à-vis women. Seigneurs (not all noblemen, although the possession of a *seigneurie* was a basis for ennoblement) retained vestiges of ancient claims, powers, and immunities. All who purchased offices from the crown received some kind of immunity or exemption along with the office. Members of the Third Estate participated abundantly in many of these privileges. Sieyès' pamphlet looked only to the privileged orders; reform-minded statesmen such as Turgot and Calonne saw in the "prodigious multitude" of special provisions a much more pervasive impediment to sound finance and administrative efficiency.[5]

The legal structure of ancien-régime society was fundamentally inegalitarian. In R. R. Palmer's summary appraisal, "what a later generation would call inequality was built into the fabric of society . . . All persons in principle had rights recognized by law or custom, but their rights . . . depended on the social category to which one belonged."[6] State-membership in this society had only a highly attenuated significance. The decisive units of membership or belonging were on the substate level. What mattered, as a determinant of one's rights and obligations, was not, in the first instance, that one was French or foreign: it was that one "belonged" to a *seigneurie*, or that one was an inhabitant of a *pays d'état*, or a bourgeois in a *ville franche*; or that one was a noble or a clergyman; or that one was a Protestant or a Jew; or that one was a member of a guild, university, religious foundation, or *parlement*.[7]

Being French did matter in one respect. The foreigner *(aubain)* could neither bequeath nor inherit property on the same terms as a Frenchman. When an *aubain* died without leaving direct French heirs, his property, in theory, reverted to the king by the traditional *droit d'aubaine*. In practice, however, the *droit d'aubaine* waned steadily in significance during the last three centuries of the monarchy. On the one hand, the jurisprudence of the *parlements* construed the *qualité de français* in a steadily more inclusive fashion between the sixteenth and the eighteenth century, so that many persons who formerly would have been considered *aubains* were now considered *français*.[8] On the other hand, the mercantilist monarchy, in order to encourage the immigration and settlement of skilled foreign workers, often exempted them from the *droit d'aubaine,* or even granted them *lettres de naturalité* completely assimilating them to Frenchmen. By the middle of the eighteenth century the *droit d'aubaine* found few defenders. Montesquieu called it "senseless" *(insensé).*[9] Necker, who argued that the impediments to economic development occasioned by the *droit d'aubaine* far outweighed the fiscal gain to the crown, proposed to abolish it. After 1750 France concluded treaties with most European states, each state reciprocally exempting citizens of the other from the *droit d'aubaine.* By the late eighteenth century only a small minority of foreigners remained subject to the *droit d'aubaine.*[10]

Although French law did not systematically discriminate against foreigners on the eve of the Revolution, the correlative statuses of French citizen and foreigner did exist in embryonic form. They had been created by the centralizing monarchy. In the feudal period the foreigner or *aubain* was defined with reference to the *seigneurie,* not with respect to the kingdom: he was the person born outside the *seigneurie.* And the *droit d'aubaine* belonged to the *seigneur,* not the king. Between the late thirteenth and fifteenth centuries, however, the kings succeeded in redefining the *aubain* as the person born outside the kingdom and in usurping the seigneurial *droit d'aubaine.*[11] During the same period the king effectively monopolized the right of naturalizing foreigners.[12] This created for the first time a kingdomwide status of foreigner and, correlatively, an embryonic legal status of French citizen or national. The legal distinction between French citizen and foreigner thus originated in the late medieval consolidation of royal authority at the expense of seigneurial rights.

Yet these statuses were not clearly defined. Today every state claiming sovereignty has its own nationality law and divides the world accordingly into citizens and foreigners. This formal legislative delimitation of the citizenry was unknown in the territorial states of medieval and early modern Europe. Citizenship remained inchoate. This is not to say that there were no rules determining who was and was not a "citizen"—who possessed the *qualité de français*—in early modern France. Although there were no codified, enacted rules, there were customary rules, supplemented by a growing body of jurisprudence. Since foreigners' rights to bequeath or inherit property were limited, the *qualité de français* mattered. When this was contested in the course of an inheritance-related dispute, the *parlements* (which were not legislative but rather the supreme judicial bodies) were called upon to settle the issue. In doing so, they did not define the criteria of citizenship in general terms, but determined citizenship status in particular cases. Legal commentators and scholars have extracted general rules from an analysis of these particular cases.[13] These rules, however, would be more accurately characterized as tendencies, for the decisions of different *parlements*, even those of the same *parlement*, were not always consistent.

Between the sixteenth and the eighteenth centuries the *parlements* moved toward a more expansive definition of the *qualité de français*.[14] In the sixteenth century one had to be born in France, have at least one French parent, and be domiciled in France to be considered French for purposes of inheritance. By the eighteenth century domicile was still necessary; but in addition to domicile, either of the first two criteria established one's status as French: it was enough to have been born in France, or to have been born of French parents.

This evolution was not driven by a changing conception of nationhood or citizenship. Whether or not one was French was incidental in this jurisprudence; the real issue was the question of inheritance.[15] The move toward more inclusive criteria of citizenship seems to have resulted from a concern that persons domiciled in France not be arbitrarily deprived of an inheritance because they had been born abroad, or born to foreign parents. Equity required that persons with a substantial connection to France be able to inherit. Since the *parlements* were not legislatures, they could not change the law of inheritance, which discriminated against foreigners. They could, and did, however, construe the *qualité de français* in a more expansive manner.[16]

Citizenship was not an independent branch of the law in the ancien régime. It was not defined independently of the rights that, in theory, were contingent upon it. Instead of inheritance rights (or other rights) depending on an independently defined citizenship, the definition of citizenship depended on beliefs about who ought to be able to inherit.[17] Thus, for example, a person claiming an inheritance from his parents had a better chance of being considered a citizen than a person claiming an inheritance from a more distant relative, even when the two were identically situated with respect to birthplace, parental citizenship, and domicile.[18]

To sum up. The pervasiveness of privilege in ancien-régime society left no room for the *common* rights and obligations that make up the substance of modern citizenship. The distinction between citizens and foreigners had neither ideological nor practical significance. Foreigners suffered few disabilities, and the most significant of these, in the domain of inheritance, had been largely removed by the late eighteenth century. Citizenship was not consistently defined or systematically codified; it was determined in an ad hoc manner in particular cases to make it accord with legal judgments about inheritance rights. The Revolution was to change all this.

The French Revolution: Four Perspectives on the Invention of Citizenship

Citizenship was central to the theory and practice of the French Revolution. This can be seen by considering the Revolution successively as a bourgeois revolution; a democratic revolution; a national revolution; and a bureaucratic, state-strengthening revolution. These perspectives are neither exhaustive nor mutually exclusive, but they bring into focus the multiple significance of the French Revolution for the development of the modern institution of national citizenship.

The Bourgeois Revolution

The "bourgeois revolution" perspective, which long dominated French Revolutionary historiography, has fallen from favor in recent decades. But what has become an exhausted, stale perspective for specialists remains valuable for other purposes. In this perspective, the revolution created the social and legal framework for the emergence of "bourgeois society." Above all, this meant the establishment of equality before the law and the consolidation of the legal right of private property. While the latter lies beyond the scope of this book, the former is central. By sweeping away the tangled skein of privilege—regional liberties and immunities, corporate monopolies, fiscal exemptions, vestigial seigneurial rights, and so on—the Revolution created a class of persons enjoying common rights, bound by common obligations, formally equal before the law. It substituted a common law for privilege (etymologically: private law), *citoyens* for *privilégiés.*

In this way the Revolution realized Sieyès' conception of citizenship as unmediated, undifferentiated, individual membership of the state: "I picture the law as being in the centre of a huge globe; all citizens, without exception, stand equidistant from it on the surface and occupy equal positions there; all are equally dependent on the law, all present it with their liberty and their property to be protected; and this is what I call the *common rights* [*droits communs*] of citizens, the rights in respect of which they are all alike."[19] Civil equality, for Sieyès, is conceptually essential to citizenship and civic virtue. He emphasizes *"la qualité commune de citoyen"* and *"l'égalité du civisme"*; he argues that members of the privileged orders, by virtue of their privilege, are *"hors du civisme."*[20] In view of the extent to which civil equality was in fact realized by the Revolution, there is some justification in calling *What is the Third Estate?* "the most successful pamphlet of all time."[21]

The Democratic Revolution

To view the French Revolution as a democratic revolution is to focus on political rights rather than civil equality.[22] The distinction is artificial in one sense, for the Third Estate demanded both civil equality and political representation, and it demanded both in the name of citizenship and the attack on privilege. "Like civil rights," Sieyès says explicitly, "political rights derive from a person's quality as a citizen."[23] Yet, in another sense, the distinction is analytically indispensable. Civil equality and political participation, though brought together by the French Revolution, are distinct components of modern citizenship, with ideological and institutional roots in different sociohistorical contexts.

Consider two ways of thinking about citizenship.[24] On the first view, citizenship is a *general* membership status. The citizenry coincides roughly with the permanent resident population of a state. Noncitizens are aliens or foreigners—generally, persons with no permanent connection to state or society. The definition of citizenship is abstract and formal, not concrete and substantive. By this I mean that citizenship is a status constituted by common rights and obligations, whatever their content, not by particular rights or obligations.

On the second view, citizenship is a *special* membership status. The citizenry is a privileged subgroup of the population. The distinction between citizens and aliens is not exhaustive. There are, besides aliens, other categories of noncitizens. These are persons who belong to the *ville* but not to the *cité*,[25] who belong to the state as a territorial administrative unit, but not to the state as a ruling organization. The definition of citizenship is substantive, not formal. Citizenship is constituted by the possession and exercise of political rights, by participation in the business of rule, not by common rights and obligations.

The conception of citizenship as a general membership status was a product of the struggle of centralizing, rationalizing territorial monarchies against the liberties, immunities, and privileges of feudal lords and corporate bodies. Through their efforts to regulate matters uniformly throughout their territory and, more generally, to monopolize the instruments and powers of rule, absolutist monarchs transformed the meaning of law. Poggi has characterized this transformation in a passage that merits quotation at length:

> In the Ständestaaat, "the law" was essentially the distinctive packages of rights and privileges traditionally claimed by the estates and their component bodies as well as by the ruler; it existed in the form of differentiated legal entitlements, generally of ancient origin . . . [I]n principle it could not be modified at the will of any one party, since it was not seen as the product of unilateral will in the first place . . . Against this background, the idea that the ruler could, by an act of his sovereign will, produce new law and have it enforced by his own increasingly pervasive and effective system of courts was wholly revolutionary. It transformed law from a *framework of* into an *instrument for* rule . . . Through such new law, the ruler addressed himself ever more clearly and compellingly to the whole population of the territory. He disciplined relations in increasingly general and abstract terms, applicable "wherever and whenever" . . . The ruler now possesses in the law a flexible, indefinitely extensible and modifiable instrument for articulating and sanctioning his will. As a result, his power ceases to be conceived as a collection of discrete rights and prerogatives . . . and becomes instead more unitary and abstract, more *potential*, as it were.[26]

The correlate of this new understanding of law and of rule was a new conception of the relationship between ruler and ruled. Just as law and power were generalized, made "more unitary and abstract," so too the condition of being a subject came to be conceived in more general, unitary, and abstract terms. And the word "citizen" (*citoyen, Bürger, Staatsbürger*) came to be used to denote the subject in general, irrespective of his corporate attachments.[27] Thus Bodin described the citizen as "no other in proper terms than a free [nonslave] subject holding of the sovereignty of another man."[28]

In the absolutist period, to be sure, the emergence of a general status of citizen was slow and halting. Privilege remained pervasive up to the eve of the Revolution in France, and into the nineteenth century elsewhere in Continental Europe. Yet the tendency toward civil equality, toward the development of citizenship understood as a general, abstract status, has its ideological and institutional roots in the program and practice of absolutism.

The social matrix of citizenship as a special, distinctively political status was the autonomous city, especially the city-state.[29] And while the understanding of citizenship as a general, abstract status was "progressive," reflecting the struggle of the territorial ruler against archaic liberties, immunities, and privileges, the understanding of citizenship as a special political status was profoundly conservative. Urban citizenship was in fact one of the archaic privilege-based institutions that territorial rulers aimed to undermine or marginalize in their efforts to construct a general state citizenship. The modern state and state citizenship were constructed *against* urban autonomy and urban citizenship.

Urban citizenship, then, was an institution on the defensive in the early modern era. With Rousseau, however, the city-state and its active, intimate, participatory, specifically political citizenship was revived as a cardinal point of reference for political theory. Rousseau lamented the eclipse of the classical, participatory definition of citizenship. Modern French authors, he complained—singling out Bodin—have "denatured" citizenship; they have "no true idea of its meaning."[30] His own participatory definition of citizenship echoed Aristotle's. For Aristotle, participation "in the administration of justice and in the holding of office" defined the citizen; for Rousseau, it was participation in the exercise of sovereignty.[31]

Paradoxically, the model of citizenship celebrated by Rousseau—"the great revolutionary of a revolutionary age"[32]—was not only an anachronism, the independent city-state being fated to disappear in a political landscape increasingly dominated by powerful territorial states. It was also essentially inegalitarian. This was notoriously the case in the classical polis. But Rousseau's native Geneva is also a case in point. As Rousseau noted in *The Social Contract*, there were four distinct orders of inhabitants in Geneva (five, including foreigners), but "only two compose[d] the Republic," that is, belonged, as citizens, to the *res publica*, the *cité*, the civic body. Nor did Rousseau consider this improper. Emphatically rejecting a territorial definition of citizenship, he pointed out that "houses make the town [*ville*] but . . . citizens make the civic body [*cité*]."[33] Citizenship was a special, not a general status; and Rousseau was proud of his own hereditary status as a citizen of Geneva.[34]

Territorial state-membership and municipal citizenship are, in some respects, polar opposites. The theory and practice of citizenship as a general, abstract status, characterized by equality of citizens before the law, was a product of the centralizing, rationalizing policies of absolutist territorial rulers. The theory and practice of citizenship as a privileged status, defined by participation in the business of rule, was a product of the defensive exclusiveness with which the politically privileged administered the affairs of the more or less autonomous classical, medieval, and early modern city. Yet the two traditions were joined in the French Revolution.

As a bourgeois revolution, the French Revolution established civil equality, realizing in a few weeks what the absolutist monarchs had struggled for over centuries. As a democratic revolution, the French Revolution institutionalized political rights as citizenship rights, transposing them from the plane of the city-state to that of the nation-state, and transforming them from a privilege to a general right. The Revolution, to be sure, did not in practice fully institutionalize political rights as general citizenship rights. Women were excluded, as were the *citoyens passifs*. Nonetheless, the Revolution was decisive for the development of the modern institution of national citizenship. As a democratic revolution, it joined the substantive and formal definitions of citizenship, the classical Republican and modern conceptions. Attaching the content of the classical definition—participation in the business of rule—to the generalizing, inclusive form of the modern definition, it made political participation a general rather than a special right. It followed the program of absolutism in making citizenship a general rather than a special status. But it also followed the classical tradition in making participation in the business of rule, if not constitutive of citizenship, at least essential to citizenship.

The National Revolution

To characterize the French Revolution as a national revolution is to suggest a dual transformation: the creation of a *nation une et indivisible*, composed of legally equal individuals standing in a direct relationship to the state, out of a patchwork of overlapping corporate jurisdictions and pervasive corporate privilege; and the substitution of a militant, mobilized nationalism for the cosmopolitanism, the prevailing indifference to nationality and citizenship, of the old regime. The Revolution thus created both the nation-state (by abolishing jurisdictional boundaries and corporate distinctions within the nation) and nationalism (by constructing new boundaries and sharpening antagonisms between nations).

The development of international at the expense of intranational boundaries during the Revolution is suggestively outlined by Lucien Febvre:

> The Revolution makes a group of subjects, vassals, and members of restricted communities into the body of citizens of one and the same state. It abolishes internal barriers between them and welds them into one powerful group which forms a coherent mass within clearly defined borders. Previously people had walked straight across the boundary; aristocrats, men of letters and merchants crossed it quite naturally. The *frontière* existed only for soldiers and princes, and only then in time of war. On the morrow of the Revolution not only did the demarcation line between France and the neighboring countries appear quite clearly, for better or for worse . . . , but the line of the national boundaries became a sort of ditch between nationalities that were quite distinct from one another, and it was backed up by a second, moral frontier. It was soon to equip itself with all the hates, bitterness and fear aroused in France and in other countries by the French Revolution.[35]

Febvre was referring to jurisdictional and territorial boundaries, but one could make a similar argument about personal boundaries defined by the law. The development of national citizenship represents a displacement of personal boundaries—that is, boundaries between personal statuses—from within to between nations. As membership of subnational units was abolished or rendered inconsequential, membership of the nation-state became more important.

This coupling of nationhood and nationalism was neither intended nor foreseen by the revolutionaries of 1789. The nation was exalted at the expense of privileged orders, corporations, guilds, provinces, and other subnational groupings, not at the expense of other nations (or their citizens). In its early stages the Revolution was ostentatiously cosmopolitan. It took over the undemonstrative, laissez-faire cosmopolitanism of the ancien régime, recast it in ideological terms, invested it with missionary fervor. Foreign enthusiasts of Revolutionary developments—*pélerins de la liberté*—were welcomed in France.[36] Liberty, Equality, Fraternity were to be France's gifts to the world: "It is not for ourselves alone, it is not for that part of the globe than one calls France, that we have conquered Liberty."[37] National boundaries as well as internal boundaries were to be transcended: "The national assembly, considering that the *droit d'aubaine* is contrary to the principles of fraternity that ought to unite all men, whatever their country or government . . . ; and that France, now free, ought to open its bosom to all the peoples of the earth, by inviting them to enjoy, under a free government, the sacred and inviolable rights of humanity, has decreed: The *droit d'aubaine* . . . [is] forever abolished."[38] The cosmopolitanism animating this decree of August 1790 was reaffirmed and consecrated in the Constitution of 1791, which devoted one of its seven sections to "the relations of the French nation with foreign nations": "The French nation renounces the aim of undertaking any war of conquest, and will never employ its forces against the liberty of any people.—The Constitution forbids the *droit d'aubaine*.—Foreigners in France, established or not, can succeed from their parents, whether these are foreigners or French.—They can make contracts, acquire and receive goods located in France, and dispose of them, in the same way as any French citizen can, by all means authorized by law.—Foreigners who find themselves in France are subjected to the same criminal and police laws as are French citizens . . . ; their person, their goods, their industry, their cult are equally protected by law."[39] The preamble to this Constitution proclaimed that there would be "no privilege, no exception to the common law of all Frenchmen." Yet outside the domain of political rights, the "common law of all Frenchmen" applied equally to foreigners. The Rights of Citizens seemed to be dissolved into the Rights of Man. The Constitution of 1793 even extended political rights to most foreigners.[40]

In ideological intent, then, the Revolution was conspicuously cosmopolitan, at least in its early phase. In practice, the status of the foreigner did not change much, for the ancien régime was also quite cosmopolitan, in theory and in practice. There was not only a "uniform, cosmopolitan culture among the upper classes of most of Europe," but a prevailing indifference to nationality in public life.[41] Skilled foreign workers were sometimes granted privileges not enjoyed by their French counterparts, without any sense of anomaly; the personal guard of the king was composed of foreigners; some high officials (notably Mazarin and Necker) were foreigners. And as has been noted, the main disability to which foreigners were subject—the *droit d'aubaine*—had been hollowed out by so many exemptions and treaties that its formal abolition during the Revolution had little effect. In its cosmopolitanism, as in other respects, the Revolution took up where the ancien régime left off.[42] It was in the xenophobic nationalism of its radical phase, not in the cosmopolitanism of its liberal phase, that the Revolution was genuinely revolutionary.[43]

This xenophobic nationalism was a product of war and factional struggle, which engendered a climate of extreme suspicion of the internal enemies that might knowingly or unknowingly be in the service of external enemies. Foreigners were not the only victims of this generalized suspicion, which embraced émigrés, refractory priests, noblemen, rebels, and political opponents. But the Convention did direct a series of repressive measures specifically against foreigners, establishing a system of registration and surveillance, ordering expulsions, imposing special criminal penalties, requiring special proofs of *civisme*, excluding foreigners from all political functions, sequestering and confiscating goods, and forbidding residence in Paris, in fortified towns, or on the coast.[44] Anarchisis Cloots, self-appointed "orator of the human race," was executed.[45] Thomas Paine was arrested. Both had been among the seventeen foreign thinkers and statesmen granted "the title of French citizen" on August 26, 1792, on the grounds that "these men who, by their writing and by their courage, have served the cause of liberty and prepared the liberation of peoples, can not be regarded as foreigners."[46]

Why this reversal, this abrupt shift from ostentatious cosmopolitanism to xenophobia and repression?[47] The pervasive fear of enemies within and enemies without, grounded in the experience of foreign war, civil insurrection, and factional struggle, but passing into paranoia, helps explain the multiplication of exclusions. But why specifically foreigners? Certain police measures directed against citizens of countries with whom France was at war are understandable. But some of the harshest measures were directed not at enemy nationals but at foreigners as such. Why were foreigners singled out?

The answer has to do with the logic of the nation-state. A nation-state is a nation's state, the state of and for a particular, bounded, sovereign nation, to which foreigners, by definition, do not belong. Legally homogeneous internally, it is by virtue of this very fact more sharply bounded externally than an internally heterogeneous state such as pre-Revolutionary France.[48] Sharp external boundedness does not dictate the terms on which resident foreigners are to be treated; but it does mark them clearly and axiomatically as outsiders—paradigmatic outsiders. By inventing the national citizen and the legally homogeneous national citizenry, the Revolution simultaneously invented the foreigner. Henceforth citizen and foreigner would be correlative, mutually exclusive, exhaustive categories. One would be either a citizen or a foreigner; there would be no third way. As a result of this stark simplification in the political geometry of membership, *l'étranger* could symbolize pure extraneity in

a manner that was not possible in the ancien régime, where the for-
eigner-citizen distinction was simply one axis of legal discrimination
among many—a relatively insignificant one at that. The Revolutionary
invention of the nation-state and national citizenship thus engendered
the modern figure of the foreigner—not only as a legal category but as
a political epithet, invested with a psychopolitical charge it formerly
lacked, and condensing around itself pure outsiderhood.[49] It is just this
definitional extraneity that, in the overheated political climate of 1793–
94, encouraged factions to accuse one another of foreign connections,
that enabled theories of a *conspiration de l'étranger* to flourish, and that
provided a veneer of justification for harsh repressive measures against
foreigners.

As a political epithet, to be sure, *"étranger"* could be used against
nationals as well as legal foreigners. Throughout the Revolutionary
period, political and legal definitions of *l'étranger* were not sharply
distinguished. This fusion—or confusion—is epitomized by Tallien's
remark: "the only foreigners in France are bad citizens." This could work
to the benefit of legal foreigners. Even at the height of xenophobic
nationalism, certain foreigners were exempted from the repressive anti-
foreigner measures. As Thibaudeau put it, "the working man can be a
foreigner in no country; he is naturalized by his work."[50] Conversely,
certain "bad citizens" could be redefined as foreigners, as nonbelongers.
"It is characteristic of a revolution," notes Vida Azimi, "to make things
foreign to it, even 'nationals' [*de rendre étranger à elle, même des nationaux*]."[51] This logic of exclusion—what Pierre Nora calls "this heavy
complex built around the notion of 'the foreigner'"—dates from 1789,
from Sieyès' definitional exclusion of the privileged orders from the
nation, not from 1793.[52] The invention of the nation-state and a national
citizenry gave new weight to the political and to the legal concept of
étranger. And precisely because the two were not consistently distinguished, *étrangers* in the legal sense could be lumped with *étrangers* in
the political sense, foreigners with émigrés, refractory priests, rebels,
aristocrats, and other political enemies.

The nation-state may, indeed must, discriminate between citizens and
foreigners. It is in this sense inherently nationalistic. Its nationalism need
not be the aggressive or xenophobic sort of 1792 and after. More often
it has a routine, normal, taken-for-granted quality. Both sorts of nationalism—the normal "background" nationalism of the nation-state and the
noisy, bellicose variety—descend to us from the French Revolution. The
harsh Revolutionary measures against foreigners had the ad hoc char-

acter of all emergency legislation. But their underlying logic illustrates Febvre's point. The Revolution created a legal frontier and a "moral frontier" between members of different nation-states. Abolishing legal and moral boundaries within the nation-state, it crystallized legal and moral boundaries and divisions between nation-states. Thus it engendered both the modern nation-state and modern nationalism.

As a national revolution, the French Revolution shaped the institution of modern citizenship in several distinct ways. By leveling legal distinctions inside the nation, it gave a common substance to citizenship: civil equality. By valorizing the nation and the idea of national citizenship, it created the ideological basis for modern nationalism, in its domestic and international expressions. And by defining precisely who was French, it provided a technical basis for denying certain rights to or imposing certain obligations on foreigners.

The Bureaucratic Revolution

The Revolution, finally, can be seen as a state-building, bureaucratic revolution.[53] By abolishing the vestiges of the seigneurial system, the tangled skein of privilege, the crazy-quilt array of jurisdictions, and the welter of corporations, the Revolution swept away obstacles to effective state action. Thus Marx: "The centralised State power . . . originates from the days of absolute monarchy . . . Still, its development remained clogged by all manner of medieval rubbish, seignorial rights, local privileges, municipal and guild monopolies and provincial constitutions. The gigantic broom of the French Revolution . . . swept away all these relics . . . , thus clearing simultaneously the social soil of its last hindrances to the superstructure of the modern state edifice."[54] And again: "with its task of breaking all separate, local, territorial, urban and provincial powers in order to create the civil unity of the nation, [the Revolution] was bound to develop what the absolute monarchy had begun: centralisation, but at the same time the extent, the attributes and the agents of governmental power."[55] The Revolution left the individual face to face with the state, unprotected by intermediary corporate bodies—the buffering institutions celebrated in the political theory informed by Montesquieu and Tocqueville.

The crucial point about citizenship, from this perspective, is that an immediate, direct form of state-membership replaced the mediated, indirect forms of membership characteristic of the ancien régime. From this transformation in the structure of membership, the state gained both greater resources and greater control. The "immediatization" of membership permitted an expansion of direct taxation, replacing the old system of tax farming, based on contracts with largely autonomous corporations. It permitted the state to demand military service from every citizen, and directly to regulate foreigners.

The strengthening of the state through the "immediatization" of membership depended, however, on the legal rationalization and codification of membership. To demand services from its citizens or to exclude or regulate noncitizens, the state had to be able to determine unambiguously who was and was not a citizen. In this domain, too, the Revolution marked a decisive stage in the development of citizenship. The Constitution of 1791 contained the first formal, explicit delimitation of the citizenry carried out by a western territorial state.[56] The formalization and codification of membership marked an important stage in the development of what Michael Mann has called the "infrastructural" power of the state, by which he means the "power to co-ordinate civil society."[57]

The development of the modern institution of national citizenship is intimately bound up with the development of the modern nation-state. The French Revolution marked a crucial moment in both. There are several respects in which the Revolution shaped the modern institution of national citizenship. As a bourgeois revolution, it created a general membership status based on equality before the law. As a democratic revolution, it revived the classical conception of active political citizenship but transformed it from a special into what was, in principle if not yet in practice, a general status. As a national revolution, it sharpened boundaries—and antagonisms—between the members of different nation-states. And as a state-strengthening revolution, it "immediatized" and codified state-membership. National citizenship as we know it bears the stamp of all these developments.

3 ◆ State, State-System, and Citizenship in Germany

The development of national citizenship followed a longer and more tortuous path in Germany than in France. There was no German nation-state, and thus no political frame for national citizenship, until 1871. Moreover, there was no pivotal event in the history of citizenship, no moment of crystallization remotely like the French Revolution. Aspects of citizenship that, as a result of the Revolutionary crystallization, were closely integrated in France—egalitarian, democratic, nationalist, and statist aspects—developed independently of one another in Germany.

This is reflected in the German vocabulary of citizenship. In French and American English, *nationalité* and *citoyenneté*, "nationality" and "citizenship," are rough synonyms.[1] "Citizenship" has participatory connotations that "nationality" lacks and "nationality" has a richer cultural resonance than "citizenship," but the words are used interchangeably to designate the legal quality of state-membership. In German, formal state-membership, participatory citizenship, and ethnocultural nation-membership are designated by distinct terms: *Staatsangehörigkeit*, *Staatsbürgerschaft*, and *Nationalität* or *Volkszugehörigkeit* respectively. The semantic overlap in French and English reflects the political definition of nationhood and the fusion of the concepts of state, nation, and sovereign people in the French, English, and American political traditions, a fusion deriving from their founding revolutions.[2] The semantic differentiation in German reflects the independent and sometimes antagonistic course of state-building, nationalism, and democracy in Germany.

This is borne out by the institutional history of citizenship. One of the first formal codifications of state-membership in Germany—a law of 1842 that, like the Constitution of 1791 in France, served as the model for all subsequent citizenship legislation—codified the status of Prussian subject, not German citizen. This underscores the prenational, predemocratic quality of the citizenship *(Staatsangehörigkeit)* that developed in the individual German states in the second half of the eighteenth and first half of the nineteenth century. I use the word "citizenship" deliberately. The ideological antithesis of subject and citizen should not blind us to the underlying structural similarity between the codification of citizenship in Revolutionary France and the codification of "subjecthood" in Restoration Prussia. Citizenship, for my purposes, is a legal institution regulating membership in the state, not a set of participatory practices or a set of specifically civic attitudes. Its meaning, in this sense, is exactly captured by the German *Staatsangehörigkeit*. This chapter examines the early, prenational and predemocratic, development of this institution in Germany, focusing on the close connection between the development of citizenship and the development of the modern state and state-system.[3]

There is an apparent paradox in this state-centered approach to the development of German citizenship. The restrictiveness of German citizenship vis-à-vis immigrants, I have argued, reflects an ethnocultural understanding of nation-state membership, according to which *Staatsangehörigkeit* presupposes and expresses *Volkszugehörigkeit*. This argument, it would seem, posits the close integration of formal-legal state-membership and ethnocultural nation-membership. Historically, however, nation-membership and state-membership were much more closely integrated in France. German citizenship law developed without reference to German ethnocultural nationality in Prussia and other German states in the first half of the nineteenth century; French citizenship law was national from its inception, defining membership of the French nation as well as membership of the French state.

The paradox is only apparent. It is true that nation and state, nationality and citizenship have always been more closely integrated in France than in Germany. Yet precisely the early and stable fusion of nation and state shaped the French understanding of nationhood as an essentially political fact, unthinkable apart from the institutional and territorial framework of the state. French citizenship has been national, even nationalist, from its inception. Yet, as I shall argue in Chapter 5, the specifically political and statist quality of French nationalism has permitted, even required, a citizenship law that would transform immigrants into Frenchmen.

German citizenship was not originally national. Nation and state, German nationality and Prussian (or other subnational) citizenship were sharply distinct. Yet that very distinctness shaped the German understanding of nationhood as an essentially ethnocultural fact, prior to and independent of the state. In 1871 Germany became a national state and acquired a national citizenship. Yet on the ethnocultural understanding of nationhood, the Bismarckian state and its citizenship were only imperfectly national. Bismarckian Germany was called an "incomplete" *(unvollendeter)* nation-state.[4] From an ethnocultural point of view, its citizenship law too was "incomplete"—too statist, and insufficiently national. The ethnonational politics that emerged in the Wilhelmine period, as we shall see in Chapter 6, sought to nationalize and "ethnicize" the citizenship law of the Empire. The major revision of citizenship law enacted in 1913 gave an ethnonational inflection to citizenship law, although an attenuated one by comparison with the vastly more radical "ethnicization" undertaken by the Nazis. The initial distinctness of nation and state—ethnic nationality and political citizenship—in Germany gave to the later nationalization of citizenship a specifically ethnocultural dimension that was muted, if not entirely absent, in France. With strong conceptual moorings independent of the territorial and institutional frame of the state, nationhood could furnish an independent, extrapolitical criterion against which German citizenship law could be measured; this was not the case in France.

Subsequent chapters examine the nationalization of citizenship in Wilhelmine Germany and the later vicissitudes of German citizenship law; they seek to explain why German citizenship law is based exclusively on *jus sanguinis* or descent. This chapter, by contrast, is concerned not with the content of citizenship law—the system of pure *jus sanguinis*—but with the development of citizenship as a legal institution regulating membership of the state. Its analytical focus is on the duality of citizenship, an institution at once inclusive and exclusive. In the last chapter we examined the ideological roots of this duality in French Revolutionary nationalism; here we discuss its institutional roots in the development of the Prussian state and German state-system. As a general, immediate, inclusive status, modern citizenship is the product of a long process of status *amalgamation;* as a formally defined, externally bounded status, it is the product of status *differentiation.* The former occurred within the developing territorial states; the latter occurred between different territorial states. The former was the product of rulers' drive toward unitary internal sovereignty, itself grounded in military competition among coordinate independent states; the latter arose from the dynamics of the early-nineteenth-century German state system, in which individual states sought to protect themselves against the increasingly mobile poor. This chapter takes up in turn these two developments.

From *Ständestaat* to Territorial State: Overcoming Internal Boundaries

Citizenship and Sovereignty: An Ideal-Typical Sketch

As a general, inclusive, immediate status, citizenship is the product of the development of the modern state in the direction of unitary internal sovereignty.[5] This involved the monopolization of the powers of rule by a single central authority; the reconceptualization of the powers of rule, traditionally understood as a bundle of limited, discrete, particular rights, now conceived more abstractly as indivisible and unlimited; and the unification of law and administration through the creation of a single, internally homogeneous, externally bounded legal and administrative space.[6] As a result, the intricate and multiform geometry of political and legal membership was starkly simplified. Before the development of unitary internal sovereignty, jurisdiction was based largely on personal status, not on territory. General law, valid for the entire territory, scarcely existed. (The very idea of general law, formulated in the early stages of rulers' drive toward sovereignty, was a revolutionary one.) Territorial rulers did claim specific regalian rights over their territories, but these were narrowly limited and impinged little on the lives of the inhabitants. Insofar as it shaped people's lives, "the law," for the most part, was neither state law nor territorial law but "special law," valid for a particular group of persons, not for a particular stretch of territory, and held as a matter of right by that group of persons, not on the discretionary sufferance of the state.[7]

Law was understood as a "strictly personal quality, a 'privilege' acquired by usurpation or grant, and thus a monopoly of its possessors who, by virtue of this fact, became 'comrades in law' *(Rechtsgenossen)*."[8] There was no general legal order, or at most a highly attenuated one. Instead there was a multitude of special legal orders, each valid only for members of particular status groups. The result, Max Weber notes, was "the coexistence of numerous 'law communities' *(Rechtsgemeinschaften)*, the autonomous jurisdictions of which overlapped, the compulsory, political association being only one such autonomous jurisdiction in so far as it existed at all . . . The idea of generally applicable norms . . . remained in an undeveloped state; all law appeared as the privilege of particular individuals or objects or of particular constellations of individuals or objects."[9] In this legal and political situation, the decisive instances of belonging were the special law communities. The territorial state, as it began to emerge, had only a secondary importance. What mattered, with respect to the legal (and thereby the social and economic) shaping of life chances, was that one belonged to a guild, or to a self-governing municipal corporation, or to the class of fief-holders.

This changed fundamentally with the development of unitary internal sovereignty. The state claimed to be the sole legitimate source of law. Ever more matters came under the direct and territorywide regulation of the state. Special law did not disappear, but special law communities lost their autonomy. Increasingly, special law lost its character as privilege, or private law, and took on the character of public law, emanating like general law from the state, special only in regulating a particular object domain. The general law of the land became increasingly important in the legal shaping of life chances. Corporate membership waned in legal significance where it did not disappear entirely. Yet it was not replaced by membership in the state. No such status yet existed: the state was not yet formally structured as a membership association. The state was structured, rather, as a territorial field of rule; all who came within that field were subject to its jurisdiction. Territory replaced membership as the organizing principle of law. This cleared the way for the invention of a new sort of membership. The new membership would be general, rather than partial; it would comprehend in a single status all persons who belonged to the state and exclude only those who belonged to other states; it would be oriented to the state as the source of general law rather than to particular law communities and their special law; it would bring individuals into direct relationship with the state, as intervening organizations and corporations lost legal significance.

The development of unitary internal sovereignty replaced the panoply of special law communities, valid only for their members, with a single general legal order, valid for the entire territory. Membership—personal belonging to an order, corporation, or association—was thereby suspended as an axial principle of social and legal organization; the state became a territorial organization, enforcing an order within a territory, indifferent to personal status. Yet the process through which territorial jurisdiction supplanted membership as a principle of law and social organization laid the foundation for a new, general, comprehensive form of membership.

The Unification of Administration: The Commissarial Bureaucracy

Central state authority developed in Brandenburg-Prussia around the standing army created in the mid-seventeenth century by Frederick William, the Great Elector. In this respect Prussia followed the common European pattern. Modern standing armies, paid, equipped, and effectively controlled by the state, emerged throughout Continental Europe in the seventeenth century, and were everywhere closely related to the development of the absolutist state.[10] Yet military and civil administration were uniquely intertwined in Prussia. The institutional link between the two was the commissarial bureaucracy that developed from an ad hoc instrument of military supervision into a permanent and general administrative apparatus.[11]

Like the French intendants, the Prussian commissaries were originally military envoys of the king, assigned to accompany and oversee royal armies on particular campaigns and to supervise their provisioning. To this end they were given broad police powers over the general population as well as over the army. With the development of the standing army, the commissaries became permanent bureaucrats, retaining broad police powers as a means of carrying out their military responsibilities. Since the standing army depended on regular tax collection, these new agencies assumed administrative responsibility for taxation; and since the extraction of tax revenue depended on general economic conditions, they assumed broad responsibility for the regulation of economic life as well. "Thus military administration became inseparably entangled with civilian and police administration; the whole internal police system that gradually developed from this bore a militaristic cast."[12] On this basis there developed an elaborate, hierarchical, centralized commissarial bureaucracy with general and far-reaching administrative responsibilities over the whole of social and economic life.

The commissaries stood outside the older system of administrative offices. Originally they were specifically extraordinary positions, justified by the urgent demands of extraordinary circumstances such as war or civil unrest. They also stood outside the law, in the sense that there was no generally acknowledged legal basis for their powers. Unlike regular officials, who were empowered by public, duly registered edict, commissaries had no "legal, publicly recognized foundation; they got the principles for their actions from secret instructions, disclosed neither to the province at large nor even to the old [official] agencies."[13] Their extraordinary, extralegal character gave them the flexibility that suited them to the emerging pattern of absolutist rule. The older, inflexible, particularistic, status-differentiated *Rechtsstaat* was bypassed by the emerging absolutist *Polizeistaat*.[14] The older offices survived, but they were overlaid and progressively eclipsed by new agencies that developed out of the war commissaries: "These agencies had no roots in the old provincial constitution and law. Their attitude toward the old order of public life was unsympathetic, indeed decidedly hostile. They became the chief implements for destroying the old system of government by Estates and for building the new absolutist military state . . . The whole apparatus . . . ran counter to the Estates and territorial custom in myriad ways . . . The old authorities . . . saw this daily increasing and encroaching power as an illegal usurpation, although they recognized that behind it was the irresistible will of the sovereign as military chief."[15]

Although the commissarial bureaucracy was extralegal in one sense, having no basis in the traditional common law, it was at the same time the vehicle for the development of a new type of law, a monarchical administrative law that ultimately developed into modern public law. Initially, however, this new administrative law was not really "law" at all, in the sense of a publicly known and publicly validated set of rules; it was, rather, a set of secret monarchical decrees and administrative rules known only to the commissarial authorities themselves. This is why the absolutist state can be characterized as a *Polizeistaat*, breaking with the older status-differentiated *Rechtsstaat*, and only later, in the age of enlightened absolutism and modern constitutionalism, becoming a *Rechtsstaat* itself. In the absolutist interlude, "this new princely administrative law fundamentally restructured all of political and legal life."[16]

One aspect of this "fundamental restructuring"—the aspect that concerns us here—was the restructuring of political and legal membership. The commissarial bureaucracy, with its territorywide reach and broad administrative mandate, centrally directed through the emerging monarchical administrative law, gradually transformed the Hohenzolleren territories from a congeries of disparate jurisdictions into a unitary administrative field.[17] All inhabitants of the territory, independently of the special law communities to which they belonged, were gradually drawn into this administrative field as objects of central bureaucratic authority. To an initially small but gradually increasing extent, the legal framework for their lives was set by monarchical administrative law, through the commissarial bureaucracy.

State penetration of society through centralized bureaucracy and administrative law contributed to the development of modern citizenship by bringing all inhabitants of the territory into direct and immediate relationship to the state. But not into an *equal* relationship to the state. The *Verstaatlichung*[18] of administration under the Great Elector and especially under King Frederick William I (1713–1740) occurred at the expense of the *ständisch* polity, but not at the expense of the *ständisch* social order. The legal foundations of that social order were undisturbed—"hereditary subjection of peasants . . . , sharp [legal] separation of town and country, social privileges of the the nobility, exclusive noble right to the possession of *Rittergüter,* tax exemption for the nobility in many provinces, preference for the nobility in the upper civil and military administration."[19] The absolutist state accepted, even confirmed, these foundational legal inequalities. Legal equality—a second component of modern citizenship—began to develop only under Frederick the Great, in the second half of the eighteenth century.

Toward the Unification of Law: The Allgemeines Landrecht

The first major, though limited, step toward legal equality occurred with the *Allgemeines Landrecht* (ALR), the legal code that was prepared under Frederick the Great and enacted under his successor in 1794. The ALR is a richly contradictory document, at once individualist and corporatist, liberal and authoritarian, progressive and conservative, sweepingly general and minutely particular. In its philosophical underpinnings and general formulations, it looked beyond the corporate society and authoritarian polity that its detailed provisions nonetheless confirmed.[20] Its chief architect, Karl Gottlieb Suarez, trained in natural law jurisprudence, championed personal freedom, civil equality, judicial independence, and limited state power. Yet Frederick the Great's commitment to the *ständisch* social order, and to the privileges of the nobility in particular, set limits to Suarez's work from the outset, while the political reservations of the more conservative government of Frederick William II occasioned substantial emendations of the original version.[21] The result was a document at war with its expressed intentions. The introduction proclaimed the equality of all before the law, without regard to their *Stand,*[22] yet the law codified *ständisch* inequalities. The title promised general law; the text articulated a mass of special law.[23] The ALR described peasants as "free citizens of the state" yet confirmed their hereditary subjection to rural lords.[24] It invoked membership of the state, but codified membership of the *Stände.*

These contradictions notwithstanding, the ALR furthered the development of citizenship in three ways. First, it gave public legal form to the military-administrative state. Previously the state had been constructed, organized, and run largely through the medium of secret monarchical decrees; now it had something like a public constitution, a body of public law that was truly public. This "legalization" of the state laid the groundwork for the later legal definition of state-membership; it constituted the state as a legal entity of which one could be a member. It did not do so directly and explicitly. Despite its quasi-constitutional character, the ALR was not a constitution, and it did not formally "constitute" the state as a constitution would. But by repeatedly invoking "the state" in various substantive contexts and detaching it from the person of the monarch, the ALR in effect constituted it as an impersonal, legal, distinctively public entity. In so doing it gave legal expression to the political philosophy of enlightened absolutism, as epitomized in Frederick the Great's famous self-characterization as "the first servant of the state."[25]

Second, to the legalization of the state corresponded a *Verstaatlichung*—an increasing state-centeredness—of law and membership. The ALR did not transform Prussian territories into a unitary state, governed by a single generally valid law. But it did establish a general, statewide legal frame within which legal unity could be realized gradually. For political reasons, Frederick the Great was unwilling to abolish *ständisch* privileges or regional particularisms, so long as they did not affect the security or strength of the state. Unlike his father, Frederick William I, Frederick the Great was not engaged in a perpetual battle with the nobility. He had successfully "Prussianized" the nobility, transforming them into a statewide service nobility, which monopolized the officer corps of the army and the high positions in the administration. The achievement was remarkable: the various provincial nobilities, fierce opponents of the centralizing military-bureaucratic state under the Great Elector and Frederick William I, were not only reconciled to that state under Frederick the Great, but, through the medium of the officer corps, were welded into a single, supraprovincial, statewide nobility, and as such became the social carriers of a statewide Prussian patriotism and nationalism.[26] Yet the achievement had a price. Having coopted the nobility, Frederick the Great was unwilling to challenge their social or legal privileges, or to impose legal unification on the provinces. In the domain of private law, therefore, the ALR was intended systematically to unify existing law, insofar as a common denominator could be found, not to create new law. In most private law matters, where the ALR diverged from prior law or established rights, the latter took precedence. Yet despite these limitations on the validity—and thus on the generality—of the "general law of the land," the ALR furthered the development of citizenship even in its capacity as a private law codification. For the continued—and in the domain of private law superordinate—validity of provincial law, special statutes, and other established rights now depended on express state confirmation.[27] Even if the state did not claim an exclusive or overriding validity for state-made, statewide law, it did claim the exclusive right to *validate* law. The autonomy of substate "law communities" was thereby denied, and the state's legislative sovereignty affirmed, even if not fully exploited.[28] The legal prerequisites of "unitary internal sovereignty" were established, even if the territory was not yet transformed into a single, internally homogeneous legal space.

Third, the ALR codified *Stand*-membership and assigned particular rights and duties to the members thus defined. This seems the direct antithesis of modern citizenship. Yet if we think historically and comparatively of citizenship as a "conceptual variable,"[29] we can see how the codification of *Stand*-membership in the ALR furthered the development of modern citizenship. In the middle ages the *Stände*, corporations, guilds—what Weber called special law communities—were autonomous. They possessed privileges, exercised internal jurisdiction over their members, and defined their own membership as a matter of autonomous, quasi-private right. These rights were not integrated into or derived from any overarching public legal order; no such public legal order existed. This very lack of integration gave the medieval "legal order" its specific complexity: it was not a single legal order at all. Administrative absolutism had undermined the autonomy of the *Stände*; the ALR abolished it. It transformed the *Stände* into state-defined and state-regulated corporations, differentiated by their function in the total political economy of the state and assigned specific rights and duties corresponding to that function. The *Stände* thereby became *"staatliche Berufstände,"* state-chartered vocational orders.[30] The ALR formulated explicit rules defining membership in the *Stände*, using a combination of ascriptive and functional criteria.[31] As a result, the *Stände* were no longer purely hereditary; they depended on occupation and state recognition as well as birth. Moreover, the *Stände*, previously provincial bodies, were now defined as statewide corporations—a step toward a more generalized, wider membership.

A further move in this direction was the definition of the *Bürgerstand*.

As a *ständisch* category, *Bürger* previously meant *Stadtbürger*, the holder of municipal citizenship rights in a town. Every town had its *Stadtbür-gertum*, or citizenry, which did not coincide with the urban population as a whole, but represented a legally privileged subgroup. The ALR retained this traditional definition for some purposes. But it was over-laid by a new and more general *Bürger*-concept. This new *Bürgerstand* was defined on a statewide basis, rather then within the limits of a particular town; and it was residually rather than positively defined. It was no longer constituted by persons possessing specific urban privi-leges, but rather by all persons not belonging to the noble or peasant *Stände*.[32] Numerically this was a small fraction of the state's population. But conceptually it was a move toward general citizenship.[33] Should legal privileges of the nobility or the legal disabilities of peasants be lifted—as they were, to a large extent, during the reform period of the early nineteenth century—then nobility and peasantry would collapse into this more general legal category of *Bürger*, which would become a general citizenship status.

The transformation of the *Stände*—from autonomous urban and pro-vincial bodies into statewide, state-constituted, state-regulated corpora-tions—prepared the way for a more general state-membership. Mem-bership was now defined *by* the state and *for* the state as a whole (rather than for particular provinces and towns). Membership *of* the state re-mained undefined in the ALR. *Stand*-membership was codified; state-membership was not. Yet if general state-membership was not codified, it was nonetheless repeatedly invoked in the ALR, along with other comprehensive *Stand*-transcending concepts.[34] For the ALR contained general *Landrecht* as well as particular *Standrecht*. While the latter was addressed to persons in their particular capacities as members of a *Stand*, the former was addressed to persons in their general and common capacity as inhabitants *(Einwohner)*, subjects *(Untertanen)*, or members of the state *(Mitglieder des Staates)*. The ALR neither defined these nor consistently distinguished between them. But their assimilative, in-clusive, generalizing function is clear. Through such constructions, the state could deliberately abstract from *ständisch* qualifications and disqualifications. This abstraction is a crucial element of the develop-mental history of citizenship. The legal historian Rolf Grawert has aptly characterized modern citizenship as an *"Abstraktionsleistung,"* a work of abstraction.[35] By abstracting from *ständisch* privileges and liabilities in this manner, the ALR staked out an egalitarian legal space, an extra-*ständisch* zone of legal equality and generally valid law, a region of general citizenship. This region was not yet substantively significant, but it was capable of substantive enrichment.[36]

Toward Legal Equality: The Prussian Reform Legislation

Our understanding of citizenship is based largely on the theory and practice of the French Revolution. As a result, we tend to think of citizenship as developing against the *Stände* and against the absolutist monarchy. In Prussia, however, the foundations of citizenship were established *by* the absolute monarch and *through* the *Stände*. Citizenship emerged gradually, through the *Verstaatlichung* and generalization of the *Stände*, not through their outright destruction, as in France. It was imposed piecemeal from above, rather than conquered integrally from below.[37] The Prussian state destroyed the autonomy of the *Stände*, transforming them into state-constituted, state-defined, state-regulated corporations. And it defined the *Stände* in an increasingly general fashion, both by stretching their territorial frame to fit that of the state as a whole, and by defining one *Stand*—the *Bürgerstand*—in residual rather than positive terms, marking it as a relatively general and inclusive status in contradistinction to the special statuses of noble and peasant.

From this point, the development of citizenship involved two further steps. The first was the emergence of a region of legal equality. In France this occurred once and for all in the Revolution; in Prussia it was effected piecemeal. The early-nineteenth-century reform legislation did not abolish the *Stände* and their privileges outright. The most glaring survival was that of the *Stand*-specific courts. Nobles and the high state bourgeoisie came under the jurisdiction of special state courts, while many peasants continued to be subject to the patrimonial justice of rural lords.[38] But in the economic domain, most *Stand*-specific privileges and obligations were abolished. Peasants were freed from hereditary subjection, service obligations, and the exit fees formerly levied on those who moved out of the local judicial district. Nobles were free to enter formerly "bourgeois" occupations—and to incorporate previously protected peasant holdings into their own. Bourgeois were free to buy formerly noble estates. Guild monopolies were dissolved, and complete freedom of occupation introduced. These reforms amounted to an abolition of the *Stände* as economically significant categories.[39]

In the economic domain, then, persons met as free and equal individuals. But not as citizens. To be sure, citizenship presupposes legal equality, and legal equality was realized in the economic domain. Internal boundaries between persons (*Stand*-specific rights and obligations) and between regions (tolls and taxes on the movement of goods and persons) were abolished. The result was a unitary, homogeneous space, within which all persons were formally free and equal economic actors. But this state of affairs has an ambiguous relationship to citizenship. For citizenship is an externally bounded as well as an internally egalitarian status. This external boundedness did not yet exist. A region of legal equality had been created. But this region was territorially bounded, not personally circumscribed. The equality of citizenship, however, is a personal, not a territorial equality; it obtains among citizens of a state, not among inhabitants of a territory. In this sense, the equality of citizenship is a *ständisch* equality; citizenship is a *Stand,* a status. It is a general, inclusive status, embracing virtually the entire population of the state. This distinguishes modern citizenship sharply from ancient and medieval municipal citizenship and from the welter of special, partial statuses that together comprised the population of the early modern state. But citizenship is nonetheless a personal status. This is what links citizenship and membership. A purely liberal economy—or a purely territorial state—is indifferent to membership, to status. It is indifferent to the old *ständisch* distinctions, but equally indifferent to citizenship. To abolish *ständisch* inequalities, then, was not *ipso facto* to create citizenship. It was to suspend membership as an organizing principle of social life, while the development of citizenship involved the reconstruction of membership as an organizing principle. This was the second step I alluded to. The reconstructed membership was a statewide, inclusive, general, immediate membership of the state. It replaced the regional (or local), exclusive, particular memberships of the *Stände* that had yielded statemembership only in a mediated fashion. But modern citizenship shared with the old *Stände* the quality of being a membership status, and thereby an instrument of social closure. This is too often forgotten or ignored in discussions that focus on the internal political development of citizenship at the expense of the *Stände*. Such discussions emphasize the inclusive, egalitarian aspect of citizenship, but neglect its external boundedness. Yet, as we saw in Chapter 1, the external boundedness of citizenship is essential to the modern state.

As a territorial organization, the modern state is largely indifferent to citizenship (and to personal status in general). Committed to establishing its authority throughout a territory, the state tolerates neither territorial enclaves where its writ does not run nor personal immunities from its jurisdiction. Its jurisdiction is territorially, not personally circumscribed. Yet the modern state is also a membership organization, with citizenship as its axial principle. The state has special claims on its citizens (claims to loyalty, for example, or to military service), and they have special claims on the state (rights of entry and residence, for example, or rights to political participation, or claims to diplomatic protection abroad). These claims have a personal, not a territorial basis.[40] They are rooted in membership, not in residence. They are not generated by passing or extended residence, nor do they lapse with temporary or prolonged absence. These claims presuppose the boundedness of citizenship, the distinction between citizens and foreigners.

How did this distinction emerge? Or rather, since the distinction is an ancient one, how was it rationalized and codified? How did citizenship come to be defined as a status that was not only general and internally inclusive but bounded and externally exclusive? The ALR, I have noted, used the language of membership, addressing the "members of the state" *(Mitglieder des Staates).* But it did not distinguish residence from membership, *Einwohner* from *Mitglieder.* Resident foreigners were expressly included among the *Mitglieder.* The ALR is an inward-looking document, wholly concerned with the internal social and legal order of the Prussian state. It was concerned to redefine this order by making the state its central and pervasive point of reference, by effecting a *Verstaatlichung* of the legal order. The language of state-membership must be understood in this context. In the expression "members of the state," the emphasis was on the state, not on membership. Membership of the state was not set against nonmembership; it was set against membership of the *Stände.* The rhetoric of state-membership was an instrument of *Verstaatlichung;* it did not announce the development of a bounded state-membership. It was connected to the development of the state as a territorial organization, with a unitary *Staatsgebiet* or territory, not to the development of the state as a membership organization.

Nor did the liberalizing economic legislation of the Reform period create an externally bounded citizenry; it was essentially indifferent to personal status and thus to membership. This indifference, however, led indirectly to the codification of citizenship in 1842. The new economic openness ultimately required political closure; the destruction of the internally closed *Stände* required the construction of an externally closed citizenry. The connecting link was migration, more precisely the migration of the poor. Prussian state-membership was codified as a means of shielding the state against foreign poor, while preserving freedom of movement within the state.

Migration and Membership: Defining External Boundaries

Closure against the migrant poor had been an essential part of municipal politics throughout the early modern era.[41] The late fifteenth and sixteenth centuries had marked a fundamental transformation in the theory and practice of poor relief. Responsibility for and control of poor relief were secularized, politicized, and rationalized. Everywhere, towns asserted secular jurisdiction over the poor. Begging, central to the medieval pattern of poor relief, was strictly regulated and limited to the local poor, who were registered and issued special permits. "Foreign" beggars—those that did not "belong" to the city—were barred. With municipal control went municipal responsibility. Imperial legislation of 1530 required "every town and [village] commune to nourish and lodge its poor."[42] But who were "its" poor? About towns' responsibility for those who legally "belonged" to them—either as full municipal citizens or as less privileged *"Beisassen"*—there was no doubt.[43] But urban populations always included various categories of nonmembers as well. And now that they were obliged to support their own poor, towns had an incentive to define membership more restrictively. Previously, de facto domicile had sufficed to establish membership (though not full municipal citizenship). Now towns increasingly made membership contingent on formally approved domicile. In this way local authorities could prevent the poor—or persons who might become poor—from establishing municipal membership and thereby a claim to municipal support. Municipal closure against the poor, then, had a double edge: "foreign" poor were excluded from the town, and the potentially poor were excluded from municipal membership.[44]

In the wider perspective of the territorial state, responsible for maintaining order throughout a territory, municipal closure against the migrant poor was problematic. The state could not permit towns to externalize poverty, to export their unwanted at will. This would endanger the peace and order of the wider state. Destitute persons expelled from one town would have to be accommodated elsewhere. To limit "homelessness"—the legal condition of those who lacked a legal home or *"heimat"* in which they had secure residence rights—states began to interfere in the politics of communal membership in the seventeenth and eighteenth centuries.[45] Communal membership was no longer determined autonomously by the towns but, at least to some extent, heteronomously by the state. The aim of the state was to coordinate membership policies so as to ensure the "full coverage" of the population;

ideally, everyone would be a member of some town or village commune. Towns would thus have to accept some poor as members—not necessarily as full citizens, but at least as members with rights of residence and support.

The autonomous regulation of municipal membership was only one of the many aspects of municipal autonomy that were challenged and curtailed by the developing territorial state. Yet the conflict over the control of membership was particularly revealing. It brought into sharp and poignant focus the tension and ultimate incompatibility between the rich bonds and narrow horizons of municipal citizenship and the weaker, more abstract bonds and wider horizons of the emerging state citizenship.[46] The conflict was protracted; it was still being played out in the nineteenth century. In fact it reached a peak of intensity in the early nineteenth century. Before that time states had moved cautiously, asserting in principle their ultimate right to regulate membership, but respecting in practice, to a considerable extent, the traditional autonomy of the communes, abridging this autonomy only at the margins.[47] In the early nineteenth century, however, the liberation of the peasants and the opening of all occupations to all comers, coupled with a growing state interest in the free movement of persons, supported by the newly influential economic liberalism, brought the conflict to a head.[48] It was particularly sharp in Prussia, where the state was most strongly committed to freedom of movement. From the point of view of the Prussian state, the communes were essentially "subdivisions of the territory and citizenry of the state, organized so as to facilitate the execution of the laws." On this understanding, it was unacceptable that the "communes close or make inaccessible to the state a part of the state's territory or a portion of its citizenry."[49] Yet from the municipal point of view, if the state were to deprive communes of the right to control entry and membership, "one would have to renounce the attempt to maintain any community of meaning [*Gemeinsinn*] in the communes [*Gemeinde*] . . . To maintain their personality, communes must have the decisive say in the choice of their members. To force them to accept everyone would destroy their common spirit [*Gemeingeist*]."[50] Although the legislation that was eventually enacted in 1842 did not require the communes to accept everyone, it sharply curbed municipal autonomy and established freedom of movement for all but the actually destitute. Towns could deny entry only to persons currently in need of public support, not to persons whom the town feared might need such support in the future. By divorcing the right to residence and welfare from communal citizenship, and sharply limiting communal rights of exclusion and expulsion, the state reduced communal citizenship to insignificance.[51] Other states, more responsive to towns' fears of an influx of the migrant poor and less committed to freedom of movement, did not go so far. But they did enact *Heimatgesetze* fixing the criteria of communal citizenship, and assuring that everyone had a communal home or *Heimat* in which they would have secure residence rights and the right to support in case of need. States allowed communes to restrict the settlement of persons not possessing the local citizenship or *Heimatrecht*, and to expel such persons for broadly defined reasons.[52] Yet if municipal closure against the migrant poor thereby remained vigorously in force outside Prussia, it was now heteronomously regulated by the states, not autonomously by the communes themselves.

So long as one focuses on movement of the poor—or potentially poor—across *communal* boundaries, then state citizenship appears essentially inclusive, municipal citizenship essentially exclusive. But the matter appears otherwise when one considers movement across *state* boundaries. The state response to the interstate mobility of the poor, like the communal response to their intercommunal mobility, involved closure against nonmembers and the restriction of access to membership.

Territorial states' closure against the migrant poor was much more rudimentary than municipal closure in the early modern period. Like municipal ordinances, territorial police ordinances and laws barred foreign beggars from the territory.[53] But the concept of the foreigner was much more nebulous on the level of the territorial state than on the level of the city. Municipal membership was codified and formalized; state-membership was not. Towns knew exactly who their members were; states did not. More fundamentally, the town was a membership association; the state was not. It was a territorial organization exercising authority over persons in a number of different domains, and distinguishing, for a number of specific purposes—emigration, poor support, eligibility for offices, military service, taxation, inheritance—between insiders and outsiders, between bearers and non-bearers of specific rights and obligations. There were a number of context-specific insider statuses; but there was no general status of state-membership.[54] About the status of persons born, raised, and settled in the territory, there was seldom any doubt. But the status of the vagabond, the itinerant, the immigrant, was uncertain.[55] This lack of precision on the state level should come as no surprise. In relation to the scope of its jurisdiction, municipal administration was much more dense, much more intensive, than territorial state administration. As a result, towns could control residence and membership much more efficiently than states. Membership was routinized—that is, integrated into administrative routines—in the towns, but not in the states. The rationalized, formalized, bureaucratized administration of membership on the scale of the territorial state required administrative resources—infrastructural power, in Mann's phrase—that the state did not yet have.[56]

It also required incentives that the state did not yet have. Towns had to be able to ascertain membership status precisely. For membership status was crucial in a number of routines of municipal life. The right of permanent residence, the right to pursue a *"bürgerlich"* trade, the right (and obligation) to hold office and to participate in municipal politics, the right to own certain types of real property, the right to municipal support in case of need—all of these were membership rights. "The commune was a Bürgergemeinde of citizens, not an Einwohnergemeinde of inhabitants. Simply living in the town space did not confer membership rights."[57]

If membership was crucial in the municipal context, it was marginal to the business of rule in the territorial state. Legal status of course mattered to the state, but what mattered was status within the state, not membership of the state: *Stand*-membership, not state-membership. And as absolutist legislation took an increasingly general form, deliberately bypassing *ständisch* distinctions, then the state became an *Einwohnergemeinde* of inhabitants, not—yet—a *Bürgergemeinde* of citizens.[58] The territorial state was just what its name implied: a territorial, not a membership organization. State-membership was not, as it was later to become, a prerequisite for public rights and duties.[59] The state did not discriminate systematically between foreigners and subjects; it tended rather to assimilate resident foreigners to subjects, treating the foreigner as a *subditus temporarius*, a temporary subject.[60] As such, the foreigner was treated the same way as other subjects, except that he had somewhat more freedom than permanent subjects—most important, the freedom to emigrate, to leave the territory of the state without obtaining special permission or paying a special tax.[61] In the era of mercantilism, state-membership was less a barrier to entry than to exit. If the foreigner were a skilled worker, he might benefit from other privileges granted by the mercantilist state as a means of promoting immigration.[62] To be a foreigner, in short, was not to be systematically outside the political or legal community of the territorial state. Insofar as the status of foreigner had legal consequences, these were privileges as often as liabilities.

A new situation developed in the early nineteenth century with the breakup of the *ständisch* social order. The liberation of the peasants and the opening of all occupations to all comers coincided with massive rural overpopulation. This was a joint result of rapid population growth since the late eighteenth century and the slow tempo of industrialization, which did not begin to absorb this surplus population until the middle of the nineteenth century.[63] The combination of rural overpopulation, the sudden lifting of restrictions on freedom of movement and occupation, the concomitant dissolution of estate-based poor relief, and the lifting of restrictions on the incorporation of peasant land into noble (or formerly noble) estates engendered a massive, uprooted class of migrant poor. It made pauperism the "most burning social problem of the time."[64]

Pauperism, to be sure, was nothing new. Early-nineteenth-century pauperism was not, as some contemporary observers believed, a consequence of industrialization; it was rather the "last instance of the old, pre-industrial poverty."[65] But the political context of migrant poverty differed from that of the early modern period. Responsibility for the poor had shifted, in principle, from the commune to the state. This was expressed in the ALR, which formally guaranteed every poor "Bürger" the right to state support. The actual practice of poor relief was not carried out by the state, except in the last instance, for those few poor for whom no other body was responsible. The state had neither the financial nor the institutional resources to take over day-to-day responsibility for poor relief. It continued to hold families, guilds, corporations, rural lords, and municipalities responsible for supporting "their" poor. But this responsibility was now formally fixed and assigned by the state, which assumed overall responsibility for organizing the system of poor relief.[66]

This shift in overall responsibility for the poor from commune to state, in conjunction with the breakup of the *ständisch* social order and its restrictions on freedom of movement, confronted the state with problems of membership like those formerly confronted by the towns. "Like the town before it, the state now had to define who 'its' poor were." The communalization of poor relief in the fifteenth and sixteenth centuries had given rise to intercommunal disputes over responsibility for the support of the migrant poor. Such disputes persisted throughout the early modern period; indeed they persist to this day. But with the *Verstaatlichung* of poor relief, interjurisdictional disputes over responsibility for the poor assumed a new form: interstate disputes emerged alongside the older intercommunal disputes. No more than the town could the state exclude or expel the poor or otherwise unwanted at will. Constraints on the town were imposed by the state, constraints on the state by other states. The problem was the same in both instances: what was expedient for a single jurisdiction—the exclusion or expulsion of the unwanted poor—imposed unacceptable costs on neighboring or encompassing jurisdictions.[67] It was the attempt to limit these costs that led states, initially on a bilateral, later on a multilateral basis, formally to assign persons to states and thereby to create an embryonic institution of citizenship.

Numerous bilateral treaties designed to foster freedom of movement between German states had been concluded in the early nineteenth century. With the establishment of the German Confederation in 1815, these provisions were extended to cover all member states. Yet the free-movement clauses were far from absolute. They abolished controls on exit but not on entry. A person could leave any state without obtaining special permission or paying the traditional exit fees, but could settle in another state only with its permission.[68] States retained the right to exclude and expel unwanted immigrants. Doubtless there would be many more such immigrants than there had been in the past. In conjunction with the liberation of the peasants, the growth of an uprooted rural proletariat, and the establishment of freedom of occupation, the provisions facilitating freedom of movement were bound to occasion a dramatic increase in interstate migration. How were the expulsions of the unwanted to be handled?

Traditionally, expulsions had been a unilateral affair. As late as 1827, a document of the Prussian Interior Minister candidly admitted that "the expellee is often brought secretly over the border without notifying foreign officials," with generally unsatisfactory results, in that the expellee "either returns to Prussia or joins with other expelled criminals in bands of thieves or robbers."[69] If such unilateral expulsions were unsatisfactory to the expelling state, they were much more so to the receiving state. With the problem threatening to get much worse as a result of increasing mobility, states sought to coordinate and rationalize their expulsion practices. Numerous early-nineteenth-century treaties articulated two basic principles: that a state could expel into the territory of another state only a member (*Angehöriger*) of the second state; and that a state was bound to admit into its territory its own members when they were expelled from other states. And since state-membership was not yet codified, the treaties even spelled out who were to count as the state-members (*Staatsangehörige*) whom the individual states were obliged to admit.[70] Thus citizenship, as a formally defined, externally bounded membership status, was not the product of the internal development of the modern state. Rather, it emerged from the dynamics of interstate relations within a geographically compact, culturally consolidated, economically unified, and politically (loosely) integrated state system.

The term and concept of *Staatsangehörigkeit* appeared for the first time in bilateral treaties enacted to regulate and coordinate expulsion practices. Initially this was a functionally specific concept, limited to the domain of entry, residence, and poor relief. As such it took its place amidst the welter of concepts that made up the membership vocabulary of the late eighteenth and early nineteenth century: native, resident, state-citizen *(Staatsbürger)*, subject, member of the state. But because of the fundamental importance of the right of entry into and secure residence in the territory of a state—a presupposition for the effective exercise of other rights—this originally functionally specific status gradually became a general membership status, to which legal consequences in various domains (military obligations and political rights, for example) were attached.[71]

There is one further respect in which migrant poverty occasioned the rationalization and codification of state-membership. In the early modern period membership and residence were not sharply distinguished. But to the extent that they were distinguished, residence, more precisely domicile, was the more fundamental category, while membership, that is, subjecthood, was understood to follow from it. *Domicilium facit subditum*—domicile makes the subject—was a universally accepted maxim.[72] Membership had a territorial base. In the face of migrant poverty, just this was problematic. It left the state open to the accession of new members by osmosis, as it were, through entry and settlement in its territory, even without its knowledge or approval. Moreover, it was uncertain just when one became or ceased to be a subject; and this unclarity was increasingly problematic.[73] Effective closure against the migrant poor required a sharper separation of membership and residence, and a reversal in their causal relationship.[74] Domicile should be contingent on membership, not membership on domicile. Membership, defined independently of residence, should be the fundamental category.

Such a transformation was effected in the 1842 "Law on the acquisition and loss of the quality of Prussian subject." This was one of a trio of laws enacted on the same day; the others governed freedom of movement within the Prussian state and the conditions under which communes were obliged to admit intrastate migrants. There was a close connection between these laws on internal migration and the codification of state-membership. The law on internal freedom of movement was explicitly addressed to Prussian subjects alone, on the grounds that this would permit the state to "exclude unwanted—that is, poor—foreigners and in so doing to keep under control the stream of foreign migrants that had been stimulated by the new freedom of occupation."[75] To this end it was necessary to define precisely who was a foreigner and who a subject. The increased interstate mobility of the poor had given the state the incentive it formerly lacked to define membership systematically and precisely as a legal quality independent of residence. The quality of Prussian subject, according to the new, explicit definition, is founded on descent, legitimation, marriage, or bestowal (naturalization), not—and this is explicitly highlighted in the text—on domicile, which "shall not in the future by itself establish the quality of Prussian [subject]."[76] The inclusion of this purely negative provision, together with its wording ("in the future"), is significant. The state now appeared (and was legally defined) as a membership association; it was no longer merely a territorial organization. Membership was no longer simply a reflex of residence. Defined independently of residence, state-membership could now serve as an instrument of closure against the migrant poor.[77]

As a legal institution regulating membership of the state, citizenship was now established. Citizenship had crystallized as a formally defined and assigned status, distinct from residence. The citizenry was externally exclusive as well as internally inclusive. Citizens, regardless of *Stand*, town, or province, stood in an immediate relationship with the state. Citizenship could henceforth serve as the legal point of attachment for certain common rights and obligations in the domain of immigration law, military service, or (later) political rights. It could serve as an instrument and object of closure.

As we have seen, the development of citizenship is inextricably bound up with that of the modern state and state system. Two phases of this dual development have been outlined. In the first, the construction of unitary internal sovereignty at the expense of *ständisch* and regional inequalities, itself grounded in military competition among coordinate territorial states,[78] laid the foundation for modern citizenship as a general, internally inclusive, immediate status. In the second, state closure against the migrant poor in the context of an increasingly integrated state system laid the foundation for citizenship as a formally defined, externally exclusive status distinct from domicile.

The emergence of the institution of citizenship cannot be understood apart from the formation of the modern state and state system. But the converse is equally true: the formation of the modern state and state system cannot be understood apart from the emergence and institutionalization of citizenship. Conceiving the modern state as a territorial organization and the state system as a system of territorial states, political sociology has for the most part neglected citizenship and membership. It has made too little of the fact that the state is a membership association as well as a territorial organization; that the state constitutes itself, and delimits the field of its personal jurisdiction, by constituting its citizenry; and that political territory, as we know it today—bounded territory, within a system of territorial states, to which access is controlled by the state—*presupposes* membership, presupposes some way of assigning persons to states, and distinguishing those who enjoy free access to a particular state territory from those who do not. The emergence of the institution of citizenship therefore marks a crucial moment in the development of the infrastructure of the modern state and state system.

The dual developmental history traced in this chapter reflects the intrinsic duality of modern citizenship, a status at once universal and particularistic, internally inclusive and externally exclusive. The literature on citizenship has emphasized its universality and inclusiveness. But citizenship is inherently bounded. Exclusion is essential both to the ideology of national citizenship (as we have seen in the discussion of French Revolutionary nationalism) and to the legal institution (as we have seen in the discussion of migration and membership in Germany).

Yet if all states control access to citizenship, the manner in which they do so varies widely. French citizenship is attributed, and has been attributed since 1889, to most persons born on French territory. As a result, a substantial fraction of postwar French immigrants has French citizenship. German citizenship has always been attributed only to descendants of German citizens. As a result, a negligible fraction of postwar German immigrants—except for ethnic Germans from Eastern Europe and the former German Democratic Republic—has German citizenship. The following chapters seek to explain this sharp and consequential difference in the legal definition of citizenship.

II · DEFINING THE CITIZENRY: THE BOUNDS OF BELONGING

4 • Citizenship and Naturalization in France and Germany

Citizenship, we have seen, is inherently bounded; it is everywhere an instrument and object of social closure. Yet the bounds of belonging are drawn differently in different polities. This was true in ancient Greece where, as Aristotle observed, "the man who is a citizen in a democracy is often not one in an oligarchy."[1] And it remains true in modern Europe, where the immigrant who would be a citizen in France would often not be one in Germany—unless he happened to be of ethnic German origin. The rate of civic incorporation for migrant workers and their descendants is more than ten times higher in France than in Germany. And the gap is even greater for second- and third-generation immigrants. A generation of young Franco-Portuguese, Franco-Algerians, and Franco-Moroccans is emerging, claiming and exercising the rights of French citizenship. In Germany, by contrast, nearly half a million second-generation Turkish immigrants, born and raised in Germany, remain outside the community of citizens.

The sharply differing definitions of citizenship are particularly striking in view of the similar French and German experiences with migrant labor in the last quarter-century.[2] In both countries foreign workers were recruited in large numbers in the 1960s and early 1970s in response to labor shortages. Organized recruitment was suspended in 1973–74, partly in response to the oil shock and ensuing recession, partly in response to the growing concern about the social and political consequences of large-scale immigration. Nonetheless, populations of immigrant origin have continued to grow in both countries, largely through family reunification.

Immigrants in both countries have become dramatically more visible in everyday life during the last two decades. During the 1950s and early 1960s most foreign workers were either single or separated from their families. Many lived in isolated workers' hostels. Outside the workplace they were largely invisible, participating little in the social, cultural, or political life of the host society. In the last two decades, however, the sojourners have become settlers. Single workers were joined by their families, or formed new families. Immigrants became neighbors, schoolmates, and joint users of public spaces. An increasingly vocal second generation emerged, tenuously rooted in the culture of the parents' generation, yet economically and socially marginalized in the country of residence. Groups marked by dress, language, religion, and custom as "culturally distant" comprised the fastest-growing segment of the immigrant community. Immigrants in both countries have clustered in particular regions and, within cities, in particular neighborhoods.[3] All these developments made immigrants much more visible.

In both countries immigrants comprise a substantial fraction of the manual working class and are overrepresented in dirty, dangerous, unpleasant, ill-paid, and menial occupations. They are also overrepresented among the unemployed. As a relatively young group, with comparatively high fertility rates, immigrants play a similar demographic role in France and Germany, which share concerns about low fertility and aging populations. This has implications for the labor market, the social security system, and, in the longer run, for military conscription— if peacetime conscription survives the great geopolitical reconfiguration now under way.

Discourse about immigration and immigrants follows similar patterns in both countries. There is an inclusionary discourse that stresses the economic and cultural contribution of immigrants to the host society and the values of tolerance and diversity. And there is a counterdiscourse stressing the unassimilability of immigrants, the dangers of excessive cultural heterogeneity, the social strains and economic costs of immigration, and the prospect of Islamic fundamentalism and interethnic strife. Finally, there are striking similarities in immigration policies. Since the mid-1970s all French and German governments, left and right, have pursued the same threefold policy, seeking to impose strict limits on further immigration, to encourage voluntary return migration, and to facilitate the integration of second-generation immigrants.[4]

There are of course significant differences between French and German experiences with immigration. Many immigrants to France have come from former French colonies and protectorates, while immigration to Germany has lacked this colonial connection. Both countries have been concerned with undocumented immigration and with an upsurge in the number of persons seeking political asylum, but the French have been particularly preoccupied with the former, the Germans with the latter. Jean-Marie Le Pen's National Front has fared much better in France than any far-right xenophobic party in Germany. France is particularly concerned about migration from the south, from the Maghreb and sub-Saharan Africa, Germany about migration from the east, especially from Poland and the ex-Soviet Union. And since the massive exodus thirty years ago of colonial settlers from postindependence Algeria, there has been no French analogue to the great migration of ethnic Germans from Eastern Europe and the Soviet Union, which brought over a million immigrants to Germany between 1988 and 1991.

Patterns of Naturalization and Definitions of Citizenship

Despite these differences, the overall picture is one of similar migration processes, comparable immigrant populations, and converging immigration policies. In the context of these thoroughgoing similarities, the sharply differing policies and politics of citizenship stand out as a striking anomaly. In the first place, German naturalization policies, although recently liberalized, remain more restrictive than those of France. Ten years' residence is ordinarily required in Germany, five years in France. More important, candidates for naturalization must ordinarily renounce their original citizenship in Germany, but not in France.[5] Besides these specific differences in requirements, there are more general differences in attitudes toward naturalization. Germany lacks a political culture supportive of naturalization. This is clearly expressed in the administrative regulations governing naturalization, which state unambiguously that "the Federal Republic is not a country of immigration [and] does not strive to increase the number of its citizens through naturalization."[6] In countries of immigration like the United States and Canada naturalization is expected of immigrants; the failure to naturalize is anomalous. In France too, which alone in Continental Europe has a tradition of immigration for purposes of permanent settlement, naturalization has been considered the normal and desirable outcome of permanent settlement. In German self-understanding, by contrast, one cannot join the nation-state by voluntary adhesion (the North American model) or state-sponsored assimilation (the French model).

Immigrants' attitudes toward naturalization, moreover, differ in France and Germany. In 1985 only 6 percent of German migrant workers and family members, and 9 percent of those aged fifteen to twenty-four, intended to naturalize, while about a quarter of young foreigners in France intend to become citizens.[7] The very low propensity to naturalize among German immigrants, many of whom clearly would qualify for naturalization, reflects a desire to retain their original citizenship.[8] Beyond this, though, the differential interest in naturalization may reflect different understandings of what naturalization means in France and Germany. To a greater extent in Germany than in France, it appears, naturalization is perceived as involving not only a change in legal status, but a change in nature, a change in political and cultural identity, a social transubstantiation that immigrants have difficulty imagining, let alone desiring. Evidence of this blurring, in the minds of immigrants, between legal citizenship and a richer, more diffuse notion of ethnocultural nationality can be found in France as well. In France, however, a larger fraction of the immigrant population seems to have adopted a more instrumental, "desacralized" understanding of citizenship, seems to have divorced the legal question of citizenship from broader questions of political loyalty and cultural belonging.[9]

These differences in policies and attitudes toward naturalization are reflected in naturalization rates that are four to five times higher in France than in Germany for the main groups of migrant workers and their dependents (see Tables 1 and 2).[10] Italians naturalize at rates five times higher, Spanish at rates ten times higher in France than in Germany. And Tunisians and Moroccans in France naturalize at rates nearly ten times higher than that of Turks in Germany. Of the 1.5 million Turks in Germany, over 1 million of whom have resided there ten or more years, and more than 400,000 of whom were born there, only about 1,000 acquire German citizenship each year. Even if rates increased tenfold, naturalizations would still be far outweighed by the 25–30,000 new Turkish citizens born each year in the Federal Republic.[11]

The German government has been saying since the mid-1980s that it favors the naturalization of second-generation immigrants, observing that "no state can in the long run accept that a significant part of its population remain outside the political community."[12] And in 1990 the legal provisions governing naturalization were liberalized for persons brought up in Germany and educated at German schools, as well as for persons having resided more than fifteen years in Germany.[13] Over time, a modest increase in naturalization rates is to be expected as the immigrant population becomes increasingly settled. Yet patterns of naturalization are unlikely to change dramatically. The most important obstacle to naturalization—the requirement that candidates give up their original citizenship—was not touched by the 1990 reform. Moreover, the

Table 1. Naturalizations in France by original citizenship, core immigrant groups, 1981–1989.

Original citizenship	A Resident population, 1982 Census	B Resident population with 7+ years' residence (1982)	C Annual naturaliza-tions[a]	D Average annual naturaliza-tions per 1,000 residents [C/A]	E Average annual naturalizations per 1,000 residents with 7+ years' residence [C/B]
Algerians	800,000	700,000	2,787	3.5	4.0
Moroccans	430,000	310,000	3,528	8.2	11.4
Tunisians	190,000	150,000	1,883	9.9	12.6
Portuguese	760,000	680,000	7,145	9.4	10.5
Spanish	320,000	300,000	5,109	16.0	17.0
Italians	330,000	310,000	3,644	11.0	11.8
Total for these groups	2,830,000 (three-fourths of total foreign population)	2,450,000	24,096	8.5	9.8

Source: Recensement Général de la Population de 1982, *Les étrangers* (Paris: La Documentation Française, n. d.), pp. 20, 106; *Journal Officiel*, Assemblée Nationale, Débats parlementaires, Nov. 3, 1986, pp. 4019–4021, Written questions, response to questions no. 4033 and 10393; Sous-Direction des Naturalisations, Direction de la Population et des Migrations, Ministère des Affaires Sociales et de la Solidarité, Annual Reports, 1984–1989; *Annuaire Statistique de la France* (Paris: Institut National de la Statistique et des Etudes Economiques, 1990), p. 87.

a. This includes acquisitions of citizenship by declaration on the part of spouses of citizens and French-born children of foreign parents. Since the breakdown of such declarative acquisitions by original citizenship has been available only since 1984, the figures in this column, and the rates in columns D and E, represent the 1981–1989 annual averages for discretionary naturalizations plus the 1984–1989 averages for declarative acquisitions. Column C also includes "reintegrations," meaning reacquisitions of French citizenship on the part of persons formerly possessing it and subsequently having lost it. This category is significant for Algerians, accounting for 52 percent of all voluntary acquisitions of nationality by Algerians between 1985 and 1989; but it is negligible for all other core immigrant groups.

barriers to naturalization lie not only in the restrictiveness of legal provisions but equally in the political culture of naturalization, embodied in attitudes of Germans and immigrants alike. Without a changed understanding of what it is to be—or to become—German, the liberalization of naturalization policy will not produce a dramatic surge in naturalization.

Naturalization rates, then, are four to five times higher in France than

Table 2. Naturalizations in the Federal Republic of Germany by original citizenship, core immigrant groups, 1981–1988.

Original citizenship	A Resident population (1985)	B Resident population with 10+ years' residence (1985)	C Annual naturalizations	D Average annual naturalizations per 1,000 residents [C/A]	E Average annual naturalizations per 1,000 residents with 10+ years' residence [C/B]
Turks	1,400,000	760,000	1,021 [1,244[a]]	0.7 [0.9[a]]	1.3 [1.76[a]]
Yugoslavs	590,000	450,000	2,194	3.7	4.9
Italians	530,000	350,000	821	1.5	2.3
Greeks	280,000	220,000	247	0.9	1.2
Spanish	150,000	130,000	206	1.4	1.6
Total for these groups	2,950,000 (two-thirds of total foreign population)	1,930,000	4,489	1.5	2.3

Source: Heinrich Meyer, "SOPEMI 1986. Federal Republic of Germany" (Organization for Economic Co-operation and Development, Système d'observation permanent sur les migrations internationales), p. 16; Deutscher Bundestag, 10. Wahlperiod, Drucksache 10/863, p. 40; Henning Fleischer, "Einbürgerungen 1982," *Wirtschaft und Statistik* 2/1984, pp. 95–97, and "Entwicklung der Einbürgerungen seit 1983," *Wirtschaft und Statistik* 1/1987, pp. 46–51; Bundesminister des Innern, "Ermessenseinbürgerungen nach ausgewählten Staatsangehörigkeiten," 30. F.; *Statistisches Jahrbuch 1990 für die Bundesrepublik Deutschland* (Stuttgart: Metzler-Poeschel Verlag, 1990), p. 60.

a. 1984–1988 annual averages.

b. Figures are not yet available for naturalizations of Greeks and Spanish in 1988; hence columns C, D, and E give 1981–1987 averages.

in Germany. But patterns of civic incorporation diverge even more sharply than this suggests. It is not enough to consider the voluntary acquisition of citizenship by naturalization or individual declaration. We must also consider the attribution of citizenship by the state. Naturalization patterns and policies must be understood in conjunction with the rules specifying whom states unilaterally define as citizens. Working invisibly and automatically, independently of the will—and sometimes even the knowledge—of the persons concerned, the rules governing the ascription of citizenship have been all but ignored by the meager literature on immigration and citizenship. Yet they are more important than naturalization rules in shaping patterns of civic incorporation in France and Germany. Ascription constitutes and perpetually reconstitutes the citizenry; naturalization reshapes it at the margins. The striking difference in the civic incorporation of immigrants in France and Germany is chiefly a consequence of diverging rules of ascription. Differing naturalization rules and rates reinforce this difference but are not its fundamental source.

The central difference between French and German ascription rules turns on the significance attached to birth and prolonged residence in the territory. While French citizenship is ascribed, at birth or majority, to most persons born on French territory of foreign parents, German citizenship is ascribed only on the basis of descent. Birth and prolonged residence in Germany have no bearing on citizenship status. French citizenship law automatically transforms most second- and third-generation immigrants into citizens; German citizenship law allows immigrants and their descendants to remain foreigners indefinitely.

In both France and Germany, to be sure, as throughout Continental Europe, citizenship is ascribed to children of citizens, following the principle of *jus sanguinis*. In Britain and the Americas, by contrast, citizenship is ascribed to all persons born in the territory, following the principle of *jus soli*.[14] What I want to highlight here is the sharp difference in the extent to which France and Germany, sharing the same basic principle of *jus sanguinis*, supplement this principle with elements of *jus soli*. France and Germany represent polar cases: French citizenship law includes a substantial territorial component; German citizenship law includes none at all. Most other Western European *jus sanguinis* countries include some complementary elements of *jus soli*, without going as far as France.[15]

Although based on *jus sanguinis*, French citizenship law incorporates substantial elements of *jus soli*. Thus, French citizenship is attributed at birth to a child born in France if at least one parent was also born in France—including Algeria and other colonies and territories before their independence. This means that the large majority of the roughly 400,000 children born in France of Algerian parents in the quarter-century following Algerian independence are French citizens.[16] Moreover, citizenship is acquired automatically at age 18 by *all* children born in France of foreign parents, provided they have resided in France for the last five years and have not been the object of certain criminal condemnations. By this means roughly 300,000 persons became French between 1973 and 1991.[17] More than a million foreign residents are under age 18. At least two-thirds of them were born in France and are destined to become French at age 18.[18] Thus, although the citizenship law of the United States is based on *jus soli,* while that of France is based on *jus sanguinis,* the result—as far as second-generation immigrants are concerned—is similar: almost all persons born in France and residing there at majority have French citizenship. German citizenship law, in contrast, is based *exclusively* on *jus sanguinis.* Birth in the territory, even coupled with prolonged residence, has no bearing on citizenship. Second-generation and even third-generation immigrants can acquire German citizenship only through naturalization.

Table 3 shows the combined effects of differing rules of ascription and rates of naturalization on the civic incorporation of the major immigrant groups (excluding ethnic German immigrants to Germany). Of the nearly three million foreign residents from the core immigrant groups in Germany, fewer than 5,000 acquire German citizenship each year, and nearly half of these are Yugoslavs. France, on the other hand, gains more than 53,000 new citizens each year from a slightly smaller core immigrant population. This includes about 16,600 persons defined as French at birth each year by virtue of birth in France in conjunction with the birth of at least one parent in preindependence Algeria, and another 12,700 persons born in France and defined as French on attaining legal majority. The overall rate of civic incorporation for these core immigrant groups is thus more than ten times higher in France than in Germany.

For second- and third-generation immigrants, the difference in rates of civic incorporation is greater still. In both France and Germany new immigration declined precipitously after 1973. As a result, a steadily increasing fraction of the population of immigrant origin consists of persons born in France or Germany. In France almost all of these persons are either defined as French at birth or programmed to become French automatically at age 18. In Germany, which lacks any mechanism of automatic civic incorporation, second- and third-generation immigrants will have to naturalize if they want to become citizens. And there is no indication that they will do so in large numbers.

One further peculiarity of German citizenship law should be noted. While the citizenry is defined restrictively vis-à-vis non-German immigrants, it is defined expansively vis-à-vis ethnic Germans. This ethnic inclusiveness has two aspects. First, the citizenry recognized by the Federal Republic of Germany always included the citizens of the German Democratic Republic. As far as citizenship law is concerned, the division of Germany never happened. Or rather it happened only from

Table 3. Combined effects of naturalization and the ascription of citizenship on the civic incorporation of core immigrant groups in France and Germany (annual averages).[a]

Manner of becoming a citizen	France	Germany
Naturalization and declarative acquisition	24,100[b]	4,500[c]
Attribution of citizenship to persons born in country, one parent also born in country	16,600[d]	—
Attribution of citizenship at majority to persons born in country and residing there for last five years	12,700[e]	—
Total acquiring citizenship or having it attributed to them	53,400	4,500

Source: Tables 1–2, except as otherwise indicated.

a. The core immigrant groups include Algerians, Moroccans, Tunisians, Portuguese, Spanish, and Italians in France, and Turks, Yugoslavs, Italians, Greeks, and Spanish in Germany.

b. 1981–1989. Includes reintegrations (see note to Table 1).

c. 1981–1988.

d. 1981–1986, calculated from André Lebon, "Attribution, acquisition et perte de la nationalité française: un bilan (1973–1986)," *Revue européene des migrations internationales* 3 (1987): 10.

e. Lebon's estimate of 16,930 annually for 1981–1986 (ibid., p. 12) is for the foreign population as a whole. Since core innigrant groups account for three-fourths of the total foreign population, I have assumed that they account for three-fourths of these cases.

the East German side. From 1967 through 1990, there was a separate East German citizenship, but there never was a separate West German citizenship. Not wanting to validate the division of Germany, the West German authorities insisted on the continued validity of a single German citizenship. As the two Germanies consolidated their separate statehoods, this insistence on a single citizenship came to seem increasingly anomalous. Yet it took on dramatic new meaning in the fall of 1989 and spring of 1990, for it was the common German citizenship that guaranteed every East German, as a German citizen, the constitutional right to enter, reside, and work in West Germany. Common citizenship paved the way for the reestablishment of common statehood.

The second aspect of the ethnic inclusiveness of German citizenship pertains to the ethnic German immigrants from Eastern Europe and the Soviet Union. These immigrants are treated very differently from non-

German immigrants. They are legally defined as Germans and immediately accorded all the rights of citizenship.[19] The liberalization of emigration and travel policies in Eastern Europe and the Soviet Union has engendered a great exodus of ethnic Germans from this region, particularly from Poland, Romania, and the Soviet Union, reversing the centuries-old *Drang nach Osten* of Germans into Slavic lands. Over a million ethnic Germans arrived in Germany between 1988 and 1991; at this writing, the flow continues unabated.

The policies and politics of citizenship are strikingly different in France and Germany. Naturalization policies and practices are more liberal and naturalization rates four to five times higher in France. French citizenship, moreover, is automatically attributed to French-born children of immigrants at their majority, while German citizenship is based solely on descent. As a result, the rate of civic incorporation for migrant workers and their families is more than ten times higher in France than in Germany. Yet while German citizenship is closed to non-German immigrants, it is remarkably open to ethnic German immigrants from Eastern Europe and the Soviet Union. The following chapters seek to explain the origin and persistence of these sharply differing definitions of citizenship.

5 ✦ Migrants into Citizens

The Crystallization of *Jus Soli* in Late-Nineteenth-Century France

The expansiveness of French citizenship vis-à-vis immigrants, we have seen, rests less on liberal naturalization policies and practices than on a system of *jus soli* that automatically transforms second- and third-generation immigrants into citizens. Commentators have suggested that demographic and military interests led the French state to establish *jus soli*. Yet although concern with the "anguishing problem of natality" did play a crucial role in the liberalization of naturalization provisions in 1927,[1] neither demographic nor military concerns were decisive in 1851, when *jus soli* was introduced for third-generation immigrants, or in 1889, when it was extended to cover second-generation immigrants;[2] and the system of 1889 remains in place today. *Jus soli* was not the product of a deliberate effort by the state to enlarge the population and the pool of military recruits.[3] The problem to which the government responded by introducing and extending *jus soli* was ideological and political, not demographic or military.

The crux of the problem was the politicized resentment, in frontier departments, of the exemption of long-settled foreigners from military service. That resentment intensified in the 1870s, as the military induction rate increased among French males, and especially in the 1880s, as Republican doctrines of universal and equal military service gained ground. The impulse behind the extension of *jus soli*, then, was social resentment, not demographic or military concern. But why did resentment of the privileged situation of established immigrants lead to a more inclusive definition of citizenship? Why did it not lead to a military service requirement for foreign residents,[4] to a more restrictive immigration policy, or to an exclusive xenophobic nationalism? The decisive extension of *jus soli* in 1889 can be explained only with reference to a distinctively state-centered and assimilationist understanding of nationhood, deeply rooted in political and cultural geography and powerfully reinforced in the 1880s by the Republican program of universal primary education and universal military service.

Although I reject the prevailing instrumental explanation of the expansiveness of French citizenship law, I do not propose a purely cultural explanation in its place. Instead, I seek to show how a state-centered and assimilationist idiom of nationhood, despite the incipient emergence of a more ethnocultural counteridiom, was reinforced and activated in a particular historical, institutional, and political context; and how this idiom of nationhood then shaped perceptions and judgments about what was in the interest of the state. The citizenship law reform occurred in a period of Republican political ascendancy and in the context of a particular sequence of institutional reform, involving the establishment of universal conscription and of free, compulsory, secular primary education. In this context, the traditional idiom of nationhood—state-centered and assimilationist—was powerfully reinforced. Opinion-shaping and decisionmaking elites came to define the exclusion from citizenship (and from military service) of legally foreign but socially French second- and third-generation immigrants as anomalous and intolerable, and to advocate their civic and military incorporation as natural and necessary.

The Revolutionary and Napoleonic Legacy

While the French system of *jus soli* dates from 1889, French citizenship was markedly open to immigrants for a century before. The initial Revolutionary and Napoleonic codifications of state-membership laid the foundations for an expansive citizenship law in France. The French Revolution dramatically enriched and transformed the legal and political meaning of citizenship and occasioned the first formal codification of state-membership by a Western territorial state. But it did not radically transform the criteria that distinguished French from foreigners. Citizenship had become a much more salient and significant status, but the question "Who is French?" was answered much as it had been in the jurisprudence of the *parlements* of the ancien régime, in a manner combining the principles of birthplace, descent, and domicile. The old criteria of membership were well suited to the new understanding of nationhood. This understanding called for an inclusive definition of citizenship; the old criteria afforded an inclusive definition.[5] Driven by the concern to guarantee legitimate inheritance rights, the jurisprudence of the *parlements* concerning the *qualité de français* had become more inclusive during the last centuries of the old regime. By the eighteenth century it sufficed, in order to establish that one was French, to have been born in France or descended from a French father, provided that one was domiciled in France. The 1791 Constitution confirmed and codified these rules, supplementing them to make citizenship still more inclusive by recognizing domiciled and socially integrated foreigners as citizens after five years' residence, and by allowing the descendants of religious émigrés to claim citizenship by establishing their domicile in France.[6]

The initial Revolutionary codification of state-membership did depart from ancien régime jurisprudence in one respect. Persons born abroad of French parents and descendants of expatriated Protestants were required to take a civic oath as well as settle in France in order to be considered French. Also required to take the civic oath were foreigners granted citizenship after five years' residence in France. This insistence on the civic oath reflected a newly voluntaristic understanding of membership. Yet despite the ideological emphasis on voluntary allegiance, the civic oath remained marginal to the determination of citizenship. Persons born in France of French parents—the great majority of citizens—were not required to manifest their will to be French; citizenship was attributed to them independently of their will.

The 1791 Constitution distinguished between *citoyens français* and *citoyens actifs*. The former were nationals or citizens in the modern sense, including all members of the nation-state; the latter comprised the subclass of persons with political rights. Through this distinction, the Constituent Assembly aimed to combine a universalist, egalitarian civil citizenship with a graded scheme of political citizenship. Subsequent Revolutionary constitutions did not make this distinction. They were not concerned with the extent of the citizenry in the modern sense, but only with the extent of the active citizenry. They did not ask: Who is French? but rather: Who shall enjoy political rights? They abandoned the notion of citizenship as a general status for the older notion of citizenship as a special, specifically political status.[7]

The question of citizenship in the modern sense of general membership of the state arose again with the preparation of the Civil Code. It was universally agreed that all Frenchmen should enjoy equal civil rights. Foreigners, however, were to enjoy civil rights only on the basis of reciprocal agreements with other states. It was therefore necessary to specify who was French and who foreign. The Code adopted the basic principle of *jus sanguinis:* citizenship was to be transmitted by descent, from a father to his children, regardless of birthplace. There was considerable debate, though, about the extent to which the basic principle of *jus sanguinis* should be complemented by elements of *jus soli.* It was agreed that birth in France should have some bearing on French citizenship. But what bearing? Should birth in France by itself constitute a sufficient criterion of French citizenship, or should it confer only a conditional right to that citizenship? Should the child born in France of foreign parents be automatically and unconditionally French, or must he demonstrate the will to be French by establishing domicile in France?[8]

Napoleon made the strongest case for the former. Reasoning explicitly from the interests of the state, he was more concerned with the military obligations that could be imposed on citizens than with the civil rights they would enjoy.[9] The wars in which France had been embroiled, he remarked, had led to the settlement in France of many foreigners. It could only serve French interests to accord French citizenship to their children: otherwise "one would not be able to subject [them] to conscription and other public obligations." Napoleon, moreover, emphasized the assimilative power of France. Children born in France of settled foreign parents have "the French way of thinking, French habits, and the natural attachment that everyone has for the country in which he was born."[10]

While Napoleon focused on the children of settled foreigners, opponents of an unconditional *jus soli* rule focused on children of transient visitors. "The son of an Englishman can become French; but should he be French simply because his mother, passing through France, gave birth to him in this territory to which she and her family are foreign? [In such a case,] one's country would depend less on one's affection for it, one's choice, or one's domicile than on the accident of birth."[11] Critics of unconditional *jus soli* agreed with its proponents that French citizenship should be defined in an expansive manner. But they insisted that citizenship reflect an enduring and substantial, not merely an accidental, connection to France, and that it reflect the will to belong. "However rich we are in population, we can be richer. Let us open our doors to foreigners, let us profit from the chance that brings their children into the world in France; but let us not seize these children in spite of themselves. [French citizenship] is an offer that we must make them, a benefit that we accord them, not a servitude that we impose on them."[12]

The latter view prevailed. In the final version of the Civil Code, children born in France of foreign parents did not have French citizenship attributed to them, but were able to claim French citizenship at majority by declaring their intention of fixing their domicile in France (and, in the case of those residing abroad, by establishing their domicile in France within a year). This system prevailed over unconditional *jus soli* because it would be "too unjust" and "too ill suited to national dignity" to confer French citizenship on a person who, although born in France, had "neither resided in France nor manifested the desire to establish himself there."[13]

The Civil Code defined two types of members: actual and potential. The former—persons born of a French father, whether in France or abroad—had French citizenship attributed to them independent of any evidence of attachment to France or manifestation of will on their part. The latter—persons born in France of a foreign father, as well as persons born abroad of a father who had once possessed but subsequently lost French citizenship—had to "recover" or "claim" their citizenship through a voluntary act. If they refrained from doing so, they would be treated as foreigners. Yet French citizenship was theirs to claim. The vocabulary *(recouvrer, réclamer)* is telling. These persons did not *become* French; they did not *acquire* French citizenship, as an ordinary foreigner would do through naturalization. They *recovered* or *claimed* a legal quality that in a sense was already theirs. They activated a latent membership, transformed a potential into an actual citizenship.[14]

The expansive definition of citizenship in the Civil Code reflects a markedly Francocentric set of presumptions about the attachments and loyalties of persons connected to France by birthplace or parentage. For persons born in France of a French father, the presumption of attachment to France was so strong and self-evident that this group is not even mentioned in the Civil Code—their citizenship literally went without saying. For persons born abroad of French parents, the presumption of attachment was almost as strong. It was presumed that the parents, being sojourners, not settlers abroad, would return to France. As Boulay put it, "our attachment to our land [*sol*] and to our compatriots has always persuaded us that one leaves them only temporarily and always with the desire to see them again. Thus the old rule, now an axiom: the Frenchman always harbors the intention of returning [*le Français conserve toujours l'esprit de retour*]."[15] Interestingly, the transmission of citizenship by descent was justified not with reference to a nonterritorial ethnicity but rather by the presumed force of the attachment to French territory.

The Francocentric bias extended to persons born in France of foreign parents. They too benefited from a presumption of attachment. But here the logic was reversed. While the intention to return was imputed to

French citizens residing abroad, the intention to settle was imputed to foreign citizens residing in France. Emigration was presumed temporary, immigration definitive. "The majority of these sons of foreigners," it was argued, "will not withdraw to the country of their father, but will remain on French soil."[16] Yet some persons born in France, it was acknowledged, would not develop strong attachments—for example, a person born in France to foreign parents on a passing visit and raised abroad.[17] The Francocentric presumption of attachment warranted according potential citizenship to persons born in France of foreign parents; it did not justify the attribution of actual citizenship. The presumption would have to be confirmed by evidence of attachment before the potential citizenship could be actualized.

In explaining the expansiveness of French citizenship law vis-à-vis immigrants, commentators have stressed the material—especially the demographic, military, and economic—interests of the state. Yet these interests do not appear to have been decisive in shaping the Civil Code. Napoleon's proposal for unconditional *jus soli*, based explicitly on such state interests, was rejected by the Tribunate, chiefly for ideal reasons. Napoleon's statist approach to the question of citizenship seemed too exclusively concerned with the vertical dimension of citizenship, with the obligations the state could impose on its citizens, and too little with the horizontal dimension, the bonds of nationhood, the ties to the land and the links among people that make nationhood a substantial social reality.[18] As such it was reminiscent of the traditional citizenship law of England, according to which every person born within the domain of the English king was an English subject. England was held up as an antimodel: its citizenship law "remains informed by feudalism and is in no way to be imitated."[19] That French citizenship might be conferred on some persons lacking any substantial connection to France was repeatedly emphasized by opponents of unconditional *jus soli*. To confer French citizenship unconditionally on someone who "has neither resided in France, nor shown any desire to establish himself there," was "incompatible with national dignity . . . It is a duty of whomever the [citizenship] law of a country has adopted to show himself worthy of this favor, and to associate himself with the destiny of his adoptive country by establishing his residence there."[20] To bestow French citizenship too widely, without regard for the substantial ties of nationhood, would devalue the status, depriving it of dignity and prestige.[21]

This is not to say that ideal interests favored a restrictive definition of citizenship. Quite the contrary. One of the powerful and enduring myths engendered by the Revolution was that of France as custodian—and midwife—of liberty for the world. "It is not for ourselves alone," said the Girondin Vergniaud, "it is not for that part of the globe called France, that we have made the conquest of Liberty."[22] Externally this myth favored territorial expansion. It could be used to justify war as a *guerre contre les tyrans* and imperialism as a *mission libératrice*. Internally the myth favored an openness to immigration and an expansive definition of citizenship. It engendered an ideal interest in the prestige of France as an open country, a country of refuge for those fleeing despotism, a land of opportunity where careers were open to talents. To define French citizenship expansively was to distribute the prestige of association with France more widely. In the absence of an ethnonational self-understanding, France was confidently assimilationist: to permit French-born children of foreigners to claim French citizenship as a matter of right was to expand and strengthen the nation, not to dilute its ethnocultural substance.[23] Another, older myth, reinforced by the Revolution, envisioned France as the center of European and world affairs. The Revolution and the wars it occasioned stimulated national pride; they reinforced the Francocentric worldview to which the French were already prone. France was presumed to exert a nearly irresistible attraction for immigrants and emigrants alike, and this presumption of attachment favored an expansive definition of citizenship. In short, French ideal interests in an expansive definition of citizenship were grounded in an understanding of nationhood in which political, institutional, and territorial motifs were strong, ethnocultural motifs weak.

Midcentury Reforms

The Civil Code defined persons born in France of foreign parents as potential citizens, and authorized them to claim French citizenship at majority. But few availed themselves of this right. Most of those concerned preferred to live in France as foreign citizens, thereby escaping military service.[24] In response to this perceived anomaly, the extension of *jus soli* was first proposed in 1831, in the form of an amendment attached to a law on military recruitment. The amendment would have declared French all persons born in France of long-domiciled foreign parents.[25] That this was proposed thirty-five years before the size of the army emerged as an issue and even longer before demographic stagnation was widely recognized as a problem clearly shows that the impulse to extend *jus soli*—in the mid-nineteenth century, at least—did not spring from military or demographic interest.

Yet while there was no *military* interest in transforming immigrants into citizens, and thus into potential conscripts, there was a *political* interest in doing so. Military service was far from universal in the early nineteenth century. Even the principle of universal service—to say nothing of the practice—was abandoned between 1814 and 1872. Conscription was formally abolished in the constitutional Charter of 1814. Obligatory service was reintroduced in 1818, but the obligation was neither universal nor personal. A lottery *(tirage au sort)* determined on whom the obligation would fall, but those drawing a bad number were not obliged to serve personally; they could hire a substitute.[26] During the 1820s the numbers actually drafted were small (between 10,000 and 50,000 out of nearly 300,000 eligible each year). Yet for those unfortunate enough to draw a bad number and too poor to hire a substitute, military service was an onerous burden, lasting six to eight years.[27] In the 1820s there was a particular reason to resent foreigners' complete exemption from this burden. Until 1830 census data on the total population, including foreigners, was used to calculate the number of persons to be recruited from each canton. As a result, large concentrations of foreigners entailed higher draft rates for the French.[28] It is not surprising, then, that foreigners' exemption from the draft was resented in the Paris region and in frontier departments, where foreigners clustered.[29]

The issue arose again in the aftermath of the Revolution of 1848. The "active part that many foreigners played in the glorious events of February" led the Provisional Government to issue a decree facilitating naturalization in late March of 1848. The decree was rescinded after three months: 2400 persons had been naturalized during this time, alarming the government, which felt that too little control was being exercised over admission to citizenship of persons offering no guarantees (such as birth or upbringing in France) of their suitability as citizens.[30] A law of December 1849 established extremely restrictive preconditions and procedures for naturalization.[31]

Yet even as the government limited the *acquisition* of citizenship, it considered expanding its *attribution*. The contradiction is only apparent. Proposals to restrict the acquisition of citizenship applied to persons born abroad, some of whom had resided in France only briefly; proposals to expand the attribution of citizenship applied to persons born and raised in France. The former had no presumptive connection to France, the latter a strong presumptive connection. It is not surprising that the same legislative commission that endorsed the restrictive naturalization law of December 1849 seriously considered a more expansive attribution policy—especially since it was not liberality that inspired the proposal to expand the attribution of citizenship, but resentment of the foreign families that had established themselves definitively on French soil, "disdaining the advantages of naturalization while profiting from the hospitable liberty of our laws and escaping the charges that our nationals must support." That this was a "very serious abuse" was beyond doubt; but the remedy was open to dispute. Opposed solutions were suggested: on the one hand, to make naturalization more difficult for persons born in France of foreign parents who failed to claim French citizenship at majority; on the other, to attribute French citizenship to all or some persons born in France of foreign parents. The restrictive proposal aimed to prevent persons born in France of foreign parents from reaping the benefits of French citizenship once past the age of conscription; the expansive proposal aimed to prevent such persons from escaping military service by remaining foreign.[32]

For a technical legal reason, neither proposal was adopted in 1849.[33] In 1851, however, the expansive proposal—actually an attenuated version of it[34]—was adopted. The 1851 law declared French every person born in France of foreign parents, at least one of whom was also born in France (although it gave these persons the opportunity to renounce French citizenship at majority). Why was an expansive rather than a restrictive solution adopted in 1851? Not, to be sure, because of Republican universalism. The legislative assembly that enacted the law of February 1851 was dominated by monarchists. There are two reasons for the expansive turn. The restrictive proposal, in the first place, would not have helped solve the problem at hand. The French-born children of foreign parents who, in order to avoid military service, declined to claim French citizenship at majority would not have behaved differently under the "naturalize now or never" condition that the restrictive proposal would have established. Faced with the alternative of claiming French citizenship at majority or remaining a lifelong foreigner in France, they doubtless would have chosen the latter. Compared to the risk of being subjected to seven years of military service, the advantages conferred by French citizenship were slight indeed.[35]

More important is the midcentury weakness of ethnic motifs in national self-understanding, and the correlative lack of emphasis on common descent as a criterion of French nationhood. In this political-cultural context, the expansive proposal was invulnerable to ideological attack. It could be presented and defended as mere common sense. The proposal was in fact quite modest; it applied only to third-generation immigrants—to persons born in France, at least one of whose parents was also born in France. For such persons, the presumption of attachment to France was strong. "Were they not French in fact and in intention, by their affections, their mores, their habits?"[36] If so, why were they not French in law? If they were members of the *pays réel*, why were they not members of the *pays légal*?[37] It would be dangerous to let such persons remain outside *"la grande famille française."* The proposed reform could be understood as a straightforward means "of regularizing this abnormal situation."[38]

Parliamentary opposition to the expansive proposal was not ideological but prudential. Nobody objected in principle to the attribution of French citizenship to third-generation immigrants. But it was feared that foreign governments would respond by attributing their citizenship to, and imposing military service on, the French residing abroad, who were, at this epoch, at least as numerous. To avoid this eventuality, the attribution of French citizenship to third-generation immigrants was made conditional; those concerned would be able to renounce French citizenship at majority. This was justified in voluntaristic terms: there was no wish, it was said, to make a *"Français malgré lui,"* a Frenchman in spite of himself. Yet the underlying concern was more prosaic—a wish to avoid provoking foreign governments into attributing their citizenship to French residing abroad.

It is worth underscoring the routine, noncontroversial character of the reform. Reservations concerned only the practical implementation of the reform, not its principle. The principle of the reform—to transform long-settled immigrants into Frenchmen—was accepted by all. The French nation-state was clearly understood by the elite as something that could, in principle, accommodate new accessions through immigration. This essentially political, statist conception of nationhood was a nonpartisan cultural idiom, not a partisan ideology.[39] In the 1880s, however, understandings of nationhood were more contestatory and contested. Elements of an alternative, more ethnic national self-understanding began to coalesce; and at the same time the traditional, state-centered understanding of nationhood was powerfully reinforced.

Jus Soli or Jus Sanguinis?

Debate on the cautious and limited midcentury reform turned not on the principle of extending *jus soli* and transforming long-settled immigrants into Frenchmen, but on the practical means to do so. The radical reform of 1889 was more controversial. Its legislative career was long and tortuous. The legislation that emerged in 1889 bore little resemblance to the original proposal of 1882, and still less to an intervening proposal of the Council of State in 1884. What was originally proposed as a purely technical rationalization of French citizenship law ended as a fundamental political restructuring. This occasioned sharp disagreement about the foundations of citizenship law, some endorsing a system of pure *jus sanguinis*, others calling for the extension of *jus soli*.

Initially it seemed that the partisans of *jus sanguinis* would prevail. A proposal by the Council of State to limit *jus soli* was adopted by the Senate on first reading. *Jus sanguinis* was explicitly affirmed as the fundamental principle of French citizenship law, *jus soli* explicitly repudiated. Representing the Council of State before the Senate, Camille Sée argued that "Nationality must depend on blood, on descent, [not on] the accidental fact of birth in our territory." *Jus soli* was rejected as a feudal survival, *jus sanguinis* endorsed as a specifically modern principle: "Why revive," Sée asked rhetorically, "this feudal principle of nationality based on birth in the territory, when all of Europe, except for England and Portugal, tells us that nationality depends on blood, and when the progress of science permits an individual to move in a few hours from one end of Europe to the other. The Council of State could not say, nearly a century after the French Revolution, that an individual born in French territory is French by virtue of the principle that makes a man a dependency of the soil." *Jus soli*, in this perspective, was tantamount to "*mainmise* on foreigners born in France."[40] Thus the critique of *jus soli* was framed in terms of an opposition between feudal and modern ideas on social and political membership.

The assault on *jus soli*, however, was largely rhetorical. The actual proposal of the Council of State was much more modest than its rhetoric would suggest. On this proposal, a person born in France of a foreign father would no longer have the right to claim French citizenship at majority. Instead, he would have to apply for naturalization like any other foreigner, although he would be permitted to do so after satisfying a less stringent residence requirement than ordinary foreigners. Since very few persons had exercised this right to become French at majority, the consequences of this reform would have been negligible.[41]

More important was what the Council of State did not propose. Third-generation immigrants had been defined as French *jure soli* since 1851. The Council of State acknowledged that "it would have been more consistent with [our] principles" to abolish this provision. But it could not bring itself to do so. Too many foreigners were permanently established, *"de père en fils,"* in French territory. Attributing French citizenship to third-generation immigrants born in France was justified as "a law of defense . . . against . . . international vagabondage," a law designed to forestall the development of "a population of uncertain nationality, enjoying most of the advantages, without supporting the obligations, of our nationals."[42]

Still, it is significant that both the Council of State and the Senate explicitly affirmed the principle of *jus sanguinis* and sharply criticized *jus soli.* The principle of *jus sanguinis,* moreover, was affirmed, or at least acknowledged, by all parties to the debate, in the more radically Republican Chamber of Deputies as well as in the more conservative Senate. Nobody attacked it directly. Even those who wished to extend *jus soli* did not, during the debates of the 1880s, challenge the *principle* of *jus sanguinis.* Arguing that theoretical considerations had to yield to practical necessities, they conceded in effect the superiority of *jus sanguinis* over *jus soli* as a principle of citizenship law. Thus, Anton Dubost, *rapporteur* of the Chambre proposal to extend *jus soli* to second-generation immigrants, criticized advocates of *jus sanguinis* for their "purely doctrinal point of view" and their consequent neglect of "social necessities."[43]

By 1886 it was generally agreed, in principle, that citizenship ought to be based on descent, not birthplace. *Jus sanguinis* had been explicitly affirmed, *jus soli* sharply criticized, both for the first time. And a bill limiting *jus soli* had been approved in first reading by the Senate. Its passage seemed imminent. Yet the law that emerged two and a half years later provided for the radical extension, not the curtailment, of *jus soli.* This reversal poses a twofold problem. First, what accounts for the general and explicit preference for *jus sanguinis*? Second, how are we to explain that the reform, as enacted, overrode this preference and substantially extended *jus soli*?

Part of the answer is that there was less to the affirmation of *jus sanguinis* and the criticism of *jus soli* than meets the eye. Commitment to *jus sanguinis* was remarkably superficial. Nowhere in the debates of the 1880s was *jus sanguinis* affirmed or defended on its own merits. It was affirmed, as it were, by default; its only justification was purely negative. Its sole virtue was to be free of the defects of *jus soli.* What were these alleged defects? First, that *jus soli* was a feudal relic, treating man as a dependency of the soil; second, that it attached citizenship to the accidental fact of birthplace, which, in an age of improved international transportation and consequently increased short-term international migration, might bear no relation to real attachments and loyalties.

These arguments had no bearing on the citizenship status of second- and third-generation immigrants. They were arguments against absolute and unconditional *jus soli,* not against the forms of limited and conditional *jus soli* that were being considered as a means of bringing established second- and third-generation immigrants into full membership of the state. No serious consideration had been given to simple and unconditional *jus soli* in France since Napoleon proposed it during the debate on the Civil Code. The law of 1851 touched only third-generation immigrants, persons born in France, one of whose parents was also born there. The birth of two successive generations in French territory could scarcely be accidental. It was taken as sufficient proof of definitive establishment in France.

To be sure, proponents in the 1880s of *jus soli* focused on second-generation immigrants, not on the third-generation immigrants about whose rootedness in France there could be no doubt. But they did not believe that birth in France was alone sufficient to warrant the attribution of citizenship. They admitted that birth in France might be merely accidental. Thus they proposed making the attribution of citizenship contingent on some further sign of durable attachment.[44] The criticisms of unconditional *jus soli* that were advanced in the 1880s were irrelevant to the forms of conditional *jus soli* under consideration. There was no principled objection to the latter.

Nor was there any principled argument in favor of *jus sanguinis.* An autonomous, positive justification of *jus sanguinis* is readily conceivable. It would have involved an appeal to an understanding of the nation as a community of descent. Yet no such positive justification was forthcoming. The only justification was purely negative, based on the critique of *jus soli.* Yet this critique had a straw-man character; it was directed against a form of unconditional *jus soli* that was never under serious consideration in late-nineteenth-century France.

The debate of the 1880s, then, affords no evidence of a strong ideal commitment to an exclusively descent-based citizenship law. In view of the larger argument of this book, this should come as no surprise. The requisite ideological base for such a commitment—an understanding of the nation as a community of descent—was missing. The ethnic strand in national self-understanding has always been relatively weak in France. More generally, it has been consistently weaker in the old, continuous "state-nations" of England and France than in the young nation-states of central Europe. Yet this provides only the beginning of an explanation. We must still explain why *jus sanguinis* was explicitly affirmed, even if this did not entail a commitment to an exclusively descent-based citizenship law. And we must explain the general concurrence in the affirmation of *jus sanguinis*. What accounts for this general and newly explicit endorsement of *jus sanguinis*?

The Incipient Ethnicization of Nationhood

Although the ethnic strand in national self-understanding has always been comparatively weak in France, it did become more salient in the late nineteenth century (although by no means as salient as in late-nineteenth-century Germany). And while the high point of this ethnic self-understanding was reached only later, during and after the Dreyfus Affair, its incipient emergence may well have contributed, in a diffuse way, to the affirmations of *jus sanguinis* during the debates of the 1880s.

This incipient and limited ethnicization of French national self-understanding was the product of several related developments. One was the sympathetic interest of French intellectuals in the national movements of the nineteenth century—especially those of the Greeks, Belgians, Poles, Hungarians, Italians, Romanians, and Germans. Support for national movements was particularly strong on the left.[45] Until the mid-1860s such movements were seen, in a perspective deriving from the Revolution and reinforced by the efflorescence and repression of the national movements of 1848, as struggles against the ancien régime, as campaigns for liberation from reactionary dynastic regimes. In this perspective, the political aspect of national movements was essential, the ethnic aspect secondary. The carriers of national movements were seen as historic peoples deprived of liberty, not prepolitical ethnocultural groups. National movements, in the words of one contemporary observer, constituted a "work of regeneration" through which arbitrarily divided nations sought to reconstitute themselves and to "reestablish their former unity."[46]

Yet even in this political perspective, it was increasingly difficult to ignore the ethnocultural basis of nineteenth-century national movements. Awareness of ethnic nationalism is apparent in the increasing use, after 1830, of the new word *"nationalité"* to designate ethnocultural community, and consequent community of political aspiration, in the absence of autonomous political organization.[47] *"Nationalité"* was not synonymous with *"nation,"* which, in French at least, implied autonomous political organization (though not, necessarily, ethnocultural community).

The link between ethnocultural community and political aspiration was crystallized in the "principle of nationality," first articulated by Mazzini, and current after midcentury. This implied a sharp conceptual distinction between nationality and state, and a political program of redrawing the political to accord with the ethnocultural map.[48] Both the conceptual distinction and the political program, central to the national movements of central Europe, had been foreign to the cultural and political experience of northwestern Europe.[49] Yet French sympathy for the political program may have helped "naturalize" the distinction between ethnocultural nationality and state and may have fostered the associated tendency to conceive of the "nationals" of the state in ethnocultural terms.[50]

The legal nationality conferred by the state and the ethnocultural nationality invoked by the "principle of nationality" are of course different things; the former may be conferred in utter disregard of the latter. Yet the thrust of the principle of nationality was precisely to connect the two[51]—not directly, through state redefinition of legal nationality in ethnocultural terms, but indirectly, via the redrawing of political boundaries so as to make legal and ethnocultural nationality converge.

It was only after midcentury that members of the French state were first routinely called *nationaux*, and state-membership first called *nationalité*.[52] In other words, the new word *"nationalité"* acquired first an ethnocultural meaning, firmly established by 1848, and subsequently a legal meaning. The prior ethnocultural meaning appears to have "contaminated" the legal meaning. Talk of *"nationalité"* in the legal sense carried with it shades of meaning belonging to *"nationalité"* in the ethnocultural sense. Indeed the very adoption of *"nationalité,"* whose ethnocultural meaning had already been established, to designate what had hitherto been known in ethnoculturally neutral terms as the *"qualité de français,"* suggests an interest in asserting the ultimate or ideal ethnocultural basis of statehood. Calling formal state-membership and ethnocultural community by the same term, *nationalité*, suggests an awareness of, and a desire to emphasize, the affinity between the two.

Although their sympathy for the principle of nationality was grounded politically rather than ethnically, many French intellectuals came to envision the congruence of legal and ethnocultural nationality as a desirable and "natural" state of affairs, toward the realization of which the whole course of nineteenth century history seemed to be tending. "All of Europe, except for England and Portugal, tells us that nationality depends on blood," argued Camille Sée in the Senate on behalf of *jus sanguinis*.[53] Even persons skeptical of or hostile to the principle of nationality, fearing its disruptive geopolitical potential, acknowledged the strength of this tendency. This may help explain why, during the debates of the 1880s, the claim that nationality ought to be based on descent provoked no opposition.

The second development fostering a limited ethnicization of national self-understanding was a critical revaluation of the universalist, individualist, and rationalist elements in the French Revolutionary tradition, beginning in the 1860s and intensifying after the 1870 defeat.[54] The revolt against rationalism was a general European phenomenon. Yet this broad European movement of ideas did not mature until the 1890s—too late to bear on the French parliamentary debates of the 1880s. The shock of military defeat, however, and the dominance of rationalist and universalist elements in the French political-cultural heritage, occasioned a precocious critique of rationalism and universalism in France.[55]

French intellectuals' assertive confidence in the universal mission of France—so robust throughout the nineteenth century—was profoundly shaken by the French collapse. Their consequent self-questioning, framed by implicit or explicit Franco-German comparisons, centered on a critique of universalism. Historically, French patriotism had a universalist thrust. (In this respect, the Revolution only strengthened a tendency already well established in the seventeenth century.) Patriotism and universalism were easily reconciled when France was the dominant European power.[56] Now, however, universalism was criticized for sapping national strength. The new geopolitical situation, it was argued, required a new type of patriotism. Defeated, weak, and vulnerable, France needed a particularist patriotism, a *reserrement*, a contraction and concentration of values and commitments. In this respect France had to imitate Germany.[57]

The particularism affirmed in the aftermath of defeat was in the first instance a political, not an ethnic particularism. Intellectuals adopted a Francocentric, but not necessarily an ethnocentric orientation. They turned their attention to the rebuilding of French national strength, to the achievement of French national interests, but there was nothing specifically ethnic about this narrowing of the horizon of attention. Particularism implied a disciplined and exclusive political commitment to the fortunes of the French state—an *"égoïsme national,"* as the nationalist Paul Déroulède called it—not, necessarily, an ethnic redefinition of the French nation.[58] Still, the new mood among French intellectuals indirectly favored a certain ethnicization of national self-understanding. The older universalist patriotism, supported by a rationalist social theory that denied the existence of fundamental differences between people,[59] made it difficult to think of nationhood in ethnic terms. The new nationalism, in contrast, emphasized the specifically and distinctively French, and the original and ultimate character of Franco-German differences. The ethnicization of self-understanding was one way—though not the only or, in the end, the most common way—of interpreting the Franco-German antagonism.[60]

A final, closely related development favoring the ethnicization of French self-understanding was what might be called the nationalization of racial and ethnic categories. "Racial" explanations of social phenomena were common in nineteenth-century France.[61] Not only Gobineau, the most systematic theorist of race, but leading intellectuals including Augustin Thierry, Ernest Renan, and Hippolyte Taine made race a central category of social and historical analysis. Until about 1870, however, French race-thinking was both conceptually and politically antinational.[62] Race was linked to class, not to nation; it was invoked to explain certain tensions, divisions, and weaknesses within the French nation, not to distinguish the French from foreign nations. The French aristocracy, it was argued, was distinguished by its Germanic descent from the rest of the French population, considered to be of Gallic descent.[63] That France was composed of a fusion of races was a commonplace. Whether this fact was celebrated, as by Michelet, or lamented, as by Gobineau, it was universally acknowledged.[64] Not only was race conceptually distinct from nation; but the partisans of race had no special sympathy for nationalism or patriotism. Gobineau was militantly antipatriotic, referring to patriotism as a "monstrosity."

Following the Franco-Prussian war, however, race-thinking became increasingly nationalized. In the aftermath of defeat, social and political analysis was dominated by Franco-German comparisons and contrasts.[65] In this context, race was dissociated from class and associated with nation; it was interpreted as a basis of international, rather than intranational conflict. Whether pro-German, like some early diagnoses of the collapse of 1870, or anti-German, many analyses of Franco-German differences invoked racial categories. Gobineau had emphasized, and deplored, the racially mixed character of France. After 1870, French race-thinking stressed international at the expense of intranational racial differences. Pessimists contrasted the decadence and decay of the Latin nations of France, Spain, and Portugal with the vigor and expansion of the "Anglo-Saxon" nations of England, the United States, and Germany. Others saw the "Latin civilization" of France as threatened by "German barbarism." "One is a barbarian by birth," wrote François Combes in 1870. "Germany is always such to us who are the bulwark of the Latin races."[66]

The corollary of the nationalization of race was a certain racialization or ethnicization of nationhood. A racial or ethnic dimension was added to institutional, historical, or geographical accounts of national differences. This was particularly true of accounts of Franco-German differences: the ethnicization of differences between hostile nations served to underscore their ultimate, irreducible, fatal character and to mobilize sentiment in the national struggle. Yet the tendency was more general and may help explain the newly explicit affirmations of *jus sanguinis* during the debates of the 1880s. The currency of race-thinking was illustrated during the debates themselves by this remark of the Senator Isaac: "France is not only a race, but especially a *patrie* . . . she possesses that eminently colonial capacity of absorbing in herself the peoples to whom she transports civilization."[67] Arguing from the left for the attribution of French citizenship to African workers recruited during the 1850s and 1860s for labor in the Antilles, Isaac himself was not sympathetic to the understanding of the nation as a community of descent. But the opening phrase of his remark—"France is not *only* a race" (my emphasis)—suggests the currency of vaguely racial or ethnic thinking at that time.[68]

The ethnic strand in French self-understanding did not crystallize until the time of the Dreyfus Affair. Even then, it remained much less pronounced than the ethnic strand in German national self-understanding. Barrès and Maurras, despite their anti-Semitism, lack a consistently ethnic understanding of nationhood like that routinely articulated by nineteenth-century German intellectuals. In the 1880s the ethnic aspect was weaker still, although by comparison with earlier periods, when it was virtually undetectable, it had become much more salient. This incipient and limited ethnicization of self-understanding, prepared by sympathetic midcentury interest in the principle of nationalities and by the currency of vaguely racial explanations of social phenomena, and stimulated by the emergence of a particularistic nationalism at home following the defeat of 1870, may help account for the general preference for *jus sanguinis* over *jus soli* as a foundational principle of citizenship law.

Demographic and Military Interests

Despite the critique of *jus soli* and the explicit affirmation of *jus sanguinis* as the foundational principle of French citizenship law, the legislature ended by substantially extending *jus soli* in 1889. What accounts for this reversal? Legal scholars have stressed the demographic, and especially the military, interests of the French state. "The shadow of the bureau of recruitment hovers over this text," wrote Niboyet, the outstanding authority on international private law of the early twentieth century, and his view remains widely accepted.[69] Yet these state interests were not decisive. To interpret the reform of citizenship law in purely instrumental terms is to overestimate military manpower needs in the 1880s and to underestimate the specifically political and ideological interests in the legal assimilation of long-settled foreigners to Frenchmen.

The instrumentalist argument at first sight seems strong. The dramatic Prussian victory over Austria in 1866 did generate concern about the size of the French population and the size of the army. France suddenly faced a North German Confederation with a population of 29 million, 10 million larger than Prussia alone. In this new incarnation, Prussia "could no longer be counted as France's military or demographic inferior."[70] This held *a fortiori* after the Franco-Prussian War and the establishment of the German Empire, when a diminished France (having lost Alsace-Lorraine) faced an enlarged Germany with a population not only larger than its own (41 vs. 36 million in 1872) but growing much more rapidly.[71] Now that railway-based supply systems had diminished constraints on effective army size, numbers loomed as decisive. War, it seemed, would be reduced to demographic arithmetic. Napoleon III was only voicing conventional wisdom when he noted in 1867 that "the influence of a nation depends on the number of men that it can place under arms."[72]

Yet the reform of citizenship law cannot be understood in instrumental terms as a state response to this conjuncture of demographic stagnation, geopolitical realignment, and emerging mass armies. In the first place, the importance of population size should not be anachronistically exaggerated. As Allan Mitchell has shown, "the most pressing issue [in the aftermath of the Franco-Prussian War] was not size but organization."[73] Population size gradually became a more salient issue as the demographic gap widened between France and Germany and as conscription schemes in both countries moved toward full utilization of available manpower.[74] In the 1870s and 1880s, however, the size of the French army was not limited by the size of the French population. If the full mobilized strength of the French army failed to match that of the German army in these decades, this reflected the more thoroughgoing universalism of conscription and the longer duration of reserve liability in Germany than in France. The French military reform of 1872 had introduced only the principle, not the reality, of universal service. Important exemptions and privileges survived, and even some who were neither exempt nor privileged were prevented by budgetary constraints from completing the full five-year term of service.[75]

In the 1870s and 1880s the material interest of the state in increasing the size of the army could be better served by universalizing service for Frenchmen and increasing the duration of reserve liability than by turning foreigners into Frenchmen. By the late 1880s the foreign population in France slightly exceeded one million, of whom 200,000 were males under the age of 20.[76] Of these, a substantial fraction—perhaps three-quarters—were born in France.[77] It is probable that from 6,000 to 8,000 foreign males born and residing in France came of age each year in the 1880s. These were the persons who, under the terms of the law of 1889, would henceforth be defined as French and therefore liable to military service.[78] Added to the 300,000 French males who came of age each year, they would enlarge the pool of recruits by approximately 2–2½ percent.[79] This marginal gain was insignificant compared to the gains to be made by universalizing service among the French.

The universalization of military service was already on the legislative agenda. When the extension of *jus soli* first was endorsed by the Chamber of Deputies, it was already clear that the system of military recruitment would be reformed in a universalistic direction. In this context it was not necessary to transform foreigners into Frenchmen in order to increase the size of the army. The conscription reform engendered, in fact, the opposite problem: too many recruits. Even though the term of service was shortened from five to three years, budgetary constraints prevented all recruits from serving the full three years: one-third were designated by lottery to serve only a single year.[80]

Republicanism and the Making of Frenchmen

Yet if the civic incorporation of immigrants was not, in the 1880s, a *military* necessity, it did come to be defined, in the context of an emerging reform of the conscription system, as a *political* necessity. The extension of *jus soli* to include second-generation immigrants was conceived in the Chamber of Deputies as a response to two problems. Both were defined in political and ideological rather than in demographic and military terms. The first and dominant was the "shocking inequality" that permitted long-established foreigners to remain in their homes—and workplaces—while Frenchmen spent up to five years in the barracks.[81] This was especially galling now that military service had become, in theory if not yet in fact, a personal obligation of every Frenchman. Although the details remained to be worked out, it was evident by the mid-1880s that the new conscription law would provide for shorter and more universal service. In this context of increasingly, if still imperfectly, universal service for Frenchmen, the exemption of second-generation foreign immigrants, while of small military import, was ideologically scandalous and politically intolerable.

Throughout the 1880s the ideologically charged debates on military recruitment formed the backdrop to debates on citizenship law.[82] The drive to reform conscription legislation was led by Republican zealots in the Chamber of Deputies with a passionate, if sometimes impolitic, commitment to equality.[83] As Challener notes, "the desire to reduce the length of conscription and the hope of ending the split contingent, the special exemptions for teachers and priests, and the system of one-year volunteers . . . were . . . but subordinate corollaries of the main egalitarian theme."[84] The extension of *jus soli* was another corollary of Republican egalitarianism. It is scarcely surprising that Republican deputies, hostile to privileges and exemptions for priests, students, schoolteachers, and the wealthy, would be equally hostile to exemption based on citizenship—especially when the foreign citizenship, as in the case of persons born and raised in France, seemed a spurious one, a legal fiction ungrounded in social fact. As a response to this unjustifiable privilege, this "shocking inequality," the move to extend *jus soli* was defined and defended in political and ideological rather than demographic or military terms.

The second problem motivating the extension of *jus soli* was the incipient development of "different nations within the French nation."[85] Although Belgians comprised the largest group of foreigners throughout the nineteenth century, concern focused on Italian immigrants, perceived as a more solidary—and culturally foreign—community.[86] In the Bouches-du-Rhône, where Italians comprised 12 percent of the population, it was reported that Italian "chefs de colonie" were actively cultivating an Italian "national spirit" and pursuing a "politics of isolation" through the means of associations, journals, and so on.[87] Such solidary ethnic communities, real or imagined, directly challenged the unitarist French political formula. Since the Revolution, the self-styled *"nation une et indivisible"* has been violently intolerant of anything that could be interpreted as a "nation within the nation." This unitarist attitude, at once intolerant of constituted groups and inclusive of their constituent members as individuals, is epitomized by the famous formula of the Comte de Clermont Tonnère during the Revolution: "One must refuse everything to Jews as a nation and grant everything to Jews as individuals . . . They must be citizens as individuals."[88] The Chamber's attitude toward established immigrants was similar: better that they become individually citizens, than that they remain collectively foreigners, a foreign nation within the French nation, and, as such, a "veritable peril."[89]

The threat posed by solidary communities of foreigners was perceived as even more acute in Algeria, where, among colonists, the French barely outnumbered foreigners.[90] In Algeria, to a greater extent than in metropolitan France, foreigners, overwhelmingly Spanish and Italians, tended to live in "compact and solidary groups," "true foreign colonies, the less susceptible of being absorbed in the French nationality as they are more dense."[91]

The extension of *jus soli*, then, was defined by the Republicans of the Chamber as a means of eliminating the "odious privilege" enjoyed by long-settled foreigners and preventing the emergence of nations within the nation. But even if the Republicans' diagnosis of these problems was accepted, what made the extension of *jus soli* an effective and acceptable solution? After all, various objections could be made to the proposal to define second-generation immigrants as French. Might it not be dangerous to incorporate such persons into the army, especially now that military service was conceived in specifically national rather than statist terms, as the expression of the "nation in arms" and no longer as a "tribute exacted by an oppressive and alien state"?[92] And how could a formal legal transformation solve the sociopolitical problem of the nation within the nation? Would not the formal "nationalization" of the foreign population leave underlying social realities untouched? A stroke of the pen might turn foreigners into Frenchmen, might make them members of the *pays légal*—but would it make them members of the *pays réel*? Or would they remain *"Français de papier"*—as naturalized Frenchmen were stigmatized by Action Française in the interwar period?[93]

If Republicans of the Chamber were not susceptible to such doubts, if they did not hesitate to transform foreigners into French soldiers and French citizens, it was because of their robust confidence in the assimilatory powers of France. Thus A. Dubost, the *rapporteur* of the bill, called for the extension of French citizenship to persons who, "having lived long on the soil on which they were born, have acquired its mores, habits, and character, and are presumed to have a natural attachment for the country of their birth."[94] Maxim Lecomte commended the "peaceful, equitable, necessary annexation of a numerous population, attached to its native soil, a population that will be rapidly assimilated by the whole of the nation."[95] Similarly A. Naquet, a leading radical Republican in the Senate, and a lone advocate of *jus soli* in that body, invoked the process by which "foreigners who are born in France, who have learned our language from their birth, who frequently speak no other, who have been educated among us, who have learned to love France . . . [become] French at heart [*Français par le coeur*]."[96]

The assimilationist motif is an old one in France. But there was a new and specifically Republican tinge to the assimilationism of the 1880s. It was not mere residence or work in France that was credited with assimilatory virtue; it was participation in the newly Republicanized and nationalized institutions of school and army. Sweeping Republican reforms of the early and mid 1880s had made publically funded primary education universal and compulsory.[97] By the end of the decade, *l'école obligatoire* was not only a principle but, to a large extent, a reality, holding foreign as well as French children in its powerfully assimilationist embrace. Moreover, primary education was now secular. The negative, violently anticlerical component of Republican educational reforms is often stressed. But "laicization" had a positive as well as a negative content. It did not simply mean eliminating religious instruction from the classroom and members of religious orders from the ranks of teachers. It meant replacing religious with civic training in the classroom, the servant of God with the servant of the state at its head, the heavenly father with the earthly fatherland in the hearts and minds of schoolchildren.[98] Jules Ferry wished to "establish humanity without a God and without a King"—but not without a substitute.[99] That substitute was the nation. It was, more exactly, "that religion of the Fatherland, . . . that cult and that love at once ardent and reasoned, with which we want to penetrate the heart and mind of the child."[100]

Secular education, in short, meant national education, in a double sense. Education, first, had a national administrative frame. From teacher-training in the normal schools to textbooks such as the history and civics manuals of Lavisse, schooling was standardized throughout the national territory.[101] The nation, second, was at the heart of the intellectual and moral curriculum of the schools. History and geography, which had pride of place in the Republican school curriculum, made the nation a central cognitive and moral category, using new textbooks to render concrete, palpable, and emotionally resonant the previously distant and abstract notion of France and to surround patriotic duty with a penumbra of dignity and grandeur.[102] The nation was thus central to the moral and civic indoctrination so characteristic of Republican schools. Patriotism was deliberately, strenuously, and—as 1914 would show—successfully cultivated.

If assimilation was "begun by *l'école obligatoire*," in the words of one participant in the debate on citizenship law, it was "continued by military service."[103] School and army reinforced each other: the school inculcated military virtues; the army taught language, literacy, and citizenship.[104] Second-generation immigrants were already subjected to the assimilatory workings of the school; the extension of *jus soli* would subject them to the assimilatory workings of the army. The "institutionalized migration and kneading together" that was inherent in military service and that contributed to the assimilation of French peasants would henceforth work in exactly the same way on immigrants.[105]

Immigrants' previous exemption from military service was not only resented as an "odious privilege" but feared as an impediment to assimilation. Exempt foreigners, it was argued, would naturally "associate with others in the same situation and . . . retain a spirit indifferent or hostile to the grandeur and prosperity of the French nation."[106] To define second-generation immigrants as French, on the other hand, would "work as a sort of solvent" on the solidary communities of foreigners of whose existence the French state was so intolerant.[107]

Republican confidence in *jus soli* rested on Republican faith in assimilation. Overlaid on the traditional, diffuse French belief in the assimilatory virtues of the territory and its institutions was a specifically Republican faith in the assimilatory virtues of school and army. To assimilate means to make similar: and school and army, in their Republican reincarnations, entrusted with "the mission of retempering the French soul," were powerfully equipped to do just that.[108] They could assimilate persons long legally French, reshaping their habits of thought and feeling to make them fit the wider frame of the nation. But they could also assimilate foreigners and the newly naturalized. Foreign and French children alike attended school; and after 1889, military service would be obligatory not only for old-stock French but for those newly defined as French by the reform of citizenship law. Internal and external assimilation were sociologically identical: if school and army could turn "peasants into Frenchmen," they could turn native-born foreigners into Frenchmen in the same way.[109]

The extension of *jus soli* was driven by political and ideological rather than demographic and military concerns. The problem to which the reform of citizenship law was addressed was construed in terms of the "shocking inequality" through which long-settled foreigners were able to escape the increasingly universal obligation of conscription and in terms of the threatened development of "different nations within the French nation." And the civic incorporation of long-settled foreigners was construed as an acceptable solution because the legal transformation, it was believed, would be accompanied by a social transformation: immigrants could be redefined legally as Frenchmen because they would be transformed socially into Frenchmen through the assimilatory workings of compulsory schooling and universal military service.

Somewhat surprisingly, in view of its earlier proposal to curtail *jus soli*, the Senate acquiesced readily in the Chamber's proposal to extend *jus soli*. Following the arguments advanced in the Chamber, the Senate report on the bill justified *jus soli* as a response to the "deplorable abuse" through which second-generation immigrants were able to escape from military service by invoking foreign citizenship.[110] The Senate, to be sure, lacked the fervent ideological commitment to equality that animated Republicans in the Chamber. In the debate on conscription it had insisted on protecting the privileges of students and seminarians—an insistence before which Chamber Republicans had to yield.[111] But the Senate was not interested in protecting the privilege of foreigners. On this issue it could adopt the moralizing rhetoric of the Chamber. Thus the Senate report called for an end to the "manifest injustice" that permitted exempt foreigners to advance their careers while their French counterparts were spending three years in the barracks. Again following the reasoning of the Chamber, the Senate report also endorsed the extension of *jus soli* as a means of impeding the formation of dangerous "agglomerations of foreigners, many of whom could be called to serve in enemy armies," and as the "only means of assuring the predominance of the French element" in Algeria.[112]

Why did the Senate not reassert its earlier claim that citizenship ought to be based on descent rather than birthplace? Part of the answer lies in the persistent weakness of the ethnic strand in national self-understanding. This weakness is nicely illustrated by the remark just quoted. If the "preponderance of the French element" can be assured by redefining long-settled foreigners as Frenchmen, then clearly "the French element" is not understood in ethnic terms. Frenchness is acquired, not inherited.

It is acquired, to be sure, in the family, as well as in workshop and marketplace, classroom and barracks. But it is the family as socializing agency, not the family as genetic unit, that is decisive.

The earlier endorsement of *jus sanguinis* may have reflected the incipient ethnicization of self-understanding in the 1870s and 1880s. But the preference for *jus sanguinis*, while expressly formulated for the first time in the 1880s, remained limited and superficial. The preference for *jus sanguinis* was tied to a critique of *unconditional jus soli*, but it did not stand in the way of the extension of *conditional jus soli* proposed by the Chamber. The Senate objected to the attribution of citizenship on the basis of the single arbitrary fact of birthplace. But it proved willing to accept the attribution of citizenship on the basis of the conjoined facts of birthplace and residence at majority. For these two facts, taken together, permitted one to presume a third: a person born in France and residing there at majority could be presumed to have lived in France during his or her formative years.[113] Such a person, the Senate report argued, would be "attached to France by powerful ties. France is his native country, he has been raised there, he knows no other country."[114] Rather than let such persons continue to live in France as *prétendus étrangers*, persons who claim to be foreigners, it would be better to "absorb [them] into the French nationality, which is so strong and so alive, as long as the circumstances of their birth and residence warrant the hope that they will become devoted citizens of their new country."[115] The phrase *prétendus étrangers*, used by a participant in the earlier Senate debate on citizenship,[116] is revealing. Ethnic nationalists would be more likely to refer to *prétendus français* than to *prétendus étrangers*.

Thus the Senate too was confident of the assimilatory virtues of France, although this confidence was more traditional and less specifically Republican than that of the Chamber. The Senate's original preference for *jus sanguinis* may have been tinged by the incipient and limited ethnicization of national self-understanding. But the ethnic strand remained too weak to stand in the way of an extension of *jus soli* that accorded so well with a more deeply rooted assimilationist and expansive conception of French nationhood.

Continuities in the French Politics of Citizenship

The legislation of 1889 gave enduring form to the rules governing the attribution of French citizenship. Subsequent major revisions of citizenship law—in 1927, 1945, and 1973—modified provisions concerning naturalization, the effect of marriage on citizenship, and the attribution of citizenship *jure sanguinis*,[117] but did not touch the principle of *jus soli* for second-generation immigrants.

The 1880s were not, assuredly, a typical decade, and it would be foolhardy to draw from the debates of that decade broad conclusions about the political and cultural meaning of French citizenship. Yet debates about the citizenship status of immigrants during the 1880s were remarkably similar, in their broad outlines and their characteristic figures of argument, to those of the Revolutionary and Napoleonic period, nearly a century earlier, and to those of today, a century later. There is, in France, a well-established dominant style of thinking and talking about citizenship in relation to immigration. This style, with roots in the Revolutionary period, crystallized during the 1880s. To be sure, it has not since gone unchallenged. Around the turn of the century, in the interwar period, and again since the mid-1980s, the dominant discourse on citizenship and immigration has been challenged by a counterdiscourse. Except for a brief interval during the Vichy regime, however, it has been this dominant discourse, not its challengers, that has informed the politics of citizenship. Three leitmotifs of this dominant discourse on citizenship may be noted.

The rhetoric of inclusion. For two centuries French debates on the citizenship status of immigrants have been conducted in an expansive idiom.[118] With few exceptions, all parties to the debates have proclaimed their support for an expansive definition of citizenship. Such proclamations have been obligatory, whatever one's substantive position. Even authors of restrictive proposals have sought to deny or minimize rather than to emphasize their restrictiveness. During the debates of the 1880s the one person who openly advocated a restrictive stance—and he alone—was repeatedly interrupted and derided by his colleagues.

Expansive rhetoric is one thing, expansive policy another. Yet the two are not unconnected. At the very least, as we will see in Chapter 7, the rhetoric of inclusion raises the political cost of advocating or imposing a more restrictive definition of citizenship. The rhetoric of inclusion is not disembodied or free-floating. It is grounded in a distinctive national self-understanding, in a sense of the grandeur of France, the assimilatory virtues of French territory and institutions, and the universal appeal and validity of French language and civilization. Even if today this self-understanding lacks its former robustness, it remains distinctive, sharply differentiated from German habits of national self-understanding. The idea of North African immigrants being or becoming French remains much more plausible and natural than the idea of Turkish immigrants being or becoming German.

The weakness of ethnicity. The weakness of the ethnic moment and the correlative strength of the assimilationist moment in French self-understanding have been repeatedly stressed in this book. Both are amply documented in the debates of the 1880s. To characterize long-settled foreigners as "those who claim to be foreigners," as "persons everyone would consider French," as "French in their hearts," or as "truly French elements" or to propose to redefine foreigners as citizens in order to "assure the predominance of the French element" is to define Frenchness in social and political rather than ethnic terms, as a matter of social becoming rather than intrinsic being.[119]

The faith in assimilation had a specifically Republican tinge in the 1880s that reflected Republican confidence in universal education and universal military service. Yet Republican assimilationism was a variant of, and was superimposed on, traditional French confidence in assimilation. This traditional assimilationism informed the initial shaping of citizenship law during the Revolutionary and Napoleonic periods; it informed the extension of *jus soli* to third-generation immigrants in 1851; it informed the liberal 1927 law on naturalization; and it informed the major postwar citizenship law reforms of 1945 and 1973. Dissenting voices have of course been heard. They crystallized into a coherent body of opinion during the Dreyfus Affair and had their hour under the Vichy regime, which denaturalized many recently naturalized citizens.[120] Such voices were raised again in the 1980s, stressing the ethnic moment in French nationhood and the unassimilability of many resident foreigners. But even a government partly sympathetic to these voices was unable to enact a mildly restrictive reform of citizenship law in 1986–87.

The ambiguities of nationalism. The weakness of ethnicity is not the same thing as the weakness of nationalism or xenophobia. Both nationalism and xenophobia have flourished in France; both flourished, indeed, during the 1880s. Yet French nationalism and xenophobia have had a peculiarly double character, engendering two distinct responses toward immigrants—one assimilationist, the other exclusionist.

During the 1880s, as during the Revolutionary period, the assimilationist response predominated. Not only did nationalism and xenophobia not stand in the way of an inclusive definition of citizenship, they furnished powerful emotions and arguments for an inclusive definition. Patriotically vilified "cosmopolites"—persons of "floating nationality" who "claim to belong to no country and fulfill nowhere the most sacred of duties"—could be defined out of existence by fixing their citizenship as French.[121] Strengthening national unity after the collapse of 1870—the chief focus of 1880s nationalism—required not only the "nationalization of the masses"[122] through school and army but also the breaking up of solidary communities of foreigners. These projects dovetailed nicely. The latter could be accomplished via the former by including second-generation immigrants in the ambit of universal primary education and universal military service. And the exorbitant privileges enjoyed by long-settled foreigners[123]—the chief focus of 1880s xenophobia—could be remedied by redefining foreigners as French. Thus the expansiveness of French citizenship is a legacy of a moment of heightened nationalism.

At the same time, a new nationalism of the right was developing, defining itself against the Republican and anticlerical animus of the still-dominant assimilationist nationalism. More sympathetic to the central European conception of the nation as a community of descent, the new nationalism and its attendant xenophobia—the nationalism of Barrès, of Maurras, of Vichy, and today of Le Pen—nourished an exclusionist rather than an assimilationist politics of citizenship. Hence Action Française's critique of the *"français de papier"* created by naturalization; hence the denaturalizations of Vichy; and hence the proposal of Le Pen to rid French citizenship law of every trace of *jus soli*.[124]

French nationalism and xenophobia have had a double face, now assimilationist, now exclusionist. Both assimilation and exclusion are inherent in the nation-state as a bounded and relatively homogeneous political and cultural space. Yet the particular forms assumed by nationalism and xenophobia, and the relative strength of their assimilationist and exclusionist moments have varied considerably among nation-states. France has been distinctive in the strength of its assimilationist nationalism. This very strength, to be sure, has elicited in response an exclusionist "counternationalism."[125] Today this counternationalism is again strong, while elite confidence in the possibility and legitimacy of assimilation is much less robust than it was in the 1880s. Yet the prevailing understanding of nationhood remains much more inclusive and assimilationist in France than in Germany. As a result, the civic incorporation of immigrants through the automatic workings of *jus soli* continues in France, while a system of pure *jus sanguinis* remains in place in Germany.

6 ◆ The Citizenry as Community of Descent

The Nationalization of Citizenship in Wilhelmine Germany

German citizenship law, although markedly expansive toward ethno-cultural Germans, is markedly restrictive toward non-German immigrants. Naturalization rules are strict, and naturalization rates are very low. More important than naturalization policies and practices in accounting for the long-term civic exclusion of non-German immigrants, however, is the German system of pure *jus sanguinis*. While French citizenship law automatically transforms most second- and third-generation immigrants into citizens, German citizenship law is based exclusively on descent, allowing immigrants and their descendants to remain indefinitely outside the community of citizens.

The unusually strict and consistent German definition of the citizenry as a community of descent crystallized in 1913. The new law was inclusive toward emigrants and exclusive toward immigrants. On the one hand, it allowed Germans residing abroad—the *Auslandsdeutsche*—to retain their citizenship indefinitely and transmit it to their descendants, whereas previously citizenship had been lost after ten years' residence abroad. On the other hand, the government and the Reichstag majority emphatically rejected, as unacceptable encroachments of *jus soli*, several amendments that would have accorded the right of naturalization to persons born and raised in Germany. The new law marked the nationalization, even the ethnicization, of German citizenship. While late-nineteenth-century French nationalism, state-centered and confidently assimilationist toward foreigners, permitted, even required, the transformation of immigrants into citizens, turn-of-the-century German nationalism, ethnoculturally oriented and "dissimilationist" toward immigrants from the east, required their civic exclusion.

Emigration and the Politics of Citizenship: The Preservation of Germandom Abroad

Before 1913 German citizenship law was internally inconsistent.[1] It stood between two models—an older model of the citizenry as a territorial community, and a newer model of the citizenry as a community of descent, the former a product of the absolutist territorial state, the latter of the emerging national state. Provisions governing the acquisition of citizenship did not correspond to those governing its preservation and loss. With respect to acquisition, the citizenry was defined as a community of descent; with respect to preservation and loss, the citizenry was defined as a territorial community. Prolonged residence in the territory no longer sufficed to acquire citizenship.[2] Prolonged absence from the territory, however, still occasioned the loss of citizenship (unless one took the special step of registering with a consulate).

By facilitating the preservation of citizenship by *Auslandsdeutsche*, the 1913 law severed citizenship from residence and defined the citizenry more consistently as a community of descent. Under the new law, residence abroad—however prolonged—had no bearing on citizenship. In theory, a family could reside abroad indefinitely, each succeeding generation assigned German citizenship at birth *jure sanguinis*, retaining it despite continued residence abroad, and transmitting it to descendants. In practice this was not so easy, for the new law, while uncoupling citizenship and residence, introduced two new grounds for the loss of citizenship: becoming a citizen of another state, and failing to fulfill military obligations. There were, however, significant exceptions and qualifications to these new provisions: naturalization abroad did not always entail the loss of German citizenship, and various measures made it easier for *Auslandsdeutsche* to fulfill military obligations.[3] The law of 1913, moreover, facilitated not only the preservation of German citizenship but also its reacquisition by former citizens and their descendants, even those long domiciled abroad.[4] This too gave greater weight to descent at the expense of territory as a constitutive principle of citizenship.

The demand for the civic inclusion of *Auslandsdeutsche* had a strong nationalistic coloration. There were two currents of nationalist thought and feeling: a focused, consistent ethnocultural nationalism, and a diffuse national pride in which statist and ethnocultural motifs were mixed. Although the demand for the revision of citizenship law stemmed from the first, the widespread support it elicited reflected the second.

The automatic loss of citizenship after ten years' residence abroad had been under sharp attack since the last decade of the nineteenth century. The attack was led by the Pan-German League, which was devoted to the "preservation of German *Volkstum*."[5] At its first convention in 1894, the League proposed making it easier for Germans living abroad to retain citizenship, and making naturalization more difficult for foreigners.[6] In December of that year, Ernst Hasse, President of the Pan-German League and a National Liberal deputy, introduced a resolution in the Reichstag with this double aim.[7] A consistent ethnonational outlook underlay both aims.[8] For Hasse and the Pan-Germans, immigration was unnecessary, given Germany's rapidly growing population and the persisting emigration.[9] More important, it was harmful, in that the *"Sprachen- und Rassenfremde"*[10] among the immigrants, especially Poles and Jews, aggravated the already difficult task of realizing an ethnoculturally homogeneous nation. Even if a certain amount of immigration was unavoidable under modern conditions, there was no need to grant migrants citizenship. *Volksfremde*—foreigners to the *Volk* and its ethnic culture—should not, as a rule, be naturalized. The Empire could draw on a more desirable stock of potential immigrants and citizens from dissatisfied emigrants and their descendants and from beleaguered ethnic German communities, subject to increasing assimilationist pressures, in the Baltics and Hungary. These ethnic Germans, and they alone, should have a right to naturalization. To facilitate the return of emigrants, German citizens living abroad should be able to preserve their citizenship indefinitely and transmit it to their descendants, even after acquiring foreign citizenship; and emigrants having lost German citizenship should be able to reacquire it. Restricting the naturalization of non-Germans, facilitating the naturalization of ethnic German immigrants, and allowing German emigrants to retain their citizenship abroad (or easily reacquire it) would further the goal of promoting an ethnoculturally homogeneous Empire. For Hasse, allowing *Auslandsdeutsche* to retain their citizenship indefinitely was just one part—and not the most important part—of a larger plan to remake Germany into a true nation-state.[11]

Hasse's attack on the automatic loss of citizenship through prolonged residence abroad was widely supported. It was taken up by other nationalist organizations[12] and supported in the Reichstag by all parties. A spate of scholarly articles and legal dissertations called for reform.[13] No one defended the status quo. Only the government was initially reluctant, but by 1901 it had agreed in principle to the change.[14] The popularity of the reform reflected its broad nationalist appeal. Only a few small right-wing parties, to be sure, shared Hasse's consistent ethnocultural outlook and agenda.[15] The nationalism informing the widespread support for the civic inclusion of *Auslandsdeutsche* was not an intellectual's nationalism, consistently articulated and elaborated, like that of Hasse; it was rather a diffuse set of habits of thought and feeling about the Reich, *Deutschtum,* and the *Auslandsdeutsche.* Nor was it consistently ethnocultural; it oscillated uncertainly between a statist and an ethnocultural pole, with the status of the *Auslandsdeutsche* understood now in relation to the Reich, now in relation to *Deutschtum* as a whole—sometimes in the course of a single speech.[16]

The statist perspective emphasized the close ties of the *Auslandsdeutsche* to the Reich. The old provisions governing the loss of citizenship through residence abroad, it was argued, no longer suited the times.[17] Earlier emigrants had left without intending to return; they had severed their ties to the Reich or allowed them to atrophy. Moreover, the Reich had been in no position to protect those emigrants who might wish to retain their citizenship.[18] But things had changed. Improved transportation and communication and the development of a lively German language press abroad permitted *Auslandsdeutsche* to maintain their ties to the homeland. And, unlike earlier emigrants, recent emigrants had not gone overseas "in order to separate themselves economically and politically from their Fatherland," but, in many cases, "in order to work economically and politically in the service of the Fatherland."[19] A strong *Reichsnational* consciousness had developed: "*Civis Germanus sum*"—formerly an empty phrase—was now a "proud avowal of membership of a large and powerful state."[20] And that state now had the means—a network of consulates and a strong navy—to protect its foreign citizens effectively. The connection between the *Auslandsdeutsche* and the Reich, finally, would be assured by making the preservation of citizenship contingent on fulfilling military obligations and on not voluntarily acquiring a foreign citizenship.

The ethnocultural perspective emphasized the "preservation of Germandom abroad" *(Erhaltung des Deutschtums im Ausland).* Not only the far-right nationalist parties but the National Liberals, the Center Party, and even the government invoked this as the central value to be realized through the reform of citizenship law.[21] *Deutschtum* (Germandom) was an ethnocultural, not a legal category. It was both more and less inclusive than the legal category of *Reichsdeutsche* (citizens of the Reich), including millions of *Volksdeutsche* (ethnic Germans) outside the Reich but excluding *Reichsdeutsche* who were not ethnic Germans, notably Poles. In this perspective, the reform sought to preserve and strengthen *Deutschtum* abroad by making German citizenship more widely available to *Auslandsdeutsche*.

But to which *Auslandsdeutsche* was citizenship to be made more accessible? The statist argument focused on current and future emigrants, who would be allowed to retain their citizenship (assuming that they satisfied military obligations and acquired no other citizenship) or to reacquire citizenship if they had lost it under existing law through ten years' residence abroad. The ethnocultural argument focused on the wider circle of persons addressed by the law—descendants, in any generation, of former citizens.[22] Such descendants were eligible for naturalization even if they continued to reside abroad, even if they were descended only on the maternal side,[23] and even if they possessed a foreign citizenship. Such persons, it is true, were not accorded an unconditional right to naturalization,[24] and the government indicated that demands for naturalization under this provision by persons possessing a foreign citizenship would be closely scrutinized.[25] But apart from statist reservations about dual citizenship, it was clear that the federal government, the individual states, and all political parties agreed on the desirability of naturalizing ethnocultural Germans.

There were two sides, then, to the wide extension of citizenship to *Auslandsdeutsche*. On the one hand, it would strengthen *Deutschtum* abroad by binding it more closely to, and placing it under the protection of, the Reich. On the other hand, it would bind the Reich more closely to *Deutschtum*; it would make the German Empire more German. Only Hasse and the small ultranationalist parties consistently and explicitly followed this second line of thought, but it was implicit in the position of the government and the National Liberals as well.[26] Germany had "an interest in strengthening return migration to our homeland," argued von Richthofen, and thus in facilitating the reacquisition of citizenship by *Auslandsdeutsche*; but as a demographically vigorous country, it had "not the least interest" in the immigration of "complete foreigners" *(Vollausländer)*.[27]

Yet despite Germany's demographic vigor, the immigration of "complete foreigners" had increased sharply. Between 1890 and 1910 the number of resident foreigners tripled—from 430,000 to 1,260,000.[28] Alone among European states, Germany had both a huge emigrant population (roughly three and a half million) and a substantial immigrant population in the early years of the twentieth century.[29] The Wilhelmine citizenship reform must be understood in this dual context. The new law made citizenship more accessible to emigrants permanently settled outside,[30] and less accessible to immigrants permanently settled inside, the Reich. The traditional German distinction between nation and state, *Volk* and *Staat,* was now projected onto the plane of citizenship law. The definition of the citizenry was nationalized—brought into closer relation with the ethnocultural frame of the nation and detached from the territorial frame of the state. The citizenry was defined by genealogical rather than territorial coordinates, by descent rather than residence. The full significance, then, of the new openness toward emigrants can be seen only in the context of closure against immigrants.

Immigration and the Politics of Citizenship: The Preservation of Germandom at Home

Severing citizenship from residence, the Wilhelmine reform defined the citizenry more consistently as a community of descent in two ways. First, as we have just seen, it made citizenship more accessible to emigrants and their descendants. Second, and more important, it denied a right to citizenship to persons born and brought up in Germany. This did not involve a change in the law.[31] But in the context of a large and growing immigrant population and demands for easier naturalization, particularly for persons born and raised in Germany, the decision to preserve pure *jus sanguinis* invested that legal principle with new meaning, transforming it from a taken-for-granted fact into a self-conscious normative tradition.

Jus soli and *jus sanguinis,* strictly speaking, are principles governing the unilateral attribution or ascription of citizenship by the state, not the voluntary acquisition of citizenship by an individual through naturalization. In this strict sense, *jus soli* was not rejected in 1913; it was not even discussed. Since the early nineteenth century, the attribution of citizenship in individual German states, the North German Confederation, and the German Empire had based exclusively on *jus sanguinis.*[32] Pure *jus sanguinis* was a well established legal tradition. It is a measure of the strength of this tradition that nobody proposed to tamper with it in 1912–13. There was extended and vigorous debate about other facets of citizenship law, but none about rules of attribution. Even those who presented themselves as advocates of *jus soli* did not propose to *attribute* German citizenship to persons born in Germany; instead, they proposed to give such persons a right to naturalization. The difference is significant. The attribution of citizenship *jure soli*—not only the unconditional *jus soli* that prevailed in the Americas, but also the conditional *jus soli* adopted in France and elsewhere to supplement *jus sanguinis*—was unthinkable in the German setting. In the age of nationalism the automatic transformation of immigrants into citizens through the workings of *jus soli* presupposed confidence in the assimilatory powers of the state—confidence that characterized France in the 1880s but not Wilhelmine Germany. Not even the attribution of citizenship *jure soli* to *third*-generation immigrants—persons born in Germany whose parents were also born in Germany—was considered. That the citizenry was fundamentally a community of descent, legally constituted through the attribution of citizenship to the children of German citizens, was beyond dispute. The contrast with the French debate of the 1880s is sharp. Not only did France end by adopting a system of conditional *jus soli* that automatically transformed most second-generation immigrants into citizens; French parliamentary discussions even considered the more radical possibility of adopting unconditional *jus soli* and attributing French citizenship automatically to every person born in the territory (as Napoleon had proposed during the debates on the Civil Code). Neither alternative was conceivable in Germany, despite the burgeoning immigrant population. The first point to underscore, then, is that the universe of discourse was more narrowly bounded in Germany than in France; the attribution of citizenship *jure soli* lay beyond the horizon of the possible.

Although the attribution of citizenship *jure soli* was not even under consideration, there was nevertheless a vigorous debate about the principle of *jus soli*, both in the legislative committee that examined and reworked the original government proposal and on the floor of the Reichstag. The debate was occasioned by a series of Social Democratic proposals to liberalize naturalization by making it a matter of right for certain persons, particularly those born and raised in Germany. Thus one proposal would have given a right to naturalization to persons born in Germany and residing there without long interruptions until majority; another to persons born and raised in Germany and willing to serve in the army; a third to persons born in Germany of a resident foreign father and an (originally) German mother.[33] All these proposals sought to ground a right to naturalization on birth and residence in the territory. Their opponents seized on this territorial aspect to brand the proposals as vehicles of *jus soli*. The Social Democrats did not deny wanting to introduce elements of *jus soli* into German citizenship law—as a principle of naturalization, though not of attribution. After all, they argued, the citizenship laws of almost all other major states contained elements of *jus soli*.[34] Leading legal scholars, they pointed out, had argued for the introduction of elements of *jus soli* to complement the system of attribution based exclusively on *jus sanguinis*. Persons born and raised in Germany, most fundamentally, were German in fact and ought to have the right to become German in law.[35] The Social Democrats were seconded in this line of argument by the Progressives, Poles, and, to some extent, by the Center Party.

The government, however, vehemently rejected the Social Democratic proposals, and the Reichstag majority concurred in this rejection.[36] The taint of *jus soli* was enough to disqualify them from serious consideration. This is evident from the several occasions on which the sole or decisive criticism of a proposed amendment was that it would introduce *jus soli*.[37] In no form, however modest, was *jus soli* acceptable. Its introduction, according to one government representative, "would run against our entire outlook."[38] Ultimately the state governments, dominated by Prussia, threatened to withdraw support for the bill as a whole if any of the Social Democratic proposals were adopted.[39] What accounts for this deep, consistent hostility?

By rejecting the Social Democratic proposals to grant a right of naturalization to certain immigrant groups, the states preserved their freedom of action, including, most important, the freedom to expel immigrants deemed "burdensome" *(lästig)*. This was a freedom of which Prussia, in particular, had made extensive use. But the rejection of *jus soli* cannot be explained solely in terms of such purely practical and statist considerations. There was an important symbolic or ideological element in the absolute rejection of *jus soli* and the assertive emphasis on *jus sanguinis*. The original government proposal, for example, specified that birth to a German father (or illegitimate birth to a German mother) bestowed citizenship, "even when it occurs abroad." To the proposal to eliminate the quoted phrase as superfluous, the government responded by conceding that the phrase did not alter the legal meaning of the provision. Yet "it seemed desirable to retain it in the text in order to express unambiguously for the layman just this highest principle: that citizenship is acquired through descent without regard for place of birth."[40] Consider a second example. The original proposal contained no provision regulating the citizenship status of children of unknown parents who were found abandoned in the territory. The citizenship law of most European states contained some such provision, and there was wide agreement that German citizenship law should have one. It was proposed in the commission that such a child "be considered a citizen of that state in whose territory he was found."[41] Because of the reference to territory, however, this phrasing ran afoul of the suspicion of *jus soli*. The government expressed "grave reservations" about it, for it "would mean a breakthrough of *jus soli* at the expense of *jus sanguinis,* which had been purely and consistently carried through in the original proposal."[42] In the end, an alternative phrasing was found that, without altering the legal force of the provision, expressed the principle of *jus sanguinis*: a child found in the territory of a state was to be presumed to be "the child of a citizen of that state."[43] Proof of citizenship, to take a final example, is very difficult in systems based solely on *jus sanguinis.* Since one's citizenship status depends on the citizenship status of one's parents, and their citizenship status on that of their parents, and so on, citizens *jure sanguinis* face an infinite regress in trying to prove their citizenship.[44] Noting this difficulty, the Social Democrats proposed that a person born in Germany and residing there until majority be provisionally considered German, until proof of the contrary, if his father had also resided in Germany since birth. This proposal would not have altered the bases of citizenship, only the mode of proof of citizenship. Birth and residence in the territory over two successive generations would not, under this proposal, have conferred citizenship; but they would have established the presumption that one was a citizen *jure sanguinis.* While conceding the point, the government nonetheless rejected the proposal on the grounds that it amounted to "the introduction of *jus soli* under the formal guise of a change in the mode of proof."[45]

Government opposition to *jus soli* went far beyond what would be necessary or useful from a purely statist point of view. Opposition focused on the principle itself, rather than on the consequences of introducing it into citizenship law in particular and limited forms. *Jus soli* was intrinsically objectionable. Not without reason did the representative of the Danish minority in North Schleswig complain to the Reichstag, "I simply do not understand this exaggerated fear *(Ängstlichkeit)* of *jus soli.*"[46] The question remains: What accounts for this deep and consistent opposition?

State-National and Ethnonational Opposition to Jus Soli

To understand variations in citizenship law it is necessary to consider the political and cultural meaning of *jus soli* and *jus sanguinis* as well as the legal operation of these principles. *Jus soli* defines the citizenry as a territorial community, *jus sanguinis* as a community of descent. There is an affinity between *jus soli* and the self-understanding of classical countries of immigration, with its emphasis on the assimilationist workings of birth and upbringing in the territory. And there is an affinity between *jus sanguinis* and the self-understanding of Continental European nation-states. The latter affinity, however, is complex, differing for state-national and ethnonational modes of self-understanding. By a "state-national" self-understanding, I mean one in which the nation is understood as embedded in and inseparable from the institutional and territorial frame of the state. An ethnonational self-understanding, on the other hand, is one in which the nation is understood as an ethnic or ethnocultural community independent of the institutional and territorial frame of the state.

From a state-national point of view, such as was predominant in Revolutionary and post-Revolutionary France and in early-nineteenth-century Prussia, *jus sanguinis* is preferable to *jus soli* because descent creates a more substantial community than the "accidental fact" of birthplace. Descent binds the individual more closely to the destiny of the state; and the strength of the ties between state and citizen is a central concern in the age of the nation-state, particularly at the historical moment of the nation-in-arms. The nation-state demands more of its citizens than its dynastic-absolutist predecessor; it is therefore less indifferent to the composition of the citizenry. From an ethnonational point of view, the affinity between *jus sanguinis* and national self-understanding is stronger and more immediate. *Jus sanguinis* creates a community of descent; and on the ethnonational understanding, the nation *is* a community of descent. From an ethnonational point of view, *jus sanguinis* preserves, while *jus soli* might undermine, the identity and the substance of the nation.

Corresponding to the elective affinity with *jus sanguinis* is a "disaffinity" with *jus soli*. But this holds in sharply differing forms for state-national and ethnonational modes of self-understanding. From a state-national point of view, there is nothing intrinsically objectionable about basing membership on territorial rootedness. Birthplace alone, in an increasingly mobile age, might well be an accidental fact, and a poor indicator of enduring ties. But the same cannot be said of birthplace in conjunction with other indicators of attachment, such as prolonged residence, parental domicile, or parental birthplace. The state-national objections to *unconditional jus soli*, in short, do not extend to *conditional jus soli*. They do not extend, that is, to the type of *jus soli* that was established in France. From the ethnonational point of view, however, conditional and unconditional *jus soli* are equally objectionable. Both base citizenship on presence in the territory, rather than membership of the *ethnos*. From a state-national point of view, it is the *strength* of attachment that is decisive; hence conditional *jus soli* is acceptable, even if unconditional *jus soli* is not. From an ethnonational point of view, it is the *kind* of attachment that matters: *jus soli*, conditional as well as unconditional, is rejected because it grounds citizenship in territory rather than descent.

In early-nineteenth-century France debates on citizenship law in connection with the framing of the Civil Code expressed the state-national argument for *jus sanguinis* and the corresponding state-national critique of unconditional *jus soli*. And in the 1880s, despite a faint ethnic tinge to the debate, the state-national point of view again prevailed—a point of view that, in the political circumstances of the 1880s, not only permitted but required the transformation of second-generation foreigners into citizens through the workings of conditional *jus soli*.

The state-national perspective also prevailed in the individual German states of the early and mid-nineteenth century. All the citizenship laws adopted by these states were based on *jus sanguinis*, yet this reflected state-national rather than ethnonational considerations.[47] The same holds for the common North German citizenship that was established in 1870.[48] That law was a work of codification, not of construction. It was drafted so as to embody, as far as possible, the existing provisions of the citizenship laws of the individual German states. Since all these states attributed citizenship solely on the basis of descent, pure *jus sanguinis* was established for the North German Confederation—and for the German Empire a year later—because it was already established in the individual German states. There was no debate about whether the basic principle of *jus sanguinis* ought to be supplemented by elements of *jus soli*. That the question did not even arise is not surprising. In 1871 there were only about 200,000 foreigners in Germany out of a total population of 40 million, and there was no reason to expect substantial immigration in the future.[49] Germany was then in the midst of a substantial emigration wave: between 1864 and 1873 more than a million Germans left for overseas destinations alone.[50] The demographic vigor of the country—in the 1870s births exceeded deaths by about half a million per year—obviated the need for immigration. Substantial internal migration was expected; and freedom of movement within Germany was an intensely contested question. But substantial immigration from outside the Reich was not expected. There was thus no reason to consider introducing elements of *jus soli* to complement the basic principle of *jus sanguinis*. In 1870, then, pure *jus sanguinis* had a different meaning than it had in 1913; it reflected not so much hostility to *jus soli* as indifference. The issue of *jus soli* simply did not arise. Pure *jus sanguinis* was enacted, as it were, by default.

By 1913 the demographic situation had changed dramatically. Germany remained demographically vigorous, but overseas emigration, following a last great surge in 1880–1893, declined precipitously, while immigration sharply increased. The last five years of the century showed a positive migration balance—more immigrants than emigrants—for the first time.[51] By 1910 there were one and a quarter million foreigners in the Reich.[52] Well over 200,000 of them had been born in the Reich and presumably had lived there most of their lives.[53] With the emergence of this substantial group of second-generation immigrants, the absence of any elements of *jus soli* became legally and politically problematic. Leading jurists noted the anomaly and recommended changes.[54] And Social Democrats, with some support from other parties, proposed giving a right to naturalization to persons born and raised in Germany. Yet, as we have seen, even the most modest proposals for the introduction of elements of *jus soli* met with the vehement opposition of the government and of conservative nationalists. To explain the depth and consistency of this opposition, we need to take account of the significant ethnonational strand in Imperial German politics.

The ethnonational rejection of *jus soli* was most clearly and directly expressed by the Conservative deputy Giese: "We are happy that the principle of *jus sanguinis* has been carried through in pure form in the law, and that therefore . . . descent and blood are decisive for the acquisition of citizenship. This provision serves excellently to preserve and defend the ethnonational [*völkisch*] character and the German essence [of the Reich]. Consequently, we reject all amendments that seek to introduce *jus soli* in any form."[55] Neither the government nor the Reichstag majority shared this consistent ethnonational point of view. In a more subtle form, however, ethnonational considerations did decisively influence the governmental stance on *jus soli*.

The Ethnonational Perspective

As a *kleindeutsch*[56] but by no means *reindeutsch* (purely German) state, the Bismarckian Empire was doubly imperfect from the ethnonational point of view.[57] It excluded ten million Austro-Hungarian Germans, and it included substantial non-German national minorities: French in Alsace-Lorraine, Danes in North Schleswig, and, above all, two and a half million Poles in the Prussian east. The Empire thus offered two distinct fields for ethnonational concerns and activities. Ethnonational politics could be oriented toward ethnic Germans outside the Reich; or it could be oriented toward national minorities within the Reich. Both varieties flourished in Imperial Germany,[58] and both contributed to the reshaping of citizenship law, the former bearing on the citizenship status of emigrants, the latter on the citizenship status of immigrants.

Ethnopolitical concern with *Volksdeutsche* outside the Reich took various forms, ranging from purely cultural efforts to preserve and support German schools, language, and culture abroad, to demands for state intervention on behalf of beleaguered ethnic Germans abroad, notably in the Baltic region and in Hungary, and, at the extreme, to renewed *grossdeutsch* demands to bring Germans excluded from the Bismarckian settlement into the Reich. The purely cultural activities—for example, those of the German School Association[59]—received widespread moral but little material support. And they did not touch fundamental issues of Imperial German politics. The *grossdeutsch* project, on the other hand, did address fundamental issues; it challenged the right of the Empire to legitimate itself as a nation-state.[60] Yet despite its revival in the last years of the nineteenth century, the *grossdeutsch* project remained marginal.[61] Bismarck had set the tone by emphatically rejecting not only further territorial expansion in Europe but also all demands for state intervention on behalf of *Volksdeutsche* abroad; his successors adhered to the same policy. Only the collapse of the Habsburg Empire reopened the fundamental question of the fit between nation and state.

Informing both the purely cultural support for the ethnic Germans outside the Reich and the demand for state intervention on their behalf was a sense of ethnonational community that was indifferent to distinctions of formal citizenship, a sense of nationhood that transcended—and, in the case of the *grossdeutsch* project, challenged—state boundaries. This ethnocultural understanding of nationhood was not the only or even the dominant one in Imperial Germany. In the crucial domain of international politics, nationalism and national consciousness were framed by and oriented toward the territory, the institutions, and the citizenry of the state, not to the crosscutting category of the ethnocultural nation.[62] Yet the new state-centered nationalism did not displace the old ethnocultural understanding of nationhood. The two coexisted uneasily. This is reflected in the ambiguity of such terms as "national" and

"German" in Imperial Germany, which sometimes referred to the state and its citizenry as a whole, sometimes to ethnocultural Germandom alone. It was just such a mixture of state-national and ethnonational assumptions that underlay the widespread support for making citizenship more accessible to *Auslandsdeutsche* and their descendants.

Complementing ethnopolitical support for *Volksgenossen* (ethnocultural "comrades") outside the Reich was ethnopolitical concern about *Volksfremde* (ethnocultural foreigners) inside the Reich. The former sought to preserve Germandom abroad, the latter to preserve Germandom at home, by maintaining or strengthening the German character of the Empire, by Germanizing its ethnic borderlands, especially in eastern Prussia.[63] Prussian-German *Polenpolitik*,[64] to be sure, was informed by state-national as well as ethnonational concerns. Indeed, the very existence of the Reich, in its *kleindeutsch* but not *reindeutsch* form, represented a triumph of the state-national over the ethnonational principle. As the Poles themselves pointed out, a consistent application of the "principle of nationality," according to which state boundaries should reflect ethnocultural boundaries, would have barred the incorporation of the Polish districts of Prussia into the Reich. The Poles accused the Germans of inconsistency. While Germans appealed to the principle of nationality to justify the incorporation of ethnocultural Germans in Alsace-Lorraine, they flouted this principle in the Prussian east. To this ethnonational protest against incorporation into the new German Reich, Bismarck replied in classically statist terms: the Poles belonged "to no other state and to no other people than the Prussian, to which I myself belong."[65]

Theodor Schieder has argued that Prussia's assimilationist language policy in the decades after the establishment of the Empire expressed the state-national political philosophy according to which the unitary and homogeneous nation is the deliberate and artificial creation of the state, rather than something prior to and independent of the state.[66] What Schieder does not sufficiently emphasize, notwithstanding his subtle and illuminating analysis, is the impossibility, after the unification of Germany, of a consistent state-national outlook and practice in the Prussian east. Even before unification, Prussian *Polenpolitik* was not—and could not be—confidently assimilationist in the manner of the French state vis-à-vis peripheral regional cultures and immigrants. The late-eighteenth-century partitions of Poland had saddled Prussia with a fiercely independence-minded nobility, who vigorously protested moves toward full administrative incorporation into the Prussian state as well as incipiently assimilationist language policies.[67] Still, it had been possible to treat Poles as Prussians (even if as Prussians who were particularly refractory to administrative centralization). But it was impossible, after unification, to treat Poles consistently as Germans or Germans-in-the-making. The Polish presence was simply too large, too consolidated, and—increasingly—too defiantly nationalistic.[68]

Prussian-German *Polenpolitik,* as a result, was informed by a mixture of state-national and ethnonational assumptions. While the former were assimilationist, the latter were essentially "dissimilationist." After the mid-1880s, except for a break in the early 1890s under Caprivi's chancellorship, the latter gained in importance, especially with the emergence of a more intransigent German nationalism and a popular Polish counternationalism. Increasingly, in habits of thought, political rhetoric, legal texts, and administrative practice, Poles were distinguished from other citizens of the Reich. "National" and "German" were used less often in their inclusive state-national meaning and more often in their discriminatory ethnonational meaning. The *Reichspolen*—Polish-speaking citizens of the Reich—were characterized as Poles, or, in more cautious public formulations, as our "Polish fellow-citizens," certainly not as Germans or German citizens *tout court;* they were stigmatized as *Reichsfeinde* (enemies of the Reich); they were legally and administratively treated as second-class citizens.[69]

The Vicissitudes of Prussian-German Polenpolitik

It is difficult to distinguish ethnonational from state-national concerns in Prussian and German *Polenpolitik.*[70] Yet one can discern a shift in accent from the statist concern to secure the political loyalty of Poles to the Prussian (and later the German) state, to a nationalist concern to Germanize the *Reichspolen,* and ultimately to an ethno-demographic concern to Germanize the eastern territories of the Reich by colonization.[71] Even under Bismarck there are significant traces of this shift in accent. Bismarck's distance from the ethnonational point of view is well known.[72] Yet he was not equally distant from the two sorts of ethnonational concerns I have distinguished. Toward the national aspirations of Germans outside the Reich, Bismarck was indifferent; toward demands for intervention on their behalf, or, in the case of Austro-Germans, for their incorporation into the Reich, he was hostile.[73] This hostility was based on considerations of both foreign and domestic policy. On the one hand, Bismarck wanted to assure the international community of the "saturation" of the Reich and of its lack of interest in further territorial acquisitions; on the other hand, he wanted to preserve North German-

Protestant-Prussian dominance in the Empire and was resolutely opposed to residual *grossdeutsch* demands for the incorporation of the Austro-German Catholics.[74]

Yet toward the internal ethnonational composition of the Reich, and more particularly the Prussian east, Bismarck was by no means indifferent. The *Kulturkampf* had a crucial anti-Polish dimension. On Bismarck's own account, it was the "rapid advance of the Polish nationality at the expense of the German in Poznania and West Prussia" that moved him to launch the *Kulturkampf*.[75] Historians have discounted this explanation, emphasizing instead Bismarck's desire to isolate Catholic France by strengthening ties with anticlerical Italy and Orthodox Russia; or his manipulative internal coalition-building strategy of "negative integration," based on the branding of the Catholic Center Party (and later the Social Democrats) as *Reichsfeinde;*[76] or (as context) the general European conflict between militant liberalism, allied with the secular state, and a Church that had recently condemned liberalism in the Syllabus of Errors and asserted papal infallibility. Yet whatever occasioned the *Kulturkampf,* there is no doubt that, in the Prussian east, it took the form of a campaign against Polish nationality as well as against the Catholic Church and the Center Party.[77]

The Prussian School Supervision Law of 1872, which placed all schools under the supervision of state-supported school inspectors, was directed chiefly against the Polish clergy, whose dominant influence in the schools of Poznan and parts of West Prussia and Silesia Bismarck blamed for the "Polonization" of those regions. This measure was grounded in state-national rather than ethnonational concerns. Unlike his National Liberal allies, Bismarck did not view Germanization as intrinsically necessary or desirable. He sought to weaken Polish nationalism, which he viewed as a threat to the Reich, rather than to suppress Polish nationality. To weaken Polish nationalism, in Bismarck's view, it was necessary to attack its traditional social carriers: the clergy and the nobility. Yet other measures of the *Kulturkampf* era were aimed more broadly against Polish nationality as such. In 1872 Bismarck proposed to expel all noncitizen Poles from Prussia. Although not carried out at the time, this proposal anticipated the mass expulsions of the 1880s.[78] In 1872 and 1873 German was made the compulsory language of instruction for all subjects in elementary schools in Upper Silesia and West Prussia, and for all subjects except religion in Poznan. Polish-speaking teachers were transferred from the east to other parts of Prussia. And in 1876 German was made the sole language of public life.[79]

To some extent these measures too could be justified in state-national terms. The insistence on German as the medium of elementary-school instruction was, for Bismarck, a means of ensuring competence in German and thereby exposure to German-language public discussion, which, he thought, would promote loyalty to the Prussian state and the German Reich.[80] And the imposition of German as the sole official language (Staatssprache), it was argued, did not entail a desire to curb Polish as a popular language (Volkssprache).[81] Yet the harsh, compulsory character of the new school and public language legislation marked a sharp break with previous Prussian policy. Even Oswald Hauser, while emphasizing the statist orientation of Bismarck's Polish policies, admits that the language legislation "brought the Prussian government to a most dangerous borderline between a policy of energetic defensive measures against a danger to the state, and national intolerance aimed at a homogeneous nation-state."[82]

Here the relative weight of state-national and ethnonational motives and motifs in Bismarck's Polenpolitik is less important than the change in the basic orientation of Prussian-German Polenpolitik between the partitions of Poland in the late eighteenth century and the early twentieth century. The change pivoted on the unification of Germany.[83] Until 1848, and to a considerable extent until 1866, the fundamental aim was to make loyal Prussian subjects out of Poles. The means to this end varied widely from benign neglect to intrusive bureaucratic centralism, and from support for Polish language and culture to efforts to foster German language and culture, the latter supported by the untroubled conviction of German cultural superiority. But even at its most assimilationist, policy aimed at Prussianization, not Germanization. What Hagen writes of the late eighteenth century was true through the middle of the nineteenth: "The national question was essentially one of patriotism. What counted was neither language, nor secular aesthetic or literary culture, nor religion, but rather loyalty and devotion to the state."[84]

Loyalty to the Prussian state was one thing, loyalty to a German nation-state another altogether. Even the former, it was clear after 1848, was not to be hoped for from the independence-minded Polish nobility and clergy.[85] The latter was much more problematic. In the constituent North German Reichstag in 1867, Polish deputies objected to incorporation in a German nation-state: "What common part, for heaven's sake, can we have in a nationally based federation that exists to represent, defend, cultivate, and further common German interests?" And again in the German Reichstag of 1871: "We want to remain under Prussian rulership, but we do not want to be incorporated into the German Reich."[86]

Bismarck continued to hope that ordinary Poles—peasants and an emerging middle class—might become loyal citizens of the Reich, if only they were insulated from Polish-nationalist propaganda of the nobility and clergy.[87] Hence the special severity of anticlerical measures in Polish districts; hence the language policies mentioned earlier; and hence Bismarck's support, in 1886, for a "Settlement Law" that committed state funds to buy up Polish estates and settle German colonists on the lands.[88]

The Settlement Law was an ambiguous measure. It could be justified as a weapon against the Polish nobility, or it could be considered a weapon against the Polish population as such. For Bismarck, it probably had the former meaning; but for the National Liberals and other nationalists who supported the bill, it clearly had the latter.[89] The Settlement Law marked a new phase in *Polenpolitik*, in which ethnodemographic interests came to the fore. This occurred with the increasingly general acknowledgment of the failure of attempts at assimilation.[90] The failure was twofold. That Prussian-German *Polenpolitik* had failed to make Poles loyal German citizens was shown by the development of a mass-based Polish nationalism;[91] that it had failed to make Poles German-speaking citizens was shown by census data recording increasing concentrations of Polish speakers in the Prussian east.[92] Having failed to win the political loyalty of the Poles and to assimilate them to German culture, the government now sought to displace Poles by Germans in the eastern frontier districts, lest these districts become increasingly Polish. Having failed to Germanize the people, it now sought to Germanize the soil, to build a "living bulwark against the Slavic flood."[93]

Even before the inauguration of the internal colonization program, the new ethnodemographic inflection of Prussian-German *Polenpolitik* was apparent in the mass expulsions of 1885.[94] Bismarck's chief concern was with nationalist agitators among the immigrants. But he and his ministers were moved by ethnodemographic concerns to undertake an indiscriminate mass expulsion of noncitizen Poles and Jews, without regard to political activity.[95] As Bismarck and Prussian Culture Minister Gossler wrote in an administrative letter to Interior Minister Puttkamer, demanding the general expulsion, "even the [Polish] masses who remain untouched by political agitation disturb our state organism by Polonizing the border provinces, whereas our state task [*staatliche Aufgabe*] is to Germanize them." Defiantly defending the expulsions in the Prussian *Landtag*, moreover, Bismarck put it more bluntly: "we want to get rid of foreign Poles, because we have enough of our own."[96]

Although the internal colonization program inaugurated a year later was to endure until the outbreak of war and result in the resettlement

of over 20,000 peasants—with their families a total of 120,000 Germans—
it failed to achieve its aims.[97] First, the counterorganization by the Polish
community of credit and "parceling" associations enabled Poles to
outdo Germans in their own game of estate subdivision and peasant
colonization. Second, powerful currents of internal migration continued
to draw more Germans than Poles from the agrarian east to the industrial districts of western Germany. The evident failure to gain ground in
the "struggle for the soil" engendered a demand for harsher measures.[98]
A law of 1904 required local administrative approval for all "new set-
tlements." This discriminated blatantly against Poles, in view of the
formal government order of 1898 making the "furthering of Germandom" *(Förderung des Deutschtums)* a duty of administrative officials.[99]
Discriminatory legislation culminated with the Expropriation Law of
1908 permitting expropriation as a means of "strengthening Germandom" in West Prussia and Poznan.[100] Restrained by sharp criticism of
the law in Germany and abroad, the Prussian government used these
powers of expropriation only once, in 1912; and this, like the mass
expulsions of 1885, occasioned a formal resolution of censure in the
Reichstag.[101] But the law itself was eloquent testimony to the bitterness
of the nationality struggle in the prewar years. It was this hard nationality struggle—this standoff between mobilized and opposed national-
isms—that formed the backdrop to the revision of citizenship law, especially to the debates about *jus soli* and naturalization policy.

Migration and Nationality

The politics of ethnocultural nationality in the Prussian east was linked
to both internal and international migration. Internal migration has
already been mentioned. The most important reason for the demographic gains of Poles at the expense of Germans in the Prussian east
was their differential rates of out-migration. Both groups left the agrarian east for the higher wages of the industrial west in the late nineteenth
and early twentieth century, but Germans at considerably higher rates
than Poles. By the 1880s the aggregate emigration rate was high enough
to cause a labor shortage, which steadily intensified until the outbreak
of war. For labor, the agrarian interests turned to immigrants from
Russian and Austrian Poland, but this only accentuated the ethnonational shift caused by the disproportionate out-migration of Germans. This
process had already begun in the 1880s, and concern over its consequences for the "Polonization" of the Prussian east was among the

factors leading to the mass expulsions of 1885. The expulsions occasioned agrarian protests, though not particularly vehement or sustained ones, for the labor shortage was not yet acute, and Bismarck was able to ignore them.[102]

Following the expulsions of 1885, further Polish immigration was banned. Yet the labor shortage intensified, not only because of continued migration to the industrial west, but also because of the displacement of extensive by intensive cultivation, of grain by sugar beets in the Prussian east. The pressure of agrarian interests for the readmission of Polish labor increased in the late 1880s. In 1890, after Bismarck's fall, a compromise was reached that seemed to satisfy both the economic interest in expanding the labor supply and the political interest in preventing further erosion of Germandom in the Prussian east. Russian and Austrian Poles were readmitted, but under strict conditions intended to prevent their permanent settlement. Only unmarried Poles were admitted; they were restricted to agricultural work in frontier districts; and, most important, they were required to return to Russia or Austria during the winter.[103] Seasonal migrant labor seemed suited both to the new intensive agriculture, with its large seasonal variations in labor demand, and to the nationalist desire to prevent immigrant Poles from reinforcing the Polonization of the Prussian east.[104] Yet even this arrangement was objectionable from the nationalist point of view. Max Weber claimed that not all seasonal workers in fact left the country in the winter, that even seasonal migration opened the door to harmful settlement. Moreover, he argued, even if strictly seasonal migration were enforceable, it would still be objectionable. For it would displace German workers and their families who could not compete with the Poles, whose modest wants reflected their "low cultural level." This would induce further internal emigration of Germans and reinforce the demand for immigrant Poles. Weber therefore demanded the "absolute exclusion of Russian-Polish workers from the German east."[105] In general, nationalistic conservatives remained opposed to Polish immigration—even for seasonal agricultural work—until the outbreak of war.[106] But in vain: seasonal migration increased steadily in the prewar decades; by 1913 about 240,000 Polish seasonal workers were employed in Prussian agriculture.[107]

Only about 40 percent of all foreign workers in Prussia in the early twentieth century were employed in agriculture;[108] and only about two-thirds of these were Poles. Of the larger number of foreign workers in industry, mining, and other sectors, only 5–10 percent were Poles. Data on ethnic nationality are not available from other German states. Yet the fact that Prussia accounted for between three-fourths and four-fifths of all foreign workers[109] and that Poles comprised a higher proportion of the foreign workforce in Prussia than elsewhere means that only about a third of all foreign workers in Germany were Poles. And since most of the Poles were seasonal agricultural workers, a much smaller fraction of all resident foreigners were Poles. Yet public discussion of immigration was dominated by the question of Polish agricultural migration into Prussia, and, more generally, by the idea of a massive flood of Slavic and Jewish immigrants from the east.[110] Immigration was seen through the prism of the nationality conflict.[111] To the extent that it did not engage the nationality question, immigration in Imperial Germany was uncontroversial and largely invisible. This identification of immigration as such with a particular component of the immigrant flow—with the ethnonationally undesired Slavic and Jewish migration from the east—was one of the underlying assumptions that shaped the debate about citizenship law.

Nationality and Citizenship

The vehement rejection of every trace of *jus soli* by the government and conservative parties during the shaping of the law of 1913 can be understood only in the dual context of Prussian-German *Polenpolitik* and the nationality struggle in the Prussian east; and the partly real and partly imagined Slavic *"Drang nach Westen"* (drive to the west) that, reversing the historic German *"Drang nach Osten,"* threatened, in nationalist perspective, to flood Germany with millions of Slavs and Jews. Legally these were entirely distinct. The former was a question of *Minderheitenpolitik* (minorities policy) toward German citizens who happened to be ethnocultural Poles; the latter a question of immigration policy toward foreign citizens. Socially and politically, however, they were inseparable. Immigration was perceived—and misperceived—in an ethnonational perspective oriented toward the nationality struggle in the Prussian east; and the nationality struggle was fundamentally conditioned by the dynamics of interregional and international migration. Both *Polenpolitik* and immigration policy were shaped by deep assumptions about ethnonational struggle in that historic zone of ethnopolitical tension: the German-Slav borderlands of central Europe.[112]

The politics of citizenship was shaped by the same assumptions. Naturalization policy was subordinated to immigration policy. In order to prevent the permanent settlement of ethnonationally undesired migrants, it was essential, as a last resort, to prevent their naturalization. Since individual German states conducted largely autonomous naturalization policies, Prussia—as the state most directly concerned both by the nationality struggle and by immigration from the east—was free to pursue a particularly restrictive policy toward Poles and Jews. As early as 1881 Interior Minister Puttkamer instructed governors of Prussia's eastern provinces to grant German citizenship to Russian subjects—almost all of whom were Poles or Jews—only in exceptional cases. And in early 1885, as the mass expulsions were being planned, Bismarck forbade the naturalization of Russian subjects anywhere in Prussia.[113] Exceptions were still permitted in particular circumstances, so the Prussian Interior Minister, concerned that local officials were interpreting this too liberally, decreed in 1895 that all naturalizations would have to be approved in advance by his office.[114] Since this proved too cumbersome, central approval was required after 1899 only for suspect categories: clergy, Poles and Moravians, and Jews (not only those with Russian but also those with Austrian citizenship). This policy remained in force until the war. As Wertheimer shows, the policies of Saxony and Bavaria—the other German "frontline" states directly exposed to immigration from the east—were equally restrictive. And archival materials, including naturalization files and internal administrative reports, enable him to show that practice was as restrictive as these policy guidelines.[115]

Naturalization policy in the larger German states had a pronounced ethnonational component; chances for legal citizenship depended on ethnocultural nationality. A Bavarian decree of 1871 made this explicit. Naturalization policy was to be liberal except with respect to "elements that as a consequence of their economic, political, *or national* status are viewed as unwanted additions to the population."[116] These ethnoculturally "unwanted elements" were those who had for centuries shared with Germans the zone of ethnoculturally mixed settlement on the eastern and southeastern frontiers of Germany: Slavs (above all, Poles) and Jews. They were unwelcome because Germany already had a nationality problem and migration—especially permanent immigration, sealed by naturalization—was expected only to make it worse. "If Prussia follows a firm [*feste*] practice in naturalization," argued a representative of the Imperial Interior Ministry in the 1913 debate, responding to charges of Prussian anti-Semitism, "this is not determined by religious considerations; it occurs on national grounds, in order to hold back the stream of foreigners from the east who seek to enter our land."[117]

The same ethnonational assumptions that underlay the restrictive naturalization policies of the individual German states—the same concern to protect Germandom against an influx of eastern Poles and Jews—informed the vehement opposition to *jus soli* at the level of the Reich. In the German context, it will be recalled, the *attribution* of citizenship *jure soli* was not even discussed; it was out of the question. The debate about *jus soli* was a debate about whether persons born and brought up in Germany should have a right to naturalize. The Social Democratic proposals to this effect, according to Dr. Lewald of the Imperial Interior Ministry, "completely overlook the particular geographic situation of the German Reich": "We stand in a completely different situation than the other European nations . . . The pull of nations [*Zug der Nationen*] goes largely from East to West, and the Eastern masses who are set in motion by this pull first run into [*stossen auf*] the German Empire . . . , with its flourishing economy, with its free institutions [laughter from Social Democrats] . . . , with its highly developed social policies that treat foreigners and citizens equally. . . . It is therefore only natural that the push to be admitted to the German Reich is an extraordinarily strong one among many elements of the eastern European population."[118]

The specter of mass migration from the east was raised not only by the government and the conservative nationalist parties.[119] Even the National Liberals and the Center Party, who had criticized Prussian naturalization policy for excluding Jews, rejected a right of naturalization for foreigners and alluded to the dangers of the flood from the east.[120] Thus a Center party deputy: "We distance ourselves from all anti-Semitism . . . But you will understand that we do not want a massive naturalization of Galician peddlers [*Hausierern*]. The religious aspect is of no concern here. But such a mass naturalization would be no gain for Germany. Just as little do we want the mass naturalization of thousands of destitute agricultural workers who come from the east to work on the harvests . . . We are obliged to protect our communes from the naturalization of morally or economically questionable [*bedenklich*] elements."[121] Without mentioning them explicitly, Belzer was referring to Jews (peddlers) and Poles (agricultural workers) and rejecting Social Democratic proposals for *jus soli* because they would open the door too widely to the naturalization of these "questionable elements."

In the final round of the debate the government reiterated its opposition to the Social Democratic proposals to ease access to citizenship for "ethnically foreign [*stammsfremde*] elements":

While the tendency of the government proposal is to facilitate the preservation and hinder the loss of citizenship on the part of Germans living abroad and their descendants, the discussions [in the Reichstag] manifested for a certain time the opposite tendency, [namely] to ease the acquisition of citizenship on the part of ethnically foreign [*stammsfremde*] elements. [The Social Democrats] went so far as to propose that foreigners, under certain circumstances, be given a right to naturalization. The federated [state] governments had to take a stand against this tendency; and on their behalf I expressly reject this tendency today . . . The Social Democratic proposals would break through the hitherto upheld principle [of *jus sanguinis*]. I note expressly that these proposals [if adopted by the Reichstag] would make the proposed law unacceptable to the federated [state] governments.[122]

The emphatic rejection of *jus soli*, like the strict state naturalization policies, had a clear ethnonational inflection. It reflected the concern of "frontline" states—above all Prussia, but also Saxony and Bavaria—and of the Prussian-dominated Reich to preserve ethnic Germandom in the eastern borderlands of the Reich in the face of a perceived double threat: from the Polish-nationalist *Reichspolen in* the Prussian east, and from the flood of would-be immigrants *into* the Prussian east. The nexus between immigration, citizenship, and nationhood was very different in Wilhelmine Germany and late-nineteenth-century France. The French formula of unitary state-nationhood permitted and (in the special political circumstances of the early Third Republic) required the transformation of immigrants into citizens, just as it permitted and required the transformation of "peasants into Frenchmen." In turn-of-the-century Germany, however, the discrepancy between ethnocultural nationhood and state territory—and the concern, arising from this discrepancy, to nationalize the state's population—required the exclusion of eastern immigrants (who, in the public mind, stood for all immigrants) from settlement and from citizenship.

7 ◆ "Etre Français, Cela se Mérite"

Immigration and the Politics of Citizenship in France in the 1980s

For a century France has defined second-generation immigrants as citizens.[1] Although anomalous in Continental Europe,[2] this practice was uncontested until recently. In the mid-1980s, however, *jus soli* came under sharp attack from the far right. "Etre Français, cela se mérite" (to be French, you have to deserve it), proclaimed Jean-Marie Le Pen's National Front.[3] Under pressure from the National Front, the center-right parties took up the theme during the 1986 legislative campaign, proposing in their joint platform to suppress "automatic" acquisitions of French citizenship. Second-generation immigrants would no longer become French *jure soli;* they would have to demand French nationality expressly, and that demand would have to be accepted by the state. Once in office, the new government of Jacques Chirac backed away from the radical proposal to abolish *jus soli,* but it did propose to limit it in order to restore "will," "value," and "dignity" to the acquisition of French citizenship.[4] Yet the proposal provoked strong opposition, and eventually it was withdrawn from the legislative agenda. A commission appointed to study the issues, while favoring the voluntary acquisition over the automatic attribution of citizenship, at the same time recommended enlarging rather than restricting access to French citizenship.[5]

The challenge to *jus soli* arose in the context of a number of converging developments: the emergence of a large population of second-generation North African immigrants, many possessing dual citizenship; increasing concern about the emergence of Islam as the second religion of France; a Socialist government perceived as "soft" on immigration; the emergence on the left of a "differentialist," cultural-pluralist discourse on immigration; the rise of the National Front; and the approaching legislative elections of 1986. These converging developments created a political opening for a nationalist critique of *jus soli*. But while that critique was politically profitable as an opposition strategy, it was politically costly as a government program. Voluntarism was a winning theme, but the exclusion of second-generation immigrants from citizenship on nationalist grounds was not. The government tried to frame its proposed reform of citizenship law in voluntarist terms, but critics adroitly focused on the question of exclusion, repeatedly invoking the incompatibility between the prevailing understanding of nationhood and the civic exclusion of second-generation immigrants. The government was obliged to retreat from its initial proposal, to affirm its commitment to an inclusive citizenship law, even, in the end, to affirm its commitment to *jus soli.*

Second-Generation Algerian Immigrants: Citizens against Their Will?

The French debate on citizenship has centered on North African, especially Algerian, immigrants.[6] Curiously, it was not the xenophobic right, or even the center-right, that first questioned *jus soli.* The issue was raised by proimmigrant voices on the left, articulating and relaying the grievances of certain second-generation Algerian immigrants, their families, and the Algerian government.[7] The roots of Algerian immigration extend deep into the colonial period.[8] Before the First World War a few thousand Algerians worked in France. During the war as many as 160,000 served in the army and another 80,000 worked in the civilian economy in France, some as volunteers, others as conscripts.[9] Almost all returned to Algeria immediately after the war, but immigration began again in the 1920s, and by 1930 there were 120,000 Algerians in France, although with the Depression the number declined. In the 1950s women and children began to join male workers in France, and the Algerian community there assumed a more settled character. By 1961 there were 80,000 Algerian children out of a total Algerian community of 350,000.[10] At the moment of independence, the Algerians in France, like the native population of Algeria, had to opt for French or Algerian citizenship. Apart from those who had fought on the French side during the Algerian war, almost all chose the citizenship of the new nation-state.[11] Yet the French-born children of these expatriate Algerians (roughly 400,000 in the quarter-century following independence) continued to be defined as French—not conditionally, on attaining legal majority, according to the century-old French way of transforming second-generation immigrants into citizens, but unconditionally, at birth, in the manner reserved in

France for *third*-generation immigrants. Second-generation Algerian immigrants, in other words, have been incorporated as citizens as if they were third-generation immigrants.

French citizenship law contains two provisions embodying the principle of *jus soli:* Article 23, attributing citizenship at birth to third-generation immigrants, and Article 44, attributing citizenship at age 18 to second-generation immigrants who were born in France and have resided there since age 13—provided that they have not opted out of French citizenship during the preceding year and that they have not been convicted of certain crimes. Since most *second*-generation immigrants are already transformed into citizens by Article 44, Article 23's provision transforming *third*-generation immigrants into citizens is largely redundant. For Algerians, however, Article 23 comes into play for *second*-generation immigrants. This is not by virtue of any special provision in French citizenship law for citizens of Algeria or other ex-colonial countries. The language of Article 23 is entirely general.[12] But the timing of Algerian immigration in relation to decolonization gave that legal provision an unintended and anomalous application to second-generation immigrants. Article 23 attributes French citizenship at birth to persons born in France when at least one parent was also born in France. But "France" has changed in extent. Since Algeria was an integral part of France until 1962, persons born in Algeria before its independence count, for the purpose of citizenship law, as having been born "in France." And when such persons emigrated to France, as they did in large numbers during the war of independence and the decade following independence, their French-born children have had French citizenship attributed to them at birth by virtue of Article 23.[13]

Even without Article 23, most French-born children of Algerians would have become French automatically on attaining legal majority by virtue of Article 44. Why then the fuss about Article 23? The answer lies in a legal technicality that became politically charged in the historical and political context of Algerian immigration to France. The attribution of French citizenship to second-generation immigrants according to Article 44 is conditional on the tacit consent of those concerned. In the year preceding the age of majority, one can decline French citizenship by simple declaration.[14] But the attribution of citizenship by virtue of Article 23, in most cases, is unconditional. If only one parent was born in France (or French Algeria), one can decline French citizenship by declaration. But when both parents were born in French Algeria—the normal case for the children of Algerian parents that were born in France in the 1960s and 1970s—the attribution of French citizenship is definitive and unconditional.

In the postcolonial context of Algerian immigration to France, the unconditional attribution of French citizenship to second-generation immigrants was resented by some Algerians.[15] The French state appeared again as the colonial power, unilaterally claiming as its own the citizens of the new Algerian nation-state. As Stanislas Mangin put it, "The father is stupefied to discover today that, because he came to work in France and because his children were born there, France takes them back from him. He experiences this as a vengeance, a punishment; above all, he sees in the acquisition of French nationality the prospect of a rupture with the home country, of an essential breach in family relations, of mixed marriage, of the acquisition of European manners."[16] The issue arose only in 1979, when the first group of children born in France of Algerian parents after Algerian independence reached the age of 16. Upon applying for residence permits—obligatory from age 16 on for all resident foreigners—they were astonished to learn that they possessed French nationality. Previously they had considered themselves Algerians and had reported their nationality as Algerian to schools, census workers, and other officials.[17] They were jolted again at age 18 when they were obliged to register for military service—in France and in Algeria. In 1984 France and Algeria negotiated an agreement providing that Franco-Algerian dual nationals be permitted to perform their military service in either France or Algeria, regardless of their place of residence.[18] Until then, however, the young Franco-Algerians were subject, in principle, to the claims of both states. Some immigrants welcomed their dual nationality, noting that French nationality protected them against expulsion. Yet others "experienced the attribution of French nationality as a violation of their personality, their familial attachments, and their membership of a newly emancipated nation—a violation all the greater in that nobody had warned their parents . . . about this French identity that would be imposed on them by the accident of the date and place of their birth."[19] Many formally requested to be "released from the bonds of allegiance" to the French state. But while this request is routinely granted for persons settled abroad, it is routinely denied for persons domiciled in France.[20] The demand for release from French citizenship peaked in 1984, when nearly 2949 requests were made, 2506 of them refused—with young Franco-Algerians who wanted to continue residing in France accounting for almost all of the refusals.[21]

The Algerian government too objected to the unilateral imposition of citizenship on "its" emigrants.[22] That "two hundred fifty thousand of its children were reclaimed by the French government after the years of murderous conflict aimed precisely at giving them their own nationality" was regarded as a neocolonial affront to Algerian sovereignty.[23] Particularly sensitive, as a new nation-state, to symbols of sovereignty, it demanded that France release from its citizenship all young Algerians born in France. Ideally, from the Algerian point of view, such a measure would be "collective and mechanical, that is, it would not take account of the opinion of the persons concerned and would not wait for them individually to request such release."[24] Proimmigrant groups in France, while not necessarily endorsing so sweeping a measure, echoed the Algerian criticism of Article 23.[25] And the Socialist government that came to power in 1981 seemed receptive to the idea of modifying Article 23.[26] On a visit to Algeria in autumn 1981, Interior Minister Gaston Defferre discussed the issue with his Algerian counterpart. He said to reporters afterward: "It will be necessary for us to find a solution . . . The Algerians who come to France do not intend to establish themselves definitively and melt [*se fondre*] into French society. They are migrant workers and not immigrants. French law could be modified to take account of this situation. I will make some proposals in this direction to the government. If they are realized, young people born in France of Algerian parents would no longer automatically have French nationality. They would have to ask for it to obtain it."[27] Talks between the French and Algerian governments on this issue did not lead to an agreement on nationality. They did, however, lead to an agreement on military service for dual nationals.[28] And once the question of military service for Franco-Algerian dual nationals was resolved, proimmigrant groups, the parties of the left, and the Socialist government lost interest in the citizenship status of second-generation immigrants.[29]

The Rise of a Nationalist Politics of Citizenship

Between 1983 and 1986, under the approaching horizon of legislative elections, and in the context of a broader debate about immigration and national identity,[30] policy intellectuals, clubs, and parties of the far right and mainstream right developed a threefold critique of French citizenship law. From a *voluntarist* perspective, citizenship law was criticized for transforming second-generation immigrants into French citizens without their knowledge and, in some cases, against their will. From a *statist* perspective, it was criticized for permitting certain foreigners to circumvent restrictions on immigration. From a *nationalist* perspective, it was criticized for turning foreigners into Frenchmen on paper without making sure that they were "French at heart" *(Français de coeur).*

The first two points had been raised by the Socialists, the first publicly, the second within the Ministry of Social Affairs. The right now took over these arguments and extended them. The nationalist critique of French citizenship law and naturalization practice, however, was new in post-war France. And the nationalist attack on *jus soli*—on the transformation of second-generation immigrants into citizens—was unprecedented even in longer-term historical perspective. In the interwar period nationalists had criticized rising naturalization rates and stigmatized the newly naturalized as *"français de papier,"* but they had not challenged the attribution of citizenship *jure soli* to second-generation immigrants. Not even under the Vichy regime, which rescinded 15,000 naturalizations, was the French system of *jus soli* challenged.[31] Moreover, a 1973 reform of citizenship law, prepared and enacted by a center-right government, confirmed *jus soli* at a moment when immigration had reached unprecedented levels and when large numbers of children were being born in France to foreign parents.[32] This reform was uncontroversial, and the parliamentary rhetoric remained assimilationist.[33] Yet a decade later *jus soli* came under sharp attack, not only from a voluntarist but also from a nationalist point of view. Why did the century-long consensus on *jus soli* break down in the mid-1980s? And why did the nationalist challenge to *jus soli* fail?

The nationalist attack on *jus soli* is best understood as a reassertion of fundamental norms of nation-statehood, perceived as threatened or undermined by immigration, especially of North African Moslems.[34] A nationalist response to immigration can be found in all European and North American countries of immigration. Faced with what they perceive as the devaluation, desacralization, denationalization, and pluralization of citizenship, nationalists defend the traditional model of the nation-state, reasserting the value and dignity of national citizenship and stressing the idea that state-membership presupposes nation-membership. They demand of immigrants either naturalization, stringently conditioned upon assimilation, or departure.[35] But conditions for a nationalist response were particularly ripe in France in the mid-1980s. The expansiveness of French citizenship law, in conjunction with the weakening of the ideology and practice of assimilation, gave French nationalists a particularly inviting target. It had transformed large numbers of second-generation immigrants—particularly North Africans—into French citizens, but citizens indifferent, sometimes antagonistic, to that citizenship. In Germany, by contrast, where very few immigrants, even of the second generation, had acquired German citizenship, there was no corresponding opening for a politically profitable nationalist response.

Dual Citizenship

The nationalist politics of citizenship focused on three related issues: dual citizenship, the desacralization and devaluation of French citizenship, and the putative unassimilability of North African immigrants. Dual citizenship comes about in three main ways. First, now that citizenship law throughout Europe has become gender-neutral, permitting transmission of citizenship by maternal as well as paternal filiation, most children of mixed-nationality marriages inherit both the father's and the mother's citizenship. Second, almost all second-generation immigrants to whom citizenship is attributed *jure soli* also inherit their parents' citizenship *jure sanguinis*. Finally, many immigrants who acquire citizenship by naturalization retain their original citizenship. There are no reliable statistics on the incidence of dual citizenship, but three sources of variation in that incidence may be noted, corresponding to the three ways in which dual citizenship arises. First, the incidence of dual citizenship varies with the rate of mixed-nationality marriages. Second, dual citizenship is more frequent in countries whose citizenship law is based at least in part on *jus soli*. Third, dual citizenship is more frequent where naturalization is not contingent on the renunciation of previous citizenship. Intermarriage rates are similar in France and Germany.[36] But the French system of *jus soli*, together with the fact that France permits foreigners to naturalize without giving up their original citizenship, while Germany does not, engenders a higher incidence of dual nationality in France than in Germany.

The nationalist politics of citizenship has drawn freely on traditional legal and political arguments against dual citizenship, especially on the classical political argument that citizenship presupposes allegiance; that allegiance is by definition unconditional and absolute; and that dual allegiance and dual citizenship are therefore impossible.[37] Yet the core concern is not dual citizenship as such but the way in which it has been a vehicle for the desacralization and devaluation of French citizenship.[38]

The Desacralization of Citizenship

The desacralization of citizenship is a general aspect of modern Western politics, rooted in the emotional remoteness of the bureaucratic welfare state and in the obsolescence of the citizen army. Yet mass Franco-Algerian dual nationality has raised the issue of desacralization in a conspicuous and pointed manner.[39] Traditionally the sacralization of citizenship has found its central and most poignant expression in the obligation to perform military service for the state, to fight for the state and die for it if need be.[40] Dual citizenship relativizes this obligation. No man can serve two states if they happen to be fighting at the same time or, worse, fighting each other. Moreover, the obligation to fight and die for more than one state, even if the states are not at war, devalues the commitment implied to each of them. The problem may not be acute in peacetime for persons holding the citizenship of two allied states and performing military service in their state of residence. But Franco-Algerian dual nationals are a special case. The French-Algerian accord on military service for dual nationals leaves dual nationals free to choose where to perform military service.[41] And although Algeria requires two years of service and France only one, a substantial fraction of young Franco-Algerians residing in France has opted for service in Algeria.[42] That Algerian immigrants to France should possess French citizenship yet perform military service for the Algerian state has outraged French nationalists, who stress the "indissoluble bond between the acquisition of nationality . . . and armed service."[43]

Nationalist indignation has been further provoked by the rhetorical desacralization of French citizenship on the part of certain young dual nationals. Asked about the meaning of French citizenship, most immigrants have stressed its purely instrumental significance. Remarks such as the following are characteristic: "one has French papers for convenience."[44] "I got my blue [French] papers because I needed them to go on vacation in Spain."[45] "To have peace with the cops, it's worth having a French identity card."[46] "Being French is a practical decision: it makes things easier for controls [police controls of identity], for the job, for the bureaucracy . . . Having French nationality doesn't take away the right to Algerian nationality. So you don't lose anything by taking it [French nationality]. If it was an alternative [i.e. if one had to choose French or Algerian nationality], I wouldn't have made this choice [becoming French]."[47]

This instrumentalist way of talking about French citizenship is by no means restricted to Algerians. Yet for historical reasons it is more pronounced in the Algerian case. The current generation of Franco-Algerian dual nationals are the children of Algerians who fought against France for Algerian independence—and for the right to have Algerian rather than French nationality. Nationality is therefore a highly charged subject for the parents. Algerian nationality is highly sacralized, as befits the nationality of a state whose independence was attained within living memory through a long and bloody war. This accounts for the consternation of Algerian families when they learned that French nationality had been imposed on their children because they happened to be born in France. Yet the very fact that French nationality was imposed, rather than chosen, provided a means of coming to terms with it. To choose French nationality would be to betray one's family;[48] but to be French through no fault of one's own insulated one from reproach. As one twenty-five-year-old Franco-Algerian put it, "these kids [to whom French nationality was attributed at birth] are lucky because one obliged them [to be French], so you can't condemn them [for being French], you can't say they betrayed anyone."[49] The imposition of French nationality on many second-generation Algerian immigrants, it has been suggested, might help legitimize even the voluntary acquisition of French nationality on the part of Algerian immigrants. "[If] a son, 'French' by necessity, solely by virtue of being born in France, remains, in the eyes of his parents, . . . just as 'good' a son . . . , just as 'good' an Algerian, and just as 'good' a Moslem, ... how could one consider his brother a 'bad' son, 'bad' Algerian, and 'bad' Moslem just because he acquired voluntarily the French nationality that his brother . . . received automatically?"[50] The experience of living involuntarily as dual nationals, Sayad suggests, might lead to a general desacralization, "laicization," and "banalization" of nationality, by showing in practice that religion and nationality were distinct, by divesting nationality of its "syncretistic connotations of a religious and communitarian nature" and engendering a more "strictly political and administrative" understanding of nationality.[51]

The discourse of young Franco-Maghrebin dual nationals reveals a desacralized, instrumental attitude toward French nationality (although not toward the nationality of their parents). They characterize their French nationality in instrumental terms as a contingent administrative fact that facilitates everyday life in France, and their Algerian, Moroccan, or Tunisian nationality in more expressive, emotional terms as an unalterable condition, an undifferentiated amalgam of religious, ethnocultural, national, and familial affiliations that provides the basis for their "identity."[52] In terms of Talcott Parsons' "pattern variables," they experience their French nationality as functionally specific, affectively neutral, and self-oriented, and their North African nationality as diffuse, affectively charged, and collectivity-oriented.[53]

Nationalists seized on evidence of this instrumental relation to French citizenship to deplore the fact that certain second-generation immigrants have French citizenship, while remaining indifferent or even hostile to French culture and the French state. "On the pretext of humanism . . . France has received and conferred its nationality on families whose sole bond of attachment to the national community consists in pecuniary advantages. What is more, the persons concerned preserve their original allegiance and often take French nationality as one takes the Carte Orange [the subway and bus pass used by Parisian commuters]."[54] To grant citizenship to such persons, they argued, devalues and desacralizes French citizenship: "To be French means something. It is not only a paper, a formality, but a value. The current legislation cheapens that value . . . Today, we feel the need to revalorize belonging to France . . . One cannot acquire French nationality out of simple convenience. It is necessary to recognize the value of being French, to become French for other reasons than for the social and economic advantages it entails."[55] Dual nationals were stigmatized as "false citizens, citizens of nowhere. When it suits them, they say they are French. When it doesn't, they say they are Algerians, or something else . . . It's detestable. Many sons of Algerians found themselves French without having asked for it: one made them citizens by force. These people don't necessarily share our values. If they don't feel French, well, we don't want them either! Before admitting someone to a club, one verifies that he is capable of exercising his rights and fulfilling his duties. One will accord French nationality in 98 percent of the cases. But we will reject those who denigrate us. I say this in the name of all those who died for the country."[56] In nationalist perspective, citizenship should possess dignity and command respect. It should not be sought for convenience or personal advantage. It should possess intrinsic, not merely instrumental value. It should be sacred, not profane. For one attribute of sacred objects, on Durkheim's account, is the respect they command—a respect that "excludes all idea of deliberation or calculation."[57] The nationalist argument is that citizenship should induce respect for what it is rather than calculation about what it entails.

The nationalist campaign against the desacralization and devaluation of French citizenship had an especially tempting target. Not only did those North African immigrants who possessed French citizenship emphasize its strictly instrumental meaning. At the same time, proimmigrant voices on the French left called for a further desacralization and devaluation of citizenship. This was particularly true in the early days of the Socialist government. Two ideas were current on the left. First, substantive citizenship rights should be divorced from formal citizenship—for example, by permitting immigrants without French nationality to vote, first in local elections, eventually in national elections. This would objectively devalue formal citizenship by making less depend on it. Second, persons wanting to naturalize should be able to do so with a minimum of social and psychological friction. Citizenship and naturalization should be desacralized, deformalized, deritualized.[58] This sort of discourse on the left, as much as attitudes toward citizenship of immigrants themselves, gave nationalists an opportunity to score political points by reemphasizing the value, dignity, and sacredness of citizenship.

An Unassimilable Immigration?

The final target of the nationalist politics of citizenship was the alleged unassimilability of today's immigrants—North African Moslems in particular.[59] Nationalists made three points. First, unlike earlier waves of immigrants, today's immigrants do not want to assimilate. Second, the traditional French institutions of assimilation no longer function the way they used to. Third, today's immigrants, being more "culturally distant" from the French than earlier immigrants, are objectively less assimilable.

In support of the first claim—that immigrants do not want to assimilate—nationalists pointed to the wide currency of differentialist rhetoric. There was, indeed, much talk of the *droit à la différence*—the "right to be different"—in the early 1980s. Most of this talk came from the French, not from immigrants,[60] and reflected less a refusal of assimilation on the part of immigrants than the rejection of the traditional Republican formula of assimilationist civic incorporation on the part of the French left.[61] But this did not prevent nationalists from seizing on differentialist rhetoric to indicate the impossibility of assimilation.[62]

The second argument—that French institutions have lost much of their former assimilatory power—is by no means restricted to nationalists. The diminishing efficacy of schools, army, church, trade unions, and political parties as instances of socialization, integration, and assimilation for French and foreigners alike has been widely remarked.[63] In place of these "universalist national institutions," as Dominique Schnapper has called them, custodial and remedial institutions—social workers, the medical establishment, the criminal justice system—increasingly are charged with the social management of marginal populations.[64] The school, in particular, is no longer thought to have its former socializing and assimilating power.[65] Particularly galling in nationalist perspective is the instruction given immigrants' children in their "language and culture of origin" in French primary school classes, with instructors chosen and paid by governments of countries of origin.[66]

The third and most important nationalist argument is that Moslem immigrants are unassimilable—or, less categorically, that today's Moslem immigrants are less easily assimilable than earlier Catholic and Jewish immigrants.[67] Nationalists assert a basic incompatibility between the political and legal culture of Islam and that of "the West." Islam, they argue, cannot be reduced to the sphere of the merely private. It inevitably generates public and political demands, and these conflict irreconcilably with what is held to be a simultaneously Christian and Republican tradition of the rights of man.[68] Like other antiassimilationist arguments, this one is advanced not only by nationalists but also, in more nuanced form, by almost all parties to the debate on immigration. Thus, Gaston Defferre, former Socialist Interior Minister: "When Poles, Italians, Spanish, and Portuguese live in France and decide to naturalize, it matters little whether they are Catholics, Protestants, Jews, or atheists . . . But the rules of Islam are not simply religious rules. They are rules of living that concern . . . marriage, divorce, the care of children, the behavior of men, the behavior of women . . . These rules are contrary to all the rules of French law on the custody of children in case of divorce, and they are contrary to [French rules on] the rights of women with respect to their husbands. What is more, in France we don't have the same habits of living."[69] All parties agree that Islam—at least some forms of Islam—poses special difficulties for assimilation. What distinguishes the nationalist position is its undifferentiated, essentialist characterization of Islam. Ignoring the varieties of Islam in France,[70] the nationalists characterize Moslem immigrants as if all were Islamic fundamentalists, although evidence suggests that fundamentalism holds only marginal appeal for Moslems in France.

Jus soli was not the only target of this nationalist critique of French citizenship law. Nationalists objected also to the ease with which citizenship could be acquired by spouses of French citizens and to insufficiently strict control over naturalizations. But *jus soli* seemed particularly objectionable. In conjunction with the citizenship law of North African states, which attributed citizenship *jure sanguinis* and held to the doctrine of perpetual allegiance, French *jus soli* automatically engendered dual citizenship. From the nationalist point of view, *jus soli* furthered the desacralization of citizenship by attributing it to persons who remained loyal to and identified emotionally and culturally with other states. It devalued citizenship by bestowing it automatically on persons, irrespective of their will, even of their knowledge. Finally, it denationalized citizenship by automatically conferring it on persons who were not assimilated, and, on some arguments, could not assimilate, to French culture.

The nationalist attack on *jus soli* was not confined to the radical right. It figured in a number of programmatic statements produced by groups and parties of the mainstream right as the legislative elections of March 1986 approached. Thus, for example, the Club '89, closely affiliated with the Gaullist *Rassemblement pour la République* party (RPR), argued in its 1985 program, "A strategy for government," that naturalization must not be

> considered a convenient legal means of obtaining social advantages and the right to remain in France. This is why the Code of Nationality must be amended in order that the acquisition of French nationality be truly the result of a personal choice, based on the will to integrate and to adopt . . . the system of values of the host country. Becoming a French citizen must be considered . . . a solemn pact based on mutual recognition and the will to live together . . . To this end, automatic attributions of French nationality by virtue of birth in France to foreign parents will be suppressed . . . French nationality will be accorded to any foreigner (including those born in France) who can satisfy a certain number of requirements (mastery of the French language, civil or military service, francization of surnames, virgin judicial dossier [no trouble with the law], sponsorship by nationals, and so on).[71]

And a 1985 report on immigration in the name of the Union for French Democracy (UDF), besides the RPR, the other major parliamentary group of the mainstream right, also adopted the nationalist critique of *jus soli:*

> The automaticity [associated with *jus soli*] appears very contestable in the sense that a large number of children of foreigners acquire French nationality without their knowledge and sometimes against their will, without

the slightest control on their effective integration . . . Henceforth, the acquisition of French nationality by children born in France of foreign parents should be the object of a demand at the age of majority and should presuppose . . . the acceptance of the consequences linked to citizenship, notably those concerning national service.[72]

The common platform of the RPR and UDF limited itself to a shorter and more general statement, though one tending in the same direction. Nationality "must be requested [by the individual] and accepted [by the state]; its acquisition should not result from purely automatic mechanisms."[73]

There was, then, a broad consensus on the right concerning the need to rid French citizenship law of *jus soli.* In legislative elections of March 1986, the right was returned to power. On assuming office as Prime Minister, Jacques Chirac declared that he would submit to the legislature "a modification of the nationality code tending to make the acquisition of French nationality depend on a prior act of will."[74] Yet the promised reform remained unrealized. Chirac did introduce legislation to modify French citizenship law, although it was much more modest than what the right had proposed while in opposition. But even this relatively modest proposal unleashed a torrent of criticism, and it was eventually withdrawn from the legislative agenda.

The Retreat from Exclusion

Why did the attack on *jus soli* fail just when it seemed to be on the verge of success? In the first place, the reform encountered an unforeseen legal obstacle. *Jus soli,* we have seen, was embodied in two provisions of the nationality code: Article 23, attributing French citizenship at birth to third-generation immigrants, and Article 44, attributing it at majority to most second-generation immigrants. The clubs and parties of the right objected to both. Once the new government began to draft an alternative citizenship law, however, it discovered that abolishing Article 23 would also abolish the most convenient and straightforward way of proving one's nationality—not only for second- and third-generation immigrants, but also for persons of French descent. To establish one's nationality using Article 23, it sufficed to provide two birth certificates, showing that the person concerned and at least one parent were born in France. To prove that one was French by virtue of descent from French parents, however, involved an infinite regress. Unless an ancestor had some other title to French nationality—a certificate of naturalization, for example—it was impossible to establish definitively that one was French.

There were political costs too to abolishing *jus soli* for third-generation immigrants. The underlying rationale for Article 23 was that birth (and presumed residence) in France over two successive generations reliably indicated an enduring attachment to France. The critique of *jus soli* did not challenge this underlying rationale. A few voices on the far right refused *jus soli* in principle and insisted on a system of pure *jus sanguinis*, but they were marginal.[75] The main thrust of the critique of *jus soli* did not concern the principle of Article 23—that the presumptive integration of third-generation immigrants warranted the attribution of French nationality to them—but rather its anomalous application to *second*-generation Algerian immigrants.

If it was difficult to argue against Article 23 in general terms, it was equally difficult to make a special case against its applicability to second-generation Algerian immigrants. The language of Article 23 was perfectly general: it attributed French nationality to a person "born in France, at least one of whose parents was also born there." To exclude second-generation Algerian immigrants would have required legislators to specify that "France" meant France in its present boundaries, so that the parents of the second-generation immigrants, themselves born in preindependence Algeria, would not count as having been born "in France." But this would have amounted to a denial of the French colonial past, in particular the long-standing claim that Algeria was an integral part of France.

Special legal and political difficulties, then, stood in the way of the abolition of Article 23. As a result, the government reluctantly refrained from proposing to alter it. On the other hand, it did propose to alter Article 44.[76] Second-generation immigrants would no longer automatically become French on attaining legal majority. Instead, those wishing to become French would have to make a formal declaration between the ages of 16 and 20.[77] This was the voluntarist aspect of the proposal. But there was also a restrictionist aspect, which stood in tension with the voluntarist aspect.

The declaration that would be required of second-generation immigrants wishing to become French would not itself suffice to establish French nationality—the rhetoric of choice and self-determination notwithstanding. The granting of nationality would be conditional. This in itself would not have changed existing law. The automatic attribution of French nationality to second-generation immigrants at majority was already conditional, excluding persons not meeting the residence requirement as well as persons having been convicted for certain offenses. The proposed reform, however, made these conditions more stringent in three respects: it considerably enlarged the list of offenses barring acquisition of citizenship; it added a formal condition of assimilation; and it required an oath of allegiance.[78]

The proposal satisfied no one. The failure to touch Article 23 disturbed the entire economy of the project. Both the voluntarist and the nationalist critique of *jus soli* had centered on Article 23. From a voluntarist point of view, Article 23, which transformed third-generation immigrants (and second-generation Algerian immigrants) into French citizens irrespective of their will, was more objectionable than Article 44, which allowed for choice, permitting second-generation immigrants to decline French nationality by declaration during the year preceding their legal majority. From a nationalist point of view too Article 23 was the chief offender, for it was the legal vehicle through which about 400,000 French-born children of Algerian immigrants had been transformed into French citizens of doubtful loyalty and assimilability. Thus the decision to leave Article 23 in place provoked criticism from the right. Both the National Front and Chirac's own party, the RPR, had already submitted reform proposals of their own to the National Assembly; both included provisions abolishing Article 23. When the government's own proposal was published, the National Front asserted that the reform had been "largely emptied of its content."[79]

But while the far right criticized the government's project for not going far enough, other voices, more numerous and more clamorous, criticized it for going too far, for seeking to restrict access to French citizenship. The restrictive tendencies of the proposal, actual or asserted, unleashed a storm of criticism. The Council of State, in its consultative opinion, which was leaked to the press, rejected the central elements of the proposal.[80] Parties and political groups of the left, trade unions, churches, human rights associations, organizations concerned with immigration, and immigrants' own associations attacked the reform with unusual vehemence. Even centrists within the parties of government expressed reservations.

In response to the initial round of criticism, the government dropped the oath of allegiance, lengthened the span of time within which second-generation immigrants could declare their intention of acquiring citizenship, and retreated from its proposal to require spouses of French citizens—previously eligible to acquire citizenship by declaration—to apply for naturalization. Yet the criticism did not abate. When, in November 1986, the proposal was formally adopted by the Council of Ministers and submitted to the National Assembly, President Mitterand declared through a spokesman that it was "inspired by a philosophy that he did not share."[81] The League of the Rights of Man initiated a campaign against the reform, enlisting the support of two hundred organizations. And SOS-Racism launched its own campaign against the project.

At the same time, high school and university students were beginning to mobilize against another legislative project: a reform of higher education that was perceived by students as restricting access to the university. A wave of strikes, occupations, and demonstrations swept Parisian and provincial *lycées* and universities. In early December a huge march in Paris ended with violent confrontations between protesters and police, which left several students injured, some seriously. The following evening there were further violent clashes, and one student died after being beaten by the police. That he was of Algerian origin, as were many of the protesting students, provided a dramatic symbolic link between the debate on education reform and that on citizenship law. Even before the violence, SOS-Racism, with a strong organizational presence in high schools and universities, had linked the two issues in an attempt to bring some of the political energies mobilized by students to bear against the reform of nationality law. Initially it had limited success, for the students insisted on the "nonpolitical" character of their mobilization and resisted efforts to broaden its agenda. But after the violent clashes with police, student protests took on an increasingly radical, antigovernment edge. Faced with the prospect of further violence, and confronting increasing dissent within the parties of government, Chirac withdrew both the education and the citizenship bills from the legislative agenda.

There were striking similarities between the two controversies. In both cases the proposed reform was moderate, a compromise between proponents of a more radical reform and opponents of any change. In both cases the controversy occurred on a largely symbolic battleground, with opposition focusing less on the specific provisions of the proposed reform than on its ideological penumbra. In both cases the project was presented by its opponents as a vehicle of selection and exclusion; in both cases it was presented as offending against symbols, values, and principles central to French political culture. In both cases the government was surprised by the magnitude of the opposition to an apparently so innocuous reform, and in both cases it initially refused to take the opposition very seriously. Yet in both cases in the end the government yielded to the symbolically resonant opposition.

From Exclusion to Inclusion

The initial defeat of the citizenship law reform owed much to the conjunctural accident that bound its fate to that of the university reform. But the citizenship reform was by no means dead; it had simply been withdrawn provisionally from the legislative agenda. Under pressure from some of its own hard line supporters, and from Le Pen, whose presidential bid threatened to undermine Chirac's own campaign, the government repeatedly reaffirmed its commitment to the reform of citizenship law. It might have reintroduced its original proposal, perhaps in slightly modified form, after passions had cooled and students had demobilized. Instead, it took a conciliatory route. Justice Minister Chalandon, responsible for preparing the initial proposal, announced in January 1987 that the proposed reform would be "remodeled" after a "vast national consultation" with all of the movements and associations concerned by the matter, as well as with the "religious and moral authorities" of the country.[82] Chalandon even indicated that the reform might actually *liberalize* access to French citizenship. Existing nationality law was "severe, ambiguous, and dangerous" and "did not offer sufficient guarantees to young foreigners destined to become French."[83] A reform might improve their position. Young foreigners born in France might be protected against expulsion until they had the chance to acquire citizenship, and they might be able to become French despite minor trouble with the law. And naturalization procedures might be accelerated.[84]

Chirac endorsed Chalandon's decision, adding that it was necessary to correct "misunderstandings" raised by the proposed reform. There had never been any intention to exclude: on the contrary, "it is a joy for France to receive supplementary children [that is, naturalized citizens]." But since it is "an honor to become French," "the manner in which one can become French is very important."[85] The reform, he implied, was essentially concerned with the *manner* of becoming French, not with the *fact* of becoming French. The government did not want to restrict access to French nationality, only to make access to nationality voluntary rather than automatic.

This marked a sharp change in orientation. As an oppositional strategy, the nationalist attack on citizenship law, mixing voluntarist, statist, and nationalist motifs, was politically profitable. As a governmental program, however, a reform of citizenship law inspired by the nationalist critique proved a political liability. Voluntarism was a winning theme; but exclusion on statist or nationalist grounds was not. While the government tried to frame its project in voluntarist terms, critics focused on the issue of exclusion. In so doing they decisively altered the terms of debate.

The reform proposed by the government was an awkward halfway measure.[86] Originating in the radical nationalist critique of citizenship law that had been elaborated by the right while it enjoyed the freedom and irresponsibility of opposition, the proposal that was finally submitted to parliament was modest and limited, reflecting the moderation and circumspection imposed by the responsibilities of government. Yet while this moderation disappointed the far right, it did not reconcile the left or even the center. For if the governmental proposal was moderate, measured against nationalist demands, this was a difference in degree, not in kind. The governmental proposal was simply a diluted version of the nationalist project, without an expressly nationalist rationale, yet lacking a distinctive rationale of its own. In the eyes of its opponents, the project was irrevocably tainted by its nationalist origin.

The government had attempted to seize the moral and political high ground by emphasizing the voluntarist aspect and minimizing the statist and nationalist aspect. The basic question, it insisted, was the *manner* in which one became French. Persons becoming French should do so deliberately, by virtue of their own free and conscious choice, and not by virtue of an ascriptive act of state. The statist and nationalist arguments—that France must prevent fraudulent and purely instrumental uses of nationality law, prevent delinquent immigrants from becoming French, and guarantee the assimilation of new citizens—were soft-pedaled. Nationalist arguments were retained only insofar as they could be interpreted in voluntarist terms, as in the claim that the substitution of voluntary for automatic acquisition of French nationality would enhance the sense of nationhood and give greater meaning and dignity to the acquisition and possession of French nationality.

The broad public opposition to the project was crucial in altering the terms of the debate. The government had addressed its Janus-faced reform to two audiences: to its own right-wing supporters and possible Le Pen voters, and to the public at large. By emphasizing the voluntarist aspect of the reform, the government had hoped to let the statist and nationalist restrictions on access to citizenship—included to satisfy its own hard-line supporters and to undercut the appeal of Le Pen—pass more or less unnoticed by the public at large. The surprisingly strong opposition to the project among those with access to the media upset this dual-track strategy and forced the government to define its project more consistently, to choose, in effect, between voluntarism and restrictionism. It was no longer possible to mask a restrictionist project with voluntarist rhetoric. The government would have to alter the project to fit the voluntarist rhetoric or alter the rhetoric to fit the project. The former was the strategy of consensus, the latter of confrontation. The government chose the former.

The choice was not made once and for all at any particular moment. The matter continued to be debated within the government—and among the parties and groups of the center and right—for the next several months. Some still advocated pushing the original reform, or something like it, through the legislature before the presidential election as a means of drawing support away from Le Pen. But at every crucial juncture, Chirac opted for the consensual route. This was evident in his decision to withdraw the project from the legislative agenda in December; in his approval of Chalandon's announcement of a "vast national consultation" in January; in his announcement in March that he would appoint a nonpartisan Commission, "representing all tendencies of opinion," to study the issue;[87] in his instructions to the Commission when it was actually appointed in June;[88] in his announcement, in September, that the reform would not be taken up before the presidential election of April 1988 unless a "general consensus" were achieved;[89] and in the fact that the issue played virtually no part in his presidential campaign.[90]

The retreat from the confrontational nationalist politics of citizenship was particularly striking insofar as it concerned *jus soli*, which had been the central target of nationalist ire. The parties of the mainstream right, as we have seen, took up this nationalist critique of *jus soli* in the legislative campaign of 1986, proposing in their joint platform to abolish "automatic" acquisitions of nationality. Technical and political considerations had already forced an initial retreat from this aim and kept the government from proposing to modify Article 23 of the Nationality Code, conferring citizenship at birth on third-generation immigrants (and second-generation Algerian immigrants). But now the government dropped its attack on *jus soli* altogether. Accused by opponents of calling the French tradition of *jus soli* into question, members of the government and of mainstream right parties denied this and even emphasized their commitment to maintaining *jus soli*.[91] They continued to argue that the acquisition of citizenship by second-generation immigrants should be voluntary. But they backed away from the argument of the common electoral platform of the center-right parties—that nationality must be "demanded *and accepted*," that candidates wishing to become French must be screened for their suitability as citizens. Under pressure from centrists in its own ranks as well as from members of the opposition and from organized opponents of the reform, who kept harping on the theme of exclusion, the government now suggested that the voluntary act it wished to introduce for second-generation immigrants would be sufficient to make them citizens; it would not be an application for citizenship that the government could refuse. Only in a few precisely delineated extreme cases—severe criminality, for example—would second-generation immigrants be barred from becoming French. In other cases they would have the right to become French by simple declaration—which might even make their citizenship status and chances more rather than less secure.[92]

Why did the government retreat from contestation here, disavowing the restrictive implications of its own proposal and proclaiming its commitment to an inclusive citizenship law? The question can be answered on various levels. The initial withdrawal of the project from the legislative agenda owed much to an accident of timing. The student mobilization having made clear the potential costs of a confrontational strategy, the government opted for consensus. But the subsequent conciliatory posture of the government owed more to deep divisions within the parties of government. Centrists, on whose votes the government depended, turned increasingly against the exclusionary aspects of the proposal and against a partisan, confrontational reform. Initially they had been cautiously favorable to the proposal, which they rightly perceived as moderate by comparison with campaign proposals or by comparison with the proposals submitted to the legislature by the National Front and the RPR deputies.[93] They were strong supporters of the principle of voluntary choice. As opponents of the reform increasingly focused attention on exclusion, however, and as the magnitude of the opposition became clear, the reticence of centrists increased. A UDF deputy close to Raymond Barre, Jacques Chirac's chief presidential rival on the mainstream right, characterized the government's reform as "dangerous, for it called into question *jus soli* . . . One can establish an act of confirmation, but without conditions. On this point, we will not cede. *Jus soli* must be maintained."[94] And Jacques Barrot, president of the Center of Social Democrats (CDS), now insisted that "one does not solve so delicate a problem as that of citizenship in a confrontational climate."[95] Clearly the centrists were not going to let the government ram a heatedly contested reform through parliament in the setting of an approaching presidential election.

But this simply pushes the problem one step back. Why did the reform divide the parties of the majority? Why were centrists among the parties of the majority so concerned about inclusion? Why did even hard-liners in the majority feel compelled to adopt the rhetoric of inclusion?[96] Why was the government apparently willing to *liberalize* access to French citizenship—on the condition that second-generation immigrants be required to declare their desire to become French?

Political Conjuncture and Political Culture

There are both situational and political-cultural reasons for the retreat from exclusion, arising from the configuration of the French political field and from enduring characteristics of French political culture. The key situational feature was the strong presence of Jean-Marie Le Pen. The debate on nationality law was decisively shaped by the emergence of Le Pen and his party as a major force in the French political field. The National Front did not initiate the nationalist critique of citizenship law. That critique was first developed in a 1984 book by UDF deputy and *Figaro* magazine columnist Alain Griotteray.[97] But it was taken up and elaborated in a 1985 book by Jean-Yves Le Gallou and the Club de l'Horloge, a political club on the extreme right with close links to the National Front;[98] and it was adopted by the National Front in the legislative campaign in the spring of 1986. It was only later, however, in the face of the government's stepwise retreat from a radical modification of citizenship law, that the National Front made the issue a salient one. The increasingly conciliatory posture adopted by the government and mainstream right parties induced Le Pen to give increasing play to the issue. It offered him the chance to contrast the distinctiveness and consistency of his own position with the government's waffling retreat toward a position only marginally different from that of the Socialists. In the spring of 1987 Le Pen made nationality the centerpiece of the early phase of his presidential campaign, successfully mobilizing huge crowds around this issue in Paris and Marseilles. Polls showed him to be a major threat to the right in the presidential campaign. In these circumstances, it was impossible to take a position on citizenship law without taking a position on Le Pen.

The government's moves toward a conciliatory posture were self-reinforcing. For as the government moved in this direction, the issue became more salient in the rhetoric of the National Front, the idea of restricting access to citizenship became more closely identified with the National Front and more clearly marked as "extremist," and the government and parties of the mainstream right had to distance themselves further from a restrictive stance. As the proposal's positional coordinates changed—as it drifted toward the right and toward the extreme regions of French political space—so too did the way the mainstream right parties and the government positioned themselves on the issue.

The government and the center-right parties were in a difficult position. Charged by the Socialists with flirting with Le Pen, and by the National Front with retreating to a position indistinguishable from that of the Socialists, they had to mark and maintain two distances simultaneously, clearly differentiating their position from that of the National Front and from that of the Socialists. To this end, it was expedient to differentiate sharply between the voluntarist and the restrictionist aspects of a possible citizenship law reform, or, more abstractly, between the *manner of access* to French citizenship and the *degree of openness* of French citizenship. To mark their distance from the Socialists, the government and conservative parties could proceed with their voluntaristic critique of the automatic attribution of citizenship to second-generation immigrants and emphasize the need to transform the *manner* of becoming French. By making the acquisition of French citizenship depend on a voluntary act, the government could claim to be restoring "value" and "dignity" to the acquisition and possession of French citizenship. At the same time, to mark its distance from the National Front, the government could emphasize its commitment to an open and inclusive citizenship law. In the domain of citizenship law, as in other domains, it could argue, according to the standard formula, that the National Front provided "bad answers to good questions."

There were of course differences within the government and center-right parties on just how this delicate task of positioning should be accomplished. Some put more weight on competing with Le Pen for potential voters, others on unambiguously repudiating his message. But all agreed on the need to mark and maintain a double distance in French political space, to define their own position through a sort of political triangulation vis-à-vis the positions of the Socialists and the National Front. The "multidimensionality" of the question of citizenship, the fact that there were two independent axes of variation—manner of access and degree of openness—facilitated this political triangulation. The structure of French political space after the rise of Le Pen, in short, favored the increasingly sharp distinction, on the part of the government and its supporters, between the voluntarist and the exclusionist aspects of the reform.

A purely situational analysis, however, would miss the underlying political-cultural reasons for the retreat from exclusion. The unitary nation, in the prevailing French elite self-understanding, is a product and project of the state rather than (as in the German tradition) its preexisting, independently defined, and autonomously valuable substrate. In this statist and assimilationist tradition, the civic incorporation of immigrants, particularly second- and third-generation immigrants, is a matter of course. It is the civic exclusion of immigrants, not their civic incorporation, that demands special justification.

The nationalist discourse on immigration, citizenship, and national identity supplied such a justification. Conceding the tradition of assimilation in France, it argued against this tradition, asserting the unassimilability of today's North African Moslem immigrants, and deducing from this the need to restrict access to citizenship. In so doing it drew on other aspects of the French tradition. It appealed to the principle of *laicité*, to the sacralization of national citizenship, and, most powerfully, to the sense of a consolidated, relatively homogeneous national culture. Yet these appeals—with the exception of the second, the least powerful and most anachronistic of the three—had more bearing on immigration than on citizenship policy. All parties agreed that France ought to limit further immigration, but it did not follow from this that France ought to restrict access to citizenship on the part of second-generation immigrants, the large majority of whom, it was widely agreed, would remain in France.

In the specific domain of citizenship law, then, restrictionists were arguing against a distinctive and deeply rooted national tradition. As a result, it was they who bore the burden of persuasion. The rhetorical playing field, as it were, was not a level one. Opponents of a restrictive reform could and did mobilize the rich symbolic and rhetorical resources associated with the French assimilationist tradition. Their arguments were saturated with references to "French tradition," "Republican tradition," "the tradition of French law," and so on.[99] Proponents of a restrictive reform, on the other hand, could not appeal so directly to tradition.

Yet to show the bearing of the distinctively French tradition of nationhood on the contemporary politics of citizenship, it is not enough to point to the centrality and frequency of appeals to tradition on the part of opponents of a restrictive reform of citizenship law. In the first place, there is no way to gauge the persuasiveness of those appeals. More fundamentally, politics cannot be reduced to persuasion. Even if one could show that the currency of an expansive, assimilationist idiom of nationhood made it more difficult in France than, say, in Germany to justify restricting access to citizenship, this would not explain the failure of a restrictive reform in France. Policy outcomes, obviously, are not determined primarily by the strength or persuasiveness of competing arguments.

Chirac retreated from an exclusionary reform as its political costs became more apparent and as he realized that it might even fail to muster a legislative majority. The reform provoked broad and vocal opposition within the political class, not only from partisan sources but also from official bodies such as the Council of State, the High Council on Population and the Family, and the Human Rights Commission, from civic groups such as the League of the Rights of Man and SOS-Racism, and from "moral authorities" such as a number of prominent Catholic bishops. More important—and partly because of this surprisingly broad and vocal opposition—the reform threatened to divide the government and the center-right parties and damage Chirac's presidential bid. Faced with the actual, probable, and possible political costs of exclusion—or even the appearance of exclusion—the government backed away from a restrictive reform.

This outcome was not inevitable. Had the student mobilization not occurred—perhaps even after that mobilization, had hard-liners prevailed—the government might have pushed through the original proposal. My argument is probabilistic. The prevailing idiom of nationhood disposed a substantial fraction of the French political and cultural elite—including, crucially, those who were members or supporters of the government or at least not actively hostile to it—to conceive and articulate reservations about and opposition to the exclusionary aspects of the proposed reform. This opposition, in turn, raised the political cost of the reform to the government, and thereby made the government less likely to push it through.

By "idiom of nationhood" I mean a manner of thinking and talking about cultural and political belonging at the level of the nation-state. It is an instance of a larger class of idioms of collective identification— ways of thinking and talking about (and thereby in large part constituting)[100] "identities" of various kinds—class, gender, national, ethnic, religious, or generational. These in turn are instances of a still more general class of "cultural idioms," to use the expression of Theda Skocpol. As distinguished from ideologies ("idea systems deployed as self-conscious political arguments by identifiable political actors"), cultural idioms "have a longer-term, more anonymous, and less partisan existence."[101] Cultural idioms, as I argued in the Introduction, are not neutral vehicles for the expression of preexisting "interests": they *constitute* interests as much as they express them. Unlike "objective" or "material" interests, these culturally mediated and thereby culturally constituted interests do not exist prior to, or independently of, the cultural idiom in which they are expressed.[102]

The idiom of nationhood that concerns us here is that of the French political and cultural elite, the literate and articulate public with dominant positions in institutions and access to (as well as habits of using) the media of public expression. It is important to stress this, for popular idioms of nationhood may differ considerably from elite idioms,[103] and the gulf between the two appears particularly pronounced in the French case.[104] Moreover, the statist, assimilationist idiom of nationhood is not the only available one, even among the elite. This "prevailing" idiom of nationhood has been contestatory and contested; it has "prevailed" only though a series of fateful political struggles. There has long been a counteridiom, originating in the conservative-organicist response to the French Revolution and decisively formed in response to the militantly secular Republicanism of the late nineteenth century.[105] The counteridiom stresses cultural homogeneity and refers, implicitly or explicitly, to the myriad respects in which French culture has been fashioned by Catholicism. Le Pen and the National Front have revived this discourse, yet it remains a counterdiscourse, and its very presence on the French political scene has called forth a reaffirmation of the prevailing self-understanding.

Idioms of nationhood, like "languages of class," as Gareth Stedman Jones has shown, may succeed one another over time.[106] Yet despite renewed contestation, the prevailing French idiom of nationhood, the prevailing self-understanding, remains political rather than ethnocultural, assimilationist rather than differentialist. Indeed the idea of assimilation, and to a certain extent the word itself, shunned by the left in the 1970s and early 1980s, were revived in the late eighties in response to the rise of Le Pen and the right's assertions of the unassimilability of immigrants. To compare the discourse about immigration in the early years of the Mitterand presidency with that prevailing in his second term is to be struck by the eclipse of differentialism and the return of an integrationist, even an assimilationist discourse on the left.[107]

The prevailing state-centered, assimilationist understanding of nationhood is not politically neutral. It engenders an interest—an ideal interest, in Weberian terms—in an inclusive, assimilationist citizenship law, just as the more organic counteridiom engenders an interest in a restrictive citizenship law. The French political and cultural elite have a stake, a collective investment, in an open, inclusive definition of citizenship. To redefine the citizenry as a community of descent, as the radical nationalists proposed, would require a reorientation in ways of thinking and talking about nationhood. Over the long term major shifts in self-understanding, in idioms of collective identity, are possible. No such shift, however, had taken place by the late 1980s. As a result, even the very moderately restrictive reform proposed by Chirac entailed high political and cultural costs; and these contributed to its eventual abandonment.

At this writing, certain voices on the right, in opposition, again have begun to criticize the expansiveness of French citizenship law, as part of a broader discourse on the problems engendered by immigration.[108] As in the mid-1980s, the nationalist critique of *jus soli* may again prove politically profitable as an opposition strategy. Should a future government of the right again attempt to enact a restrictive reform of citizenship law, however, it would again encounter vigorous opposition—and not only from the ranks of the opposition. In the French context, the political cost of restricting access to citizenship would be bound to be high. This is not an absolute bar to such a reform; but it does make a fundamental restructuring of citizenship less likely.

8 ◆ Continuities in the German Politics of Citizenship

Remarkably, German citizenship today remains governed by a law of the Wilhelmine period. As a result of this continuity across two World Wars, three regime changes, and the division and reunification of the country, the marked restrictiveness of citizenship law toward non-German immigrants was carried over from Wilhelmine Germany into the Federal Republic and, in 1990, into the new German nation-state. The 1913 system of pure *jus sanguinis*, with no trace of *jus soli*, continues to determine the citizenship status of immigrants and their descendants today. In recent years, as a substantial second-generation immigrant population—and now the beginnings of a third generation—has developed, the system of pure *jus sanguinis* has become increasingly anomalous. The anomaly has been heightened by the great influx of ethnic German immigrants since 1988. For while the great majority of non-German immigrants, even of the second and third generation, remain outside the community of citizens, ethnic Germans from Eastern Europe and the Soviet Union are immediately accorded all the rights of citizenship. The marked openness toward ethnic Germans has made the continued civic exclusion of non-German immigrants at once more visible and more problematic.

The Citizenry as *Volksgemeinschaft:* The Nazi Era

Continuity arguments in recent German historiography have tended to focus on the antecedents of the Nazi dictatorship.[1] We are concerned here, however, with continuity around the Third Reich, not continuity leading up to it. To be sure, the racist citizenship legislation of the Nazi era had its antecedents. The notions on which it was based—the nation as organic *Volksgemeinschaft*, the importance of common descent, the exclusion of Jews and other *"fremdvölkisch"*—had deep roots in German history, and had already left their mark on the citizenship legislation and naturalization practice of Imperial Germany. However, to emphasize this continuity would obscure the radical novelty of Nazi citizenship policy, which differed not only in degree but in kind from Wilhelmine policy. It also would invite an anachronistic misinterpretation of earlier conceptions of nationhood and definitions of citizenship as prefigurations of Nazi ideology and policy.[2]

Compared with the late-nineteenth-century French citizenship law reform, or with the citizenship legislation of the North German Confederation, the Wilhelmine citizenship law reform had a marked ethnonational inflection. Yet, as we have seen in Chapter 6, it was informed not by a consistent ethnonational ideology, but by a national self-understanding in which ethnonational and state-national motifs were uneasily combined. Moreover, while Wilhelmine citizenship and naturalization policy sought to prevent Poles and Jews from *becoming* citizens, there was no attempt to *deprive* Polish-speaking and Jewish citizens of the Reich of their citizenship. No doubt Weimar nationalism and the rise of Nazism have to be understood in historical context, and the clamorous, contestatory nationalism of the Wilhelmine era is an important part of that context.[3] But in order to explain the restrictiveness of German citizenship toward immigrants today, and the continuity of citizenship law from the Wilhelmine era to the present, it is important to distinguish sharply between the ethnocultural aspect of the Wilhelmine citizenship law reform and the radical ethnoracial restructuring of citizenship under the Nazis.

From the point of view of Nazi ethnoracial ideology, Wilhelmine citizenship law and Weimar naturalization practice were multiply inadequate.[4] The Nazis took a number of steps to remedy these alleged defects, beginning a few months after their seizure of power with a law permitting the retrospective annulment of those Weimar naturalizations that were now seen as "unwanted." Unwantedness was to be "judged according to *völkisch*-national principles." It was to be presumed in the case of eastern Jews, except (at this point early in the National Socialist regime) for those who had fought on the German side in the First World War or those who had been of particular service to German interests.[5]

This preliminary step scarcely satisfied Nazi ideologists. The party program was much more ambitious:

4. Only *Volk*-comrades [*Volksgenossen*] can be [full] citizens [*Staatsbürger*]. And only persons of German blood, irrespective of [religious] confession, can be *Volk*-comrades. No Jew can be a *Volk*-comrade.

5. Persons who are not citizens [*Staatsbürger*] can live in Germany only as guests and must be subject to legislation governing foreigners.

6. The right to determine the leadership and laws of the state may be held only by citizens [*Staatsbürger*]. We therefore demand that every public office of whatever kind, on the *Reich*, *Land*, or communal level, be occupied only by citizens.[6]

The *Reichsbürgergesetz* of 1935—better known as one of the Nuremberg laws—realized points 4 and 6 of the party program. It distinguished full citizenship *(Reichsbürgerschaft)* from mere state-membership *(Staatsangehörigkeit)*. Only full citizens were to have political rights; mere state-members simply belonged to the protective association *(Schutzverband)* of the German Empire. The full citizens were a subclass of state-members, namely, politically loyal state-members "of German or related blood."[7] An administrative order of a few months later stated baldly that "No Jew can be a [full] citizen" and went on to spell out in detail who was to be considered a Jew.[8]

The *Reichsbürgergesetz*, however, did not realize point 5 of the Nazi party program. It excluded Jews from full citizenship, but not from formal state-membership as such. The party program, on the other hand, demanded that all who were not full citizens be considered foreigners. It demanded ethnonational purity not only for full citizenship but for state-membership as such. The *Reichsbürgergesetz* was only a partial solution, for Jews remained members of the state, *Staatsangehörige*, entitled (in theory) to its protection. In order to prevent this from being the case in the future, and to make state-membership congruent with *Volk*-membership, *Staatsangehörigkeit* with *Volkszugehörigkeit*, the Interior Ministry proposed in 1938 to exclude Jews and other "foreigners to our kind" *(Artsfremde)* from the attribution of state-membership *jure sanguinis*.[9] In 1940 the beginning of deportations focused attention on Jews' present status as *Staatsangehörige* and on the means of stripping them of that status. This was done by making the loss of *Staatsangehörigkeit*, for Jews, an automatic consequence of "taking up" (or being forced to take up) "residence" (even in a concentration camp) "abroad" (defined broadly for the purpose of the law so as to include most destinations for Jewish deportees). Thus "legally" it was "not German *Staatsange-*

hörige but stateless persons of Jewish descent" who were slaughtered in the death camps.[10]

One Nation, One Citizenship: The Postwar Reconstruction of Citizenship

The collapse of the Third Reich and the discrediting of *völkisch* ideology might have been expected to discredit German self-understanding as an ethnocultural nation as well. Instead, the peculiar circumstances of the immediate postwar period—the total collapse of the state, the massive expulsion of ethnic Germans from Eastern Europe and the Soviet Union, and the imposed division of Germany—reinforced and powerfully relegitimated that self-understanding.[11]

With the unconditional surrender and total collapse in 1945, Germany became again what it had been before unification: a nation without a state. National self-understanding, to be sure, was not oriented exclusively to common ethnicity or culture. Like Polish national self-understanding after the collapse of the Polish state and the partitions of Polish territory in the late eighteenth century, postwar German national self-understanding retained a significant historical-territorial dimension. This historical-territorial moment in national self-understanding was nourished by the partitions of German territory: the loss of the historic German *Ostgebiete*—the territories east of the Oder and the Neisse—to Poland and (in small part) the Soviet Union, and the partition of the remaining territory by the occupying powers, crystallized in 1949 with the establishment of the Federal Republic of Germany and the German Democratic Republic.

The ethnocultural moment in national self-understanding, on the other hand, was nourished by the massive and brutal postwar expulsions of ethnic Germans from Eastern Europe and the Soviet Union. Among the enormous, largely forced population flows that accompanied and followed the Second World War in Europe and Asia, only the Hindu-Moslem population exchange between India and Pakistan, involving more than 15 million persons, surpassed in magnitude the *Vertreibung* (driving out) of Germans.[12] By 1950 twelve million ethnic Germans had fled or been expelled. Two-thirds of them had been resettled in West Germany, where they comprised one-sixth of the population.[13] Somewhat more than half of the *Vertriebene* (expelled persons) came from the eastern territories of Germany that had now been incorporated into Poland; with these "*Reichsdeutsche*" the bond of common nationhood had been political as well as ethnocultural. But 40 percent—more than three million—had long been citizens of non-German states; and with these *"Volksdeutsche"* the bond of common nationhood was purely ethnocultural.[14]

The postwar reconstruction of citizenship, in conjunction with the establishment of the Federal Republic of Germany, reflected this self-understanding as a nation without a state. The architects of the new state emphasized its provisional character and wrote into the Preamble to its Constitution a commitment to the realization of German unity on the part of the "entire German people." Article 116 of the Constitution drew the conclusions of that commitment for citizenship law: "everyone is a German [*not* a West German] in the eyes of the Constitution . . . who holds German [*not* West German] citizenship or who, as a refugee or expellee of German *Volkszugehörigkeit*,[15] or as a spouse or descendant of such a person, has been admitted to the territory of the German Reich as it existed on December 31, 1937." This provision distinguishes two groups of "Germans": German citizens and ethnic German refugees and expellees from Eastern Europe. "German citizens" never meant West German citizens. There never was a separate West German citizenship. Not wanting to validate the division of Germany, the founders of the Federal Republic insisted on the continued validity of a single German citizenship.[16] This meant that the Wilhelmine citizenship law of 1913, with its system of pure *jus sanguinis*, remained in force and became the law of the Federal Republic.[17] As a result, almost all residents of the German Democratic Republic were, all along, viewed by the West German state as German citizens *jure sanguinis*.

Besides German citizens, there is a second group of legal "Germans" with identical rights and obligations. These are the ethnic German refugees and expellees. In the wake of the massive wartime dislocations their legal status had to be normalized.[18] This was done in the Constitution by defining them as "Germans" and by assigning virtually identical rights and duties to these "Germans without German citizenship" and to German citizens.[19] The ethnic German refugees, then, have been treated as citizens: they have been citizens in fact if not in name.[20]

To interpret the postwar reconstruction of citizenship in the light of the citizenship status of non-German immigrants today would be anachronistic. In the immediate aftermath of the war there were no non-German immigrants. In that ravaged land, flooded with millions of displaced persons, returned prisoners of war, and German refugees from Eastern Europe and East Germany, the prospect of labor shortages and of substantial non-German immigration was remote. Moreover, the citizenship rules of the *Grundgesetz* were intended to be provisional. Article 116 of the Constitution, conferring the legal status of "German" on ethnic German refugees, was included in a section containing "transitional" provisions. Some such measure was obviously needed to regularize the status of the refugees. The Federal Republic as a whole was established as a provisional state.[21] The division of Germany had not crystallized or solidified, and the commitment to a single German citizenship expressed a commitment to reunification. Even the German Democratic Republic initially held to the principle of a single German citizenship, although in 1967 it established a separate East German citizenship.[22] Only later, in the context of the apparent stabilization and consolidation of the two German states, culminating in their mutual recognition in 1972,[23] did the West German insistence on a single German citizenship come to seem quixotic[24]—until of course its sudden and spectacular vindication in 1989–90.[25]

Since 1988, however, the ethnonational inflection of German citizenship law has become increasingly pronounced as the contrast between its expansiveness toward fellow Germans and its restrictiveness toward non-German immigrants has become more salient. Besides the dramatic influx of East Germans in 1989–90, there has been an equally dramatic although less publicized influx of ethnic Germans from Eastern Europe and the Soviet Union—over a million between 1988 and 1991. The constitutional definition of ethnic German refugees as "Germans," originally a transitional provision defining the legal status of the millions of refugees already in the Federal Republic, has become, in effect, a "law of return" for ethnic German immigrants from Eastern Europe and the Soviet Union. This was not inherent in the constitutional provision itself, which defined as Germans only "refugees and expellees," with reference to those who had been driven out of Eastern Europe and the Soviet Union because of their German *Volkszugehörigkeit*. Strictly interpreted, this category would have applied only to the expellees of the immediate postwar years. It certainly would not have included the influx of ethnic Germans that began in the late 1980s. These resettlers were not refugees or expellees. By all accounts, the deliberate *Vertreibung* of ethnic Germans from Eastern Europe and the Soviet Union ended in 1947. Nevertheless, a law of 1953 defined "*Vertriebene*" broadly to include not only persons who were actually driven out (or who had fled before the advancing Red Army in the last months of the war) but also persons leaving Eastern Europe or the Soviet Union "as" ethnic Germans "after the end of the general expulsion measures."[26] Administrative guidelines have interpreted this law in a remarkably inclusive manner. Reasoning from the premise that "the repression of Germans in these territories continues," since Germans "are not recognized as a national group and can not protect their cultural identity," current guidelines specify that "it is generally to be assumed—without special examination—that [the repression of Germans] is the essential cause for departure."[27] So while one must prove that one is an ethnic German,[28] one need not ordinarily prove that one left as a result of the repression of ethnic Germans; this is generally assumed. What began as a transitional legal provision intended to grant a secure legal existence to millions of ethnic Germans who were quite literally *Vertriebene,* driven out of their homes and homelands, became something quite different: an open door to immigration and automatic citizenship for ethnic German immigrants from Eastern Europe and the Soviet Union. This invitation has been taken up by more than two and a half million persons since 1950, half of them in the last few years; at this writing, the influx continues unabated.[29]

Gastarbeiter: Sojourners into Settlers

The influx of Germans has occurred against the backdrop of a large and increasingly settled population of non-German immigrants. Through an irony of history, just when two World Wars and Hitler's murderous policies had succeeded in ridding Germany of its "non-German" population, the long postwar boom created a new one. The economic recovery was remarkably rapid: despite the enormous influx of more than 10 million German refugees and migrants from East Germany, dwarfing the present immigration, sectoral labor shortages began to appear in the late 1950s.[30] Migrant workers were recruited from Italy, Greece, Spain, Portugal, Yugoslavia, and Turkey. By 1973 there were 2.6 million foreign workers, comprising 11.9 percent of the labor force, and 4 million foreigners altogether, comprising 6.4 percent of the total population.[31] Until around 1970, nobody thought that this labor migration would lead to settlement on a large scale. The government repeatedly emphasized that foreign workers were sojourners, not settlers.[32] The recession of 1966–67, during which the number of foreign workers declined by 25 percent, seemed to confirm that the foreign workers were temporary labor migrants, *Gastarbeiter,* whose presence in Germany was governed by the rhythms of the business cycle.[33] Nor did the migrants view themselves as permanent settlers. Even today, surprisingly few express a firm intention to remain permanently—or even for "several more years"—in Germany.[34]

Yet by the early 1970s there were already signs of settlement.[35] The average length of stay was increasing;[36] and the sex ratio and employment rate were becoming more "normal," slowly approximating those of the nonimmigrant population.[37] Most striking was the surge in births to immigrant parents. Between 1966 and 1974 the number of births to German parents fell by almost 50 percent, while in the same period the number of births to foreign parents increased by 140 percent. As a result, foreigners' share of total births soared from 4.3 percent in 1966 to 17.3 percent in 1974.[38] These changes led to an increasing concern with the social, as distinguished from the merely economic aspects of immigration.[39] They led to attempts in some states, especially Bavaria and Baden-Wurtermberg, to discourage the settlement of migrants by instituting a system of "rotation" of foreign workers.[40] And they contributed to the federal government's decision to suspend further recruitment of foreign workers in November 1973.[41] Yet that decision only reinforced the process of settlement, sharply limiting back-and-forth migration and prompting a surge in the immigration of family members.[42] Thus while the number of foreign workers fell from 2.6 million in 1973 to 1.9 million in 1976, and to 1.6 million in 1984, the total foreign population, after remaining roughly constant between 1973 and 1978, increased from 4.0 million in 1978 to 4.7 million in 1982.[43] This population is an increasingly settled one. Of 1.5 million Turks, more than a million have resided in the Federal Republic for at least ten years, while over 400,000 were born there. For the other leading immigrant groups the average length of stay is even longer: nearly 90 percent of Spanish, about 80 percent of Greeks, Yugoslavs, and Portuguese, and about 70 percent of Italians have resided in Germany for more than ten years.[44] About a million foreigners, moreover, were born in the Federal Republic.[45]

Migrants into Citizens?

In the context of this large and increasingly settled non-German immigrant population, the surge in ethnic German immigration has underscored the ethnocultural inflection of citizenship law. For while German immigrants are automatically defined as citizens or, what amounts in practice to the same thing, as Germans, the non-German immigrants, even second- and third-generation immigrants, can become citizens only through naturalization. As we have seen, very few have done so. As the non-German immigrant population has become increasingly settled, their low naturalization rates have become increasingly problematic, and their citizenship status anomalous—especially in contrast with the automatic citizenship accorded to ethnic German immigrants from Eastern Europe (and attributed *jure sanguinis,* thoughout the postwar period, to all East Germans).

With respect to the citizenship status of second-generation immigrants, French and German definitions of citizenship are "outliers" in Continental Europe. French law departs from the Continental norm by automatically attributing citizenship *jure soli* to most second- and third-generation immigrants, German citizenship law by taking no account of birth in the territory, even over two or more generations. One might expect these outlying citizenship policies to converge toward the Continental norm, especially since immigration policies have converged remarkably in the postwar period. As we have seen, there was in fact a vigorous, although unsuccessful, campaign in the mid-1980s to rid French citizenship law of *jus soli.* There have been moves toward convergence from the German side as well. The anomaly of settlement without citizenship is widely acknowledged, and there is a large consensus about the need to promote the naturalization of second-generation immigrants. Even the present Christian-Liberal government, which came to office in 1982 insisting on the need to reduce the number of Turks residing in Germany, has proclaimed a "public interest" in the naturalization of second-generation immigrants whose "life is centered in the FRG": "for no state can in the long run accept that a significant part of its population remain outside the political community."[46]

In 1990 naturalization provisions were liberalized as part of a comprehensive reform of *Ausländerrecht* (the law governing foreigners). Officials can no longer deny or accord naturalization at will to persons brought up and educated in Germany or having resided more than fifteen years there. Yet while this reform marks a significant change in direction, it is unlikely substantially to further the civic incorporation of immigrants. In the first place, the government rejected proposals to allow immigrants to naturalize, as in France, without giving up their original citizenship. The required renunciation of their original citizenship has already deterred, for both material and symbolic reasons, many otherwise qualified candidates from seeking naturalization; there is every indication that it will continue to do so.[47] With good reason has federal *Ausländerbeauftragte* Liselotte Funcke criticized as unrealistic the attempts to facilitate the naturalization of second-generation immigrants without allowing dual citizenship.[48] More important, the rules governing the ascription of citizenship were not changed. The system of pure *jus sanguinis* remains in place. This, even more than restrictive naturalization rules, remains the chief obstacle to the civic incorporation of immigrants in Germany. What accounts for the surprising hardiness of this distinctively restrictive system of pure *jus sanguinis*?

"Wir sind kein Einwanderungsland"

This refrain—"we are not a country of immigration"—has been a leitmotif of the German discussion of immigration during the last three decades.[49] Since the mid-1970s critics have challenged this formulation, marshaling impressive evidence that temporary labor migrants had become permanent settlers.[50] Yet in a sense the critics have missed the point. For the *kein Einwanderungsland* claim articulates not a social or demographic fact but a political-cultural norm, an element of national self-understanding. The undeniable fact of immigrant settlement does not make Germany—according to its own self-understanding—a country of immigration. Nor has the massive influx of ethnic Germans, who are indeed acknowledged as settlers and citizens, altered that self-understanding. For the implicit meaning of the *kein Einwanderungsland* formula is that Germany is not a country of *non-German* immigration. Ethnic German immigration is something else altogether.

The fact that Germany does not understand itself as a country of immigration for non-Germans leaves it ill-prepared to deal with its non-German settlers.[51] A country of immigration in the strong sense is one that, on its own self-understanding, is constituted in significant part by immigration. In a weaker sense, it is one in which immigrants are deliberately sought and incorporated as integral components of the population. In neither sense is Germany a country of non-German immigration.[52] The implications for citizenship are explicitly drawn in the administrative regulations that specify the guidelines authorities are to follow in exercising the discretion granted to them in naturalization cases: "the Federal Republic is not a country of immigration [and] does not strive to increase the number of its citizens through naturalization."[53] Naturalization, in consequence, is never routine: it is, in the words of the supreme administrative court, always "an exception, that comes into consideration only in individual cases, in which it seems to be in the interest of the state."[54] The authorities must consider whether the naturalization would involve a "valuable addition to the population" *(wert-vollen Bevölkerungszuwachs).*[55]

Whether or not naturalization would involve a "valuable addition to the population" depends not only on the individual characteristics of the applicant but on the demographic, economic, political, and cultural context. It may be useful to compare the Wilhelmine and contemporary contexts. In Wilhelmine Germany total population was increasing rapidly. Nonetheless, heavy internal migration from east to west and a shift from extensive to intensive cultivation engendered labor shortages in eastern agricultural districts. A large supply of Russian and Galician Poles was eager to work in those districts. Intensifying German and Polish nationalism, however, occasioned ethnopolitical concern about the contribution of Polish immigration to the Polonization of those districts, which lay in the historic zone of mixed Polish-German settlement. The economic interest in cheap and abundant labor stood in tension with the ethnopolitical interest in the preservation of Germandom in the east. Seasonal migration was a compromise satisfying in large measure both agrarian and nationalist concerns. In this context, immigration from the east, though a valuable help to the economy, could not be seen as a "valuable addition to the population." There was an economic interest in admitting Poles to the territory, but there was neither an economic nor a demographic interest in admitting them to the citizenry.

Today the population has stabilized and is expected to decline if fertility remains low. Although unemployment is high in eastern Germany, the labor market is tight in the west. Depending on the course of economic reconstruction in the eastern part of the country, and on patterns of east-west internal migration, significant labor shortages may develop in western regions, especially in entry-level positions, as the small "baby bust" cohorts enter the labor market. Until recently, concern about the development of consolidated ethnic minorities ruled out a renewal of immigration. German unification, however, together with the liberalization of Eastern European and Soviet exit regimes, has dramatically changed the character of the available immigrants; it has made available a large pool of highly mobile ethnic Germans. While the migration of ethnic Germans to Wilhelmine Germany remained a nationalistic chimera, the migration of ethnic Germans to new German nation-state is a massive reality.

The bearing of labor market and demographic considerations on the politics of immigration and citizenship today is ambiguous. In Wilhelmine Germany there was no ambiguity. Germany needed seasonal agricultural workers, but it did not need, and did not want, settlers or citizens. What Germany needs or wants today is less clear. Since the mid-1970s high unemployment has been used as an argument for a restrictive immigration and refugee policy, but sectoral labor shortages are increasing and resettlers from eastern Germany, along with ethnic German immigrants from Eastern Europe and the Soviet Union, have been welcomed by West German employers. Germany is a densely populated country, and this too has been used as an argument against refugee admissions and in support of the claim that Germany is not and cannot become a country of immigration. But at the same time, Germany has one of the lowest birthrates ever recorded, and the positive demographic contribution of immigration has been increasingly acknowledged in government and business circles.[56]

The evident economic and demographic usefulness of ethnic German immigrants, in short, has undermined the plausibility of the standard economic and demographic arguments against the entry, settlement, and civic incorporation of non-German immigrants. The real objection to non-German immigration has not been economic or demographic, but cultural and political. The increasing salience of ethnic German immigration has exposed the ethnocultural orientation of immigration and citizenship policy. While the government sought—without great success—to induce Turks to return to Turkey, it sought at the same time to facilitate the immigration of ethnic Germans from Eastern Europe. While politicians of all parties have invoked the limited "absorptive capacity" [Aufnahmefähigkeit] of Germany, especially with respect to Turks, it remains politically unacceptable to make the same argument about ethnic Germans. And while the government has maintained its restrictive citizenship policies toward non-German immigrants, German immigrants continue to enjoy a privileged citizenship status. The availability of a supply of ethnic German immigrants, legally privileged and socially preferred to non-Germans, has revealed the marked ethnocultural inflection in the contemporary German politics of immigration and citizenship.[57]

The Bounds of the Plausible

In France the civic incorporation of immigrants proceeds largely through the workings of *jus soli*, which automatically transforms second-generation immigrants into citizens. In Germany, by contrast, almost no consideration has been given to *jus soli*. The introduction of *jus soli* for *third*-generation immigrants was proposed by the Social Democrats in 1986, only to be rejected by the Christian Democratic-dominated upper house. But the attribution of citizenship *jure soli* to the *second* generation—a system of civic incorporation like that of France—has been outside the mainstream universe of discourse, advocated only by the Greens.

If *jus soli à la française* is unimaginable in Germany, this results in part from the lack of a viable assimilationist tradition. Unilaterally to attribute German citizenship to immigrants—especially to those who, according to surveys, have remarkably little interest in acquiring it—is out of the question.[58] This is evident from the use, on the right and the left,[59] of the strongly pejorative expressions *Zwangsgermanisierung* (forced Germanization) and *Eindeutschung* (Germanization) to disavow any intention of compelling or even inducing immigrants to take on German citizenship.[60] The invocation of the specter of *Zwangsgermanisierung* reflects an historical bad conscience grounded not only in the *völkisch* imperialism of the Nazis but also in the lack of a viable assimilationist tradition in Germany. Assimilation, to be sure, has its critics in France as well, on the right and on the left. And the arrogance, verging on ruthlessness, of the Third Republic's assimilationist policies toward regional cultures is well known.[61] Nonetheless, French patterns of state- and nation-building furnished to the political elite a model of effective— and largely legitimate—assimilation, and the expansiveness of French citizenship law toward immigrants is one legacy of that assimilationist self-understanding. Instead of a similarly effective and legitimate tradition of assimilation, Germany—like ethnoculturally intermixed Central Europe in general—has an uncertain and multivalent tradition of intercourse with ethnocultural others, a tradition with at least three different faces: one benignly differentialist; a second harshly (and thus often ineffectively) assimilationist;[62] a third invidiously dissimilationist. The unthinkability of an assimilationist citizenship law in Germany reflects the lack of an assimilationist tradition and self-understanding.[63]

Not only the antimodel of forced assimilation but equally the positive historical model of benign differentialism weakens the appeal of an assimilationist citizenship policy. By "benign differentialism" I have in mind noninvidious legal differentiation along ethnocultural lines that assigns special rights or privileges to persons in their capacities as members of ethnocultural groups, typically as a means of guaranteeing the free practice of their religion, language, or culture. Central European history—the fabulously complex world of the Habsburg empire[64] and East Central Europe in the early interwar period, the golden age (quickly tarnished, to be sure) of formal minority rights—affords multiple examples of such benign differentialism.

From a legal perspective it is puzzling that this historical model should work against an assimilationist citizenship policy, for in international law only the citizens of a state qualify for legal protection as ethnocultural or ethnonational minorities.[65] Yet from a sociopolitical perspective, it is understandable. The ethnocultural inflection of German self-understanding and German citizenship law makes it difficult to reconcile—in the political imagination of Germans and immigrants alike—the preservation of Turkish cultural identity and autonomy, for example, with the acquisition of German citizenship. State-membership is too closely tied to nation-membership. To take on German citizenship, in the self-understanding of Germans and Turks alike, requires that one become German in some thicker, richer sense than merely acquiring a new passport. Persons drawn to the idea of differentialist integration have therefore tried to work out models that do not require a person to become a formal member of the state. It is only against this background that we can understand the otherwise puzzling preoccupation with voting rights for noncitizen immigrants in local—and ultimately in statewide—elections.[66] To a remarkable extent, efforts of "inclusionists" have been focused on local voting rights and not on full formal citizenship. This concern with partial civic inclusion outside of formal citizenship has distracted attention from the question of formal citizenship status and delayed full recognition of the anomalous formal citizenship status of Germany's increasingly settled immigrants.

The formal civic incorporation of second-generation immigrants has not solved the problems engendered by immigration in France, nor would it solve them in Germany. The social, cultural, and economic situation of immigrants in the two countries is similar in many respects. Yet by transforming second-generation immigrants into citizens, France has at least formally recognized and guaranteed their permanent membership of polity and society. When and whether the new German nation-state will do the same is likely to be an increasingly salient question in the years to come.

Conclusion

In the context of advancing European integration, the sharp and persisting difference between French and German citizenship policies poses both a political and an intellectual problem. Because citizenship in one state carries with it rights of entry, work, and residence in other states of the European Community, the definition of citizenship in one state necessarily affects other Community states. Member states are working to harmonize their immigration and refugee admissions policies, and there has been some discussion about harmonizing citizenship law as well. Since it is the citizenship legislation of France and Germany, along with that of Britain, that diverges most sharply from the modal European legislation, the proposed harmonization concerns these countries in particular. Moreover, this divergence from the European norm renders French and German citizenship law vulnerable to domestic criticism. The anomalous expansiveness of French citizenship law has been repeatedly invoked by French restrictionists, the unparalleled restrictiveness of German citizenship law by German inclusionists.

The continuing difference in citizenship policies and practices appears still more anomalous, and more surprising, in light of the similar migration processes, comparable immigrant populations, and converging immigration policies in France and Germany. Other things being equal, one would expect states with similar immigrant populations and immigration policies to have similar citizenship policies. And there have been moves toward convergence. On the German side, even the present Christian-Liberal government has acknowledged the anomaly of settlement without citizenship and has eased naturalization rules for second-generation immigrants. On the French side, the unique expansiveness (in Continental Europe) of citizenship law provoked a strong campaign in 1986–87 to restrict immigrants' access to citizenship, justified inter alia

179

by the need to bring French citizenship law into line with that of its continental neighbors. Yet these moves toward convergence remained largely unrealized. The French attack on *jus soli* encountered strong opposition and ultimately failed, while the liberalization of naturalization procedures in Germany, without allowing dual citizenship or introducing elements of *jus soli,* will do little to further the civic incorporation of immigrants. Why have citizenship policies so far escaped the convergence to which immigration policies have been subjected? What is special about citizenship?

To formulate the question in this way is to suggest a first part of the answer. Citizenship is special because admission to its prerogatives, within the very wide bounds set by international law, is entirely at the discretion of the state. The regulation of membership is an essential attribute of sovereignty; the principle of the liberty of the state in the attribution of citizenship is firmly established in international law. It is true that other competencies relating to immigration—notably discretion in the admission of noncitizens to the territory of the state and in the selection of the legal regime to which resident noncitizens are submitted—also belong to the traditional notion of sovereignty. But the theoretically sovereign competence of states in these domains has been eroded by numerous bilateral and multilateral agreements, treaties, and conventions and, above all, in the case of France and Germany, by membership in the European Community. Questions of citizenship, however, have been left untouched by these encroachments of supranational on national jurisdictions. Viewed against the backdrop of the loss of sovereign control over admission to the territory and access to civil and socioeconomic rights, states' continued sovereign control over admission to citizenship stands out.

In the European setting citizenship is a last bastion of sovereignty; states continue to enjoy a freedom of action in this domain that they increasingly lack in others. Yet while sovereign control over admission to citizenship permits national variation, it does not explain that variation. Why have citizenship policies not converged to reflect the underlying similarities in immigration processes, immigrant populations, and migration policies?

A second and more important part of the answer has to do with what is at stake in debates about citizenship law. Citizenship confers not only political rights but the unconditional right to enter and reside in the country, complete access to the labor market, and eligibility for the full range of welfare benefits. In a world structured by enormous and increasing inequalities between states in labor and consumer markets, welfare systems, and public goods such as order, security, and environmental quality, the rights conferred by citizenship decisively shape life chances.[1] For peaceful and prosperous states it is vital to limit the number of persons possessing these powerful rights of access—especially since demographic, economic, and political differentials on the one hand and increasingly dense networks of communication, transportation, and migration on the other have generated unprecedented and increasing migratory pressures. The question of access to the territories, labor markets, and welfare systems of the world's favored states is decisive for persons and states alike.[2]

Yet these weighty questions of access are *not* at stake in the French and German debates about the citizenship status of postwar labor migrants and their families. The debates have concerned the citizenship status of *actual*, not *potential* immigrants—of persons already in the territory, the labor market, and the welfare system. For these immigrants, and for the French and German states, the material interests at stake are relatively minor. Most of the immigrants already enjoy a secure residence status and broad economic and social rights that differ only at the margins from those of citizens. Citizenship would add complete protection against expulsion, access to public sector employment, and eligibility for those few social services and benefits that are limited to citizens. While not negligible, the marginal advantages conferred by citizenship over and above those conferred by the status of long-term foreign resident are of modest import.[3] From the point of view of the immigrants concerned, citizenship status as such does not decisively shape life chances.

Nor does the citizenship status of immigrants seriously engage vital state interests. The modern territorial welfare state, to be sure, has a vital interest in the legal, political, and administrative capacity to control access to its territory, labor market, and welfare system, and the control of access pivots on the institution of citizenship. Noncitizens are routinely excludable; citizens are not. The citizenship status of *potential* immigrants therefore matters a great deal to the state. The citizenship status of *actual* immigrants matters much less. Noncitizens can routinely be refused admission to the territory; and noncitizens admitted to the territory on a strictly temporary basis—as tourists, students, or short-term workers with fixed-duration contracts—can routinely be refused admission to immigrant status. In both cases, citizenship is a decisive instrument of closure. But noncitizens who have been admitted to immigrant status—particularly those who have lived ten, fifteen, even twenty years in the country—can no longer be excluded routinely from the territory, labor market, or welfare system.[4] They have politically and legally protected claims to membership, if not to full citizenship. With respect to these immigrants, citizenship is no longer a decisive instrument of closure. Closure based on citizenship remains crucial in the political domain. But in the social and economic domain, and in the crucial question of access to and residence in the territory, noncitizen immigrants can be excluded only in marginal ways or in exceptional circumstances.[5] And since citizenship status is no longer the axis of routine exclusion, it no longer matters to the state in the same way whether or not immigrants have citizenship. The state retains marginally greater freedom of action vis-à-vis noncitizen immigrants than vis-à-vis citizens, and can still expel them in exceptional circumstances. But this marginal gain in freedom of action is not of decisive importance to the state, just as the marginal improvements in legal position are not of decisive significance for the opportunities of individual immigrants.

It is not enough, therefore, to consider citizenship in its "functional" context, in terms of its contribution to the opportunities of immigrants or the exclusionary capacities of the state. One must also examine citizenship in its political-cultural context. For if the material stakes of citizenship law reform are relatively minor, the "moral" or symbolic stakes are considerable. Citizenship in a nation-state is inevitably bound up with nationhood and national identity, membership of the state with membership of the nation. Proposals to redefine the legal criteria of citizenship raise large and ideologically charged questions of nationhood and national belonging. Debates about citizenship in France and Germany are debates about what it means to belong to the nation-state. The politics of citizenship today is first and foremost a politics of nationhood. As such, it is a *politics of identity*, not a *politics of interest* (in the restricted, materialist sense).[6] It pivots more on self-understanding than on self-interest. The "interests" informing the politics of citizenship are "ideal" rather than material. The central question is not "who *gets* what?" but rather "who *is* what?"

This was particularly clear in the French debate about citizenship law in 1986–87. Debate centered on what it meant, and what it ought to mean, to be or become French. It pivoted on self-understanding, not on group or state interests. Both sides attempted to articulate and mobilize around "a certain idea of France." For advocates of citizenship law reform, becoming French was an honor, not a bureaucratic convenience.

It was necessary to restore "will," "value," and "dignity" to citizenship by restricting access to persons desiring and deserving to become French. France was a nation to be loved and served, not merely a state dispensing benefits; one should admit as citizens only persons who were "French at heart," and exclude those unwilling or unable to assimilate. For its opponents, the reform marked a dangerous departure from the long French tradition of assimilation and inclusion, a departure inspired by a discredited conception of the nation as a community of descent. Advocates of reform, after all, had criticized only the "automaticity" inherent in *jus soli*, not that inherent in *jus sanguinis;* they singled out for criticism the automatic attribution of citizenship to second-generation immigrants born and raised in France, while endorsing the automatic attribution of citizenship to children of French citizens, even those born and raised abroad. To opponents, this preference for the ties of blood over those of milieu was inconsistent with the assimilationist tradition of France and distastefully reminiscent of Vichy.

Recent German discussions about immigration and citizenship also have centered more on identity and self-understanding than on interest (in the narrow sense). Defenders of the existing citizenship law argue that the system of pure *jus sanguinis* properly reflects the fact that Germany is not, in a deep political-cultural sense, a country of immigration[7]—the immigration of ethnic Germans being considered a different matter altogether. They reject *jus soli* in any form as foreign to the German legal and political tradition. They argue that Germany cannot be or become a *Vielvölkerstaat*, a multinational state, and that the massive transformation of non-German immigrants into citizens would be a dangerous step in that direction.[8] Individual immigrants, in their view, can become citizens, provided that they are willing to become German; but naturalization must remain an essentially individual process, not a form of collective incorporation. Underlying this view is a marked skepticism about the eventual social and cultural assimilation of immigrants. This skepticism is shared by all parties to the debate, even those most strongly committed to the civic inclusion of immigrants. They too find it difficult to imagine immigrants being or becoming German en masse. Thus while they have criticized the restrictiveness of German citizenship law, and proposed that immigrants wishing to acquire citizenship should have the right to do so, they have not placed great importance on this. For naturalization has assimilationist connotations: to acquire German citizenship, in their minds—and in the minds of immigrants—is to become German in something more than a merely legal sense. They tend to find this both implausible and illegitimate. Instead of strongly urging the incorporation of immigrants as formal citizens, inclusionists have sought to articulate a new, postnational political formula that would allow immigrants to be citizens in Germany without being German citizens. A system of automatic civic incorporation like that of France has not been seriously considered in Germany. Many of those committed to granting immigrants full political and civil rights have hesitated to propose attributing German citizenship to them. This, in their view, would constitute a form of symbolic or cultural violence against immigrants.

The politics of citizenship vis-à-vis immigrants is similar in form in France and Germany but sharply different in content. In both cases it pivots on national self-understanding, not on state or group interests. But the prevailing elite self-understandings are very different.[9] The French understand their nation as the creation of their state, the Germans their nation as the basis of their state. There is a strong assimilationist strand in the prevailing French self-understanding that is lacking in the prevailing German self-understanding. France is not a classical country of immigration, but it is a classical country, perhaps *the* classical country, of assimilation.[10] And schemes of self-understanding referring originally to the assimilation of the French periphery by the Parisian center have been easily and in a sense automatically and unconsciously transferred to the assimilation of immigrants.[11] In the last two decades both the desirability and the possibility of assimilating immigrants have been contested, as has the legitimacy of the Jacobin-Republican model of internal assimilation. Yet the prevailing elite understanding of nationhood, while contested, remains more assimilationist in France than in Germany. As a result, the idea of North African immigrants being or becoming French remains much more plausible and natural than the idea of Turkish immigrants being or becoming German.

Despite similar immigrant populations and immigration policies, French and German citizenship policies vis-à-vis immigrants remain sharply opposed. In part, this reflects the absence of compelling state or group interests in altering definitions of the citizenry. But it also reflects the fact that existing definitions of the citizenry—expansively combining *jus soli* and *jus sanguinis* in France, restrictively reflecting pure *jus sanguinis* in Germany—embody and express deeply rooted national self-understandings, more state-centered and assimilationist in France, more ethnocultural in Germany. This affinity between definitions of citizenship and conceptions of nationhood makes it difficult to change the former in fundamental ways. In France, the center-right government headed by Jacques Chirac was unable, in 1986–87, to adopt even a mildly restrictive reform of citizenship law, in part because its opponents were able to mobilize effectively by appealing to the prevailing elite national self-understanding. In Germany, naturalization policies were liberalized in 1990. But there is no chance that the French system of *jus soli* will be adopted; the automatic transformation of immigrants into citizens remains unthinkable in Germany. And liberalized naturalization rules alone will do little to further the civic incorporation of immigrants. Immigrants as well as Germans continue to associate the legal fact of naturalization with the social and cultural fact of assimilation, yet neither German political culture in general nor the specific social, political, and cultural context of the postwar immigration is favorable to assimilation. Add to this the fact that dual citizenship is permitted only in exceptional cases, and it seems likely that naturalization rates will remain quite low, and that the citizenship status and chances of immigrants in France and Germany will continue to diverge.

I should emphasize that I am not trying to account for the fine details of particular policy outcomes. Clearly these depend on a host of factors unrelated to patterns of national self-understanding. The policymaking process is highly contingent. Yet if elite understandings of nationhood have little bearing on the timing or detailed content of legislative change, they do help explain the otherwise puzzling persistence of broadly different ways of defining the citizenry. They limit the universe of debate and make a fundamental restructuring of citizenship improbable.

It might be objected that the appeal to elite understandings of nationhood is unnecessary. In the absence of pressing interests in citizenship law reform, on this argument, differences would persist out of mere inertia. This ignores the fact that there are pressures for convergence, although these do not arise in the first instance from state or group interests. In Germany, the anomaly of settlement without citizenship has generated widespread demands, endorsed even by the present center-right government, for easier access to citizenship. In France, the automatic attribution of citizenship to immigrants who, nativists argued, were neither assimilated nor assimilable, generated a strong campaign on the right for a more restrictive citizenship law. Mere inertia explains nothing.

But suppose the argument from inertia were reformulated. French and German definitions of the citizenry, it might be argued, are resistant to fundamental modification not because they are consonant with political and cultural traditions, but simply because they are *legal* traditions. The expansive French combination of *jus sanguinis* and *jus soli* was established a century ago; its roots extend back to the Revolution and even to the ancien régime. And German states—Prussia and other states before unification, Imperial Germany, the Weimar Republic, the Third Reich, and both German states after 1949—have relied exclusively on *jus sanguinis* ever since citizenship law was first codified in the early nineteenth century. The citizenship law of both countries has been modified in detail on numerous occasions over the years. But the broad patterns—the mix of *jus soli* and *jus sanguinis* in France, the system of pure *jus sanguinis* in Germany—have long been fixed. They have taken on the inertial weight and normative dignity of tradition. This inertial force is only increased by the gravity and symbolic centrality of citizenship. States do not tinker with the basic principles of citizenship law as they might with the fine print of the tax code. The appeal to self-understanding, on this argument, is unnecessary. France and Germany continue to define their citizenries in fundamentally different ways because they have been doing so for more than a century.

This is more satisfactory than the crude argument from inertia. But tradition can not be equated with duration. The longevity of a practice alone does not establish its "traditional" quality. Tradition is a constructed, not a purely objective property.[12] The appeal to tradition is an elementary form of political rhetoric. To present a policy or practice as traditional can contribute to its preservation by investing it with normative dignity and thereby raising the political cost of challenging it. Tradition is therefore a contested category. Policies and practices are the objects of representational struggles that seek to deem them "traditional" or to deny them this dignity—instances of the general and perpetual struggle over the representation and characterization of the social world.[13] The appeal to tradition that was central to the French mobilization against the attempt to curb *jus soli* was not an appeal to endurance as such. It was an appeal to legitimate endurance, to the endurance of something deserving to endure, to an enduring consonance between a legal formula and a political-cultural self-understanding. Thus opponents of citizenship law reform characterized *jus soli* as a specifically *Republican* tradition, while proponents of the reform contested this characterization, arguing that *jus soli* reflected not Republican principles but the military and demographic needs of the state. In Germany too appeals to tradition invoked not simply the endurance of a legal form but rather the enduring congruence between a legal form *(jus sanguinis)* and a principle of political-cultural self-understanding (that Germany is not a country of immigration).

Endurance matters, but it is not alone decisive. Long-standing practices do have normative force, but only when the practices have some material or symbolic value or meaning that cannot be reduced to, although it may be strengthened by, their perdurance. The long-standing French and German definitions of the citizenry have indeed assumed the inertial weight and normative dignity of tradition. But this does not mean that self-understandings are irrelevant. If *jus soli* in France and *jus sanguinis* in Germany are construed and defended as traditions, this is not simply because of their endurance, but also because they embody and express deeply rooted habits of national self-understanding. They are understood and defended as legal traditions because of their consonance with political and cultural traditions. It is this consonance that gives their long endurance its normative force.

The crystallization of *jus soli* in France and of pure *jus sanguinis* in Germany occurred at the high noon of the European nation-state, in the decades before the First World War. Today, many observers have argued, Western Europe is moving decisively beyond the nation-state. Thus even if French and German definitions of citizenship remain sharply opposed, national citizenship may wane in significance, along with the nation-state itself. Just as the nation-state is being eroded from above and from below,[14] ceding some functions and capacities to supranational and others to subnational institutions, so too national citizenship may be eroded by the development of forms of supranational and subnational citizenship. In the postnational Europe of the future, the decisive instances of belonging, the decisive sites of citizenship, might be Europe as a whole on the one hand and individual regions and municipalities on the other.[15]

In the long run this postnational vision may come to fruition.[16] For the foreseeable future, however, the nation-state and national citizenship will remain very much—perhaps too much—with us. It is not only that, as Western Europe moves fitfully *beyond* the nation-state, multinational Yugoslavia and the Soviet Union have disintegrated *into* nation-states. It is not only that a powerful German nation-state has been recreated in the heart of Europe. It is also that throughout Western Europe nationhood has been revived as a political theme, and nativism as a political program, in response to the unprecedented immigration of the last thirty years.

Despite restrictive immigration policies in place in most Western European states for nearly two decades, the populations of immigrant origin have become larger and more diverse. This trend shows no sign of abating. For demographic reasons alone—to say nothing of economic, political, or ecological reasons—south-north migratory pressure is bound to increase. And at this writing, the countries of Western and Central Europe are bracing for a large influx of migrants from economically distressed and politically unstable regions of Eastern Europe and the former Soviet Union.

To some observers the ethnic heterogeneity that has been introduced, or reinforced, by immigration, together with the encroachments on sovereignty that are entailed by membership of the European Community, show that Western European countries can no longer be considered nation-states. But this is to mistake the nature of the nation-state. The nation-state is not only, or primarily, an ethnodemographic phenomenon, or a set of institutional arrangements. It is also, crucially, a way of thinking about and appraising political and social membership.[17] Because this way of thinking remains widely influential, debates about the citizenship status of immigrants remain in large part debates about nationhood—about what it means, and what it ought to mean, to belong to a nation-state.

We have followed these debates as they have unfolded in France and Germany, where distinctive and deeply rooted understandings of nationhood have found enduring expression in sharply opposed definitions of citizenship. But one could well follow them elsewhere. At this writing, for example, the incipient successor states to the Soviet Union are establishing their own citizenships. These are intended to serve as instruments of closure against unwanted immigrants, as means of strengthening the "stateness" of these new nation-states, and as symbolic expressions of sovereignty. The politics of citizenship, in this setting, is a politics of identity, as in France and Germany; but it is also, to a greater extent than in Western Europe, a politics of interest. In the context of proportionally much larger minority populations, high ethnic tension, and potential violence, much more is at stake. For Latvians and Estonians, for example, who comprise only a small majority of the population of their respective states, it matters a great deal how citizenship is defined; as it does, reciprocally, for the large Russian immigrant minority in these states. Some radical nationalists have urged that citizenship be restricted to descendants of citizens of interwar Latvia and Estonia; others have argued that citizenship must be open to all residents.[18] Similar debates have been occurring in other breakaway polities.

Emigration from the Soviet Union and its successor states has engendered another set of problems concerning definitions of citizenship and understandings of nationhood. The emigration, at this writing, is primarily one of ethnic affinity, comprised of persons leaving the former Soviet Union for an external homeland to which they belong in ethnocultural terms. This is the case, above all, of Jews and ethnic Germans, who have automatic citizenship rights in Israel and Germany, based on ethnoreligious and ethnocultural understandings of nationhood. But there are many other ex-Soviet nationalities with external ethnic "homelands." These include over a million Poles, 437,000 Koreans, 379,000 Bulgarians, 358,000 Greeks, and 172,000 Hungarians. How will the receiving states respond to these potential immigrants? Will they institute ethnocultural "laws of return" like those of Israel and Germany, granting automatic citizenship to immigrants? Or will they decline to acknowledge these potential immigrants as members of their nation, or—even if they are acknowledged as members of the nation—decline to grant them privileged access to membership of their state?[19]

Citizenship and nationhood are intensely contested issues in European politics, east and west. They are likely to remain so for the foreseeable future. Those who herald the emerging postnational age are too hasty in condemning the nation-state to the dustbin of history. They underestimate the resilience, as well as the richness and complexity, of an institutional and normative tradition that, for better or worse, appears to have life in it yet.

Notes

For complete names of authors, full titles, and publication data, see the Bibliography.

Introduction

1. Michelet is quoted in Girardet, *Le nationalisme français*, p. 13
2. Kohn, *The Idea of Nationalism*, esp. pp. 329ff., and *Prelude to Nation-States;* Schieder, "Typologie und Erscheinungsformen des Nationalstaats in Europa"; Szücs, *Nation und Geschichte*, pp. 21f.; Smith, *The Ethnic Origins of Nations.*
3. See especially Blackbourn and Eley, *The Peculiarities of German History.*
4. Berdahl, "New Thoughts on German Nationalism"; and Breuilly, *Nationalism and the State*, pp. 65–83.
5. Earlier versions of this and the next four sections appeared in "Einwanderung und Nationalstaat in Frankreich und Deutschland," pp. 15–27, and "Immigration, Citizenship, and the Nation-State in France and Germany: A Comparative Historical Analysis," pp. 387–398.
6. This account of monocephalic and polycephalic Europe closely follows Rokkan and Urwin, *Economy, Territory, Identity*, p. 27; see also pp. 7–12, 35–39.
7. On nationhood as a "conceived order," see Lepsius, "The Nation and Nationalism in Germany"; on the nation as an "imagined community," see B. Anderson, *Imagined Communities.*
8. E. Weber, *Peasants into Frenchmen.*
9. The 1648 Peace of Westphalia, ending the Thirty Years' War, imposed religious pluralism on Germany and provided a model for the coexistence of distinct cultural communities. This model permitted assimilation on the level of the individual principality (according to the formula *cuius regio, eius religio*), but on the scale of the nation it was pluralist and differentialist.
10. See Rokkan and Urwin, *Economy, Territory, Identity*, esp. pp. 27, 35–38, 74–76, 96, for suggestive comments on the geoeconomic and geocultural conditions underlying different patterns of state-building in France and western Germany. On the roots of the more assimilationist self-understanding of France,

see also von Thadden, "Umgang mit Minderheiten"; Elias, *The Civilizing Process;* and, building on Elias, Noiriel, *Le creuset français,* pp. 341–356.

11. Weber, *Peasants into Frenchmen.*

12. Assimilation succeeded with respect to the Polish-speaking Masuren (Conze, "Nationsbildung durch Trennung," pp. 101–105) and, in the long run, with respect to Poles who migrated from the Prussian east to the Ruhr industrial districts. But assimilation failed, as we shall see in Chapter 6, with respect to the largest and most visible groups of Polish-speaking Germans, those in the Prussian provinces of Poznan and West Prussia.

13. The French-Spanish and French-German borderlands are interesting in their own right (on the former, see Sahlins, *Boundaries*), but they are marginal to national self-understanding. Since Alsace-Lorraine belonged to Germany during the crucial phase of nation-building in late-nineteenth- and early-twentieth-century France, we cannot know how vigorously assimilationist policies would have been pursued then. Yet French tolerance for bilingualism before and after this interlude shows that this cultural borderland posed no threat to national identity.

14. The second wave of German settlers in Slavic lands, from the sixteenth century on, especially the more numerous Protestants, tended to preserve their language, religious culture, and national identity. See Hagen, *Germans, Poles, and Jews,* pp. 1–9.

15. Godechot, "Nation, patrie, nationalisme et patriotisme," p. 494.

16. The word refers to the cultivated middle classes, the bourgeoisie constituted by *Bildung* (education or cultivation), and conscious of its *ständisch* unity.

17. For Schiller's formulation, see Conze, "'Deutschland' und 'deutsche Nation' als historische Begriffe," pp. 29–30. For the distinction between *Staatsnation* and *Kulturnation,* see Meinecke, *Weltbürgertum und Nationalstaat,* chap. 1.

18. Meinecke, *Weltbürgertum und Nationalstaat,* chap. 2.

19. Article 3 of the Declaration of Rights of August 26, 1789, located "the principle of all sovereignty" in the nation, while the Constitution of 1791 was even more categorical: "Sovereignty is one [and] indivisible . . . It belongs to the Nation" (Title III, Article 1). (The Revolutionary Constitutions are reprinted in *Les Constitutions de la France.*) The "nationalization" of political authority, however, was not limited to the constitutional domain. In effect, "all that was 'royal' became . . . national: national assembly, national gendarmerie, national guard, national army, national education, . . . national domains, . . . national debt" (Godechot, "Nation, patrie, nationalisme et patriotisme," p. 495).

20. *Qu'est-ce que le tiers état?* p. 126. This political definition of nationhood was not new: Sieyès' definition echoed that given in the Dictionnaire de l'Académie of 1694, according to which a nation is constituted by "all the inhabitants of the same state, of the same country who live under the same laws and use the same language" (quoted by Soboul in "De l'Ancien régime à l'Empire," p. 58).

21. "Il n'y a d'étranger en France que les mauvais citoyens" (quoted by Azimi, "L'étranger sous la Révolution," p. 702). While Tallien's remark, as Azimi notes, cannot be taken as representative of the Revolution's attitude toward

foreigners, the remark does illustrate the strictly political definition of nationhood then prevailing. The ambivalence of the Revolutionary attitude toward foreigners will be discussed in Chapter 2.

22. Kedourie, *Nationalism,* chap. 1; Soboul, "De l'Ancien régime à l'Empire," p. 63; Godechot, *La Grande Nation,* p. 69.

23. As Meinecke notes, the right of national self-determination could be applied to nations understood historically, with the emphasis on the "historically developed personality of the nation," or rationalistically, with the nation understood as "a subdivision of humanity, an abstractly constructed frame without [distinctive] individual content." Meinecke registers his clear preference for the former and his criticism of the "deep weaknesses and errors" of the latter, "entirely formalistic doctrine of national sovereignty" (*Weltbürgertum und Nationalstaat,* p. 34). This corresponds roughly to Simmel's distinction between the nineteenth-century conception of individuality as *Einzigkeit* (uniqueness) and the eighteenth-century conception of individuality as *Einzelheit* (oneness); see *The Sociology of Georg Simmel,* pp. 58–84, esp. p. 81.

24. Both reports are reprinted in de Certeau et al., *Une politique de la langue,* pp. 291–317; the quotations are from pp. 295, 302.

25. Kohn, *Prelude to Nation-States,* pp. 90–93.

26. The reference is to Weber, *Peasants into Frenchmen,* which contains a wealth of material on assimilation, but focuses on the period 1870–1914.

27. Furet and Richet, *La Révolution française,* p. 175; Soboul, "De l'Ancien régime à l'Empire," p. 58.

28. Godechot concludes that "it is therefore absurd to speak of French *nationalism* during the first years of the Revolution: *patriotism* is an entirely different thing" ("Nation, patrie, nationalisme et patriotisme," p. 498).

29. On the internal nationalism, see Azimi, "L'étranger sous la Révolution"; Nora, "Nation"; and Chapter 2 below. The contradictions involved in the external missionary nationalism are evident: "the Grande Nation is not only the nation that, in 1789, triumphed over the monarchy; it is the nation that has triumphed over its internal and external enemies and that will deliver the oppressed patriots of all Europe . . . The expression *Grande Nation* applies to the liberating, emancipating nation, the nation that propagates the 'great principles' of 1789, the nation that must aid oppressed peoples to conquer their liberty . . . [but also to] the nation that, despite these loudly proclaimed principles, dominates, oppresses, annexes, without regard for the will of other peoples" (Godechot "Nation, patrie, nationalisme et patriotisme," pp. 499–500).

30. See especially Kohn, *Prelude to Nation-States,* pp. 168–221. Even if Kohn goes too far in claiming that the period from 1789 to 1815 "determined the character of nationalism and the rising nation-states" in Germany as well as France (p. v), there can be no doubt about its importance.

31. Müller is quoted in Kohn, *Prelude to Nation-States,* p. 188.

32. Quoted in Pinson, *Modern Germany,* p. 33.

33. In this context, the "nineteenth century" means roughly 1830 to 1914 in France, and 1815 to 1914 in Germany.

34. Schieder, "Typologie und Erscheinungsformen des Nationalstaats," p. 120.
35. On "instituting the nation," see Weber, *Peasants into Frenchmen*, p. 332.
36. On national consolidation in these and other domains, see Nora, ed., *Les lieux de mémoire*, II: *La Nation*, and Weber, *Peasants into Frenchmen*.
37. Rémond, *The Right Wing in France*, pp. 208f.; Girardet, "Pour une introduction à l'histoire du nationalisme français."
38. Girardet, *L'idée coloniale en France*.
39. Lewis, "One Hundred Million Frenchmen."
40. The assimilationist citizenship law is discussed in Chapter 5. On the quasi-colonial dimension of the Republicans' internal civilizing mission, see Weber, *Peasants into Frenchmen*, pp. 486ff.
41. Girardet, "Pour une introduction à l'histoire du nationalisme français."
42. Mommsen is quoted in Basdevant, "Le principe des nationalités," p. 90.
43. Although occasioned by the question of Alsace-Lorraine, Renan's letters—the second in particular—offer a prescient general critique of the dangers of an "ethnographic politics" that strives to adjust political to prior ethnocultural boundaries: "The division of humanity into races, besides resting on a scientific error . . . can only lead to wars of extermination, to 'zoological' wars . . . You have raised the flag of ethnographic . . . politics in place of liberal politics; that politics will be fatal to you. Comparative philology, which you invented and wrongly transposed to the terrain of politics, will serve you badly. The Slavs are passionately interested in it. How can you believe that the Slavs will not do to you what you do to others? . . . Every affirmation of Germanism is an affirmation of Slavism; every movement of concentration on your part is a movement that 'precipitates' the Slav, releases him, makes him exist separately . . . Therefore beware of ethnography, or rather do not apply it too much to politics" (Renan, "Nouvelle lettre à M. Strauss," pp. 456–457).
44. Conze, "Nationsbildung durch Trennung," p. 95; Lepsius, "The Nation and Nationalism in Germany," p. 48.
45. On Bismarck's distance from nationalism, see Schieder, *Das Deutsche Kaiserreich von 1871 als Nationalstaat*, pp. 22–26. The annexation of Alsace-Lorraine, while demanded and justified in terms of the ethnocultural principle of nationhood, was in fact determined by strategic considerations. See Gall, "Das Problem Elsass-Lothringen."
46. Thus the preamble to the Constitution of 1791: "Il n'y a plus, pour aucune partie de la Nation, ni pour aucun individu, aucun privilège, ni exception au droit commun de tous les Français" (There is no longer any privilege, or any exception to the common law of all Frenchmen, for any part of the nation, or for any individual). Reprinted in *Les Constitutions de la France*, p. 35.
47. In the case of Poles in the Prussian east provinces, it was not the Reich, but already the North German Confederation, that had the ominous character of a nation-state. Poles accepted membership of the non-national Prussian state, but protested against the incorporation of the east Prussian provinces into this newly national entity. In 1871 they renewed their protest: "we want to remain under Prussian authority, but we do not want to be incorporated

into the German Reich" (Polish deputies quoted in Schieder, *Das Deutsche Kaiserreich von 1871 als Nationalstaat*, pp. 19, 20).

48. Schieder, *Das Deutsche Kaiserreich von 1871 als Nationalstaat*; Kocka, "Probleme der politischen Integration der Deutschen." On the articulation in 1871 of the idea of the "incomplete" nation-state, see Conze, "Nationsbildung durch Trennung," p. 95.

49. The vicissitudes of French and German traditions of nationhood in the twentieth century cannot be analyzed here. Chapters 7 and 8 argue that the deeply rooted styles of national self-understanding sketched here survived the turmoil of the first half of the twentieth century and that they continue to inform the politics of immigration and citizenship today.

50. Stedman Jones, *Languages of Class*, p. xx.

51. M. Weber, "The Social Psychology of the World Religions," p. 280; translation modified; M. Weber, *Gesammelte Aufsätze zur Religionssoziologie*, I, 252.

1. Citizenship as Social Closure

1. Marshall, *Citizenship and Social Class*, p. 8.

2. Strictly speaking, the citizenry excludes not only foreigners but stateless persons.

3. See, for example, two recent sociological surveys: Turner, *Citizenship and Capitalism*; and Barbalet, *Citizenship*.

4. On codification, see especially Bourdieu, "La codification," pp. 98–99: "Codification is linked to discipline and to the normalization of practices . . . Codification is an operation of symbolic ordering . . . most often incumbent on the great state bureaucracies. As one sees in the case of automobile traffic, codification brings with it collective profits of clarification and homogenization . . . Codification minimizes equivocation and flux, especially in interactions. It shows itself to be particularly indispensable and effective in situations where the risk of collision, conflict, accident . . . are particularly great. The encounter of two groups quite distant from one another is the encounter of two independent causal series. Between people of the same group, with the same habitus, thus spontaneously orchestrated, everything, even conflicts, goes without saying . . . But with different habituses, there appears the possibility of accident, collision, conflict. Codification is important because it guarantees a minimal communication."

5. Giddens, *The Nation-State and Violence*, p. 172; Zolberg, "International Migrations in Political Perspective," p. 6; Meyer and Hannan, "National Development in a Changing World System," pp. 3, 11–12.

6. This perspective owes most to Max Weber, *Economy and Society*, esp. pp. 54–56.

7. Poggi, *The Development of the Modern State*.

8. On the "territorialization" of rule, see Sahlins, *Boundaries*, pp. 61–63, 78–89, 93–97, 168–170, 190–192.

9. Weber, *Economy and Society*, pp. 43–46; see also pp. 341–343.

10. Suggestive remarks about the essential boundedness of the political com-

munity are found in Walzer, *Spheres of Justice*, chap. 2; Freeman, "Migration and the Political Economy of the Welfare State"; Barber, *Strong Democracy*, pp. 225ff.; Balibar, "Propositions sur la citoyenneté"; and Lochak, "Etrangers et citoyens." Turner alludes to the notion of closure in *Citizenship and Capitalism* (p. 85); and Murphy mentions closure based on citizenship in passing in *Social Closure* (pp. 74, 228). Yet there has been no sustained analysis of the structure and function of citizenship as a mode of social closure.

11. See Zolberg, "International Migrations in Political Perspective," p. 7.

12. That the modern state makes spatially comprehensive claims to rule does not imply that it necessarily makes otherwise comprehensive claims. In its liberal incarnation, the modern state claims to regulate only a limited range of action—but this action, however narrowly or broadly it is defined, is regulated wherever it occurs within the territory and whoever engages in it. There are no territorial enclaves within which the state's authority is unrecognized, although in liberal and corporatist states there may be domains of action that are exempt from its sway.

13. Weber, *Economy and Society*, p. 56.

14. The demographic interests of the state extend further, of course, to such matters as fertility and mortality; this analysis is limited to migration.

15. Poggi, *The Development of the Modern State*, p. 91.

16. See Marrus, *The Unwanted*, p. 5.

17. Exceptions include the occasional willingness of new-world countries of immigration to accept old-world unwanted, and the willingness of certain countries to accept foreign citizens of shared religion or ethnicity. The most striking recent instance of complementarity was the absorption by postwar Germany of some ten million ethnic Germans expelled from Eastern Europe and the Soviet Union. (The complementarity became apparent only during the fifties as the West German economy began its phenomenal expansion.)

18. This is expressed in a law of 1810 from the German state of Baden, indicating that banishment "cannot be carried out against citizens [*Inländer*] without offending the society of states" (quoted in von Martitz, "Das Recht der Staatsangehörigkeit," p. 800).

19. The emergence of bounded citizenries in early-nineteenth-century Germany is discussed in greater detail in Chapter 3.

20. By "domestic" closure I mean any and all instances in which noncitizens present in the territory are excluded from full participation in social or political life, insofar as exclusion does not take the form of expulsion from the territory. Unlike territorial closure, which directly involves other states (since persons denied entry or expelled are compelled to remain under or are transferred to the jurisdiction of another territorial state), domestic closure is an intrastate affair in which other states are not immediately implicated.

21. J. D. B.Miller, "The Sovereign State and Its Future," p. 284.

22. See, for example, Beetham, "The Future of the Nation-State"; Mommsen, "Varieties of the Nation-State in Modern History"; Young, "Cultural Pluralism in the Third World," pp. 116–118.

23. The semantic fields of "nation" and "people" differ, but these differences are not essential to the point.

24. By "capacitarian" I mean a scheme of political citizenship the ostensible rationale of which is to apportion political rights according to persons' capacity to exercise them responsibly, where capacity is held to be indicated by such properties as age, sex, civil status, property, income, employment, literacy, or educational attainment. On the transition from functional to plebiscitarian systems of suffrage, see Bendix, *Nation-Building and Citizenship*, pp. 90f., 112f., 125.

25. In Sweden, the Netherlands, and elsewhere, noncitizens are now allowed to vote in local elections (see Just, "Europaïsche Erfahrungen mit dem kommunalen Wahlrecht für Ausländer"; Hammar, *Democracy and the Nation-State*). But the campaign for local voting rights for resident noncitizens has emphasized the categorical difference between local and national elections, local and national politics. Precisely because of this fundamental difference, it is argued, granting noncitizens local voting rights would not violate the principle of national self-determination. The argument for extending local voting rights to noncitizens concedes to citizens the legitimate monopoly on electoral participation in the politics of the national state.

26. Dunn, *Western Political Theory in the Face of the Future*, pp. 55, 56, 65.

27. This Foucaultian theme has been developed by Giddens in *The Nation-State and Violence*, esp. chap. 7; see also Noiriel, *Le creuset français*, pp. 350–353.

28. Lochak, *Etrangers: de quel droit?*, pp. 49–51.

29. This is often the case in countries in which police have broad power to conduct identity checks on vaguely specified public order grounds. In France, young men who appear to be of North African ethnic origin are singled out for frequent identity checks. (One of the first laws passed by the Chirac government in 1986 widened the power of the police to conduct such checks.) Many of these youth are in fact French citizens. Their sardonic appraisal of such practices is sociologically acute: "Ta carte d'identité, c'est ta gueule" (your identity card is your mug). For a rich assortment of comments by Turks, black Africans, and North Africans on the meaning of formal citizenship in everyday life, see the interview transcripts reprinted in "Culture islamique et attitudes politiques," particularly the responses to question 5.5: "In your opinion, if one becomes French, does this change something for a Moslem?" See also the conversations with young Franco-Algerians in Grenoble, reported by Frédéric Ploquin in *L'évenement du jeudi*, November 20–26, 1986, pp. 56–58; and Sayad, "La naturalisation," II, drawing on Goffman's *Stigma*: "One cannot be fully French in law [despite possessing French citizenship] when one is not fully French in fact . . . When particular and particularizing differences subsist, these stigmatizing differences refute the theoretical equality between nationals and naturalized nationals . . . they destroy the assimilationist illusion that underlies naturalization" (pp. 31–32).

30. This is the case in France. Violation of rules of entry and residence can be punished by one month to one year in prison and a fine of 180 to 8,000 francs. In addition, there may be a "complementary punishment" of expulsion or, in case of recidivism, of interdiction from the territory for up to a year (Richer, *Droit de l'immigration*, p. 62).

31. This is expressed in the UN Universal Declaration of Human Rights, Article

15 (1): "Everyone has the right to a nationality." Persons without a citizenship—revealingly called "stateless"—are not simply lacking a privilege, they are fundamentally anomalous, and are accommodated in our state-centered world only precariously and in an ad hoc fashion.

32. The following paragraphs draw on material that has appeared, in different form, in Brubaker, "Citizenship and Naturalization," pp. 101–102 and 108–109.

33. Schuck and Smith, *Citizenship without Consent.*

34. Similarly, the core benefits are too important to permit persons to opt *into* them at will.

35. In the intermediate case, exemplified by most European countries, some special provision is made for second- and third-generation immigrants. See Chapter 4, n. 15.

36. Brubaker, "Citizenship and Naturalization," pp. 108–109.

37. Ibid., pp. 109–120.

38. See Zolberg, "International Migrations in Political Perspective," p. 6.

2. The French Revolution and the Invention of National Citizenship

1. An earlier version of this chapter appeared as "The French Revolution and the Invention of Citizenship" in *French Politics and Society* 7 (Summer 1989): 30–49.

2. Marx, Preface to the first German edition of *Capital*, I, 9.

3. This eighteenth-century definition of privilege is from the *Encyclopédie Méthodique Jurisprudence* (1786), quoted in Behrens, *The Ancien Régime*, p. 46. This and the next paragraph are based primarily on Behrens, *The Ancien Régime*, pp. 46–62; Palmer, *The World of the French Revolution*, pp. 34–41; and Palmer, *The Age of the Democratic Revolution*, I, 28–29.

4. As Perry Anderson points out, "the Bourbon monarchy of the 18th century made very few moves of a 'levelling' type against the 'intermediary powers' which Montesquieu and his consorts cherished so intensely. The Ancien Régime in France preserved its bewildering jungle of heteroclite jurisdictions, divisions, and institutions . . . down to the Revolution. After Louis XIV, little further rationalization of the polity occurred: no uniform customs tariff, tax-system, legal code or local administration was ever created" (*Lineages of the Absolutist State*, p. 108). For a balanced account of the limits of the rationalizing efforts of the monarchy, see Furet, *Penser la Révolution française*, pp. 173–177.

5. "Prodigious multitude" of special provisions: Behrens, *The Ancien Régime*, p. 62, quoting Calonne.

6. Palmer, *World of the French Revolution*, p. 34.

7. On the social and legal structure of France under the ancien régime, see Mousnier, *The Institutions of France under the Absolute Monarchy*, vol. 1.

8. Vanel, *Histoire de nationalité française d'origine*, pp. 25–64.

9. *De l'Esprit des Lois*, Bk. XXI, chap. 17.

10. On the gradual erosion of the *droit d'aubaine*, see Villers, "La condition des étrangers en France dans les trois derniers siècles de la monarchie," pp. 146–149.

11. Boulet-Sautel, "L'aubain dans la France coutumière du Moyen Age," pp. 68–71, pp. 88–95.
12. Vanel, *Histoire,* p. 20.
13. Ibid., pp. 8–9.
14. Ibid., esp. pp. 27–29, 65–68.
15. "The problem of the distinction between citizens and foreigners was never examined directly, in itself . . . [Citizenship] was determined only when this determination was necessary for the solution of a practical problem . . . [connected with] the liquidation of a succession . . . In a system of written law, it would have been logical to make [the determination of citizenship] depend on the application of a theoretical rule. In a system of customary law, on the contrary, the theory [of citizenship] had to evolve as a function of the necessities of practice [as a function of beliefs about who ought to be able to inherit]" (ibid., pp. 70–71).
16. Vanel notes that legal opinion was "generally against the *droit d'aubaine* . . . To assure to children born in France of foreign parents the right of inheritance, it was necessary to make them French; it was necessary, as Guyot put it, to *convert into a right the accident* that had led them to be born in France" (ibid., p. 37, italics in original).
17. "A person does not inherit because he is French; he is French because it is logical that he inherit" (ibid., p. 71).
18. Ibid., pp. 40, 71.
19. Sieyès, *What is the Third Estate?,* p. 162; italics in original.
20. Sieyès, *Qu'est-ce que le Tiers état?,* pp. 212, 208, 211, respectively; italics in original.
21. Talmon, *The Origins of Totalitarian Democracy,* p. 69.
22. See generally Palmer, *The Age of the Democratic Revolution.*
23. Sieyès, *What is the Third Estate?,* p. 79, translation modified [*Qu'est-ce que le Tiers état?,* p. 145].
24. See Riedel, "Bürger, Staatsbürger, Bürgertum," esp. pp. 684f.
25. See Rousseau's note to *On the Social Contract,* I, 6 (p. 54).
26. Poggi, *The Development of the Modern State,* pp. 72–74.
27. Riedel, "Bürger, Staatsbürger, Bürgertum," p. 683; Stolleis, "Untertan—Bürger—Staatsbürger," pp. 65–74; Weinacht, "'Staatsbürger,'" pp. 44–45.
28. Bodin, *The Six Books of a Commonweale,* p. 47. Bodin rejected the older conception of the citizenry as a privileged subgroup. To define a citizen in terms of particular privileges would be to engender "five hundred thousand of definitions of citizens, for the infinite diversity of the perogatives that citizens have one against another, and also over strangers." Instead, it is "the acknowledgement and obedience of the free subject towards his sovereign prince, and the tuition, justice, and defense of the prince towards the subject, which maketh the citizen: which is the essential difference of a citizen from a stranger, as for other differences they are casual and accidentarie" (p. 64).
29. Riedel, "Bürger, Staatsbürger, Bürgertum," pp. 672–673, 676–678.
30. Rousseau, *Emile,* IV, quoted in Editor's Note to *On the Social Contract,* p. 138, n. 32; and Rousseau's note to ibid., I, 6 (p. 54).
31. Aristotle, *Politics,* 1275 a 23 (p. 93); Rousseau, *Social Contract,* I, 6 (p. 54): those who are associated in the Republic "collectively take the name *people,*

and individually are called *Citizens* as participants in the sovereign authority, and *Subjects* as subject to the laws of the State."

32. Palmer, *Age of the Democratic Revolution*, p. 114.
33. Rousseau's note to *On the Social Contract* I, 6 (p. 54; translation modified).
34. Until his bitter break with his native republic after its condemnation of *Emile* and *On the Social Contract*, Rousseau proudly signed his work, "citoyen de Genève." And his *Discourse on the Origin of Inequality* contained a dedication to Geneva, full of effusive praise for the Republic.
35. Febvre, "*Frontière*: the word and the concept," pp. 213–214. More recently, echoing Febvre: Nora, "Nation," pp. 804–805.
36. Mathiez, *La Révolution et les étrangers*, chap. 2.
37. Vergniaud, séance of August 24, 1792, quoted in Vanel, *Histoire*, p. 109. This was the day on which the Assembly debated conferring honorary citizenship on foreigners (ibid., p. 114).
38. Decree of August 6, 7, and 18, 1790, quoted in Portemer, "Les étrangers dans le droit de la révolution française," p. 540.
39. Title VI, Constitution of 1791, printed in *Les Constitutions de la France*, p. 65.
40. More precisely, it admitted most foreigners to "the exercise of the rights of French citizens." Article 4, Constitution of 1793, printed in *Les Constitutions de la France*, p. 83.
41. Palmer, *History of the Modern World*, p. 299. See Rousseau's lament in "Considérations sur le gouvernement de Pologne," p. 347: "Today there are no longer French, Germans, Spanish, or even English . . . there are only Europeans. All have the same tastes, the same passions, the same manners."
42. Mathiez, *La Révolution et les étrangers*, pp. 8f.
43. Godechot, "Nation, patrie, nationalisme, et patriotisme."
44. Garaud, *La Révolution et l'égalité civile*, pp. 190–192.
45. On the occasion of the great Festival of national Federation in 1790, Cloots wanted also to celebrate a "festival of the human race" (Soboul, "Anacharsis Cloots," p. 31). He ridiculed the very category of "foreigner" as a "barbaric expression that is beginning to make us blush" (quoted in Mathiez, *La Révolution et les étrangers*, p. 132) and dismissed the labels "French," "English" and "German" as "gothic characterizations" (quoted by Ozouf in "Fraternité," p. 734). Kristeva notes that this may have been the first critique of the concept of foreigner in history (*Etrangers à nous-mêmes*, p. 241).
46. Quoted in Portemer, "Les étrangers dans le droit de la révolution française," p. 542.
47. The harshness should not be exaggerated. Mathiez argues that the Revolutionary measures against foreigners were on the whole "much less severe and absolute than those adopted by all belligerent nations at the outbreak of the first world war" (*La Révolution et les étrangers*, p. 181). Yet this may have reflected technical limits to the repressive capacities of the revolutionary state more than the relative weakness of xenophobia.
48. Nora, "Nation," pp. 804–805; Lochak, "Etrangers et citoyens."
49. Lochak, "Etrangers et citoyens," p. 76.
50. Tallien and Thibaudeau are quoted by Azimi, "L'étranger sous la révolution," p. 702.

51. Ibid.
52. Nora, "Nation," p. 804.
53. This perspective owes much to Tocqueville, something to Marx, and has recently been elaborated by Theda Skocpol in *States and Social Revolutions*.
54. Marx, "The Civil War in France," p. 289.
55. Marx, "The Eighteenth Brumaire of Louis Bonaparte," p. 170.
56. The content of this and later Revolutionary and Napoleonic codifications of citizenship will be discussed in Chapter 5.
57. Mann, *The Sources of Social Power*, I, 477.

3. State, State-System, and Citizenship in Germany

1. Akzin, *States and Nations*, pp. 11–12.
2. Since America has no concept of the state like that of Continental Europe, this statement requires qualification. In the United States, the semantic overlap between "nationality" and "citizenship" reflects the political definition of nationhood and the fusion of the concepts of nation and sovereign people.
3. This chapter neglects the changing conceptions of state and citizenship and focuses on institutional changes. On changing conceptions of membership and citizenship, see Riedel, "Bürger, Staatsbürger, Bürgertum"; Stolleis, "Untertan—Bürger—Staatsbürger"; Weinacht, "'Staatsbürger.'" Grawert's *Staat und Staatsangehörigkeit* is a sustained analysis of both conceptual and institutional developments; my analysis in this chapter owes much to his.
4. Conze, "Nationsbildung durch Trennung," p. 95.
5. By designating predemocratic citizenship as inclusive, I do not have in mind inclusion in civil, political, and social rights, but rather the development of a single, territorially comprehensive and in this sense inclusive status of common "subjecthood" that was overlaid on, and gradually came to supersede, the multitude of particular, partial statuses.
6. Poggi, *The Development of the Modern State*, esp. pp. 74, 92.
7. Ibid., pp. 72–73.
8. Weber, *Economy and Society*, p. 696.
9. Ibid., pp. 697–698.
10. Howard, *War in European History*, p. 49, and chap. 4 *passim*; Hintze, "Military Organization and the Organization of the State," esp. pp. 198–201.
11. The following paragraphs are based on Hintze, "The Commissary and his Significance." See also Rosenberg, *Bureaucracy, Aristocracy, and Autocracy*, esp. pp. 1–56; and Braun, "Taxation, Sociopolitical Structure, and State-building," esp. pp. 268–281.
12. Hintze, "Commissary," p. 271.
13. Ibid., p. 273.
14. *Polizeistaat*, literally, police state, is best translated by "administrative state." For the development of the *Polizeistaat* in Brandenburg from the early sixteenth to the early eighteenth century, from the standpoint of legal and administrative history, emphasizing the development of the absolutist territorial state with its monopoly on legislative power, see Schulze, *Die Polizeigesetzgebung zur Wirtschafts- und Arbeitsordnung der Mark Brandenburg*

in der frühen Neuzeit, esp. pp. 110ff. Marc Raeff's *The Well-Ordered Police State: Social and Institutional Change through Law in the Germanies and Russia, 1600–1800* is a less formalistic account, from the point of view of social and intellectual history, of territorial rulers' attempts to transform social and economic reality through police ordonnances. However, it pays relatively little attention to Prussia, focusing instead on the smaller German states.

15. Hintze, "Commissary," pp. 272–274.

16. Hintze, "Preussens Entiwicklung zum Rechtsstaat," p. 105.

17. The system of *Gutsherrschaft* in the Prussian East—a system that based administrative and judicial authority on estate ownership—represented a large exception to this generalization, for the authority of the state was limited on these estates.

18. This expression denotes movement toward greater "stateness," in the various senses indicated by Nettl, "The State as a Conceptual Variable."

19. Hintze, "Der preussische Militär- und Beamtenstaat im 18. Jahrhundert," p. 428.

20. Koselleck, *Preussen zwischen Reform und Revolution,* pp. 24 and 23–77 passim.

21. Ibid., pp. 24–33; Hintze, *Die Hohenzollern und ihr Werk,* pp. 397–398; Wieacker, *Privatrechtsgeschichte der Neuzeit,* p. 331.

22. *Allgemeines Landrecht für die preussischen Staaten,* Introduction, §22 (p. 51): "Die Gesetze des Staats verbinden alle Mitglieder desselben, ohne Unterschied des Standes, Ranges und Geschlechts."

23. Koselleck, *Preussen,* pp. 39, 42, 126.

24. ALR, Part II, Title 7, §93f. (p. 436): "Wie die Unterthänigkeit entstehe"; Part II, Title 7, §147f. (p. 438): "Persönliche Freyheit der Unterthanen."

25. See ALR, Part II, Title 13 (pp. 589–590); Grawert, p. 128; Poggi, *Development of the Modern State,* p. 76; Hintze, *Hohenzollern,* p. 400; Hartung, "Der aufgeklärte Absolutismus," pp. 62–63; Koselleck, *Preussen,* pp. 34–37.

26. Hintze, *Hohenzollern,* p. 398.

27. Koselleck, *Preussen,* p. 38.

28. Even if the provisions lacked general *validity,* having to yield in case of conflict to provincial or other prior law, the general *form* of many of its provisions marked an important step toward legal unity and equality.

29. By analogy with Nettl, "The State as a Conceptual Variable."

30. Koselleck, *Preussen,* p. 74 and, more generally, pp. 70–76.

31. On membership of the peasant *Stand,* see ALR Part II, Title 7, §1 (p. 433); on membership of the noble *Stand,* see ALR Part II, Title 9, §1–13 (p. 534).

32. ALR Part II, Title 8, §1 (p. 452): "Der Bürgerstand begreift alle Einwohner des Staates unter such, welche, ihrer Geburt nach, weder zum Adel, noch zum Bauerstande gerechnet werden können; und auch nacher keinem dieser Stände einverleibt sind."

33. Koselleck, *Preussen,* p. 88.

34. Grawert, *Staat und Staatsangehörigkeit,* pp. 124–133; Koselleck, *Preussen,* pp. 56f., 660–662.

35. Grawert, *Staat und Staatsangehörigkeit,* p. 213.

36. Koselleck, *Preussen,* pp. 24, 39, 43–44.

37. This formulation overstates the difference, neglecting the generalizing, lev-

eling work of absolutism that prepared the way for the revolutionary construction of citizenship in France. Yet the absolutist foundations of citizenship, as well as the *ständisch* medium through which it developed, emerge much more clearly in the Prussian case.

38. Koselleck, *Preussen,* pp. 89, 540f.
39. Ibid., pp. 58–60, 487f., 587f.; Hintze, *Hohenzollern,* pp. 450–452, 464–465. Legal privileges remained, but were now attached to objects that were formally accessible to all, not to status as such. Thus rights of patrimonial justice were attached to the possession of "knightly estates" *(Rittergüter),* formerly restricted to noblemen, but now purchasable by anyone.
40. Bornhak, *Preussisches Staatsrecht,* pp. 238–239.
41. Discussion in this section is not restricted to Prussia. The interplay between municipal and state membership policies and politics in response to the migrant poor can be better illustrated with respect to Germany in general than with respect to relatively less urbanized Prussia alone.
42. This principle had been articulated by Luther in his celebrated 1520 tract, "To the Christian Nobility of the German Nation," but it antedated that tract by at least twenty years. Recent scholarship has shown that the secularization and rationalization of poor relief began before the Reformation, although it undoubtedly received a major impetus from the Reformation (T. Fischer, *Städtische Armut und Armenfürsorge im 15. und 16. Jahrhundert,* pp. 180–182; W. Fischer, *Armut in der Geschichte,* p. 33).
43. Breithaupt, "Öffentliches Armenrecht und persönliche Freiheit," p. 18; Rehm, "Der Erwerb von Staats und Gemeinde-Angehörigkeit in geschichtlicher Entwicklung," pp. 181–183. On the differentiation of *Bürger* and *Beisassen,* see Rehm, "Erwerb," p. 164. Actual legal reality was much more complex. There were many distinct statuses, not simply *Bürger* and *Beisassen.* The crucial point here is the basic distinction between the wider community of all persons with secure residence rights and the narrower community of full municipal citizens (Grawert, *Staat und Staatsangehörigkeit,* p. 58).
44. T. Fischer, *Städtische Armut,* pp. 180ff., 207ff., 224ff.; Rehm, "Erwerb," p. 184.
45. Grawert, *Staat und Staatsangehörigkeit,* p. 64.
46. Walker, *German Home Towns,* esp. pp. 205–211; Barber, *The Death of Communal Liberty,* esp. pp. 213–220.
47. Grawert, *Staat und Staatsangehörigkeit,* p. 61.
48. With increased mobility, there were increasing intercommunal disputes about responsibility for the support of those poor who had lived in various places before becoming impoverished (Bruch, "Armenwesen und Armengesetzgebung im Königreich Preussen," p. 46).
49. Explanatory justification of the Prussian Staatsministerium, accompanying the proposed text of a law on the freedom of movement, quoted in Schinkel, "Armenpflege und Freizügigkeit in der preussischen Gesetzgebung vom Jahre 1842," p. 467.
50. Comments of the head of the Westphalian *Landtag,* quoted in ibid., p. 473.
51. On this legislation, see Breithaupt, "Öffentliches Armenrecht und persönliche Freiheit," pp. 90ff.; Schinkel, "Armenpflege und Freizügigkeit." Protests from the towns led in 1855 to a new law that permitted towns to expel

persons who required public support during their first year of residence. Under this system, the previous commune of residence remained responsible for poor relief until a full year's residence in a new commune engendered a claim on the new commune. This was still a relatively open system: communes could not exclude all nonmembers, only currently destitute migrants or those who required public support within their first year of residence (Breithaupt, "Öffentliches Armenrecht," p. 97; Bruch, "Armenwesen und Armengesetzgebung," pp. 46–47).

52. Rockstroh, *Die Entwickelung der Freizügigkeit in Deutschland*, pp. 59ff.; Rehm, "Freizügigkeit," pp. 374–375; Breithaupt, "Öffentliches Armenrecht," pp. 58ff.

53. For Prussia, see Bruch, "Armenwesen und Armengesetzgebung," pp. 41–44.

54. Grawert, *Staat und Staatsangehörigkeit*, pp. 71, 75.

55. Ibid., pp. 118–119.

56. On "infrastructural power," see Mann, *The Sources of Social Power*. On the development of the administrative power of the nation-state, see also Giddens, *The Nation-State and Violence*.

57. Walker, *German Home Towns*, p. 140.

58. Compare Grawert, *Staat und Staatsangehörigkeit*, pp. 121–122.

59. Bornhak, *Preussisches Staatsrecht*, pp. 233–234.

60. Grawert, *Staat und Staatsangehörigkeit*, pp. 120, 126–127.

61. Rockstroh, *Die Entwickelung der Freizügigkeit*, p. 44.

62. Hinze, *Die Arbeiterfrage zu Beginn des modernen Kapitalismus*, pp. 108ff.

63. Conze, "Vom 'Pöbel' zum 'Proletariat,'" p. 335; Köllmann, "Industrialisierung, Binnenwanderung, und 'Soziale Frage,'" p. 49.

64. Rockstroh, *Die Entwickelung der Freizügigkeit*, pp. 58–59; Grawert, *Staat und Staatsangehörigkeit*, p. 133.

65. W. Fischer, *Armut in der Geschichte*, p. 56.

66. ALR, Part II, Title 19, §1 (p. 663); Koselleck, *Preussen zwischen Reform und Revolution*, pp. 129–131; Grawert, *Staat und Staatsangehörigkeit*, p. 135.

67. Grawert, *Staat und Staatsangehörigkeit*, pp. 134–135; the quotation is from p. 134. The need for the state to define "its" poor was more pressing in Germany than in France, for the smaller size of states and the cultural and economic commonalities across state borders engendered more frequent interstate migration.

68. Rockstroh, *Die Entwickelung der Freizügigkeit*, pp. 49–51.

69. Quoted in Friedrichsen, "Die Stellung des Fremden," p. 71.

70. Rönne, *Das Staatsrecht der Preussischen Monarchie*, p. 606; Bornhak, *Preussisches Staatsrecht*, pp. 235–236; Grawert, *Staat und Staatsangehörigkeit*, pp. 135–136.

71. Grawert, *Staat und Staatsangehörigkeit*, pp. 135, 138–139. On the richly differentiated membership vocabulary, see also Stolleis, "Untertan—Bürger—Staatsbürger."

72. Grawert, *Staat und Staatsangehörigkeit*, pp. 79ff.

73. Lippe, "Die preussische Heimatgesetzgebung," pp. 148, 150, 154.

74. Grawert, *Staat und Staatsangehörigkeit*, p. 174.

75. Lippe, "Die preussische Heimatgesetzgebung"; Grawert, *Staat und Staats-*

angehörigkeit, pp. 140–143; Dohse, *Ausländische Arbeiter und bürgerlicher Staat,* pp. 16–17. The quotation is from Grawert, p. 142.

76. Sec. 13, Gesetz über die Erwerb und Verlust der Eigenschaft als preussische Untertan sowie über Eintritt in fremde Staatsdienste, December 31, 1842, printed in Lichter, *Die Staatsangehörigkeit,* pp. 521–524.

77. Grawert, *Staat und Staatsangehörigkeit,* p. 174; Lippe, "Die preussische Heimatgesetzgebung," pp. 135, 137.

78. Poggi, *The Development of the Modern State,* pp. 60–61.

4. Citizenship and Naturalization in France and Germany

1. Aristotle, *Politics,* p. 93.
2. On French-German convergence, see Rist, "Migration and Marginality"; and Manfrass, "Ausländerpolitik," which notes persisting differences as well as convergences. On broader patterns of convergence among European labor-importing countries, see Hammar, "Comparative Analysis," esp. pp. 292–304; Castles, *Here for Good,* p. 9; Miller, *Foreign Workers in Western Europe,* pp. 7, 15.
3. See, generally, Castles and Kosack, *Immigrant Workers and Class Structure.* On the clustering of immigrant populations in geographic and social space, see George, *L'immigration en France.*
4. French officials sometimes stress the need to combat illegal immigration in place of the need to encourage return migration.
5. For exceptions to this rule in Germany, see "Einbürgerungsrichtlinien" (Administrative guidelines on naturalization), no. 5.3.3, printed in Groth, *Einbürgerungsratgeber,* p. 95.
6. "Einbürgerungsrichtlinien," no. 2.3, printed in ibid., p. 88.
7. The German figures are from a representative survey of 6000 migrant workers and their dependents, *Situation der ausländischen Arbeitnehmer und ihrer Familienangehörigen in der Bundesrepublik Deutschland,* pp. 484, 486. The French figures are from a 1983 study by A. Malewska-Peyre, "Crise d'identité et déviance chez les jeunes immigrés," Documentation Française, 1983, quoted in Dubet, *Immigration: Qu'en savons-nous?,* p. 85.
8. *Situation der ausländischen Arbeitnehmer,* pp. 485–487.
9. Sayad, "La naturalisation," II, 28–31.
10. "Naturalization" here includes not only discretionary grants of citizenship by the state but also, in France, the declarative acquisition of citizenship as a matter of right by spouses of citizens and French-born children of foreign parents.
11. By the end of 1988, the last year for which figures are available, 932,000 Turks had resided ten or more years in Germany, while another 200,000 had resided there from eight to ten years (Bundesminister des Innern, "Ausländer am 31.12.1988 nach nach ausgewählten Staatsangehörigkeiten und Aufenthaltsdauer," 33. F.) One can safely conclude that by the early 1990s, well over a million Turks had resided in Germany for ten or more years. As of June 30, 1988, 368,000 Turks residing in Germany were born there (Bundesminister des Innern, "Unter 16jährige, im Bundesgebiet geborene/nicht

im Bundesgebiet geborene Ausländer nach ausgewählten Staatsangehörig-keiten," 27. F. Although more recent data are not available, it is clear that, at this writing, the number is well over 400,000, given the fact that 25,000–30,000 Turkish citizens are born each year in Germany (Bundesminister des Innern, "Ausländische Lebendgeborene nach ausgewählten Staatsange-hörigkeiten," 23. F.).

12. This formulation recurs in various official statements, for example, in the Interior Ministry's "Aufzeichnung zur Ausländerpolitik und zum Auslän-derrecht in der Bundesrepublik Deutschland."

13. According to the new law, persons between the ages of sixteen and twenty-three should "generally" *(in der regel)* be granted citizenship when they (1) renounce their previous citizenship; (2) have resided legally in Germany for eight years; (3) have attended school in Germany for six years; and (4) have no criminal record (§85, Gesetz zur Neuregelung des Ausländerrechts vom 9. Juli 1990).

14. In Britain a 1981 reform of citizenship law limited *jus soli.* Under the new law, children born in Britain of noncitizen parents are citizens only if at least one parent is "settled" there—meaning lawfully resident without a time limit on his or her stay (Brubaker, "Citizenship and Naturalization," p. 106).

15. Thus, for example, Belgium and the Netherlands attribute nationality to third-generation immigrants. Austria, Belgium, Finland, the Netherlands, Norway, and Sweden permit persons born in the territory and residing there for a certain length of time to acquire nationality by simple declaration at or around the age of majority. (Residence alone, not birth in the territory, is required in Sweden.) In Italy persons born in the territory and residing there for ten years before majority acquire Italian nationality automatically at their majority. Among European countries that have experienced substantial immigration during the postwar period, only Switzerland, apart from Ger-many, has a nationality law based exclusively on *jus sanguinis.*

16. For births in France to Algerian parents between 1963 and 1974, see Jean, "Combien sont-ils," p. 258; for later years, see Lebon, "Attribution, acquisi-tion et perte de la nationalité française," p. 10.

17. Lebon conservatively estimates the number at 225,000 for the period 1973–1986 ("Attribution, acquisition et perte," pp. 11–12). Extrapolating from his annual estimates for the mid-1980s, we arrive at a figure of about 310,000 for the period 1973–1991.

18. In 1982, the last year for which census figures are available, about 1.1 million foreign residents were under eighteen. At that time, 69 percent of those under age fifteen were born in France (Recensement général, "Les étrangers," pp. 54–55).

19. Technically, in order to be legally defined as a German, these immigrants must not only be ethnic Germans (of German *Volkszugehörigkeit);* they must also qualify as *Vertriebene,* that is, as persons "driven out" of Eastern Europe and the Soviet Union because of their German *Volkszugehörigkeit.* Originally this category referred to the ethnic Germans who were physically driven out of Eastern Europe and the Soviet Union in the immediate aftermath of the Second World War. But German administrative practice has been to consider

virtually all ethnic German immigrants from Eastern Europe and the Soviet Union as *Vertriebene*, without inquiring into the actual circumstances of their emigration. Given the very large numbers of persons who have taken advantage of the status of *Vertriebene* to gain entry and citizenship in Germany, the practice of automatically granting the status of *Vertriebene* is currently being reconsidered. Even if this practice is modified, however, it appears likely that the migration of ethnic Germans will continue.

5. *Migrants into Citizens: The Crystallization of* Jus Soli *in Late-Nineteenth-Century France*

1. Bonnet, "Les pouvoirs publics français et l'immigration dans l'entre-deux-guerres," pp. 8, 153–154, 159–160.
2. Sociologically understood, a second-generation immigrant is one whose socialization occurs preponderantly in the country of immigration. It is socialization, not birth, in the country of destination that is sociologically crucial (Noiriel, *Le creuset français*, p. 213). My definition of second-generation is stricter, including only persons born in the country of immigration. I adopt this definition for convenience, since the administrative ease of recording place of birth has given it a much greater weight in citizenship law than place of socialization. By second-generation immigrant, I mean a person born in the country of immigration; by third-generation immigrant, one born in the country of immigration at least one of whose parents was also born there.
3. Throughout the nineteenth century the initiative for the reform of citizenship law came from Parliament, not the government. The government, concerned lest the extension of *jus soli* induce foreign countries to impose their citizenship on French citizens residing abroad, proceeded cautiously, modifying parliamentary initiatives to make them less rather than more expansive.
4. This was in fact considered at various points. But the citizen-soldier tradition was sufficiently firmly established that it was rejected.
5. I mean citizenship in the broad sense of membership of the nation-state, not in the narrow sense of active political citizenship.
6. Constitution of September 3, 1791, Title II, Articles 2 and 3, printed in *Les Constitutions de la France depuis 1789*, p. 37.
7. Vanel, *Histoire*, pp. 95f., 102f., 113–114. Confusion results from the ambiguity of the term *citoyen* in Revolutionary constitutions. The 1791 Constitution used the term to denote the national or state-member in the modern sense; subsequent Revolutionary Constitutions used it, in general, to denote the holder of political rights (the *citoyen actif*, in the language of the 1791 Constitution). On the confusions occasioned by this specifically political definition of citizenship, see Grawert, *Staat und Staatsangehörigkeit*, pp. 165–168. I use "citizenship" in this chapter, as elsewhere in the book, to denote formal membership of the state.
8. Locré, *Esprit*, I, 250.
9. Ibid., p. 150.
10. Quoted in Nizet, *Des effets de la naissance*, pp. 61–62.

11. Fenet, *Recueil,* VII, 166.

12. Boulay in ibid., pp. 166–167.

13. Gary, presenting the final version of the project to the Tribune, quoted in Vanel, *Histoire,* p. 137 (see also Fenet, *Recueil,* VII, 643).

14. That such persons were already latent or potential citizens is further suggested by nineteenth century jurisprudence. Throughout the nineteenth century French courts ascribed retroactive effect to the claim of citizenship: the person claiming French citizenship was considered to have been French from birth on (Nizet, *Des effets de la naissance,* pp. 89–90; Lagarde, *La nationalité française,* no. 99 [p. 83]).

15. Fenet, *Recueil,* VII, 155

16. Roederer quoted in Locré, *Esprit,* I, 252.

17. It was a commonplace at the time that the development of commerce occasioned an increasing flow of persons across state boundaries for purposes other than permanent settlement. In accordance with the Francocentric habit of thought, this observation was typically made with respect to French citizens abroad. But it was admitted that some foreigners might seek their fortune in France without intending to settle.

18. On horizontal and vertical dimensions of citizenship, see Terré, "Réflexions sur la notion de nationalité," pp. 203, 208.

19. Siméon in Fenet, *Recueil,* VII, 167.

20. Gary in ibid., VII, 643.

21. As we shall see in Chapter 7, this concern with the dignity, value, and prestige of citizenship has been salient in the recent French debates about immigration and citizenship.

22. Séance of August 24, 1792, quoted by Vanel, *Histoire,* p. 109.

23. In the late eighteenth and early nineteenth century, before the age of ethnocultural nationalism, there was no significant interest in preserving the ethnocultural substance of French nationhood. From a linguistic point of view, there was not yet much ethnocultural substance to preserve: it would have to be created before it could be preserved. Nor was there yet a self-consciously Catholic definition of French nationhood, although the Revolution had created the conditions for its emergence.

24. Noiriel, *Le creuset français,* pp. 77–78, 252.

25. The amendment was not adopted, apparently because provisions on citizenship were deemed inappropriate in a bill on military recruitment (CD 2083, p. 232; Nizet, *Des effets de la naissance,* p. 98).

26. B. Schnapper, *Le remplacement militaire.*

27. Formally, the period of service was six years between 1818 and 1825, eight years from 1825 to 1832, and seven years thereafter (Choisel, "Du tirage au sort au service universel," p. 45), although Schnapper estimates that the actual period served may have averaged four years (*Le remplacement militaire,* p. 38). The long period of service accorded with the military doctrine and political views of the time, the former holding that a long period of training and service was required in order to build a disciplined, effective force, the latter resisting universal service out of mistrust of the masses. Military and political opposition to universal service persisted into the Third

Republic, with the latter most vividly articulated by Thiers, who argued against "putting a gun on the shoulder of every socialist" (Kovacs, "French Military Institutions before the Franco-Prussian War," p. 217; Challener, *The French Theory of the Nation in Arms*, p. 39).

28. Schnapper reports that the Seine was unable to fill its contingent in the late 1820s because of the large number of foreigners in the district (*Le remplacement militaire*, pp. 38–39).

29. In principle, the system was changed in 1830 so that the foreign population was no longer counted in determining size of local contingent. In practice, it still mattered. For the new system was based on the number of persons inscribed on the lottery lists. Many long-established foreigners appeared on these lists. Yet if they drew a bad number, they could claim their foreign citizenship. So the system was still biased against cantons with many long-established foreigners, to the extent that these foreigners were represented on the *listes de tirage* (AND 2122, pp. 275–276).

30. Beudant, "De la naturalisation," pp. 121–122.

31. The candidate had to have received the authorization to establish his domicile in France and, in addition, to have lived in France for ten years since receiving this authorization. Naturalization, moreover, was accorded "only after an inquiry by the government concerning the morality of the foreigner, and only on the favorable opinion of the Council of State" (Loi des 13, 21 novembre, 2 décembre 1849 sur la naturalisation et le séjour des étrangers en France; printed in *La nationalité française: Textes et documents*, p. 59).

32. Rapport de M. de Montigny du 8 novembre 1849, quoted in Nizet, *Des effets de la naissance*, p.109.

33. Nizet, *Des effets de la naissance*, p. 108.

34. Attenuated because it applied only to third-generation immigrants. The stronger version, which would have extended French citizenship to second-generation immigrants, was not adopted until 1889.

35. The incentive to claim French citizenship at majority was particularly weak because certain significant benefits of French citizenship—like the right to attend certain government schools or to volunteer for the one-year military service—could be exercised only before the age of majority (SD 19, 373b). More generally, on the lack of strong incentives to become French, see Noiriel, *Le creuset français*, pp. 76–77.

36. Rapporteur of 1851 law, quoted in Nizet, *Des effets de la naissance*, p. 112.

37. Only later was this formula reversed, with the argument that full formal citizenship, membership of the *pays légal*, did not suffice to make immigrants—or Jews—members of the *pays réel*.

38. Benoît-Champy, quoted in Nizet, *Des effets de la naissance*, pp. 113, 114.

39. Here I follow Skocpol's characterization of cultural idioms as "longer-term, more anonymous, and less partisan . . . than ideologies" ("Cultural Idioms and Political Ideologies," p. 91).

40. S1, 1185a, 1182b. See also S1, 1179–1180. Originally a term of feudal law, denoting confiscation or seizure of goods, *mainmise* had acquired a broad pejorative meaning, implying the tyrannical and exclusive exercise of power.

41. Statistics are not available, since there was no centralized administrative

control or even registration of declarative acquisitions of French citizenship. But observers concur in emphasizing the infrequency with which persons born in France of foreign parents chose to acquire French citizenship. Indirect evidence is found in the fact that nearly 40 percent of the foreign citizens residing in France in 1891 were born in France (Noiriel, *Le creuset français*, p. 251). Had large numbers of those born in France opted for French citizenship at majority, this fraction would have been considerably lower.

42. S1, 1182c.

43. CD 2083, 234.

44. In its final form, for example, the law of 1889 attributed French citizenship to persons born in France and residing there at majority, provided that they did not claim (and prove) that they had retained their original citizenship.

45. Girardet, *Le nationalisme français*, pp. 12–13; Weill, *L'Europe du XIXe siècle et l'idée de nationalité*, p. 137.

46. Deloche, *Du principe des nationalités*, pp. vi, 31. This essentially political sympathy for national movements derived directly from the Revolution, specifically from the celebrated decree of the Convention on November 19, 1792: "La Convention nationale déclare, au nom de la Nation française, qu'elle accordera fraternité et secours à tous les peuples qui voudront *recouvrer* leur liberté" (quoted in Godechot, *La Grande Nation*, p. 75; my italics).

47. Weill, *L'Europe du XIXe siècle*, pp. 4–6.

48. In principle, there is an important difference between ethnic and cultural definitions of nationhood, a difference obscured by the word "ethnocultural." In practice, however, even cultural definitions of nationhood tend to have a much stronger ethnic tinge than do state-centered definitions of nationhood. Common culture may be independent, in the long run, of common descent. But the family plays a crucial part in the transmission of national culture—including not only language but cultural markers such as mores, gestures, and modes of thinking and feeling that are more resistant than language to formalized, organized transmission. Consequently, there is an elective affinity between the familial transmission of citizenship (*jus sanguinis*) and cultural—as well as explicitly ethnic—conceptions of nationhood. This does not mean that common culture is seen as having a biological basis. It is not common descent in a biological sense that is emphasized; rather, it is socialization in the family. Descent is taken as an indicator of socialization.

49. Akzin, *States and Nations*, pp. 11–12, 23–24, 46.

50. A further source of the increasing awareness of the opposition of ethnocultural nationality and state may be found in the increasing nineteenth century interest in the role of heredity in social life, an interest expressed in the development of ethnography, physical anthropology, human geography, and demography (Noiriel, *Le creuset français*, pp. 35f., 81–82).

51. Battifol and Lagarde, *Droit international privé*, pp. 61–62.

52. The first use of "*nationalité*" in this sense in an official text occurs only in 1874, although it occurs in legal writing at least two decades earlier.

53. S1, 1182b.

54. The following paragraphs are based on Sternhell, *La droite révolutionnaire;* Digeon, *La crise allemande de la pensée française;* Mitchell, *Victors and Vanquished;* and Hughes, *Consciousness and Society.*

55. Critical self-scrutiny did not emerge *ex nihilo* after Sedan. As Mitchell has shown, French self-criticism in relation to Germany developed after the Prussian victory over Austria at Sadowa, with an articulation of the need to strengthen the French system of conscription to compete with its newly powerful neighbor. And as Sternhell has shown, there was a mood of critical dissatisfaction with the "French tradition" in the late years of the Second Empire. He shows that thinkers who would articulate comprehensive critiques after 1870, notably Renan and Taine, articulated similar themes in the 1860s.

56. Digeon, *La crise allemande de la pensée française,* p. 75.

57. Ibid., pp. 77, 87.

58. Déroulède is quoted by Sternhell, *La droite révolutionnaire,* p. 83.

59. Digeon, *La crise allemande,* p. 76.

60. The specifically and distinctively French could be interpreted in ethnic terms, but it could also be interpreted in ideological terms. The contest over Alsace-Lorraine favored this latter interpretation.

61. Barzun, *Race;* Marrus, *The Politics of Assimilation,* chap. 2. The nineteenth-century use of "race" was quite loose. It generally referred—and I use it in this sense here—to a group united or believed to be united by common descent. What it designated, in most instances, would today be called ethnicity rather than race. Common descent was one element emphasized by race-thinkers, but not the only element, just as the invocation of ethnic categories today involves a reference to common descent, but also to other elements. The reference to common descent was combined in varying ways and proportions with an acknowledgment of other factors such as geography, climate, and institutions.

62. Arendt, *Origins of Totalitarianism,* pp. 161–163, 174.

63. In this respect, nineteenth-century race-thinking followed the early-eighteenth-century analysis of Boulainvilliers. See Arendt, *Origins,* pp.162–164.

64. For Michelet, "The French genius is thoroughly distinct from the Roman and from the Germanic genius . . . All the races of the world have contributed to the endowment of France" (quoted in Barzun, *Race,* p. 30). On Gobineau, see Barzun, *Race,* pp. 56–57; Arendt, *Origins,* pp. 171–173.

65. Digeon, *La crise allemande;* Mitchell, *Victors and Vanquished.*

66. Barzun, *Race,* pp. 137–146, quoting Combes at p. 141.

67. S2, 94c.

68. Anti-Semitism was central to the ethnicization of nationhood during the 1890s. But it was not particularly important before the late 1880s. It developed, beginning with the publication of Drumont's *La France Juive* in 1886, after the legislative affirmation of *jus sanguinis* and thus cannot explain that affirmation.

69. Niboyet, *Traité,* p. 154. For other exponents of this view, see Battifol and Lagarde, *Droit international privé,* no. 87 (p. 89); *Etre français aujourd'hui et demain,* II, 23, 25; Costa-Lascoux, "Nationaux, mais pas vraiment citoyens,"

p. 47; Massot, "Français par le sang," p. 9; Lochak, "Etrangers et citoyens," pp. 79–80. The chief dissenting view is the short but fine piece by Bruschi, "Droit de la nationalité," which recognizes the importance of the contemporary Republicanism (see esp. p. 45). The only detailed study of the debates of the 1880s is the law thesis of Nizet, *Des effets de la naissance*, which is limited to an analysis of the technical legal issues raised by the reform. Noiriel's *Le creuset français*, pp. 82f., situates the debates in their wider political, social, and cultural context, but does not analyze them in detail.

70. Mitchell, *Victors and Vanquished*, p. 3. On the shock to France of the Prussian victory at Sadowa, see also Challener, *The French Theory of the Nation in Arms*, p. 11; and Kovacs, "French Military Institutions," pp. 223–224.

71. From 1872 to 1911 the French population grew 90,000 per year, the German population 600,000 per year. On the eve of the war there were 66 million Germans, 39 million French (Armengaud, *La population française*, pp. 47, 53).

72. On railway-based supply systems, see Howard, *War in European History*, p. 99; and Challener, *The French Theory of the Nation in Arms*, pp. 49–51. On demographic arithmetic, see Vagts, *A History of Militarism*, p. 217. Napoleon is quoted in Mitchell, *Victors and Vanquished*, p. 7.

73. Mitchell, *Victors and Vanquished*, p. 20; cf. pp. 3, 72–73.

74. Challener, *The French Theory of the Nation in Arms*, pp. 79–80. Estimates of optimal army size increased substantially between 1866 and 1914. Since French military doctrine emphasized numerical parity with Germany, and since Germany kept increasing the size of its forces, French estimates were frequently revised upward. By the early years of the twentieth century, demography was indeed a central concern, as Germany began more fully to exploit a demographic base considerably larger than that of France (ibid., pp. 61, 73, 79–80). The response, then clearly motivated by demographic concern, was to extend conscription to the colonies—without, it should be noted, a parallel extension of civic rights (ibid., p. 80). In the 1870s and 1880s, however, the constraints and central concerns were not yet demographic.

75. Monteilhet, *Les institutions militaires de la France*, p. 217; Mitchell, *Victors and Vanquished*, p. 73.

76. *Les naturalisations en France*, p. 73.

77. We know that 40 percent of the total foreign population of 1891 was born in France (Noiriel, *Le creuset français*, pp. 251–252). This fraction must have varied substantially by age, with a much higher fraction of the young than the old foreigners born in France.

78. This group does not include persons who satisfied military obligations in their own country or who were not subjected to military service in their own country. Under the terms of the 1889 law, these persons could decline French citizenship.

79. Assuming that 300,000 young Frenchmen came of military age each year.

80. Mitchell, *Victors and Vanquished*, p. 108. For the budget problem, see also Challener, *The French Theory of the Nation in Arms*. In the 1880s the republican objective of universal three-year service was unrealizable: it "would have inflated the army far beyond the resources of the military budget . . . Although the French birth rate had become stationary and demographers were already pointing out that Germany's population would soon be far superior

to that of France, there were still too many young men available for induction each year for a three-year system to be established without upsetting the budget. Furthermore . . . the size of the German army at this time did not appear to warrant any great peacetime expansion of French forces . . . A considerable portion of every military debate concerned various attempts to solve the problem of an excess number of conscripts and to establish some system of exemptions which would do the least violence to egalitarian principles." The problem was eventually solved only by reducing the length of service to two years in 1905 and by the decreasing size of annual cohorts. "Thereafter, as European tensions mounted and the Germans began to conscript more men from their larger population, the French problem became not a surplus but a deficiency of potential soldiers" (Challener, *The French Theory of the Nation in Arms*, pp. 54–55).

81. CD 3904; C2, 594b.
82. The parliamentary careers of the military recruitment and citizenship legislation developed in tandem throughout the middle and late 1880s; the bills were approved within two weeks of one another in the summer of 1889. The close connection between the two reforms, both driven by intransigent Republican egalitarianism, is evident in the intertwining of the two debates. Debates on citizenship were punctuated with references to the imminent conscription reform, and debates on conscription occasioned references to the exemption of foreigners from military service and proposals to abolish it by redefining long-settled foreigners as French. In 1884, for example, during debate on a recruitment bill, the deputy Maxime Lecomte proposed an amendment defining as French, and thereby subjecting to military service, all persons born in France of foreign parents. Although it was received sympathetically, the amendment was rejected for the technical reason that a provision on citizenship was out of place in a law on recruitment (C2, 594a).
83. Monteilhet notes that legislative politics of recruitment between 1875 and 1905 pivoted on a question "plus politique et sociale que militaire" (*Les institutions militaires*, pp. 218–219). This is amply confirmed in Challener, *The French Theory of the Nation in Arms*, chap. 2. Militant Republicans, he notes, verged on a "purely moral" approach to military recruitment; "equal service for all was a 'cause'" (p. 58).
84. Challener, *The French Theory of the Nation in Arms*, pp. 58–59. "Split contingent": for budgetary reasons, the annual conscripted contingent had long been divided by lottery into two parts, only one of which was required to perform the full term of service; the other was either dispensed from service entirely or given only brief training. "One-year volunteers": the well off could "volunteer" for a stint of one year's service by paying 1,500 francs (Weber, *Peasants into Frenchmen*, p. 293).
85. C2, 595a
86. Milza, "Un siècle d'immigration étrangère," pp. 5–6. Belgium and France, moreover, maintained friendly relations, while Italy was viewed as a potential enemy (ibid.). In 1886 Belgians comprised 43 percent, Italians 24 percent of the 1.1 million foreigners in France. All foreigners together comprised 3 percent of the French population (Recensement Général, *Les étrangers*, p. 17).
87. C2, 595a

88. Quoted in Schnapper and Leveau, "Religion et politique: juifs et musulmans maghrébins en France," p. 3.
89. CD 2083, 34
90. This comparison, setting the 225,000 French against 210,000 "étrangers européens," excludes the 3.3 million "indigènes" (S2, 79a).
91. CD 1490, 265c.
92. On the "nation in arms," see Monteilhet, Les institutions militaires, chap. 5; and Challener, The French Theory of the Nation in Arms. "Tribute exacted by an oppressive and alien state": Weber, Peasants into Frenchmen, p. 295. Weber shows that the "nation in arms" was not simply a military theory but an emergent social reality in the late nineteenth century. In the 1870s, there was "little sense of national identity to mitigate the hostility and fear most country people felt for troops" (p. 297). But the war with Prussia "marked the beginning of change" (p. 298), and its "role . . . in promoting national awareness was reinforced by educational propaganda, by developing trade and commercial ties, and finally by something approaching universal service. By the 1890s there is pervasive evidence that the army was no longer 'theirs' but 'ours.' Ill feelings between troops and civilians were countered by the sense of nationality being learned in the school, and in the barracks too. At least for a while, the army could become what its enthusiasts hoped for: the school of the fatherland" (p. 298).
93. Schor, L'opinion française et les étrangers, pp. 529f.
94. CD 2083, 232b.
95. C2, 594a.
96. S1, 1186b.
97. On Republican school reforms, see Ozouf, "L'école, l'église et la République"; Gontard, "L'oeuvre scolaire de la troisième République."
98. See Azéma and Winock, La IIIe République, chapter on "Le ciment idéologique"; Girardet, Le nationalisme français, pp. 28–30; Weber, Peasants into Frenchmen, p. 336.
99. Ferry, quoted in Mayeur and Rebérioux, The Third Republic, p. 84.
100. Paul Bert, quoted in Azéma and Winock, La IIIe République, p. 149.
101. According to Nora, the Lavisse textbooks were "practically unrivaled in public education" and enjoyed a "quasi-monopoly" for decades ("Lavisse, Instituteur national," p. 267).
102. Weber, Peasants into Frenchmen, pp. 95–96, 332–336, 486. Ernest Lavisse's first-year history manual was praised by Ferdinand Buisson, collaborator of Ferry and director of primary education, as "le petit livre d'histoire vraiment national et vraiment libéral que nous demandions pour être un instrument d'éducation, voire même d'éducation morale" (Nora, "Lavisse, Instituteur national," p. 265, my italics). Bruno's Tour de France of 1877 had sold 8 million copies by 1900. Love of France is its leitmotif; its last words are "duty and fatherland" (Weber, Peasants into Frenchmen, p. 335). In general, the Republican schools "instilled a national view of things in regional minds" (ibid., p. 486). One component of this newly national perspective on the world was a new understanding of one's pays (which was previously a local or regional concept) and a new understanding of the concept of "foreigner"

(which was still used, in the mid-nineteenth century, to refer to persons from another region) (ibid., pp. 96, 98, 99).

103. CD 1490, 266b.
104. Nora, "Lavisse, Instituteur national," p. 267; Weber, *Peasants into Frenchmen,* pp. 298–299.
105. Weber, *Peasants into Frenchmen,* p. 294.
106. CD 3904.
107. CD 1490, 266.
108. Azéma and Winock, *La IIIe République,* p. 149.
109. Weber stresses the "making similar": as a result of improved communications caused by roads and railroads, a generation of Republican schooling, and universal military service, "variations in language and behavior were significantly less . . . the regions of France were vastly more alike in 1910 than they had been before Jules Ferry, before Charles Freycinet" [who was responsible for the conscription law of 1889] (*Peasants into Frenchmen,* p. 494).
110. SD 160, 283b.
111. Monteilhet, *Les institutions militaries,* pp. 226–230.
112. SD 160, 283b-c.
113. SD 160, 283b.
114. Ibid.
115. Ibid.
116. S2, 81a.
117. These reforms too were generally expansive. The 1927 reform dramatically facilitated naturalization; permitted a French woman marrying a foreign man to retain French citizenship; and assigned French citizenship to children of such a marriage, provided they were born in France. The 1945 reform assigned French citizenship to all children born of a French mother or a French father, regardless of birthplace. The 1973 reform gave the spouse of a French citizen, male or female, the right to acquire French citizenship by declaration. For the legal texts, see *La nationalité française: Textes et Documents.*
118. I refer here only to expansiveness with respect to the citizenship status of long-established immigrants, particularly those who have grown up in France. French naturalization policy vis-à-vis recent immigrants, and the rhetoric that has accompanied and informed this policy, has been more restrictive (although, compared to German naturalization policy, French naturalization policy has been quite liberal).
119. The quotations are from S2, 81a; C2, 594b; S1, 1186b; CD 3904; and SD 160, 283c.
120. A 1940 law required the administrative review of all naturalizations granted since the liberal law of 1927 was enacted. Some 15,000 persons—3 percent of the total number naturalized between 1927 and 1940— were stripped of their citizenship under these proceedings, among them 6,000 Jews. Jews were disproportionately touched by the denaturalization proceedings; some—perhaps a thousand—were deported as a direct result of their denaturalization (Marrus and Paxton, *Vichy France and the Jews,* p. 4; Laguerre, "Les dénaturalisations de Vichy," pp. 11–14).

121. The quoted phrases are from S1, 1182c, and S2, 80c.
122. To borrow the title of the book by George Mosse.
123. These included not only exemption from military service but the consequent unfair advantage enjoyed by foreigners in the labor market and, some claimed, even on the marriage market (C2, 594c).
124. Le Gallou and Jalkh, *Etre français cela se mérite*, pp. 101, 110.
125. Hoffmann, "The Nation: What For?" p. 409.

6. *The Citizenry as Community of Descent: The Nationalization of Citizenship in Wilhelmine Germany*

1. Nadelhoffer, "Einfluss familienrechtlicher Verhältnisse auf die Erwerbung und den Verlust der Reichs- und Staatsangehörigkeit," p. 293.
2. The older understanding, that prolonged residence generated membership, was expressed in the maxim *"domicilium facit subditum"* (domicile makes one a subject). The Prussian citizenship law of 1842, as we have seen in Chapter 3, broke with this tradition, specifying that domicile alone did not make one a subject.
3. Only the voluntary acquisition of another citizenship entailed the loss of German citizenship. Children of German parents born in North or South America, for example, to whom an American citizenship was attributed *jure soli*, would not thereby lose their German citizenship. And even persons naturalizing voluntarily might obtain permission to retain their German citizenship. Nonetheless, the new law fell short of the extreme nationalist demand that German citizenship never be lost, at least never against the will of a citizen (for the government's rejection of this demand, see SB 13 I 13: 250D–251A).
4. Secs. 9, 11, 13, and 31 of the law of 1913. This law is printed along with commentary in Lichter, *Die Staatsangehörigkeit*, pp. 50f.
5. League Constitution, quoted in Wertheimer, *The Pan-German League*, p. 229.
6. Resolutions of the Pan-Germanist Conference in Berlin, September 9, 1894, printed in the *Flugschriften des Alldeutschen Verbands*, no. 14, 1902, pp. 6–8, 39–41.
7. A 9 III 36.
8. For a thorough and consistent articulation of that outlook, see Hasse, *Das Deutsche Reich als Nationalstaat*.
9. In 1894, when Hasse first introduced his legislative proposals, the third great wave of overseas emigration was just ending. Thus while Hasse cited an outflow of 100,000 per year, emigration from then on averaged about 30,000 per year (Bade, "Die Deutsche überseeische Massenauswanderung," p. 264).
10. Foreigners from the point of view of language and race.
11. This account is based chiefly on Hasse's speech to the Reichstag on March 6, 1895, pp. 1277–1280, and secondarily on other Reichstag speeches (SB 9 II 42 [Feb. 6, 1894]: 1028D–1029C; SB 10 II 33 [Jan. 25, 1901]: 891C; SB 10 II 262 [Feb. 19, 1903]: 8047A), and on two more reflective works, *Das Deutsche Reich als Nationalstaat* and *Die Besiedlung des deutschen Volksboden*, esp. pp. 127–141.
12. These included the German Colonial Society (Weiss, "Erwerb und Verlust,"

p. 837) and the German School Association (Bell, "Geschichte," pp. 198–199).

13. For a survey of the legal literature, see Weiss, "Erwerb und Verlust."

14. Ibid., p. 838.

15. Thus Herzog of the Wirtschaftliche Vereinigung at SB 13 I 14: 274C-275D; von Liebert of the Reichspartei at SB 13 I 14: 271C; Giese of the Conservatives at SB 13 I 153: 5282A–5283A.

16. See the speech by Reichspartei deputy von Liebert at SB 13 I 14: 271C-D, which illustrates the "peculiar mix of völkisch and imperial goals" characteristic of the last decades of the *Reich* (Schieder, *Das Deutsche Kaiserreich von 1871 als Nationalstaat*, p. 50, following Hannah Arendt).

17. The following account is based largely on the speech by Delbrück at SB 13 I 13: 250 C-D.

18. See also von Liebert, SB 13 I 14: 271D.

19. Delbrück, SB 13 I 13: 250 C-D.

20. Ibid.; see also von Liebert, SB 13 I 14: 271D.

21. For the National Liberals, see SB 13 I 13: 260D; for the Center Party, SB 13 I 153: 5275D; for the government, A 13 I 6: 15, 19.

22. Thus National-Liberal deputy Beck at SB 13 I 13: 261B.

23. This was not generally true of German citizenship law, which, like the law of all other European states at the time, restricted the transmission of citizenship *jure soli* to paternal filiation, in order to minimize dual citizenship. Here however, the net was cast as wide as possible. See von Keller and Trautman, *Kommentar*, p. 161.

24. Like foreigners, that is, they could be naturalized at the discretion of the state without having a legal right to that naturalization.

25. A 13 I 6: 23, zu §9.

26. Hasse too was a National Liberal, but he was far more radically nationalist than his party. With respect to Hasse's demands in the Reichstag for state intervention on behalf of Hungarian Germans, the party explicitly indicated that Hasse did not speak for it (Schieder, *Das Deutsche Kaiserreich von 1871 als Nationalstaat*, p. 52). Yet there was an ethnonational strand in the arguments even of mainstream National Liberals such as Beck and von Richthofen—notwithstanding their criticisms of the restrictive Prussian naturalization policy toward Jews.

27. SB 13 I 14: 283D-284A.

28. Herbert, *Geschichte der Ausländerbeschäftigung*, p. 25.

29. For an estimate of the size of the emigrant population, see "Die Deutschen im Ausland und die Ausländer im Deutschen Reich," pp. 3*–4*.

30. It was hoped that some might eventually return to Germany, but citizenship was not made contingent on return.

31. The 1913 law did make citizenship less accessible to immigrants in other respects. Under the 1870 law the individual German states had almost complete autonomy in naturalization. Only persons meeting certain minimum conditions were eligible for naturalization; otherwise the states were free to grant or refuse citizenship as they pleased. Prussia demanded that this autonomy be abridged. For decades, it had pursued a restrictive naturalization policy toward Jews and Poles (Neubach, *Ausweisungen*, pp. 3, 4, 13, 17,

30, 41, 110; Wertheimer, *Unwelcome Strangers*, pp. 45–47, 54–60). Concerned that persons denied naturalization in Prussia might be naturalized in another German state, and then return to Prussia as legally protected citizens of the Reich, it demanded that it (or any other state) have the opportunity to express reservations about naturalization candidates in other states. Should a state raise such reservations, the matter would be decided by the Bundesrat or Federal Council, in which Prussia occupied a commanding position. This provision was bitterly contested by the Social Democrats in the Reichstag on the grounds that it would permit Prussia to impose its own restrictive naturalization policy on the other states of the Empire (SB 13 I 153: 5274A; SB 13 I 169: 5762A). Other parties too criticized Prussian naturalization policy, but their concerns about this provision were alleviated by (1) the inclusion of a clause limiting reservations to matters "justifying the concern that the naturalization of the candidate would endanger the well-being of the Reich or one of its constituent states," and (2) a formal assurance by Prussia that religion had not been and would not be taken into account in naturalization decisions (SB 13 I 153: 5285C-D; SB 13 I 169: 5764C-D). That the latter was patently contradicted by the facts, and the former an empty phrase, did not dissuade the Reichstag from approving the new provision. It is impossible to estimate its effect, for the war, the creation of an independent Polish state, and postwar economic dislocation drastically reduced the number of foreigners in Germany, so that no comparison with the Wilhelmine period is possible. It seems certain, though, that the new measure had a restrictive effect. Wertheimer notes that in Weimar Germany, "anti-semitic governments in Bavaria and Hamburg vetoed the naturalization of Eastern Jews (and also Christian Poles) who had applied for citizenship in the then far more liberal Prussia on the grounds that the applicants were 'culturally alien Eastern foreigners'" (*Unwelcome Strangers*, p. 59). For present purposes, however, this change in the law is less significant than the continued insistence on pure *jus sanguinis* and the rejection of all elements of *jus soli*.

32. Grawert, *Staat und Staatsangehörigkeit*, pp. 190–192, 203.

33. A 13 I 962: 1428, Nos. 1 and 3; SB 13 I 154: 5299D; A 13 I 962: 1452. As in most European countries at the time, the woman automatically took her husband's citizenship at marriage. Thus children born in Germany of a foreign father and a German mother were not German citizens.

34. SB 13 I 169: 5768D.

35. SB 13 I 153: 5273A; SB 13 I 169: 5761B; SB 13 I 169: 5769D.

36. The "government" means the federal government, on the one hand, the representatives of the state governments, dominated by Prussia, on the other.

37. A 13 I 962: 1430, 1452, 1453; SB 13 I 154: 5303D-5304A; SB 13 I 169: 5763D-5764A.

38. A 13 I 962: 1430.

39. SB 13 I 169: 5764A.

40. A 13 I 962: 1415. In this instance, the legislative committee rejected the government argument and excised the superfluous phrase.

41. "That state" means that individual German state within the Empire. The citizenship law of the Empire, like its constitutional structure, was federal:

imperial citizenship derived from citizenship of a particular state. Yet while states retained some autonomy in naturalization, they had none in the attribution of citizenship. Even as early as 1870, there were uniform attribution rules.

42. A 13 I 962: 1416.
43. Von Keller and Trautman, *Kommentar*, p. 64.
44. Makarov, *Allgemeine Lehren*, p. 336.
45. A 13 I 962: 1453.
46. SB 13 I 154: 5318.
47. Grawert, *Staat und Staatsangehörigkeit*, pp. 190–191.
48. Ibid., p. 203.
49. Herbert, *Geschichte der Ausländerbeschäftigung*, p. 25.
50. Bade, "Die Deutsche überseeische Massenauswanderung," p. 269.
51. Bade, "Vom Auswanderungsland zum 'Arbeitseinfuhrland,'" pp. 434ff., 443.
52. Because the census was taken in December, this figure does not include several hundred thousand seasonal workers who were required by law to return home during the winter months (Herbert, *Geschichte der Ausländerbeschäftigung*, pp. 24–25).
53. The native-born fraction of the foreign population in 1910 is not known, but in 1900 some 28 percent of all foreigners (222,000 out of 779,000) were born in Germany ("Die Deutschen im Ausland und die Ausländer im Deutschen Reich," p. 50). As a result of heavy immigration during the next decade, this fraction was probably lower in 1910, but the absolute number of native-born foreigners probably increased substantially.
54. Laband, *Das Staatsrecht des deutschen Reiches*, pp. 180–181; Cahn, "Zur Reform," pp. 21–22; von Martitz, "Das Recht der Staatsangehörigkeit," pp. 1119–1122, 1145–1146; Lehmann, "Die deutsche Reichsangehörigkeit," pp. 798–809; Ratjen, *Kampf um die Reichsangehörigkeit*, pp. 47–58. While proponents of limited *jus soli* cited numerous authorities on their behalf, opponents cited none. It appears as though authorities on public law were generally agreed on the desirability of introducing elements of *jus soli*.
55. SB 13 I 153: 5282B; for a similar statement, also presumably by Giese, in the discussions of the legislative commission that worked over the proposal, see A 13 I 962: 1429.
56. *Kleindeutsch:* "Small-German," a term opposed to *grossdeutsch* (great-German) and referring to the exclusion of Austro-Germans from the Bismarckian state.
57. Hasse, *Das Deutsche Reich als Nationalstaat.* Hasse tried to quantify the ethnonational imperfection of the Reich, claiming on the one hand that its population was only 92 percent German (the "non-German" 8 percent including German-speaking Jews as well as linguistic minorities), and on the other that it included only 68 percent of European Germandom (p. 4). For him, a true nation-state must include either all Germans or only Germans. The Reich, in his view, could not claim to be a nation-state; it was merely a territorial state (p. 49).
58. Neither, it should be noted, existed in France, where the conditions for ethnonational politics were absent. Bretons may have resisted the assimila-

tionist policies of the Third Republic, but they were not a *national* minority like the Poles in Eastern Prussia.

59. The German School Association—from 1908 on called the Association for Germandom Abroad—aimed, according to its statutes, to "preserve Germans outside the Reich for Germandom." ("German" here had an ethnocultural, not a legal meaning.) The association pursued this end by supporting German schools and libraries abroad, providing them with German books and German teachers. For a history, from within, of the association, see Bell, "Geschichte des Vereins für das Deutschtum im Ausland," esp. pp. 163–201.

60. Hasse, *Das Deutsche Reich als Nationalstaat*, pp. 1–4.

61. Schieder, *Das Deutsche Kaiserreich von 1871 als Nationalstaat*, pp. 39–54.

62. Ibid., esp. pp. 40ff.; Kocka, "Probleme der politischen Integration der Deutschen."

63. For the national question in other zones of ethnopolitical concern, North Schleswig and Alsace-Lorraine, see Hauser, "Polen und Dänen," pp. 309–317, and Wehler, "Das 'Reichsland' Elsass-Lothringen von 1870 bis 1918," esp. pp. 57–62.

64. For convenience, I will use this German word for Prussian and German policies and politics toward the ethnically Polish citizens of the Reich.

65. Quoted in Schieder, *Das Deutsche Kaiserreich von 1871 als Nationalstaat*, p. 19. As Schieder points out, Bismarck's response was disingenuous. The Poles had accepted—at least provisionally—incorporation in the *Prussian* state, but protested against incorporation into the new *German* state.

66. Schieder, *Das Deutsche Kaiserreich von 1871 als Nationalstaat*, p. 29. Schieder's emphasis on the strength of state-national consciousness in Imperial Germany is a useful corrective to earlier interpretations stressing the continuity in *völkisch* thought and practice from Herder through Hitler (p. 39).

67. The Polish *szlachta* was an unusually numerous nobility, comprising about a tenth of the population, and a substantially higher fraction of the Polish-speaking population, in the early modern era (Anderson, *Lineages of the Absolutist State*, pp. 283–284; Hausmann, "Adelsgesellschaft und nationale Bewegung in Polen," pp. 23, 44 n. 1). By the nineteenth century, to be sure, the *szlachta* was no longer nearly so numerous (pp. 25, 38–39). The impoverished petty nobility lost its noble status in the late eighteenth and early nineteenth centuries, in part because the partitioning powers refused to recognize it. But these ex-nobles, too, remained important carriers of Polish nationalist strivings (ibid., p. 39). The size of the nobility up to the late eighteenth century, coupled with the peculiar Polish political tradition of the aristocratic Republic, provided a strong social base for postpartition Polish nationalism.

68. Conze, "Nationsbildung durch Trennung," esp. pp. 105ff.

69. Wehler, "Polenpolitik," pp. 193ff.

70. Hauser, "Nationalisierung Preussens."

71. Ibid.; Hauser, "Polen und Dänen," esp. pp. 291, 299ff.; Broszat, *Zweihundert Jahre deutsche Polenpolitik*, esp. pp. 127–128, 135–136, 142–147, 156–157.

72. Rothfels, "Bimarck und der Osten"; Schieder, *Das Deutsche Kaiserreich von 1871 als Nationalstaat*, pp. 22–26.

73. For Bismarck's reserved and thoroughly statist posture vis-a-vis Baltic Germans, in the face of Russification campaigns in that region, see Rothfels, "Bimarck und der Osten," pp. 34–44; and for his relations to Germans in the Dual Monarchy, pp. 44–68.
74. Schieder, *Das Deutsche Kaiserreich von 1871 als Nationalstaat*, pp. 23–24, 42–43; Kocka, "Political Integration," p. 130; Rothfels, "Bimarck und der Osten," pp. 34–35.
75. Bismarck's Memoirs, quoted in Blanke, *Prussian Poland in the German Empire*, p. 17; see also Hagen, *Germans, Poles, and Jews*, p. 347 n. 36.
76. Wehler, *Das Deutsche Kaiserreich*, pp. 96–97. On "negative integration," see also Sauer, "Das Problem des Deutschen Nationalstaates," p. 180, who calls it "secondary integration," and Roth, *The Social Democrats in Imperial Germany*.
77. Blanke, *Prussian Poland in the German Empire*, pp. 17–37; Broszat, *Zweihundert Jahre deutsche Polenpolitik*, pp. 134–142; Hagen, *Germans, Poles, and Jews*, pp. 128–131.
78. Neubach, *Ausweisungen*, p. 4.
79. On school and language politics in the Prussian east, see Blanke, *Prussian Poland in the German Empire*, pp. 18–24; Broszat, *Zweihundert Jahre deutsche Polenpolitik*, pp. 134–135, 138–139; Hagen, *Germans, Poles, and Jews*, pp. 129–130; Hauser, "Polen und Dänen," pp. 301–302.
80. Schieder, *Das Deutsche Kaiserreich von 1871 als Nationalstaat*, p. 25.
81. Hagen, *Germans, Poles, and Jews*, pp. 127–128.
82. Hauser, "Polen und Dänen," p. 302; see also Hauser, "Nationalisierung Preussens."
83. Broszat, *Zweihundert Jahre deutsche Polenpolitik*, pp. 124–128; Schieder, *Das Deutsche Kaiserreich von 1871 als Nationalstaat*, pp. 17–20; Blanke, *Prussian Poland in the German Empire*, pp. 12–13, 17ff.; Hagen, *Germans, Poles, and Jews*, pp. 127ff.; Conze, "Nationsbildung durch Trennung," p. 96.
84. Hagen, *Germans, Poles, and Jews*, pp. 59–61, 90, 120–121; the quotation is from p. 59.
85. Hagen, *Germans, Poles, and Jews*, p. 120.
86. Quoted in Schieder, *Das Deutsche Kaiserreich von 1871 als Nationalstaat*, pp. 19, 20. Poznan, East Prussia, and West Prussia, although part of the Prussian state, had not belonged to the German Confederation between 1815 and 1866.
87. There was perhaps some basis for this hope in 1871, when the Polish Reichstag deputation was composed exclusively of wealthy landowners. But by 1912 the "great majority [of Polish Reichstag deputies] were editors, physicians, lawyers, priests, trade union leaders, etc." (Tims, *Germanizing Prussian Poland*, p. 189n.). Middle-class nationalism had emancipated itself from aristocratic sponsorship.
88. A hundred million marks were committed initially, rising over the next three decades to a total of about a billion marks (Wehler, "Polenpolitik," p. 191).
89. And to the Junkers, it meant financial rescue, for most of the money was eventually spent on the purchase of German, not Polish, estates. See Wehler, "Polenpolitik," p. 191; Tims, *Germanizing Prussian Poland*, p. 112.
90. Broszat, *Zweihundert Jahre deutsche Polenpolitik*, pp. 143, 157; Blanke, *Prussian*

Poland in the German Empire, p. 60; Wehler, *Sozialdemokratie und Nationalstaat,* p. 118.

91. Eley, "German Politics and Polish Nationality," pp. 349–355; Hagen, *Germans, Poles, and Jews,* pp.136–150, 231–265; Blanke, *Prussian Poland in the German Empire,* pp. 93–119, 147–175, 209–238.

92. Bökch, "Die Verschiebung der Sprachverhältnisse in Posen und Westpreussen."

93. Quoted by Wehler, "Polenpolitik," p. 192.

94. More than 30,000 Poles and Jews with Russian and Austrian citizenship were expelled in the operation, which was not completed until 1887. My account is based on Neubach, *Ausweisungen,* a thorough study of the expulsions and the reaction to them in Germany and abroad. See also Bade, "'Kulturkampf' auf dem Arbeitsmarkt," pp. 125–133.

95. Bismarck conceded that "many useful and nonpartisan workers were included among the expellees" (quoted by Neubach, *Ausweisungen,* p. 108).

96. Quoted in Neubach, *Ausweisungen,* pp. 32, 109.

97. Wehler, "Polenpolitik," p. 192.

98. Tims, *Germanizing Prussian Poland,* pp. 152–154.

99. Wehler, "Polenpolitik," p. 193.

100. Tims, *Germanizing Prussian Poland,* pp. 151–188; Wehler, "Polenpolitik," pp. 194–195.

101. Wehler, "Polenpolitik," p. 195.

102. Herbert, *Geschichte der Ausländerbeschäftigung,* pp. 18–19; Dohse, *Ausländische Arbeiter und bürgerlicher Staat,* p. 30. Bismarck anticipated and rejected such protests even before ordering the expulsions. Against the warning of Interior Minister Puttkammer that mass expulsions would entail "fateful disadvantages" for agrarian interests, Bismarck wrote that "scattered shortages" were "the lesser evil" than "endangering the state and its future" (quoted in Neubach, *Ausweisungen,* pp. 31–32).

103. Nichtweiss, *Die ausländische Saisonarbeiter,* pp. 27–43; Herbert, *Geschichte der Ausländerbeschäftigung,* pp. 18–24; Dohse, *Ausländische Arbeiter und bürgerlicher Staat,* pp. 33–34; Bade, "'Kulturkampf' auf dem Arbeitsmarkt," pp. 137–142; Bade, "Preussengänger," pp. 112–121. The obligatory winter return, according to an internal administrative memorandum, was "the only means of making clear again and again to foreign workers and also to the native population that they [foreign workers] are only tolerated aliens [*Fremdlinge*] and that their permanent settlement is out of the question" (quoted in Bade, "Politik und Ökonomie," p. 284).

104. M. Weber, "Die ländliche Arbeitsverfassung," p. 449; Herbert, *Geschichte der Ausländerbeschäftigung,* p. 19; Nichtweiss, *Die ausländische Saisonarbeiter.*

105. Weber, "Die ländliche Arbeitsverfassung," pp. 456–458.

106. Herbert, *Geschichte der Ausländerbeschäftigung,* p. 28. The Prussian bureaucracy attempted in the last two decades before the war, without much success, to replace Poles with foreigners who were less objectionable from the nationalist point of view (Dohse, *Ausländische Arbeiter und bürgerlicher Staat,* p. 37).

107. Bade, ed., "Arbeiterstatistik," p. 270.

108. Ibid., pp. 256–270.

109. Ibid., p. 164.
110. Herbert, *Geschichte der Ausländerbeschäftigung*, pp. 28, 48.
111. For the way in which Prussian immigration policy was shaped by the larger concerns of Prussian *Polenpolitik*, see Bade, "Preussengänger," pp. 112–121.
112. The close connection between immigration policy and *Polenpolitik* was most dramatically expressed in the mass expulsions of immigrant Poles and Jews in 1885, and in the two-day debate about these expulsions in the Prussian Landtag in January 1886. In the course of that debate, Christoph von Tiedemann, governor of the Bromberg district of Poznan, explicitly invoked the "thousand-year struggle for dominance between Germans and Poles in the land between the Elbe and the Weichsel" (quoted in Neubach, *Ausweisungen*, pp. 110–111).
113. Neubach, *Ausweisungen*, pp. 13, 17, 30.
114. Wertheimer, *Unwelcome Strangers*, p. 55.
115. Ibid., pp. 17, 45–47, 53, 54–60. Reporting an Interior Ministry ruling of 1890, Wertheimer summarizes Prussian policies as follows. Even the "sons of Poles and Russian Jewish immigrants who had lived in the country for a long period of time (i.e. since the expulsions of the mid-1880s) could be considered for naturalization only when they reached the age of military duty and only if they were fit for army service. Those young men deemed unfit were not entitled to receive citizenship, any more than were daughters of Jewish immigrants. At the beginning of the next decade, the minister also ruled that Christian converts of Jewish ancestry needed special approval. In summing up Prussian naturalization policies . . . [in Wilhelmine Germany], the following statement of policy enunciated to the cabinet by Bethmann-Hollweg, [then] minister of interior, provides an apt generalization: 'the naturalization of immigrant Jews is banned by administrative policies; it is possible for the children of immigrants to acquire citizenship only if they were born in Germany, are militarily fit, and are found unobjectionable by the central authorities.' Exceptions were made in general only 'when a particular state, economic, or communal interest can be served by the naturalization of an individual'" (p. 55).
116. Quoted in ibid., p. 58; my italics.
117. SB 13 I 154: 5304 AB.
118. SB 13 I 154: 5303C-5304A.
119. For the conservative-nationalist perspective, see the remarks by Herzog of the Wirtschaftliche Vereinigung at SB 13 I 14: 275A-D and SB 13 I 153: 5288D.
120. For the National Liberals, see the remarks of von Richthofen at SB 13 I 154: 5311C-D.
121. Belzer, SB 13 I 153: 5276C.
122. SB 13 I 169: 5763C-5764A.

7. *"Etre Français, Cela Se Mérite": Immigration and the Politics of Citizenship in France in the 1980s*

1. The legal details have been changed on several occasions, but the basic principle has remained the same. It no longer suffices, for the automatic acquisition of French citizenship, to be born in France and domiciled there

at majority. In 1927 persons who had been ordered expelled from the territory were excluded (Art. 4, Loi du 10 août 1927 sur la nationalité). In 1945 five years' residence was added as a precondition, and the state was permitted to oppose automatic acquisition for indignity, lack of assimilation, or grave physical or mental defect (Arts. 44 and 46, Ordonnance no. 45–2441 du 19 octobre 1945 portant code de la nationalité française). In 1973 persons having been condemned to prison for certain crimes were excluded (Art. 79, Code de la nationalité française, rédaction de la loi no. 73–42 du 9 janvier 1973). Besides these restrictions, there have also been liberalizations. In 1927 a person born and domiciled in France could "claim French citizenship" before attaining legal majority with the authorization of his parents (after the age of sixteen) or by parental declaration on his or her behalf before the age of sixteen (Art. 3., Loi du 10 août 1927 sur la nationalité). This provision survives today. About 5,000 such declarations were made annually between 1983 and 1987; the number jumped to over 9,500 in 1988 and 1989 (Lebon, "Attribution, acquisition et perte de la nationalité française," p. 15; Sous-direction des naturalisations, annual reports for 1987, 1988, and 1989). Current and former legal texts governing citizenship are collected in *La nationalité française: Texts et documents*. The provisions referred to above are found on pp. 74, 96, 28, and 73.

2. No other Continental state but Portugal automatically transforms second-generation immigrants into citizens.

3. This slogan was also the title of a polemical book by Jean-Yves Le Gallou and Jean-François Jalkh.

4. Jacques Toubon, General Secretary of the Gaullist *Rassemblement pour la République* (RPR), quoted in *Le Monde*, November 5, 1986.

5. For essayistic discussions of this debate, see Krulic, "L'immigration et l'identité de la France"; Costa-Lascoux, "Nationaux, mais pas vraiment citoyens"; Pinto, "L'immigration: l'ambiguité de la référence américaine"; Feldblum, "The Politicization of Citizenship."

6. During the debate on citizenship law, there was virtually no mention of Portuguese immigrants, although they comprise the largest group of foreign citizens in France.

7. This point was obscured during the debate of 1986–87, during which the left vehemently criticized the citizenship law reform proposed by the Chirac government. One of the few observers to note the reversal of positions was Costa-Lascoux, "L'acquisition de la nationalité française," p. 82. When the issue was first raised, it should be emphasized, it concerned the anomalous situation of second-generation Algerian immigrants, not second-generation immigrants in general.

8. Gillette and Sayad, *L'immigration algérienne en France*; Ageron, "L'immigration maghrébine en France."

9. Figures on wartime service: Meynier, "Les soldats algériens durant la guerre 14–18," pp. 38–43; Gillette and Sayad, *L'immigration algérienne*, p. 50; Lequin, "L'invasion pacifique," p. 344.

10. Ageron, "L'immigration maghrébine," pp. 65–66; Recensement Général, *Les étrangers*, p. 20.

11. For the Algerian immigrant community in France, there was no material incentive to choose French citizenship, for the Evian Agreement of 1962 guaranteed freedom of movement between France and Algeria. This, however, was included in the agreement mainly to protect Europeans in Algeria, far more numerous at the moment of independence than Algerians in France. Once the European community had fled, France no longer had an interest in free movement, and the Evian accords were renegotiated. See Gillette and Sayad, *L'immigration algérienne*, pp. 90ff.; Leveau and de Wenden, "Evolution des attitude politiques des immigrés maghrébins," pp. 74–75.

12. "A child born in France, whether legitimate or natural, is French when at least one parent was also born there." Article 23, Code de la nationalité française, rédaction de la loi no. 73–42 du 9 janvier 1973, reprinted in *La nationalité française*, p. 24.

13. Article 23 affects children born in France *after* independence to parents born in Algeria *before* independence. Most children born in metropolitan France *before* independence became Algerian along with their parents when their parents opted for Algerian citizenship upon Algerian independence. Yet because of the timing of Algerian immigration to France, the surge in births to Algerian parents—more than 10,000 per year since 1964, more than 15,000 per year since 1967—occurred *after* independence. (For figures on births in France to Algerian parents, see Jean, "Combien sont-ils?" p. 258.) Beginning in 1963, these French-born children of Algerian parents were defined at birth as French citizens. Today, however, an increasing fraction of births in France to Algerian parents is to parents who were born in *post*independence Algeria. Since these parents do not count as having been born "in France," Article 23 does not apply to their French-born children. If those children continue to reside in France, they will become French on attaining legal majority by virtue of Article 44, but they are not defined as French at birth. Almost all of the children of Algerian parents born in France between 1963 and the early 1980s were defined as French at birth; but that fraction has been declining in recent years. By the end of the 1990s the anomalous application of Article 23 to second-generation immigrants will have dwindled to insignificant proportions. Article 23 also concerns second-generation immigrants whose parents were born in French territories of sub-Saharan Africa. But few of these were born in France until recently, while the numbers of Algerians born in France, as we have just seen, were high even in 1960s.

14. Article 45, Code de la nationalité française, rédaction de la loi no. 73–42 du 9 janvier 1973, reprinted in *La nationalité française*, p. 26.

15. For a subtle analysis, see Sayad, "La naturalisation," II, 26ff.

16. Mangin, "Les problèmes de nationalité," p. 268. Cf. Sayad, "La naturalisation," II, 49 n. 60, reporting the reaction of Algerian parents: "How, as an Algerian, could I produce French children!"

17. GISTI (Groupe d'information et de soutien des travailleurs immigrés), "Note sur les jeunes Algériens en France," January 1983, p. 5. In the 1975 census, about 200,000 children under the age of eighteen born in France were counted as Algerians, although most of them—those born since Algerian

independence—were in fact French. In the 1982 census, about 220,000 were thus counted, almost all of whom were in fact French. See Recensement Général, *Les étrangers*, p. 39. The 1982 figure is especially interesting, since this was three years after the Algerian immigrant community—or at least some families within it—became aware of the French nationality of some of the second-generation immigrants.

18. The persons concerned were all Algerian *jure sanguinis* .

19. GISTI, "Note sur les jeunes Algériens en France," January 1983, p. 6. Sayad explores the ambivalence with which many second-generation immigrants experience their dual nationality ("La naturalisation," II, 28, 32, 37).

20. See the following official explanation in response to a written question in the National Assembly: "The administration refuses to authorize the loss of French nationality when the person concerned fails to show an evident will to expatriate himself, notably when he retains familial and professional attachments in France" (Assemblée Nationale, Débats, June 8, 1987, p. 3280, Response to Question no. 19942).

21. Statistics on administrative refusals of demands for release from French citizenship have been published only since 1983. In 1983, 544 of 758 demands were refused (for a refusal rate of 72 percent); in 1984, 2506 out of 2949 demands were refused (85 percent); in 1985, 732 out of 1034 were refused (71 percent); in 1986, 385 out of 872 (44 percent). Most refusals concern "young dual-nationals who wish to lose French nationality while remaining in the national territory" (Lebon, "Attribution, acquisition et perte de la nationalité française," pp. 21–22).

22. "Its immigrants": cf. Gallissot, "L'interrogation continue: minorités et immigration," p. 254.

23. Mangin, "Le statut des jeunes Algériens nés en France depuis l'indépendance," p. 23. Cf. Sayad, "La naturalisation," II, 26: by "refusing to accept the automatic 'naturalization' of its 'children' (of its 'naturals') and refusing the affront thus made to the integrity of *its* population, . . . and thus to its national integrity, Algeria refuses, in effect to acknowledge, even implicitly and retrospectively, the former colonial order . . . against which it had rebelled."

24. Sayad, "La naturalisation," II, 27.

25. Thus Communist deputy François Asensi proposed to remedy this "aberration" in citizenship law by allowing young Algerians to benefit from the "common law" [Article 44] according to which second-generation immigrants could declare their intention to decline French nationality in the year before attaining legal majority (Assemblée Nationale, Débats, Questions Ecrites, January 18, 1982). GISTI proposed according second-generation Algerian immigrants the right to be released on request from the citizenship attributed to them by virtue of Article 23, even if they wished to continue residing in France (GISTI, "Note sur les jeunes Algériens en France," January 1983, p. 9).

26. Weil, *La France et ses étrangers*, p. 165.

27. Defferre, quoted in *Le Monde*, October 3, 1981.

28. The agreement was signed October 11, 1983, and took effect, after parliamentary ratification, on December 5, 1984. The text is printed in *La nationalité Française*, p. 278.

29. There was some concern in the new Socialist government with the citizenship status of *first*-generation immigrants. On the one hand, the arbitrariness of discretionary naturalization procedures had been a traditional target of the French Left. On the other hand, as a party of government, committed like its predecessors to curbing further immigration, the Socialists were concerned about the way in which certain provisions of French nationality law were being exploited to circumvent restrictions on immigration. Although there was no public discussion of the issue, the Ministry of Social Affairs prepared a reform of citizenship law that would have answered to these two very different concerns, simultaneously liberalizing access to citizenship for long-settled immigrants and restricting it for certain groups of potential immigrants including spouses of citizens, citizens of former colonies residing abroad, and nonresident children of persons naturalized in France (Weil, "La politique française de l'immigration," p. 196). This preliminary proposal, however, was not prepared until 1984. By this time the National Front had emerged as a significant force on the national political scene, and the mainstream right parties, in response, had begun to step up their criticism of government "laxism" on immigration. In their discussions of immigration, both right and far right were paying increasing attention to citizenship. In this increasingly contestatory climate, the government quietly dropped its plans for a reform of citizenship law, for it did not want to provide further ammunition to the opposition by proposing to grant first-generation immigrants a right to naturalization after ten years' residence.

30. In 1985 colloquia on national identity were organized both by the nationalist and vehemently anti-Socialist Club de l'Horloge and by the pro-Socialist Espaces 89; the contributions have been published under the respective titles *L'Identité de la France* and *L'Identité française*. See also "Serons-nous encore français dans 30 ans?," the alarmist article by Jean Raspail featured in the *Figaro Magazine* of October 26, 1985.

31. Why did the Vichy regime review all naturalizations granted since 1927 and invalidate 15,000 of them, yet not attack *jus soli* ? Three reasons can be suggested: (1) The law of 1927 had dramatically liberalized naturalization policy, permitting naturalization after only three years' residence. This occasioned a flood of naturalizations, which in turn galvanized critical attention in a manner that the quiet, anonymous workings of *jus soli* did not. (2) *Jus soli* was less problematic in the interwar period than in the 1980s, for there was nothing comparable then to the anomalous and unconditional attribution of citizenship at birth to second-generation Algerian immigrants as if they were third-generation immigrants. (3) Naturalizations could be rescinded immediately: changing citizenship law of attribution would have only long-term effects. For the politics of citizenship in the interwar period, see Schor, *L'opinion française et les étrangers*, pp. 529–544; and Bonnet, "Les pouvoirs publics français et l'immigration dans l'entre-deux-guerres,"

pp. 150–170. For denaturalizations in Vichy, see Marrus and Paxton, *Vichy France and the Jews,* pp. 4, 16, 56, 323–329; and Laguerre, "Les dénaturalisations de Vichy."

32. In 1971, for example, there were more than 60,000 births in France to couples in which both father and mother were foreign citizens, accounting for 8 percent of all legitimate births (Hémery and Rabut, "La contribution des étrangers à la natalité," p. 1074). Some 18,000 of these, born to Algerian fathers, were defined as French at birth (Jean, "Combien sont-ils?" p. 258); the rest would become French automatically if they remained in France.

33. See, for example, the report on the citizenship bill by the Commission of Laws of the National Assembly, headed by Gaullist deputy Jean Foyer, arguing for reducing the residence required for naturalization from five to three years: "Despite an improvement in its demography between 1946 and 1964, France, like its neighbors, is and will remain a country of immigration. Just as Romans of the fifth century refused to serve in the imperial legions, so Europeans of the late twentieth century refuse to carry out difficult and dirty tasks. Now as then, immigration is a necessity . . . Those immigrants who do not intend to return [to their country of origin] will have to integrate themselves into our national community. Our revised law of nationality will enable them to do this . . . In the course of its long history, France has been a marvelous crucible [*creuset*]. From Gallo-Romans and Germans, it made Frenchmen. The amended text that we propose to you will facilitate this action with persons of other *ethnies*" (Assemblée Nationale, Première session ordinaire de 1972–73, No. 2545, p. 18).

34. On the challenges posed by immigration to norms of nation-statehood, see Brubaker, "Immigration, Citizenship, and the Nation-State in France and Germany," pp. 380–383.

35. Thus *La préférence nationale: réponse à l'immigration,* p. 66. "Those foreigners who cannot or will not become naturalized Frenchmen, in the etymological sense of the term [by which the author means acquiring a French "nature"] are destined to depart sooner or later, except for citizens of EC [European Community] countries."

36. Proebsting, "Eheschliessungen, Ehescheidungen, Geburten und Sterbefälle von Ausländern 1981, p. 60*; Munoz-Perez and Tribalat, "Mariages d'étrangers et mariages mixtes en France," p. 459.

37. The modern notion of allegiance derives from the feudal notion of liege fealty, meaning unconditional or absolute fealty. "There is nothing in feudal theory or practice to prevent a man from having more lords than one. In such a case he owes fealty to both . . . But he can owe *liege* fealty *(ligeantia)* to one only. He can have two lords, but not two liege lords. This was a fundamental maxim of feudalism . . . The fealty which he owes to one of them is not unqualified; it is subject always to the claim of him who is not only his lord, but his liege lord—of him to whom he owes not merely fealty but allegiance. If enmity and war shall arise between two lords, he who is in the faith of each must adhere to him in whose liegeance he is" (Salmond, "Citizenship and Allegiance," p. 51). For traditional arguments against dual citizenship in the context of debates about the citizenship status of immi-

grants, see Hammar, "State, Nation, and Dual Citizenship"; and Darras, "La double nationalité," pp. 401ff., 956.

38. Thus Darras, "La double nationalité," p. 953: "There is nothing in common between a Franco-American dual national . . . and a Moslem possessing against his will French as well as Algerian nationality."

39. There are an estimated one million Franco-Algerian dual nationals (Costa-Lascoux, "Intégration et nationalité, p. 108).

40. Walzer, "The Obligation to Die for the State"; Contamine, "Mourir pour la patrie."

41. Most other interstate accords on this issue encourage the performance of service in the state of residence by specifying that military service is to be performed in that state unless the person concerned formally declares an intention to perform military service in the other country whose citizenship he possesses. The Franco-Algerian accord permits, indeed requires, choice, for it contains no such default specification. For the texts of the Franco-Algerian and other accords, see *La nationalité française: textes et documents,* pp. 278ff.

42. As of 1987, 26 percent of Franco-Algerians born in 1967 had formally declared their intention of performing their military service in Algeria (Service d'information et de relations publiques des armées, "Le service national en chiffres," 1987, p. 19.) It is hard to know how to interpret this statistic. It does not mean that 74 percent have declared their intention of serving in France. In fact, very few have declared their intention of serving in France. At one point, statistics showed that over 90 percent of all declarations indicated the intention of serving in Algeria. Yet although this was seized upon by nationalists, it was wildly misleading. For even though Franco-Algerians are formally obliged to declare where they will serve, very few of those who in fact opt for France have previously declared their intention of doing so (Maurice Faivre, "Le service militaire des doubles-nationaux," *IRIS* No. 1, 1987, p. 35). Compliance with the declaration requirement, in short, is low, at least for those who end up serving in France. The picture is clouded further by the fact that most young Franco-Algerians have taken advantage of their right to postpone military service for a few years. Moreover, Justice Minister Chalandon claimed that there were over 2,000 Franco-Algerians out of compliance with French military requirements in the first half of 1986 (quoted in *L'Évenement du jeudi,* November 20–26, 1986, p. 64). Rates of exemption and dispensation for dual nationals, finally, have been high (over 70 percent) in both countries (Faivre, pp. 35–36). It will be some time before the evidence is sorted out. But the mere fact that significant numbers of Franco-Algerians would choose Algeria while residing in France and enjoying the rights of French citizenship was sufficient to galvanize nationalists. Thus, for example, Pierre Chaunu: "What do 85 percent of the Beurs choose? We give them a passport and a ballot, and they choose to do their national service in Algeria" (interview in *Le Quotidien de Paris,* June 23, 1987).

43. See, for example, Griotteray, *Les immigrés: le choc,* p. 110. See also the parliamentary written question posed by Bruno Chauvierre, noting the fact that certain dual nationals perform military service abroad, and asking the Min-

ister of Justice "what he intends to do so that the young persons in this case [those possessing dual nationality] who perform their national service in another country than France lose French nationality" (written question no. 13888, December 1, 1986, printed along with response in *Journal Officiel,* Assemblée Nationale, January 12, 1987). Even the moderate Albert Chalandon, Justice Minister under Chirac, characterized the decision of a dual national to perform military service in Algeria as a "rejection of France" (*L'Évenement du jeudi,* November 20–26, 1986, p. 64).

44. Quoted in "Culture islamique et attitudes politiques," p. 355; see also pp. 203, 321, 333, 367, 442, 453, 467.

45. Franco-Moroccan, quoted in *L'évenement du jeudi,* November 20–26, 1986, p. 58.

46. Franco-Algerian, twenty years old, quoted in *Libération,* September 4, 1986, p. 26.

47. *Libération,* September 4, 1986, p. 26. The same instrumental view was expressed in a document addressed to young dual nationals who were considering renouncing French citizenship: "You must think carefully before renouncing French nationality. To have two nationalities is to be able to choose the country in which you want to live" ("La nationalité des jeunes Algériens nés en France," reprinted in *Hommes et Migrations,* no. 1030, April 15, 1982, p. 10).

48. As one twenty-five-year-old Algerian secretary put it, young Algerian immigrants who do not have French nationality "don't dare say, 'I'd like to have a French [identity] card,' because they have the impression that this would be to reject their parents, because for Algerians nationality counts a lot, their parents, their uncles, their grandparents who fought during the war . . . If they fought for independence and now, just because it's convenient, the kids opt for the French card, they betray their family" ("Culture islamique et attitudes politiques," p. 467).

49. "Culture islamique et attitudes politiques," p. 467.

50. Sayad, "La naturalisation," II, 28–29.

51. Ibid., pp. 30–31. As Sayad notes elsewhere, this understanding of nationality as a legal and administrative fact and naturalization as a legal and administrative process is one that has to be learned: immigrants from third world countries, he writes, "have not yet assimilated the [legal-] rational, European definition of nationality as a legal abstraction, a fiction" ("Les droits politiques des immigrés," p. 16).

52. That French and Algerian nationality are experienced in terms of distinctive coordinates of reference is consistent with the more general argument of Jean Leca concerning the two axes in terms of which immigrants' perceptions of the "costs" and "benefits" of immigration are organized: "the axis of material [benefits]: (salary, conditions of work and lodging, schooling and professional training, purchasing power), and the axis of communal gratifications (communication, shared style of life, the morale of the reference group, collective identity, the sense of one's own history and territory). France is almost always evaluated negatively on the second axis, . . . Algeria is often evaluated negatively on the first . . . In short, Algerian immigrants seem to

be caught between an economic system (in France) more or less efficient but without cultural legitimation and (in Algeria) a cultural system more or less legitimate but economically weak" (Leca, "Une capacité d'intégration défaillante," pp. 16–17).

53. The pattern variables are outlined by Parsons in *The Social System*, pp. 58–67. Herbert Kelman distinguishes sentimental from instrumental modes of attachment to the nation-state, although he does not consider the problem of dual nationality or dual affiliations ("Patterns of Personal Involvement in the National System," pp. 280ff.).

54. Le Gallou, *La préférence nationale*, p. 83. See also Le Gallou and Jalkh, *Etre français cela se mérite*, p. 113: "La carte d'identité n'est pas la Carte Orange."

55. Jacques Toubon, General Secretary of the RPR, in *Le Monde*, Nov. 5, 1986.

56. Historian Pierre Chaunu, quoted in *L'Express*, October 24–30, 1986, p. 20.

57. Durkheim, *Elementary Forms of the Religious Life*, pp. 237–238, 356.

58. See the discussion reported in "Les droits politiques des immigrés." Thus, for example, J. P. Gomane: "Is it not possible, and is it not time, to desacralize the notion of citizenship and nationality? It is no more than a simple convenience [*commodité*]; but one attaches to it nonetheless a sacred character" (p. 33). Or Stanislas Mangin: "Once progress has been made on terrain of social equality, it will be a form of legal progress to desacralize nationality, so that one can become French much more easily without breaking completely with one's country of origin" (p. 71). Or K. Muterfi: "For us, to ask for naturalization is to break with one's past . . . Not to require us to break with the past, isn't this a way of recognizing . . . the right to be different, the right to a cultural identity? It is the right to continue to be what one has been before living in France. One could decide that after a minimum period of residence—five or ten years—the immigrant would have the right to take French nationality . . . without any procedure [*démarche*], without formality, without renouncing his previous situation" (p. 17).

59. For a subtle discussion of assertions of the unassimilability of immigrants, see Taguieff, "Les métamorphoses idéologiques du racisme," esp. pp. 45–51.

60. Charlot, "Peut-on parler d'un 'droit à la différence, pour les jeunes Algériens?," p. 162.

61. Differentialist models flourished in the early years of Socialist rule, finding some official support from Minister of Culture Jack Lang and Minister of Social Affairs and National Solidarity Georgina Dufoix. See the following collections: *Diversité culturelle, société industrielle, état national; Les minorités à l'age de l'état-nation;* and *La France au Pluriel?* See also Giordan, *Démocratie culturelle et droit à la différence.* This last was a report to Minister Lang, whose letter of commission, reprinted at the front of the volume, noted his commitment to the "furthering of regional and minority cultures" and proposed that all citizens have the "fundamental right to live their cultural differences, whether or not these have a territorial base." Shortly before the elections of 1981, Mitterand himself endorsed the "droit à la différence": "C'est blesser un peuple au plus profond de lui-même que de l'atteindre dans sa culture et sa langue. Nous proclamons le droit à la différence" (quoted in Giordan, p. 7). Embarrassment concerning the assimilationist tradition was signaled,

among other ways, by the use of words such as "integration" and especially "insertion" instead of "assimilation" (Schlegel, "Comment parler de l'immigration"). For nuanced discussions of the problem of assimilation, see Dubet, *Immigrations*, pp. 48–80, and Taguieff and Weil, "'Immigration,' fait national et 'citoyenneté,'" pp. 89–93.

62. Griotteray, *Les immigrés: le choc*, pp. 112f.; Schlegel, "Comment parler de l'immigration."

63. See for example Leca, "Capacité," pp. 12–13, 15–17; Schlegel, "Figures d'une marge," p. 15; *Etre français aujourd'hui et demain*, II, 44f. France's weakened capacity for assimilation was explicitly invoked by Pierre Mazeaud in his proposal—much more restrictive than that of the government—for the reform of citizenship law. The proposal is reported in *Actualités Migrations* 136 (July 7, 1986), p. 9.

64. Schnapper, "La 'France plurielle'?" p. 225; see also Schnapper, *La France de l'intégration*, chap. 6.

65. Le Gallou, *La préférence nationale*, pp. 122–124; Griotteray, *Les immigrés: le choc*, pp. 114–115. But see the more balanced judgments of Dubet, *Immigrations*, pp. 50–51, and Schnapper, *La France de l'intégration*, pp. 193, 213.

66. Le Gallou and Jalkh, *Etre français cela se mérite*, pp. 27–28; Le Gallou, *La préférence nationale*, pp. 122ff., 127; Griotteray, *Les immigrés: le choc*, p. 120. For pre-1981 moves toward cultural pluralism in the primary school, see Munoz, "De la pluralité ethnique à la pédagogie interculturelle." Instruction in "language and culture of origin" has not been especially successful. Thus the Commission de la Nationalité: "Not only does experience show that this orientation generates discrimination rather than integration, that it constitutes a handicap rather than an advantage, but it also fails to win the adhesion of the persons concerned: in Marseille, children of Maghrebin origin desert classes in classical Arabic, practice their Marseillaise slang and prefer Latin or German, in order to get into a good *lycée*" (*Etre français aujourd'hui et demain*, II, 88).

67. There are between 2.5 million and 3 million Moslems in France, roughly 1 million of whom have French nationality. Of the foreign Moslems, roughly 45 percent are Algerian, 25 percent Moroccan, 15 percent Tunisian, 7 percent Turks, and 6 percent from sub-Saharan Africa, primarily Senegal and Mali (Kepel, *Les banlieues de l'Islam*, pp. 12–13; Voisard and Ducastelle, "La question immigrée en France," pp. 62–63).

68. Schlegel, "Comment parler de l'immigration?" pp. 83–84. Schlegel notes the irony of "une droite devenue républicaine/laïque comme jamais."

69. Interview published in *Les Temps Modernes* 452–453–454 (March–April–May 1984), pp. 1573–1574.

70. See Kepel, *Les banlieues de l'Islam*; Schnapper and Leveau, "Religion et politique: juifs et musulmans maghrébins en France."

71. Club 89, *Une stratégie du gouvernement*, reprinted, in part, in *Hommes et Migrations* 1088 (January 15, 1986). The quotation is from pp. 60–61.

72. "L'immigration aujourd'hui et demain," report by Didier Bariani in the name of the "Commission de Synthèse" of the UDF, June 1985, pp. 51–52.

73. Reprinted in *Le Quotidien de Paris*, January 17, 1986.

74. "General Declaration of Policy" to the National Assembly, April 9, 1986, reprinted in *Actualités Migrations* 125 (April 21, 1986), p. 1.
75. See, for example, Le Gallou and Jalkh, *Etre français cela se mérite,* pp. 109–110.
76. The government proposal was submitted to the Council of State on October 7, 1986. In slightly modified form, it was approved by the Council of Ministers on November 12.
77. This was contained in the version submitted to the Council of State. In the version approved by the Council of Ministers on November 12, second-generation immigrants would be able to make the declaration between age sixteen and twenty-three.
78. This was the proposed text of the oath: "I swear to be faithful to the French Republic, to respect the constitution and the laws of the state, and to accomplish loyally the duties of a French citizen." There was a further respect in which the rhetoric of voluntarism and self-determination was misleading. Under existing law, second-generation immigrants had been able to acquire French citizenship before attaining legal majority, either through their own declaration after age sixteen or even earlier through a parental declaration on their behalf (Articles 52–54; see *La nationalité française,* p. 26). The government's proposal suppressed this possibility, despite its voluntaristic character, arguing that some parents had been demanding French nationality for their French-born children chiefly in order to protect themselves against expulsion.
79. *Le Monde,* November 14, 1986. See also the article by National Front deputy Jean-François Jalkh, criticizing the government's proposal for being "much too timid" and for representing a "retreat from its campaign promises" (*Le Quotidien,* November 22–23, 1986).
80. The text of the note formally conveying the opinion of the Council of State was published by *Libération,* November 5, 1986.
81. *Le Monde,* November 13, 1986.
82. AFP January 15, 1987, 19:31.
83. *Le Figaro,* January 16, 1987.
84. *Le Monde,* January 22, 1987, reporting suggestions made by Chalandon to representatives of the association France Plus.
85. *Le Figaro,* January 16, 1987.
86. As Chalandon himself admitted, the initial project suffered from "a certain ambiguity," reflecting a hasty "compromise between those who believe that this reform must correspond to a moral objective of revivifying [*rehaussement*] the sentiment of national belonging [by making access to citizenship voluntary rather than automatic] and those who, on the other hand, demand such a reform . . . as a means of exclusion" (quoted in *Le Figaro,* January 16, 1987).
87. *Le Monde,* March 14, 1987.
88. Chirac himself, formally installing the Commission on June 22, echoed this inclusionist rhetoric, enjoining the commission to "avoid every systematic and brutal exclusion and, on the contrary, seek the ways and means of a successful insertion into the French community." According to Chirac, the proposed reform had been misunderstood. There had never been any ques-

tion of depriving second-generation Maghrebin immigrants of French nationality. The "heart of the reform" was the idea of a voluntary declaration. "An entire conception of nationhood is expressed in this idea of voluntary choice" (*Le Figaro,* June 23, 1987).

89. "It is not in a preelectoral period that we can address a matter this important" (*Le Matin,* September 9, 1987). This declaration, on national television, was met with general satisfaction, except by the far right (*Le Figaro,* September 10, 1987).

90. In marked contrast to the 1986 legislative campaign, only Le Pen made reform of citizenship law a central theme in the 1988 presidential campaign. Chirac ignored the issue entirely except for one offhand suggestion that the matter be submitted to referendum.

91. Even before the violence of December, Justice Minister Chalandon claimed that the governmental project followed tradition and preserved *jus soli* instead of revolutionizing nationality law and rejecting *jus soli* in favor of *jus sanguinis* (interview in *Libération,* October 29, 1986). Later he asserted that he was "attached to *jus soli,* although not shocked when one demands to the beneficiary to clearly say that he wants to be French" (interview in *Le Figaro,* June 19, 1987).

92. See, for example, the remarks of Jacques Toubon, General Secretary of the RPR and President of the Commission of Laws in the National Assembly, at a briefing on the occasion of the naming of the members of the Commission of Nationality: "We favor a policy of integration, and the voluntary declaration is an instrument of this policy." But for those making this voluntary declaration, the legal obstacles to becoming French "must be reduced to a minimum." Only persons who had been ordered expelled and persons condemned to more than five years in prison for a crime would be barred from becoming French. As Toubon underscored, these exclusions would be less restrictive not only than the government's initial proposal, but also less restrictive than current law (*Le Quotidien de Paris,* June 21, 1987; *Le Monde,* June 22, 1987; *Libération,* June 20, 1987).

93. Thus, Jacques Barrot, general secretary of the Center of Social Democrats, described the reform in November as "reasonable and relatively limited . . . We feared that the project would go further." At the same time, he warned that his group would vote against the proposal if it appeared, in the course of parliamentary debate, that it was inspired by "distrust of foreigners" (*Le Figaro,* November 13, 1986).

94. *Le Matin,* January 17, 1987. Later, Barre himself indicated his opposition to a reform of nationality law, suggesting that it was better to "begin by solving practical problems" concerning housing, education, and aid to immigrants wishing to return to their country of origin. With respect to nationality law, he said, "what matters is the style with which one addresses problems: either one adopts an attitude of exclusion . . . or we adopt a pragmatic attitude in the line of the French tradition of welcome" (*Le Monde,* September 7, 1987).

95. *Le Matin,* January 17, 1987. On the divisions within the government, see the analysis of *L'Évenement du Jeudi,* September 17, 1987.

96. Pierre Mazeaud, for example, was an RPR hardliner who himself had sub-

mitted a very restrictive nationality bill to the National Assembly, calling for the complete abolition of *jus soli*, the verification of knowledge of French language and history, an oath of allegiance, the renunciation of allegiance to other states, even the retroactive loss of nationality for later criminal convictions. Yet in his capacity as reporter for the Commission of Laws of the National Assembly on the much milder proposal of the government, he indicated that the government proposal might be further liberalized, notably by limiting the cases of exclusion for trouble with the law (*Le Monde*, December 13, 1986).

97. Griotteray, *Les immigrés: le choc,* pp. 166–168. Griotteray, to be sure, had close ties with Jean-Yves Le Gallou and through him to the Club de l'Horloge and the National Front. Griotteray was not the first to criticize *jus soli:* UDF deputy Mayoud had introduced a proposal to this effect in 1983. But Griotteray's was the first developed argument; and the attention it received in political circles inaugurated the debate.

98. Le Gallou, *La préférence nationale,* pp. 83–90.

99. To cite only a few examples: The League of the Rights of Man, in an appeal signed by more than one hundred organizations, characterized the principle of *jus soli* as belonging to Republican tradition (AFP, November 13, 1986). The Council of State criticized the governmental reform as "contrary to Republican tradition" (*L'Express*, November 14, 1986). The High Council of Population and Family argued that a restrictive reform "would be contrary to the historic evolution of our law" (*Libération*, September 4, 1986). Socialist leader Lionel Jospin, appearing on television, said that "For a century . . . left and right agreed on this Republican tradition [of an expansive citizenship law] . . . France is a country of integration; it is with the old rules that we integrated men and women from Italy, from Poland, from Portugal, from Spain. If we want to remain a country that integrates, if we don't want to reject . . . young people, who have been in our territory for long years, I think we must say no to this project" (Antenne 2, November 12, 1986). And tradition was routinely invoked in the discourse of the trade unions, churches, and associations and in the left-leaning and centrist press.

100. See Bourdieu, "L'identité et la représentation."

101. Skocpol, "Cultural Idioms and Political Ideologies," p. 91.

102. Stedman Jones, *Languages of Class,* p. 22

103. The elite possesses a distinctive idiom of nationhood, partly because it is the business of the political and cultural elite to "represent" the nation. For others, however, nationhood may be a matter of little concern. Its salience is variable. Rather than a coherent idiom of nationhood, members of the popular classes may have something existing less in a state of discourse and more in the form of dispositions and habits of thought in terms of which elite discourses on nationhood may find greater or lesser resonance.

104. The popular idiom of nationhood is more "culturalist"—in the broad anthropological sense of culture—than the more assimilationist, political, statist elite conception.

105. On French "counternationalisms," see Hoffmann, "The Nation: What For?," p. 409.

106. Stedman Jones, *Languages of Class,* p. 22.

107. For a subtle and probing analysis of the way in which the differentialist rhetoric of the left was taken over by exclusionists on the right, see Taguieff, "Les métamorphoses idéologiques du racisme." On the revival of the assimilationist idiom, see Vichniak, "French Socialists and Droit à la Différence"; Noiriel, Le creuset français, p. 341; Pinto, "L'immigration: l'ambiguité de la référence américaine," p. 96; Schlegel, "Comment parler de l'immigration."

108. See, notably, the article by former president Valéry Giscard d'Estaing in the Figaro Magazine, September 21, 1991.

8. Continuities in the German Politics of Citizenship

1. Eley, Reshaping the German Right, pp. 1–8; and for a critical discussion of this tendency, Blackbourn and Eley, Peculiarities of German History, pp. 22–35. For a short statement of the continuity thesis, see Fischer, "Zum Problem der Kontinuität in der deutschen Geschichte von Bismarck zu Hitler." For probing historical analyses of Imperial Germany from the point of view of the continuity problem, see Wehler, Das Deutsche Kaiserreich, pp. 15–16 and passim; and Krisenherde des Kaiserreichs, pp. 18ff. and passim.

2. The tendency to write "German history since the middle of the last century as if the known outcome in 1933 were inscribed in every event . . . leads to a form of teleological blandness" or to "a kind of reverse Whiggism" (Blackbourn and Eley, Peculiarities of German History, pp. 33, 45). For a criticism of the tendency to misread Wilhelmine nationalism in the light of the völkisch imperialism of the Nazis, see Schieder, Das Deutsche Kaiserreich von 1871 als Nationalstaat, pp. 39–40.

3. See Blackbourn and Eley, Peculiarities of German History, p. 23.

4. For accounts of this inadequacy, see the following Nazi-era analyses: Lösener and Knost, eds., Die Nürnberger Gesetze, pp. 10–16; Beuster, "Reichsbürger und Staatsangehöriger," pp. 17–25; Zimmerman, "Staatsangehörigkeit und Reichsbürgerschaft," pp. 12f.

5. "Gesetz über den Widerruf von Einbürgerungen und die Aberkennung der deutschen Staatsangehörigkeit vom 14. Juli 1933" and "Ausführungsverordnung vom 26. Juli 1933" for the same law, both printed in Lichter, Staatsangehörigkeit, pp. 171–177. A comprehensive and exhaustively documented review of the Nazi restructuring of citizenship is provided by Majer, "Fremdvölkische" im Dritten Reich, pp. 195–221.

6. Quoted in Beuster, "Reichsbürger und Staatsangehöriger," pp. 23–24.

7. Text of law in Lösener and Knost, Die Nürnberger Gesetze, p. 28.

8. Erste Verordnung zum Reichsbürgergesetz, sec. 4 (1). See also sec. 5 (1): "A Jew is a person who descends from at least three racially fully Jewish grandparents"; sec. 2 (2): "A grandparent is considered 'fully Jewish' if he belonged to the Jewish religious community"; and sec. 5 (2), which specified that the descendant of "two fully Jewish grandparents" was to be considered a Jew in some circumstances but not in others. Text in Lösener and Knost, Die Nürnberger Gesetze, pp. 28–30.

9. Majer, "Fremdvölkische" im Dritten Reich, p. 207. This proposal was not adopted, but a new system of tiered membership was instituted in 1943 to

order relations between ethnic Germans and others in the ethnically mixed eastern districts of the Reich. The category of "revocable *Staatsangehörigkeit*" was created for those non-Germans who were considered "Germanizable" *(Eindeutschungsfähig)*; and next to it the category of protectorate membership *(Schutzangehörigkeit)* for other non-Germans. Jews and Gypsies were formally excluded not only from regular *Staatsangehörigkeit* but also from revocable *Staatsangehörigkeit* and *Schutzangehörigkeit* (Majer, pp. 215–221; Lichter, *Staatsangehörigkeit,* pp. 182–183).

10. Majer, *"Fremdvölkische" im Dritten Reich,* p. 213.
11. For a general survey of the postwar period, see Klessman, *Die doppelte Staatsgründung.*
12. Schlenger, "Das Weltflüchtlingsproblem," pp. 40–42.
13. Nellner, "Grundlagen und Hauptergebnisse der Statistik," pp. 122, 128, 130; Klessman, *Die doppelte Staatsgründung,* pp. 39–44; Bethlehem, *Heimatvertreibung, DDR-Flucht, Gastarbeiterzuwanderung.*
14. The Sudeten Germans, comprising half of these *volksdeutsche Vertriebene,* had been German citizens since the incorporation of the Sudetenland in 1938; historically, however, they had been citizens of the Habsburg empire and—in the interwar period—of Czechoslovakia. On *Reichsdeutsche* and *Volksdeutsche* among the *Vertriebene,* see Lemberg, "Der Wandel des politischen Denkens," pp. 437–442.
15. Literally "membership of the Volk." Although I refer to "ethnic Germans" for convenience in translating *"Volksdeutsche"* or *"deutsche Volkszugehörigen,"* "ethnicity" is not entirely satisfactory as a translation of the legal category of *"Volkszugehörigkeit,"* which is legally defined by subjective attitude *(Bekenntnis)* as well as by the objective markers such as language, culture, and descent that are usually associated with ethnicity. See the 1953 Law on Expelled Persons and Refugees, section 6, printed in Otto, ed, *Westwärts—Heimwärts.*
16. This required a rather complicated and implausible legal justification, according to which the German Reich did not cease to exist with the collapse of 1945 but simply became *handlungsunfähig,* incapable of action. On this view, the German state and its citizenry continued to exist after 1945; and the Federal Republic was not a new state but a reorganization of that still existing state, operating within a narrower territorial realm but otherwise identical with it. See Schwartz, "Die Staatsangehörigkeit der Deutschen," pp. 29f., 47f., 68f., 137f.
17. The Nazis had left the basic framework of the 1913 law—including its system of pure *jus sanguinis*—undisturbed. They had created a new category of full citizenship *(Reichsbürgerschaft)* within the basic state-membership *(Staatsangehörigkeit)* that remained governed by the law of 1913; and they had stripped Jews of even that basic state-membership; but they had not touched the core provisions of the 1913 law itself. That law thus remained in effect, and since the taint of Nazism did not attach to it as such, it could be taken over by the Federal Republic.
18. Strictly speaking, this applies only to those among the ethnic German refugees and expellees who did not possess German citizenship already. Most

of those expelled from the former German *Ostgebiete* were *Reichsdeutsche* who already possessed German citizenship. The special status of "German without German citizenship" was invented for the *Volksdeutsche* refugees and expellees from other Eastern European territories.

19. Thus the basic rights enumerated in the Constitution, so far as they are not granted to all persons, are granted to "Germans," not to "German citizens." These include freedom of assembly and association (Arts. 8 and 9), freedom of movement (Art. 11), and freedom of occupation (Art. 12).

20. These persons also had the right to acquire German citizenship on demand. Throughout the postwar period, such as-of-right naturalizations *(Anspruchseinbürgerungen)* have accounted for the substantial majority of German naturalizations.

21. Von Doemming et al., "Entstehungsgeschichte der Artikel des Grundgesetzes," p. 21.

22. See Schwartz, "Die Staatsangehörigkeit der Deutschen," pp. 94–115.

23. See Bender, *Neue Ostpolitik: Vom Mauerbau bis zum Moskauer Vertrag,* esp. pp. 190–195.

24. For a quarter of a century after the construction of the Berlin Wall, the "German citizenship" possessed by citizens of the GDR was anomalous and unreal. Between 1949 and 1961, 1.7 million persons moved from the GDR to the FRG (not including nearly a million *Vertriebene* who came to West Germany during that period after residing for some time in East Germany). After 1961, however, they could not enter the territory of the FRG and thus could not enjoy the rights guaranteed to them under the Grundgesetz of the Federal Republic.

25. On the crucial role of the single German citizenship in the German Revolution of 1989, see Brubaker, "Frontier Theses."

26. Gesetz über die Angelegenheiten der Vertriebenen und Flüchtlingen (Law on Expelled Persons and Refugees), §1 (2) 3, printed in Otto, ed, *Westwärts— Heimwärts?,* p. 176.

27. Richtlinien zur einheitlichen Anwendung des §1 Abs. 2 Nr. 3 des Bundesvertriebenengesetzes (Guidelines for the application of §1 Abs. 2 Nr. 3 of the Law on Expelled Persons and Refugees), printed in *Ministerialblatt des Landes Nordrhein-Westfalen,* Nr. 74 vom. 12 Sept. 1986, p. 1291. (These guidelines are valid in all West German *Länder.*) Excerpts are printed in Otto, ed, *Westwärts—Heimwärts?,* pp. 178ff.

28. Excerpts from the law and administrative regulations concerning the concept of German *Volkszugehörigkeit* and the means of determining it are printed in Otto, ed, *Westwärts—Heimwärts?,* pp. 177, 180–186.

29. For statistics since 1950 on Aussiedler, see Bundesminister des Innern, VER I 5–933 600/2, and Puskeppeleit, "Zugangsentwicklungen," p. 165. Figures for 1987: *Suddeutsche Zeitung,* November 7, 1988. For 1988, *Der Spiegel* 8, (February 20, 1989), p. 72. For 1989, *Der Spiegel* 8 (February 19, 1990), p. 29. For 1990–91, *This Week in Germany,* February 21, 1992, p. 2.

30. Recruiting efforts began, however, while unemployment remained high. Thus the first recruitment agreement, with Italy, was concluded in 1955 when the unemployment rate was still 5 percent (Dohse, *Ausländische Arbeiter und bürgerlicher Staat,* p. 145).

31. Fijalkowski, "Gastarbeiter als industrielle Reservearmee?" p. 405; *Ausländer 1986*, p. 15.
32. Bethlehem, *Heimatvertreibung*, p. 160
33. Rist, *Guestworkers in Germany*, p. 62; Bundesminister des Innern, "Sozialversicherungspflichtig beschäftigte Ausländer nach ausgewählten Staatsangehörigkeiten," 23. F.
34. Only half of all foreigners, according to a large-scale representative survey undertaken by the Friedrich-Ebert-Stiftung, plan to remain at least "several more years," with one-third uncertain and one-sixth not planning to remain that long (*Situation der ausländischen Arbeitnehmer und ihrer Familienangehörigen in der Bundesrepublik Deutschland*, p. 467). Expressed intentions, however, have proved a poor guide to actual behavior, leading some analysts to speak of the "Heimkehrillusion," the illusion of return. See Miller, "The Problem of Foreign Worker Participation," pp. 102ff., and the studies cited there.
35. On the process by which short-term labor migrants gradually redefine themselves as long-term residents, see Piore, *Birds of Passage*.
36. Despite the massive new immigration of 1968–1973, during which time the foreign population doubled, nearly half of all foreigners in 1973 had resided at least four years in Germany (Fijalkowski, "Gastarbeiter," p. 405). A representative survey of early 1972 showed that 21 percent of foreign workers had been in Germany at least seven years (Bethlehem, *Heimatvertreibung*, p. 161 n. 186).
37. The number of females per 1000 males in the foreign population increased from 451 in 1961 to 593 in 1970; in 1986 it was 751 (*Ausländer 1986*, p. 15). The employment rate for foreigners fell from 80 percent in 1961 to 65 percent in 1973, 57 percent in 1975, and 51 percent in 1982, while the rate for Germans increased from 43 percent in 1970 to 46 percent in 1982 (Fijalkowski, "Gastarbeiter," p. 404; Heckmann, "Temporary Labor Migration or Immigration?" p. 72).
38. Proebsting, "Eheschliessungen, Scheidungen, Geburten und Sterbefälle von Ausländern 1985," p. 227.
39. See, for example, Dirk Schubert, "Wohlstandskulis oder Mitbürger? Vor einer Wende in der Gastarbeiterpolitik," *Deutsche Zeitung*, October 13, 1972: The idea that foreign workers come to the Federal Republic "in order to earn as much money as possible and then return to their home countries in a few years has proved to be deceptive. Rather, it is becoming clear that more and more Gastarbeiter are making the Bundesrepublik their new home and settling here: they send for their families or marry German women . . . The Federal Republic has thus—even if against its will—become a country of immigration." For a retrospective analysis of the changing orientation of federal policy, see Bethlehem, *Heimatvertreibung*, pp. 154ff.
40. *Süddeutsche Zeitung*, December 12, 1972; *Frankfurter Allgemeine Zeitung*, February 6, 1973; *Hannoversche Allgemeine Zeitung*, September 22, 1973; Meier-Braun, *"Freiwillige Rotation"*, pp. 108ff.; Bethlehem, *Heimatvertreibung*, pp. 202ff.
41. While the decision was triggered by the dramatic increase in oil prices, and justified on labor market grounds, most scholars now agree that specifically

social concerns about the growing and more settled immigrant population played a key role in the decision. See Miller, *Foreign Workers in Western Europe*, p. 10; Rist, "Migration and Marginality," pp. 97–98.

42. Körner, "Return Migration from the Federal Republic of Germany," p. 175.

43. *Ausländer 1986*, p. 15; Bundesminister des Innern, "Sozialversicherungspflichtig beschäftigte Ausländer nach ausgewählten Staatsangehörigkeiten," 23. F. Turks accounted for most of this increase: between 1974 and 1986, the Turkish population in West Germany increased by 40 percent, while the other chief foreign populations all declined markedly: Spanish by 45 percent, Portuguese by 36 percent, Greeks by 32 percent, Yugoslavs by 17 percent, Italians by 15 percent (*Ausländer 1986*, p. 16). Yet despite these sharply differing trends in total size, all of these foreign communities have become increasingly settled.

44. *Ausländer 1986*, p. 59

45. As of June 1988, the latest date for which figures are available, 722,000 foreign residents under age sixteen had been born in the Federal Republic (Bundesminister des Innern, "Unter 16jährige, im Bundesgebiet geborene/ nicht im Bundesgebiet geborene Ausländer"). Taking account of foreign citizens born in Germany since then (more than 50,000 per year) and of foreign residents aged sixteen and over in 1988 who were born in Germany, we can estimate that, at this writing, the Federal Republic hosts about a million German-born foreign residents.

46. This formulation is found in various official statements, for example in the Interior Ministry's "Aufzeichnung zur Ausländerpolitik und zum Ausländerrecht in der Bundesrepublik Deutschland."

47. Even a long-time leading advocate of liberalized naturalization provisions, Gerhart Baum of the Free Democratic Party, admitted that second-generation immigrants might make only modest use of a right to naturalization (Baum, "Aktuelle Probleme der Ausländerpolitik," p. 9).

48. Funcke, "Doppelte Staatsbürgerschaft als Chance für Migranten, Staaten und Bürger," p. 4. The Beauftragte für Ausländerfragen is a federal official charged with making policy recommendations on all questions bearing on immigration and immigrants. The position was held throughout the 1980s by Liselotte Funcke of the Free Democrats, who upheld a consistently liberal line on *Ausländerpolitik* but who remained quite marginal in the policymaking process. On the issue of dual citizenship, see also Hammar, "State, Nation, and Dual Citizenship."

49. Bethlehem, *Heimatvertreibung*, p. 160.

50. For one of earliest challenges, see Folker Schreiber and Karl Furmaniak, "Aus Gastarbeitern werden Einwanderer," *Die Zeit* 29, 1971.

51. Thränhardt, "'Ausländer' als Objekte deutscher Interessen und Ideologien," p. 123; Hoffmann, *Die unvollendete Republik*, part I.

52. Prussia and other European states in the mercantilist era, and to a much greater extent France in the interwar period, qualify in the second sense.

53. "Einbürgerungsrichtlinien" (Administrative guidelines on naturalization), no. 2.3, printed in Groth, *Einbürgerungsratgeber*, p. 95.

54. Quoted in ibid., p. 95.

55. Quoted in Bernsdorf, *Probleme der Ausländerintegration,* p. 199.
56. At its 1989 Party Conference, the CDU noted that "with respect to the change in the age structure of the German population [a consequence of low birthrates of recent decades], the employment of foreign workers and their children will be indispensable" (37. Bundesparteitag des CDU, Bremen, September 13, 1989, Resolution C1, I, 4). In October 1991 the state labor agency in North Rhine–Westphalia estimated that Germany would need half a million foreign workers per year, even after exhausting the reserves of unemployed labor in eastern Germany, while the publisher of a business magazine said Germany might need a million foreign workers to fill the gap in the work force caused by low birthrates (*This Week in Germany,* October 18, 1991, p. 5).
57. See Hoffman, *Die unvollendete Republik.*
58. On immigrants' lack of interest in naturalization, see *Situation der ausländischen Arbeitnehmer und ihrer Familienangehörigen in der Bundesrepublik Deutschland,* pp. 483–488.
59. See Baum, "Aktuelle Probleme der Ausländerpolitik," p. 9: "The solution does not lie in transforming foreigners—forcibly—into Germans [*dass man die Ausländer—zwangsweise—zu Deutschen macht*]."
60. In 1981 Berlin Bürgermeister Richard von Weizsäcker, now president of the Federal Republic, declared that foreigners must eventually choose between remaining in Berlin and becoming German citizens or returning to their country of origin—a formulation that was widely criticized, although it simply expressed a basic norm of nation-statehood: that residence and citizenship should coincide in the long run. In another country, with a better historical conscience with respect to the assimilation of foreigners, this formulation might not have provoked the reaction it did in Germany.
61. E. Weber, *Peasants into Frenchmen,* notes the quasi-colonial character of the policies and attitudes of the center; see esp. pp. 486ff.
62. The harshness of assimilationist politics in Central Europe in the age of nationalism was nicely evoked by the leader of the Conservative fraction in the Reichstag, von Racuhhaupt: "Since they [the Poles] will not let themselves be assimilated, there is no other option but to Germanize them" (quoted in Hauser, "Nationalisierung Preussens," p. 102).
63. On differentialist and dissimilationist elements in the German tradition, see von Thadden, "Minderheiten." See also Thränhardt, "'Ausländer' als Objekte deutscher Interessen und Ideologien," p. 116.
64. On the "nationalities politics" of the Habsburg empire as an heuristic point of reference for the question of the mode of integration of immigrants today, see Fijalkowski, "Das Problem der Erweiterung der politischen Rechte für die neuen ethnischen Minderheiten der Arbeitsmigranten," pp. 39ff.
65. Kimminich, *Rechtsprobleme der polyethnischen Staatsorganisation,* pp. 118, 204–207.
66. For an introduction to the subject, see Margrit Gerste, "'Die werden uns niederstimmen!' Der Streit um das kommunale Wahlrecht für Ausländer," *Die Zeit* 37, 1987, p. 37. From the large scholarly literature, see Keskin, ed., *Menschen ohen Rechte? Einwanderungspolitik und Kommunalwahlrecht in Europa;* Sievering, ed., *Integration ohne Partizipation?: Ausländerwahlrecht in der*

Bundesrepublik Deutschland; "Kommunalwahlrecht auch für Ausländer?" (Evangelischer Pressedienst *Dokumentation* 30, 1986); Breer, *Die Mitwirkung von Ausländern an der politischen Willensbildung in der Bundesrepublik Detuschland.*

Conclusion

1. See Schuck and Smith, *Citizenship without Consent,* p. 109.
2. See Zolberg, "Contemporary Transnational Migrations in Historical Perspective."
3. Schuck, "Membership in the Liberal Polity"; Brubaker, "Membership without Citizenship."
4. By "immigrant status" I mean a status that permits noncitizens, ordinarily, to remain indefinitely in the country and, outside of the political domain, to participate in social and economic life on virtually the same terms as citizens. Persons may be admitted to the territory as immigrants, as is the case of those who enter the United States as permanent resident aliens; or they may be admitted to the territory with some other status and later become immigrants, as in the case of persons who entered France and Germany with short-term residence and work permits and only later graduated to immigrant status. The large majority of resident foreigners in European states are "immigrants" in this sense (Brubaker, "Membership without Citizenship").
5. Brubaker, "Membership without Citizenship."
6. See Cohen, "Strategy or Identity." On immigrants as "moral actors," see Zolberg, "Contemporary Transnational Migrations in Historical Perspective," esp. p. 18.
7. See, for example, Quaritsch, "Einbürgerungspolitk als Ausländerpolitik."
8. Uhlitz, "Deutsches Volk oder 'Multikulturelle Gesellschaft'?"; Stöcker, "Nationales Selbstbestimmungsrecht und Ausländerwahlrecht," p. 82; Schilling, "Einwanderung und Staatsidee."
9. Popular understandings of nationhood may be much more similar. But the politics of citizenship depends on elite self-understandings, for formal citizenship, unlike, say, immigration, is not a salient popular issue.
10. The French political and intellectual elite is itself a remarkable product of assimilation. The habitual schemes of thought and expression deployed by professionals in the representation of the social and political world—politicians, journalists, high civil servants, intellectuals, and so on—are products of the labor of "continuous normalization" imposed by centralized institutions such as the Ecole Normale Supérieure, the Ecole National d'Administration, or the Institut d'Etudes Politiques (Bourdieu, "La représentation politique").
11. On the transfer of schemes of interpretation and understanding from one domain to another, see Bourdieu's discussion of the concept of habitus in *Outline of a Theory of Practice,* pp. 82–83; and Bourdieu, *Distinction,* pp. 170–175.
12. Hobsbawm, "Introduction: Inventing Traditions."

13. On representation struggles, see Bourdieu, "L'identité et la représentation"; "La représentation politique"; and *Distinction,* pp. 479–484.
14. Kolinsky, "The Nation-State in Western Europe: Erosion from 'Above' and 'Below'?"; Beetham, "The Future of the Nation-State."
15. On the incipient development of European citizenship, see Aron, "Is Multinational Citizenship Possible?"; A. C. Evans, "European Citizenship: A Novel Concept in EEC Law"; Durand, "European Citizenship"; Grabitz, *Europäisches Bürgerrecht zwischen Marktbürgerschaft und Staatsbürgerschaft.*
16. For an account of the recasting of membership asserting—in my view, prematurely—that the fundamental organizing and legitimating principles of membership are already postnational, based on universal personhood rather than national citizenship, see Soysal, "Limits of Citizenship," chap. 8.
17. Brubaker, "Immigration, Citizenship and the Nation-State," pp. 380–383.
18. Brubaker, "Citizenship Struggles in Soviet Successor States."
19. Brubaker, "Political Dimensions of Migration from and among Soviet Successor States."

Bibliography

Primary Sources

FRENCH GOVERNMENT REPORTS

Sous-Direction des Naturalisations, Direction de la Population et des Migrations, Ministère des Affaires Sociales et de la Solidarité (name of ministry has varied). Annual Reports, 1985–1989.

GERMAN GOVERNMENT TABLES AND REPORTS

Bundesminister des Innern, "Aufzeichnung zur Ausländerpolitik und zum Ausländerrecht in der Bundesrepublik Deutschland."

Bundesminister des Innern, "Ausländer am 31.12.1988 nach ausgewählten Staatsangehörigkeiten und Aufenthaltsdauer," 33. F.

Bundesminister des Innern, "Ausländische Lebendgeborene nach ausgewählten Staatsangehörigkeiten," 23. F.

Bundesminister des Innern, VER I 5–933 600/2. "Aussiedler aus den ost- und südosteuropäischen Staaten und Vertriebenen, die über das freie Ausland in die Bundesrepublik Deutschland gekommen sind."

Bundesminister des Innern, "Ehelich Lebendgeborene nach der Staatsangehörigkeit der Eltern," 21. F.

Bundesminister des Innern, "Ermessenseinbürgerungen nach ausgewählten Staatsangehörigkeiten," 30. F.

Bundesminister des Innern, "Sozialversicherungspflichtig beschäftigte Ausländer nach ausgewählten Staatsangehörigkeiten," 23. F.

Bundesminister des Innern, "Unter 16jährige, im Bundesgebiet geborene/nicht im Bundesgebiet geborene Ausländer nach ausgewählten Staatsangehörigkeiten," 23. F., 27. F.

FRENCH PARLIAMENTARY MATERIALS

Citations in the notes indicate the document—using the abbreviations that follow— and the page. Most citations to parliamentary debates also include a letter indicating the column: 1182c = third column of page 1182.

AND 2122. Annales de l'Assemblée Nationale, Séance du 18 décember 1873, Annexe no. 2122. "Rapport fait au nom de la commission chargée d'examiner la proposition de loi de M. des Rotours, ayant pour objet de déclarer Français et d'assujetir à l'obligation du recrutement les individus d'origine étrangère nés en France, qui ne satisfont pas, dans leur pays d'origine, aux charges du service militaire," par M. Albert Desjardins.

CD 1490. Chambre des Députés, Documents Parlementaires, Session ordinaire de 1887, Séance du 25 janvier 1887, Annexe no. 1490. "Proposition de loi ayant pour objet la naturalisation des étrangers en Algérie," présentée par M. Alfred Letellier.

CD 2083. Chambre des Députés, Documents Parlementaires, Session extraordinarie de 1887, Séance du 7 novembre 1887, Annexe no. 2083. "Rapport fait au nom de la commission chargée d'examiner la proposition de loi, adoptée par le Sénat, sur la nationalité," par M. Antonin Dubost.

CD 3904. Chambre des Députés, Documents Parlementaires, Session Ordinaire de 1885, Séance du 25 juin 1885, Annexe no. 3904. "Proposition de loi relative à la nationalité des fils d'étrangers nés en France," présentée par M. Maxime Lecomte et al.

C2. Chambre des Députés, Compte Rendu, Séance du 16 mars 1889.

SD 19. Sénat, Documents Parlementaires, Session extraordinaire de 1886, Séance du 4 novembre 1886, Annexe no. 19. "Rapport supplémentaire fait, au nom de la commission chargée d'examiner la proposition de loi de M. Batbie, sur la naturalisation, par M. Batbie, sénateur."

SD 156. Sénat, Documents Parlementaires, Session ordinaire de 1882, Séance du 1er avril 1882, Annexe no. 156. "Proposition de loi sur la naturalisation," présentée par M. Batbie.

SD 160. Sénat, Documents Parlementaires, Session ordinaire de 1889, Séance du 3 juin 1889, Annexe no. 160. "Rapport fait au nom de la commission chargée d'examiner la proposition de loi, adoptée par le Sénat, modifiée par la Chambre des Députés, sur la nationalité, par M. Delsol, sénateur."

S1. Sénat, Compte Rendu, Séances du 13, 15 novembre 1886.

S2. Sénat, Compte Rendu, Séances du 3, 4, 7, 8, 11 février 1887.

S3. Sénat, Compte Rendu, Séance du 6 juin 1889.

GERMAN PARLIAMENTARY MATERIALS

(All references are to the *Verhandlungen des Reichstags.* The volumes in this series are of two types: one contains the transcripts of parliamentary debates [Stenographische Berichte]; the other includes reports, propositions, and other documents [Anlagen zu den stenographischen Berichten]. Citations in the notes use the abbreviations that follow. They also include page numbers; most citations to the Stenographische Berichte include page numbers together with a letter indicating position on the page.)

A 13 I 6. Anlagen zu den stenographischen Berichten, 13th Legislative Period, first session, Nr. 6 (Feb. 6, 1912). "Entwurf eines Reichs- und Staatsangehörigkeitsgesetzes."

A 13 I 962. Anlagen zu den stenographischen Berichten, 13th Legislative Period, first session, Nr. 962 (April 23, 1913). "Bericht der 6. Kommission zur Vorberatung der Entwürfe (a) eines Reichs- und Staatsangehörigkeitsgesetzes, (b) eines Gesetzes zur Abänderung des Reichsmilitärgesetzes sowie des Gesetzes, betreffend Änderungen der Wehrpflicht, vom 11. Februar 1888."

SB 13 I 13. Stenographische Berichte, 13th Legislative Period, first session, 13th sitting (Feb. 23, 1912).

SB 13 I 14. Stenographische Berichte, 13th Legislative Period, first session, 14th sitting (Feb. 27, 1912).

SB 13 I 153. Stenographische Berichte, 13th Legislative Period, first session, 153rd sitting (May 28, 1913).

SB 13 I 154. Stenographische Berichte, 13th Legislative Period, first session, 154th sitting (May 29, 1913).

SB 13 I 155. Stenographische Berichte, 13th Legislative Period, first session, 155th sitting (May 30, 1913).

SB 13 I 169. Stenographische Berichte, 13th Legislative Period, first session, 169th sitting (June 25, 1913).

Secondary Sources

Articles from the daily and weekly press are not listed here; citations are given in the notes. Wire service reports from Agence France Presse (AFP) are cited by date and time. In a few instances, when a published source is cited or quoted in the text but not listed in the bibliography, full bibliographic details are given in the notes.

Ageron, Charles-Robert. "L'immigration maghrébine en France: Un survol historique." *Vingtième siècle* 7 (July–September 1985): 59–69.

Akzin, Benjamin. *States and Nations*. Garden City, N.Y.: Doubleday, 1966.

———, ed. *La nationalité dans la science sociale et dans le droit contemporain*. Paris: Sirey, 1933.

Allgemeines Landrecht für die preussischen Staaten (ALR). Textausgabe, with an introduction by Hans Hattenhauer. Frankfurt am Main: Alfred Metzner, 1970.

ALR. See *Allgemeines Landrecht für die preussischen Staaten*.

Anderson, Benedict. *Imagined Communities: Reflections on the Origin and Spread of Nationalism*. London: Verso, 1983.

Anderson, Perry. *Lineages of the Absolutist State*. London: NLB, 1974.

Arendt, Hannah. *The Origins of Totalitarianism*. New York: Harcourt Brace Jovanovich, 1973.

Aristotle. *The Politics of Aristotle*. Edited and translated by Ernest Barker. London: Oxford University Press, 1958.

Armengaud, André. *La population française au XIXe siècle*. Paris: Presses Universitaires de France, 1971.

Aron, Raymond. "Is Multinational Citizenship Possible?" *Social Research* 41 (1974): 638–656.

Ausländer 1986. Statistisches Bundesamt, 1987. Distributed by Verlag W. Kohlhammer, Mainz.

Azéma, Jean-Pierre and Michel Winock. *La IIIe république (1870–1940)*. Paris: Calmann-Lévy, 1976.

Azimi, Vida. "L'étranger sous la Révolution." In *La Révolution et l'ordre juridique privé: Rationalité ou scandale?* Paris: Presses Universitaires de France, 1988.

Bade, Klaus J. "Die Deutsche überseeische Massenauswanderung im 19. und frühen 20. Jahrhundert." Pp. 259–299 in Bade, ed., *Auswanderer–Wanderarbeiter–Gastarbeiter*, vol. I.

————— "'Kulturkampf' auf dem Arbeitsmarkt: Bismarcks 'Polenpolitik' 1885–1890." Pp. 121–142 in Pflanze, ed., *Innenpolitische Probleme des Bismarckreichs*.

————— "Politik und Ökonomie der Ausländerbeschäftigung im Preussischen Osten 1895–1914." Pp. 273–299 in H. J. Puhle and H.-U. Wehler, eds., *Preussen in Rückblick*. Göttingen: Vandenhoeck and Ruprecht, 1980.

————— "'Preussengänger' und 'Abwehrpolitik': Ausländerbeschäftigung, Ausländerpolitik und Ausländerkontrolle auf dem Arbeitsmarkt in Preussen vor dem ersten Weltkrieg." *Archiv für Sozialgeschichte* 24 (1984): 91–162.

————— "Vom Auswanderungsland zum 'Arbeitseinfuhrland': Kontinentale Zuwanderung und Ausländerbeschäftigung in Deutschland im späten 19. und frühen 20. Jahrhundert." Pp. 433–485 in Bade, ed., *Auswanderer–Wanderarbeiter–Gastarbeiter*, vol. II.

—————, ed. "Arbeiterstatistik zur Ausländerkontrolle: Die 'Nachweisungen' der preussischen Landräte über den 'Zugang, Abgang und Bestand der ausländischen Arbeiter im preussischen Staate' 1906–1914." *Archiv für Sozialgeschichte* 24 (1984): 163–283.

—————, ed. *Auswanderer–Wanderarbeiter–Gastarbeiter: Bevölkerung, Arbeitsmarkt und Wanderung in Deutschland seit der Mitte des 19. Jahrhunderts*. 2 vols. Ostfildern: Scripta Mercaturae Verlag, 1984.

Balibar, Étienne. "Propositions sur la citoyenneté." Pp. 221–234 in de Wenden, ed., *La Citoyenneté*.

Barbalet, J. M. *Citizenship: Rights, Struggle and Class Inequality*. Minneapolis: University of Minnesota Press, 1988.

Barber, Benjamin R. *The Death of Communal Liberty*. Princeton: Princeton University Press, 1974.

————— *Strong Democracy: Participatory Politics for a New Age*. Berkeley: University of California Press, 1984.

Barzun, Jacques. *Race*. New York, 1937.

Basdevant, Suzanne. "Le principe des nationalités dans la doctrine." In Akzin, ed., *La nationalité*.

Battifol, Henri, and Paul Lagarde. *Droit international privé*. 7th ed. Paris: Librairie Générale de Droit et de Jurisprudence, 1981.

Baum, Gerhart. "Aktuelle Probleme der Ausländerpolitik." *Zeitschrift für Ausländerrecht und Ausländerpolitik* 1 (1981): 7–12.

Beetham, David. "The Future of the Nation-State." In Gregor McLennan, David Held, and Stuart Hall, eds., *The Idea of the Modern State*. Milton Keynes, U.K.: Open University Press, 1984.

Behrens, C. B. A. *The Ancien Régime*. London: Thames and Hudson, 1967.

Bell, Karl. "Geschichte des Vereins für das Deutschtum im Ausland." Pp. 99–348 in Erwin Barta and Karl Bell, *Geschichte der Schutzarbeit am deutschen Volkstum*. Dresden: Verein für das Deutschtum im Ausland, 1930.

Bender, Peter. *Neue Ostpolitik: Vom Mauerbau bis zum Moskauer Vertrag*. Munich: Deutscher Taschenbuch Verlag, 1986.

Bendix, Reinhard. *Nation-Building and Citizenship*. New ed. Berkeley: University of California Press, 1977.

Berdahl, Robert M. "New Thoughts on German Nationalism." *American Historical Review* 77 (1972): 65–80.

Bernsdorff, Norbert. *Probleme der Ausländerintegration in verfassungsrechtlicher Sicht*. Frankfurt am Main: Lang, 1986.

Bethlehem, Siegried. *Heimatvertreibung, DDR-Flucht, Gastarbeiterzuwanderung*. Stuttgart: Klett-Cotta, 1982.

Beudant, Charles. "De la naturalisation." *Revue critique de législation et de jurisprudence* 7 (1855): 113–144.

Beuster, Horst. "Reichsbürger und Staatsangehöriger." Dissertation, Friedrich-Wilhelms-Universität Berlin, 1939.

Blackbourn, David, and Geoff Eley. *The Peculiarities of German History*. Oxford: Oxford University Press, 1984.

Blanke, Richard. *Prussian Poland in the German Empire (1871–1900)*. Boulder, Col.: East European Monographs, 1981.

Bodin, Jean. *The Six Books of a Commonweale*. Edited by Kenneth Douglas McRae. Cambridge, Mass.: Harvard University Press, 1962 (facsimile reprint of English translation of 1606).

Bökch, R. "Die Verschiebung der Sprachverhältnisse in Posen und Westpreussen." *Preussische Jahrbücher* 77 (1894): 424–436.

Bonnet, Jean-Chales. "Les pouvoirs publics français et l'immigration dans l'entre-deux-guerres." Thèse du troisième cycle, Université Lyon II, 1974.

Bornhak, Conrad. *Preussisches Staatsrecht*, vol. 1. Freiburg: JCB Mohr, 1888.

Boulet-Sautel, Marguerite. "L'aubain dans la France coutumière du Moyen Age." Pp. 65–96 in *Recueils de la Société Jean Bodin*, vol. X, *L'Etranger* (second part). Brussels: Editions de la Librairie Encyclopédique, 1958.

Bourdieu, Pierre. "La codification." Pp. 94–105 in *Choses Dites*. Paris: Minuit, 1987.

—— *Distinction: A Social Critique of the Judgement of Taste*. Translated by Richard Nice. Cambridge, Mass.: Harvard University Press, 1984.

—— "L'identité et la représentation. Éléments pour une réflexion critique sur l'idée de région." *Actes de la recherche en sciences sociales* 35 (November 1980): 63–72.

—— *Outline of a Theory of Practice*. Translated by Richard Nice. Cambridge: Cambridge University Press, 1977.

—— "La représentation politique. Éléments pour une théorie du champ politique." *Actes de la recherche en sciences sociales* 36–37 (February-March 1981): 3–24.

Bracher, Karl Dietrich, et al., eds. *Nationalsozialistische Diktatur 1933–1945: Eine Bilanz*. Bonn: Bundeszentrale für politische Bildung, 1986.

Braun, Rudolf. "Taxation, Sociopolitical Structure, and State-building: Great Britain and Brandenburg-Prussia." Pp. 243–327 in Tilly, ed., *The Formation of National States in Western Europe.*

Breer, Dietmar. *Die Mitwirkung von Ausländern an der politischen Willensbildung in der Bundesrepublik Deutschland durch Gewährung des Wahlrechts, insbesondere des Kommunalwahlrechts.* Berlin: Duncker & Humblot, 1982.

Breithaupt, Georg Wolfgang. "Öffentliches Armenrecht und persönliche Freiheit." *Zeitschrift für die gesamte Staatswissenschaft,* Ergänzungsheft 51, 1915.

Breuilly, John. *Nationalism and the State.* Chicago: University of Chicago Press, 1982.

Broszat, Martin. *Zweihundert Jahre deutsche Polenpolitik.* Rev. ed. Frankfurt: Suhrkamp, 1972.

Brubaker, [William] Rogers. "Citizenship and Naturalization: Policies and Politics." Pp. 99–127 in Brubaker, ed. *Immigration and the Politics of Citizenship.*

———— "Citizenship Struggles in Soviet Successor States." Forthcoming in *International Migration Review.*

———— "Einwanderung und Nationalstaat in Frankreich und Deutschland." *Der Staat* 28 (1989): 1–30.

———— "Frontier Theses: Exit, Voice, and Loyalty in East Germany." *Migration World Magazine,* Vol. 18, No. 3/4, 1990, pp. 12–17.

———— "Immigration, Citizenship, and the Nation-State in France and Germany: A Comparative Historical Analysis." *International Sociology* 5 (1990): 379–407.

———— "Membership without Citizenship: The Economic and Social Rights of Non-Citizens." Pp. 145–162 in Brubaker, ed., *Immigration and the Politics of Citizenship.*

———— "Political Dimensions of Migration from and among Soviet Successor States." Paper presented at conference on International Migration and the Security and Stability of States, Center for International Studies, Massachusetts Institute of Technology, December 5–6, 1991.

————, ed. *Immigration and the Politics of Citizenship in Europe and North America.* Lanham, Md.: German Marshall Fund and University Press of America, 1989.

Bruch, Ernst. "Armenwesen und Armengesetzgebung im Königreich Preussen nach seinem Bestand vor 1866." Pp. 25–67 in A. Emminghaus, ed., *Das Armenwesen und die Armengesetzgebung in europäischen Staaten.* Berlin: F. A. Herbig, 1870.

Brunner, Otto, et al., eds. *Geschichtliche Grundbegriffe,* vol. I. Stuttgart: E. Klett, 1972.

Bruschi, Christian. "Droit de la nationalité et égalité des droits de 1789 à la fin du XIXᵉ siècle." Pp. 21–59 in Laacher, ed., *Questions de nationalité.*

Bundesminister des Innern. See Primary Sources, German Government Tables and Reports.

Büsch, Otto, and James Sheehan, eds. *Die Rolle der Nation in der deutschen Geschichte und Gegenwart.* Berlin: Colloquium Verlag, 1985.

Cahn, Wilhelm. *Zur Reform des Reichs- und Staatsangehörigkeitsgesetzes.* Berlin: J. Guttentag, 1908.

Castles, Stephen (with Heather Booth and Tina Wallace). *Here for Good: Western Europe's New Ethnic Minorities.* London: Pluto Press, 1984.

Castles, Stephen, and Godula Kosack. *Immigrant Workers and Class Structure in Western Europe*. 2nd ed. Oxford: Oxford University Press, 1985.

Certeau, Michel de, Dominique Julia, and Jacques Revel. *Une politique de la langue. La Révolution française et les patois: L'enquête de Grégoire*. Paris: Gallimard, 1975.

Challener, Richard D. *The French Theory of the Nation in Arms 1866–1939*. New York: Russell & Russell, 1965.

Charlot, Martine, ed. *Des jeunes Algériens en France: leur voix et les nôtres*. Paris: CIEMM, 1981.

—— "Peut-on parler d'un 'droit à la différence' pour les jeunes Algériens?" Pp. 159–178 in Charlot, ed., *Des jeunes Algériens en France*.

Choisel, Francis. "Du tirage au sort au service universel." *Revue historique des armées* no. 2, 1981: 43–60.

Cohen, Jean. "Strategy or Identity: New Theoretical Paradigms and Contemporary Social Movements." *Social Research* 52 (Winter 1985): 663–716.

Les Constitutions de la France depuis 1789. Presented by Jacques Godechot. Paris: Garnier-Flammarion, 1979.

Contamine, Phillipe. "Mourir pour la patrie." Pp. 11–43 in Nora, ed., *La Nation*, vol. III.

Conze, Werner. "'Deutschland' und 'deutsche Nation' als historische Begriffe." Pp. 21–38 in Busch and Sheehan, eds., *Die Rolle der Nation in der deutschen Geschichte und Gegenwart*.

—— "Nationsbildung durch Trennung." Pp. 95–119 in Pflanze, ed., *Innenpolitische Probleme des Bismarckreichs*.

—— "Vom 'Pöbel' zum 'Proletariat': Sozialgeschichtliche Voraussetzungen für den Sozialismus in Deutschland." *Vierteljahrschrift für Sozial- und Wirtschaftsgeschichte* 41 (1954): 333–364.

Costa-Lascoux, Jacqueline. "L'acquisition de la nationalité française, une condition d'intégration?" Pp. 81–118 in Laacher, ed., *Questions de nationalité*.

—— "Intégration et nationalité." Pp. 89–121 in de Wenden, ed., *La Citoyenneté*.

—— "Nationaux, mais pas vraiment citoyens." *Projet* 204 (March–April 1987): 45–57.

"Culture islamique et attitudes politiques dans la population musulmane en France." Transcripts of interviews conducted in 1985 by the Centre d'Etudes et de Recherches Internationales, Paris, under the direction of Remy Leveau.

Dann, Otto, ed. *Nationalismus und sozialer Wandel*. Hamburg: Hoffmann und Campe, 1978.

Darras, Loïc. "La double nationalité." Thesis in Law, Paris, 1986.

Deloche, Maximin. *Du principe des nationalités*. Paris: Guillaumin, 1860.

"Die Deutschen im Ausland und die Ausländer im Deutschen Reich." *Ergänzungsheft zu der Vierteljahresheften zur Statistik des Deutschen Reiches*, 1905.

Digeon, Claude. *La crise allemande de la pensée française 1870–1914*. Paris: Presses Universitaires de France, 1959.

Diversité culturelle, société industrielle, état national. Actes du Colloque. Paris: L'Harmattan, 1984.

Doemming, Klaus-Berto von, Rudolf Werner Füsslein, and Werner Matz. "Entstehungsgeschichte der Artikel des Grundgesetzes." *Jahrbuch des öffentlichen Rechts der Gegenwart.* New series, vol. I, 1951.

Dohse, Knuth. *Ausländische Arbeiter und bürgerlicher Staat: Genese und Funktion von staatlichen Ausländerpolitik und Ausländerrecht.* Königstein: Hain, 1981.

"Les droits politiques des immigrés." Compte rendu du Colloque des 5 et 6 décembre 1981, published in brochure form by the review *Etudes,* Paris, n.d.

Dubet, François. *Immigrations: Qu'en savons-nous?* Paris: La Documentation française, 1989.

Dunn, John. *Western Political Theory in the Face of the Future.* Cambridge: Cambridge University Press, 1979.

Durand, Andrew. "European Citizenship." *European Law Review* 4 (1979): 3–14.

Durkheim, Emile. *The Elementary Forms of the Religious Life.* Translated by Joseph Ward Swain. New York: Free Press, 1965.

Eley, Geoff. "German Politics and Polish Nationality: The Dialectic of Nation-Forming in the East of Prussia." *East European Quarterly* 18 (September 1984): 335–374.

———— *Reshaping the German Right: Radical Nationalism and Political Change after Bismarck.* New Haven: Yale, 1980.

Elias, Norbert. *The Civilizing Process,* vol. 1: *The History of Manners.* Translated by Edmund Jephcott. New York: Urizen Books, 1978.

Etre français aujourd'hui et demain. Report of the Commission de la Nationalité. Vol. I: "Les auditions publics"; Vol. II: "Conclusions et propositions de la Commission de la Nationalité." Paris: La Documentation Française, 1988.

Evans, A. C. "European Citizenship: A Novel Concept in EEC Law." *American Journal of Comparative Law* 32 (1984): 679–715.

Febvre, Lucien. "*Frontière*: The word and the concept." Pp. 208–218 in Lucien Febvre, *A New Kind of History and Other Essays,* edited by Peter Burke, translated by K. Folca. New York: Harper, 1973.

Feldblum, Miriam. "The Politicization of Citizenship as a Function of Immigration Politics: The Case of France, 1981–1988." Paper presented at the Seventh International Conference of Europeanists, Washington, D.C., March 23–25, 1990.

Fenet, P. A. *Recueil complet des travaux préparatoires du Code civil.* Vol. 7. Paris: Videcoq, 1836.

Fijalkowski, Jürgen. "Gastarbeiter als industrielle Reservearmee?" *Archiv für Sozialgeschichte* 24 (1984): 399–456.

———— "Das Problem der Erweiterung der politischen Rechte für die neuen ethnischen Minderheiten der Arbeitsmigranten." Unpublished paper.

Fischer, Fritz. "Zum Problem der Kontinuität in der deutschen Geschichte von Bismarck zu Hitler." Pp. 770–782 in Bracher et al., eds., *Nationalsozialistische Diktatur.*

Fischer, Thomas. *Städtische Armut und Armenfürsorge im 15. und 16. Jahrhundert.* Göttingen: Otto Schwartz, 1979.

Fischer, Wolfram. *Armut in der Geschichte: Erscheinungsformen und Lösungsversuche der "Sozialen Frage" in Europa seit dem Mittelalter.* Göttingen: Vandenhoeck & Ruprecht, 1982.

La France au pluriel? Centre de Relations Internationales et de Sciences Politiques d'Amiens and Revue Pluriel-Débat. Paris: L'Harmattan, 1984.

Freeman, Gary P. "Migration and the Political Economy of the Welfare State." *Annals of the American Academy of Political and Social Science* 485 (1986): 51–63.

Friedrichsen, Hans H. "Die Stellung des Fremden in deutschen Gesetzen und Völkerrechtlichen Verträgen seit dem Zeitalter der französischen Revolution." Dissertation, Göttingen, 1967.

Funcke, Liselotte. "Doppelte Staatsbürgerschaft als Chance für Migranten, Staaten und Bürger." Paper presented to a conference on dual citizenship ("Doppelte Staatsbürgerschaft—ein europäischer Normalfall?") in West Berlin, Oct. 18–20, 1989.

Furet, François. *Penser la Révolution française.* Paris: Gallimard, 1978.

Furet, François, and Mona Ozouf, eds. *Dictionnaire critique de la Révolution française.* Paris: Flammarion, 1988.

Furet, François, and Denis Richet. *La Révolution française.* Paris: Hachette, 1965.

Gall, Lothar. "Das Problem Elsass-Lothringen." Pp. 366–385 in Schieder and Deuerlein, eds., *Reichsgründung.*

Gallissot, René. "L'interrogation continue: minorités et immigration." Pp. 248–254 in *La France au pluriel?*

Garaud, Marcel. *La Révolution et l'égalité civile.* Paris: Recueil Sirey, 1953.

George, Pierre. *L'immigration en France.* Paris: Armand Colin, 1986.

Giddens, Anthony. *The Nation-State and Violence.* Berkeley: University of California Press, 1987.

Gillette, Alain, and Abdelmalek Sayad. *L'immigration algérienne en France.* 2nd ed. Paris: Entente, 1984.

Giordan, Henri. *Démocratie culturelle et droit à la différence.* Report to Minister of Culture Jack Lang. Paris: La Documentation Française, 1982.

Girardet, Raoul. *L'idée coloniale en France de 1871 à 1962.* Paris: Pluriel, 1978.

———— "Pour une introduction a l'histoire du nationalisme français." *Revue française de science politique* 8 (1958): 505–528.

————, ed. *Le nationalisme français: Anthologie 1871–1914.* Paris: Seuil, 1983.

Godechot, Jacques. *La Grande Nation: L'expansion révolutionnaire de la France dans le monde de 1789 à 1799.* Paris: Aubier Montaigne, 1983.

———— "Nation, patrie, nationalisme et patriotisme en France au XVIIIe siècle." *Annales historiques de la Révolution française* 206 (1971): 481–501.

———— See also *Les Constitutions de la France depuis 1789.*

Gontard, Maurice. *L'oeuvre scolaire de la troisième République.* Toulouse: Centre régional de documentation pédagogique, n. d.

Grabitz, Eberhard. *Europäisches Bürgerrecht zwischen Marktbürgerschaft und Staatsbürgerschaft.* Cologne: Europa Union Verlag, 1970.

Grawert, Rolf. *Staat und Staatsangehörigkeit.* Berlin: Duncker & Humblot, 1973.

Griese, Hartmut, ed. *Der gläserne Fremde.* Opladen: Leske und Budrich, 1984.

Griotteray, Alain. *Les immigrés: le choc.* Paris: Plon, 1984.

Groth, Klaus-Martin. *Einbürgerungsratgeber.* Frankfurt: Alfred Metzner, 1984.

Hagen, William W. *Germans, Poles, and Jews: The Nationality Conflict in the Prussian East, 1772–1914.* Chicago: University of Chicago Press, 1980.

Hammar, Tomas. "Comparative Analysis." Pp. 237–304 in Hammar, ed., *European Immigration Policy*. Cambridge: Cambridge University Press, 1985.

—— *Democracy and the Nation-State: Aliens, Denizens, and Citizens in a World of International Migration*. Aldershot: Avebury, 1990.

—— "State, Nation, and Dual Citizenship." Pp. 81–95 in Brubaker, ed., *Immigration and the Politics of Citizenship in Europe and North America*.

Hartung, Fritz. "Der aufgeklärte Absolutismus." Pp. 54–76 in Karl Otmar Freiherr von Aretin, ed., *Der aufgeklärte Absolutismus*. Cologne: Kiepenheuer & Witsch, 1974.

Hasse, Ernst. *Die Besiedlung des deutschen Volksboden*. Munich: J. F. Lehmann, 1905.

—— *Das Deutsche Reich als Nationalstaat*. Munich: J. F. Lehmann, 1905.

Hauser, Oswald. "Polen und Dänen im Deutschen Reich." Pp. 291–318 in Schieder and Deuerlein, eds., *Reichsgründung*.

—— "Zum Problem der Nationalisierung Preussens." Pp. 95–108 in Ernst-Wolfgang Böckenförde, ed., *Moderne deutsche Verfassungsgeschichte*, 2nd ed. Königstein/Ts: Athenäum, Hain, Scripter, Hanstein, 1981.

Hausmann, Kurt Georg. "Adelsgesellschaft und nationale Bewegung in Polen." Pp. 23–47 in Dann, ed., *Nationalismus und sozialer Wandel*.

Heckman, Friedrich. "Temporary Labor Migration or Immigration? 'Guest Workers' in the Federal Republic of Germany." Pp. 69–84 in Rogers, ed., *Guests Come to Stay*.

Hémery, S., and O. Rabut. "La contribution des étrangers à la natalité en France." *Population* 28 (1973): 1063–1077.

Herbert, Ulrich. *Geschichte der Ausländerbeschäftigung in Deutschland 1880 bis 1980*. Berlin and Bonn: Dietz, 1986.

Hintze, Otto. "The Commissary and his Significance in General Administrative History: A Comparative Study." Pp. 269–301 in *The Historical Essays of Otto Hintze*.

—— *The Historical Essays of Otto Hintze*. Edited by Felix Gilbert. New York: Oxford University Press, 1975.

—— *Die Hohenzollern und ihr Werk: Fünfhundert Jahre vaterländischer Geschichte*. 9th ed. Berlin: Paul Parey, 1916.

—— "Military Organization and the Organization of the State." Pp. 180–215 in *The Historical Essays of Otto Hintze*.

—— "Preussens Entwicklung zum Rechtsstaat." Pp. 97–163 in Hintze, *Regierung und Verwaltung*.

—— "Der preussische Militär- und Beamtenstaat im 18. Jahrhundert." Pp. 419–428 in Hintze, *Regierung und Verwaltung*.

—— *Regierung und Verwaltung: Gesammelte Abhandlungen zur Staats-, Rechts- und Sozialgeschichte Preussens*. (*Gesammelte Abhandlungen*, vol. III). Göttingen: Vandenhoeck & Ruprecht, 1967.

Hinze, Kurt. *Die Arbeiterfrage zu Beginn des modernen Kapitalismus in Brandenburg-Preussen 1685–1806*. Berlin: Walter de Gruyter, 1963.

Hobsbawm, Eric. "Introduction: Inventing Traditions." Pp. 1–14 in Hobsbawm and Ranger, eds., *The Invention of Tradition*.

Hobsbawm, Eric, and Terence Ranger, eds. *The Invention of Tradition.* Cambridge: Cambridge University Press, 1983.

Hoffmann, Lutz. *Die unvollendete Republik: Zwischen Einwanderungsland und deutschen Nationalstaat.* Cologne: Papy Rossa Verlag, 1990.

Hoffmann, Stanley. "The Nation: What For? Vicissitudes of French Nationalism, 1871–1973." Pp. 403–442 in *Decline or Renewal? France Since the 1930s.* New York: Viking, 1974.

Horowitz, Donald. "Europe and America: A Comparative Analysis of 'Ethnicity.'" *Revue Européene des Migrations Internationales* 5, no. 1 (1989): 47–59.

———. "Immigration and Group Relations in France and America." Pp. 3–35 in Donald Horowitz and Gérard Noiriel, eds., *Immigrants in Two Democracies: French and American Experience.* New York: New York University Press, 1992.

Howard, Michael. *War in European History.* Oxford: Oxford University Press, 1976.

Hughes, H. S. *Consciousness and Society.* New York: Knopf, 1961.

L'Identité de la France. Papers presented to meeting organized by the Club de l'Horloge, April 28–30, 1985. Paris: Albin Michel, 1985.

L'Identité française. Papers presented to meeting organized by Espaces 89, March 22–24, 1985. Paris: Tierce, 1985.

Jean, Martin. "Combien sont-ils?" Pp. 251–259 in Charlot, ed., *Des jeunes Algériens en France.*

Just, Wolf-Dieter. "Europaïsche Erfahrungen mit dem kommunalen Wahlrecht für Ausländer." Pp. 1–19 in *Kommunalwahlrecht auch für Ausländer?* Evangelischer Pressedienst Dokumentation, No. 30, 1986.

Kedourie, Elie. *Nationalism.* London: Hutchinson, 1985.

Keller, F. von, and P. Trautmann. *Kommentar zum Reichs- und Staatsangehörigkeitsgesetz vom 22. Juni 1913.* Munich: C. H. Becksche, 1914.

Kelman, Herbert. "Patterns of Personal Involvement in the National System: A Social-Psychological Analysis of Political Legitimacy." In Rosenau, ed., *International Politics and Foreign Policy.*

Kepel, Gilles. *Les banlieues de l'Islam.* Paris: Seuil, 1987.

Keskin, Hakki. *Menschen ohne Rechte? Einwanderungspolitik und Kommunalwahlrecht in Europa.* Berlin, 1984.

Kimminich, Otto. *Rechtsprobleme der polyethnischen Staatsorganisation.* Mainz and Munich: Grünewald and Kaiser, 1985.

Klessman, Christoph. *Die doppelte Staatsgründung: Deutsche Geschichte 1945–1955.* 4th ed. Bonn: Bundeszentale für politische Bildung, 1986.

Kocka, Jürgen. "Probleme der politischen Integration der Deutschen, 1867 bis 1945." Pp. 119–136 in Busch and Sheehan, eds., *Die Rolle der Nation in der deutschen Geschichte und Gegenwart.*

Kohn, Hans. *The Idea of Nationalism.* New York: Collier Books, 1944.

——— *Prelude to Nation-States: The French and German Experience, 1789–1815.* Princeton: Van Nostrand, 1967.

Kolinsky, Martin. "The Nation-State in Western Europe: Erosion from 'Above' and 'Below'?" Pp. 82–103 in Tivey, ed., *The Nation-State.*

Köllmann, Wolfgang. "Industrialisierung, Binnenwanderung, und 'Soziale Frage.'" *Vierteljahrschrift für Sozial- und Wirtschaftsgeschichte* 46 (1959): 45–70.

"Kommunalwahlrecht auch für Ausländer?" Evangelischer Pressedienst *Dokumentation* 30, 1986.

Körner, Heiko. "Return Migration from the Federal Republic of Germany." Pp. 175–186 in Kubat, ed., *The Politics of Return.*

Koselleck, Reinhart. *Preussen zwischen Reform und Revolution: Allgemeines Landrecht, Verwaltung und soziale Bewegung von 1791 vis 1848.* Stuttgart: Ernst Klett Verlag, 1967.

Kovacs, Arpad F. "French Military Institutions before the Franco-Prussian War." *American Historical Review* 51 (1946): 217–235.

Kristeva, Julia. *Etrangers à nous-mêmes.* Paris: Fayard, 1988.

Kritz, Mary M., ed. *U.S. Immigration and Refugee Policy.* Lexington, Mass.: Lexington Books, 1983.

Kritz, Mary M., Charles B. Keely, and Silvano M. Tomasi, eds. *Global Trends in Migration.* New York: Center for Migration Studies, 1981.

Krulic, Joseph. "L'immigration et l'identité de la France: mythes et réalités." *Pouvoirs* 47 (1988): 31–43.

Kubat, Daniel, ed. *The Politics of Return: International Return Migration in Europe.* New York: Center for Migration Studies, 1984.

Laacher, Smaïn, ed. *Questions de nationalité: histoire et enjeux d'un code.* Paris: Harmattan, 1987.

Laband, Paul. *Das Staatsrecht des Deutschen Reiches,* vol. I. 5th ed. Tübingen: J. C. B. Mohr, 1911.

Lagarde, Paul. *La nationalité française.* Paris: Dalloz, 1975.

Laguerre, Bernard. "Les dénaturalisés de Vichy 1940–1944." *Vingtième siècle* (October–December 1988): 3–15.

Lebon, André. "Attribution, acquisition et perte de la nationalité française: un bilan (1973–1986)." *Revue européene des migrations internationales* 3 (1987): 7–34.

Leca, Jean. "Une capacité d'intégration défaillante?" *Esprit* 102 (June 1985): 9–23, 102–106.

Lefebvre, Georges. *The French Revolution,* vol. II. London: Routledge and Kegan Paul, 1964.

Le Gallou, Jean-Yves, and Jean-François Jalkh. *Etre français cela se mérite.* Paris: Albatros, 1987.

Le Gallou, Jean-Yves, and the Club de l'Horloge. *La préférence nationale: réponse à l'immigration.* Paris: Albin Michel, 1985.

Lehmann, Bodo. "Die deutsche Reichsangehörigkeit." *Annalen des deutschen Reichs* (1899): 776–856.

Lemberg, Eugen. "Der Wandel des politischen Denkens." Pp. 435–474 in Lemberg and Edding, eds., *Die Vertriebenen in Westdeutschland,* vol. III.

Lemberg, Eugen, and Friedrich Edding, eds. *Die Vertriebenen in Westdeutschland.* 3 vols. Kiel: Ferdinand Hirt, 1959.

Lepsius, M. Rainer. "The Nation and Nationalism in Germany." *Social Research* 52 (Spring 1985): 43–64.

Lequin, Yves. "L'invasion pacifique." Pp. 335–352 in Lequin, ed., *La mosaïque France: Histoire des étrangers et de l'immigration en France.* Paris: Larousse, 1988.

Leveau, Remy, and Catherine Wihtol de Wenden. "Evolution des attitude politiques des immigrés maghrébins." *Vingtième siècle* 7 (July–September 1985): 71–83.

Lewis, Martin Deming. "One Hundred Million Frenchmen: The 'Assimilation' Theory in French Colonial Policy." *Comparative Studies in Society and History* 4 (1962): 129–153.

Lichter, Matthias. *Die Staatsangehörigkeit nach deutschem und ausländischem Recht.* 2nd ed. Berlin: Carl Heymanns Verlag, 1955.

Lippe, Hans Heinrich. "Die preussische Heimatgesetzgebung vom 31. Dezember 1842." Dissertation, Göttingen, 1947.

Lochak, Danièle. "Etrangers et citoyens au regard du droit." Pp. 73–85 in Wenden, ed., *La Citoyenneté.*

——— *Etrangers: de quel droit?* Paris: Presses Universitaires de France, 1985.

Locré, J. G. *Esprit du Code Napoléon, tiré de la discussion.* Vol 1. Paris: Imprimerie Impériale, 1807.

Lösener, Bernhard, and Friedrich Knost, eds. *Die Nürnberger Gesetze mit den Durchführungsverordnungen und den sonstigen Vorschriften.* 4th ed. Berlin: Franz Vahlen, 1941.

Majer, Diemut. *"Fremdvölkische" im Dritten Reich.* Boppard: Harald Boldt, 1981.

Makarov, Alexander N. *Allgemeine Lehren des Staatsangehörigkeitsrechts.* 2nd ed. Stuttgart: W. Kohlhammer Verlag, 1962.

Manfrass, Klaus. "Ausländerproblematik in europäischen Industrieländer: ein Vergleich Frankreich - Bundesrepublik Deutschland." Pp. 758–783 in Bade, ed., *Auswanderer–Wanderarbeiter–Gastarbeiter,* vol. II.

Mangin, Stanislas. "Les problèmes de nationalité des jeunes Algériens élevés en France." Pp. 261–274 in Charlot, ed., *Des jeunes Algériens en France.*

——— "Le statut des jeunes Algériens nés en France depuis l'indépendance." *Le Monde,* December 25, 1980, reprinted in *Hommes et Migrations* no. 1011 (May 1, 1981): 21–25.

Mangoldt, Hans von. "Einbürgerungsanspruch für zeitweise in Deutschland aufgewachsene Ausländerkinder?" *Juristenzeitung* 37 (1982): 174–178.

Mann, Michael. *The Sources of Social Power,* vol. I: *A History of Power from the Beginning to A.D. 1760.* Cambridge: Cambridge University Press, 1986.

———, ed. *The Rise and Decline of the Nation State.* Cambridge, Mass.: Blackwell, 1990.

Marrus, Michael R. *The Politics of Assimilation: The French Jewish Community at the Time of the Dreyfus Affair.* Oxford: Oxford University Press, 1971.

——— *The Unwanted: European Refugees in the Twentieth Century.* New York: Oxford University Press, 1985.

Marrus, Michael R., and Robert O. Paxton. *Vichy France and the Jews.* New York: Schocken, 1983.

Marshall, T. H. *Citizenship and Social Class and Other Essays.* Cambridge: Cambridge University Press, 1950.

Martitz, F. von. "Das Recht der Staatsangehörigkeit im internationalen Verkehr." *Annalen des deutschen Reichs* (1875): 794–836, 1113–1170.

Marx, Karl. *Capital,* vol. I. New York: International Publishers, 1967.

—— "The Civil War in France." Pp. 274–313 in Marx and Engels, *Selected Works in One Volume.*

—— "The Eighteenth Brumaire of Louis Bonaparte." Pp. 97–180 in Marx and Engels, *Selected Works in One Volume.*

Marx, Karl, and Friedrich Engels. *Selected Works in One Volume.* New York: International Publishers, 1968.

Massot, Jean. "Français par le sang, Français par la loi, Français par le choix." *Revue européene des migrations internationales* 1 (December 1985): 9–18.

Mathiez, Albert. *La Révolution et les étrangers.* Paris: La Renaissance du Livre, 1918.

Mayeur, Jean-Marie, and Madeleine Rebérioux. *The Third Republic from its Origins to the Great War, 1871–1914.* Translated by J. R. Foster. Cambridge: Cambridge University Press, 1984.

Meier-Braun, Karl-Heinz. *"Freiwillige Rotation": Ausländerpolitik am Beispiel der baden-wurttembergischen Landesregierung.* Munich: Minerva, 1979.

Meinecke, Friedrich. *Weltbürgertum und Nationalstaat.* 5th ed. Munich: R. Oldenbourg, 1919.

Meyer, John W., and Michael T. Hannan. "National Development in a Changing World System." Pp. 3–16 in Meyer and Hannan, eds., *National Development and the World System.* Chicago: University of Chicago Press, 1979.

Meynier, Gilbert. "Les soldats algériens durant la guerre 14–18." *Actualités de l'emigration* 64 (November 1986): 38–43.

Miller, J. D. B. "The Sovereign State and its Future." *International Journal* 39 (1984): 284–301.

Miller, Mark J. *Foreign Workers in Western Europe: An Emerging Political Force.* New York: Praeger, 1981.

—— "The Problem of Foreign Worker Participation and Representation in France, Switzerland and the Federal Republic of Germany." Ph.D. dissertation, University of Wisconsin, 1978.

Milza, Pierre. "Un siècle d'immigration étrangère en France." *Vingtième siècle* 7 (July–September 1985): 3–17.

Les minorités à l'age de l'état-nation. Groupement pour le droit des minorités. Paris: Fayard, 1985.

Mitchell, Allan. *Victors and Vanquished: The German Influence on Army and Church in France after 1870.* Chapel Hill: University of North Carolina Press, 1984.

Mommsen, Wolfgang J. "Varieties of the Nation State in Modern History: Liberal, Imperialist, Fascist and Contemporary Notions of Nation and Nationality." Pp. 210–226 in Mann, ed., *The Rise and Decline of the Nation State.*

Monteilhet, J. *Les institutions militaires de la France (1814–1924).* Paris: Librairie Félix Alcan, 1926.

Mousnier, Roland. *The Institutions of France under the Absolute Monarchy 1598–1789.* Vol. 1: *Society and the State.* Chicago: University of Chicago Press, 1979.

Munoz, Marie-Claude. "De la pluralité ethnique à la pédagogie interculturelle." Pp. 181–195 in *La France au pluriel?*

Munoz-Perez, Francisco, and Michèle Tribalat. "Mariages d'étrangers et mariages mixtes en France: Évolution depuis la Première Guerre." *Population* 39 (1984): 427–461.

Murphy, Raymond. *Social Closure: The Theory of Monopolization and Exclusion.* Oxford: Clarendon, 1988.

Nadelhoffer, Emil. "Einfluss familienrechtlicher Verhältnisse auf die Erwerbung und den Verlust der Reichs- und Staatsangehörigkeit." *Annalen des deutschen Reichs* (1906).

La nationalité française: Textes et documents. Paris: La Documentation Française, 1985.

Les Naturalisations en France 1870–1940. Ministère des Finances, Direction de la Statistique Générale. Paris, 1942.

Nellner, Werner. "Grundlagen und Hauptergebnisse der Statistik." Pp. 61–143 in Lemberg, ed., *Die Vertriebenen in Westdeutschland,* vol. I.

Nettl, J. P. "The State as a Conceptual Variable." *World Politics* 20 (July 1968): 559–597.

Neubach, Helmut. *Die Ausweisungen von Polen und Juden aus Preussen 1885/86.* Wiesbaden: Otto Harrassowitz, 1967.

Niboyet, J.-P. *Traité de droit international privé français,* vol. 1. Paris: Recueil Sirey, 1938.

Nichtweiss, Johannes. *Die ausländischen Saisonarbeiter in der Landwirtschaft der östlichen und mittleren Gebiete des Deutschen Reiches.* Berlin: Rütten & Loening, 1959.

Nizet, Charles. *Des effets de la naissance sur le sol français au point de vue de la nationalité.* Thesis, Faculté de Droit de Nancy. Nancy: Imprimerie Crépin-Leblond, 1896.

Noiriel, Gérard. *Le creuset français. Histoire de l'immigration XIXe-XXe siècles.* Paris: Seuil, 1988.

Nora, Pierre. "Lavisse, instituteur national." Pp. 247–290 in Nora, ed., *La République.*

———— "Nation." Pp. 801–812 in Furet and Ozouf, eds., *Dictionnaire critique de la Révolution française.*

————, ed. *Les lieux de mémoire,* I: *La République;* II: *La Nation* (3 vols.). Paris: Gallimard, 1984–1986.

Olzak, Susan, and Joane Nagel, eds. *Competitive Ethnic Relations.* Orlando, Fla.: Academic Press, 1986.

Otto, Karl A., ed. *Westwärts—Heimwärts?: Aussiedlerpolitik zwischen 'Deutschtümelei' und Verfassungsauftrag.* Bielefeld: AJZ, 1990.

Ozouf, Mona. *L'école, l'église et la République 1871–1914.* Paris: Armand Colin, 1963

———— "Fraternité." Pp. 731–741 in Furet and Ozouf, eds., *Dictionnaire critique de la Révolution française.*

Palmer, R. R. *The Age of the Democratic Revolution,* 2 vols. Princeton: Princeton University Press, 1959 and 1964.

———— *History of the Modern World.* 2nd ed., revised with the collaboration of Joel Colton. New York: Knopf, 1960.

———— *The World of the French Revolution.* New York: Harper & Row, 1971.

Parsons, Talcott. *The Social System.* New York: Free Press, 1951.

Pflanze, Otto, ed. *Innenpolitische Probleme des Bismarckreichs.* Munich: R. Oldenbourg, 1983.

Pinson, Koppel. *Modern Germany.* New York: Macmillan, 1966.

Pinto, Diana. "Immigration: L'ambiguité de la référence américaine." *Pouvoirs* 47 (1988): 93–101.

Piore, Michael J. *Birds of Passage: Migrant Labor and Industrial Societies.* Cambridge: Cambridge University Press, 1979.

Poggi, Gianfranco. *The Development of the Modern State.* Stanford: Stanford University Press, 1978.

Portemer, Jean. "L'étranger dans le droit de la révolution française." Pp. 533–552 in *Recueils de la Société Jean Bodin,* vol. X, *L'Etranger* (part two). Brussels: Editions de la Librairie Encyclopédique, 1958.

Proebsting, Helmut. "Eheschliessungen, Ehescheidungen, Geburten und Sterbefälle von Ausländern 1981." *Wirtschaft und Statistik* 2/1983: 79–85.

Puskeppeleit, Jürgen. "Zugangsentwicklungen, Ungleichverteilung, und ihre Auswirkung auf die Kommunen." Pp. 161–175 in Otto, ed., *Westwärts—Heimwärts?*

Quaritsch, Helmut. "Einbürgerungspolitik als Ausländerpolitik?" *Der Staat* 27 (1988): 481–503.

Raeff, Marc. *The Well-Ordered Police State: Social and Institutional Change through Law in the Germanies and Russia, 1600–1800.* New Haven: Yale University Press, 1983.

Ratjen, Hans. *Der Kampf um die Reichsangehörigkeit.* Hamburg: Lucas Gräfe, 1908.

Recensement Général de la Population de 1982, *Les étrangers.* Série "Boulier," RP 82/5. Prepared by the Institut National de la Statistique et des Etudes Economiques and the Ministère des affaires sociales et de la Solidarité nationale. Published by La Documentation Française as No. 6 in the Collection "Migrations et Sociétés" (n. d.).

Rehm, Hermann. "Der Erwerb von Staats- und Gemeinde-Angehörigkeit in geschichtlicher Entwicklung nach römischem und deutschem Staatsrecht." *Annalen des deutschen Reichs* (1892): 137–281.

——— "Freizügigkeit." In *Handwörterbuch der Staatswissenschaften,* vol. 4. 4th ed. Jena: Gustav Fischer, 1927.

Rémond, René. *The Right Wing in France From 1815 to de Gaulle.* Translated by James M. Laux. 2nd American ed. Philadelphia: University of Pennsylvania Press, 1969.

Renan, Ernest. "Nouvelle lettre à M. Strauss." Pp. 449–462 in *Oeuvres Complètes,* vol. I.

——— *Oeuvres Complètes.* Paris: Calmann-Lévy, 1947.

——— "Qu'est-ce qu'une nation?" Pp. 887–906 in *Oeuvres Complètes,* vol. I.

Richer, Laurent. *Le droit de l'immigration.* Paris: Presses Universitaires de France, 1986.

Riedel, Manfred. "Bürger, Staatsbürger, Bürgertum." Pp. 672–725 in Brunner et al., eds., *Geschichtliche Grundbegriffe,* vol. I.

Rist, Ray. *Guestworkers in Germany.* New York: Praeger, 1978.

——— "Migration and Marginality: Guestworkers in Germany and France." *Daedalus* 108 (Spring 1979): 95–108.

Rockstroh, Hans Wilhelm. *Die Entwickelung der Freizügigkeit in Deutschland unter besonderer Würdigung der preussischen Verhältnissen.* Halle: Heynemann'sche Buchdruckerei, 1910. Dissertation, Jena, 1910.

Rogers, Rosemarie, ed. *Guests Come to Stay: The Effects of European Labor Migration on Sending and Receiving Countries.* Boulder, Col.: Westview, 1985.

Rokkan, Stein, and Derek Urwin. *Economy, Territory, Identity: Politics of West European Peripheries.* London: SAGE, 1983.

Rönne, Ludwig von. *Das Staatsrecht der Preussischen Monarchie,* vol. 1. 4th ed., 1899.

Rosenau, James N., ed. *International Politics and Foreign Policy: A Reader in Research and Theory.* New York: Free Press, 1969.

Rosenberg, Hans. *Bureaucracy, Aristocracy and Autocracy. The Prussian Experience 1660–1815.* Cambridge, Mass.: Harvard University Press, 1958.

Roth, Guenther. *The Social Democrats in Imperial Germany: A Study in Working-Class Isolation and National Integration.* Totowa, N.J.: Bedminster, 1963.

Rothfels, Hans. "Bismarck und der Osten." Pp. 1–125 in *Bismarck, der Osten und das Reich.* Stuttgart: W. Kohlhammer, 1960.

——— "Die Nationsidee in westlicher und östlicher Sicht." Pp. 7–18 in *Osteuropa und der Deutsche Osten,* Series 1, Book 3. Cologne-Braunsfeld: Rudolf Müller, 1956.

Rousseau, Jean-Jacques. "Considérations sur le gouvernement de Pologne." Pp. 337–417 in J.-J. Rousseau, *Contrat social, ou Principes du droit politique* (Selected works). Paris: Garnier Frères, 1914.

——— *On the Social Contract.* Translated by Judith R. Masters, edited by Roger D. Masters. New York: St. Martin's Press, 1978.

Sahlins, Peter. *Boundaries. The Making of France and Spain in the Pyrenees.* Berkeley: University of California Press, 1989.

Salmond, John W. "Citizenship and Allegiance." *Law Quarterly Review* 17 (1901): 270–282, 18 (1902): 49–63.

Sauer, Wolfgang. "Das Problem des Deutschen Nationalstaates." *Politische Vierteljahresschrift* 3 (1962): 159–186.

Sayad, Abdelmalek. "La naturalisation, ses conditions sociales et sa signification chez les immigrés Algériens." Parts I and II. *Greco 13: Recherches sur les migrations internationales* 3 (1981): 23–46, 4–5 (1982): 1–51.

Schieder, Theodor. *Das Deutsche Kaiserreich von 1871 als Nationalstaat.* Cologne: Westdeutscher Verlag, 1961.

——— "Typologie und Erscheinungsformen des Nationalstaats in Europa." Pp. 119–137 in *Nationalismus,* ed. Heinrich August Winkler. 2nd ed. Königstein/Ts.: Athenäum, 1985.

Schieder, Theodor, and Ernst Deuerlein, eds. *Reichsgründung 1870/71.* Stuttgart: Seewald Verlag, 1970.

Schilling, Jürgen. "Einwanderung und Staatsidee: Wird die Einheit der Nation durch die Ausländerpolitik gefährdet?" *Deutschland Archiv* 13 (1980): 156–158.

Schinkel, Harald. "Armenpflege und Freizügigkeit in der preussischen Gesetzgebung vom Jahre 1842." *Vierteljahrschrift für Sozial- und Wirtschaftsgeschichte* 50 (1964): 459–479.

Schlegel, Jean-Louis. "Comment parler de l'immigration?" *L'Esprit* 102 (1985): 82–88.

———— "Figures d'une marge." Unpublished paper, 1987.

Schlenger, Herbert. "Das Weltflüchtlingsproblem." Pp. 36–60 in Lemberg, ed., *Die Vertriebenen in Westdeutschland*, vol. I.

Schmitter, Barbara E. "Immigration and Citizenship in West Germany and Switzerland." Ph.D. dissertation, University of Chicago, 1979.

Schnapper, Bernard. *Le remplacement militaire en France*. Paris: S.E.V.P.E.N., 1968.

Schnapper, Dominique. *La France de l'intégration: Sociologie de la nation en 1990*. Paris: Gallimard, 1991.

———— "La 'France plurielle'?" *Commentaire* 61 (Winter 1987–88): 220–227.

Schnapper, Dominique, and Rémy Leveau. "Religion et politique: juifs et musulmans maghrébins en France." Paper presented at conference "Les musulmans dans la société française," organized by the Association Française de Science Politique. Paris, January 29–30, 1987.

Schor, Ralph. *L'opinion française et les étrangers 1919–1939*. Paris: Publication de la Sorbonne, 1985.

Schuck, Peter H. "Membership in the Liberal Polity: The Devaluation of American Citizenship." Pp. 67–79 in Brubaker, ed., *Immigration and the Politics of Citizenship*.

Schuck, Peter H., and Rogers M. Smith. *Citizenship without Consent: Illegal Aliens in the American Polity*. New Haven: Yale University Press, 1985.

Schulze, Reiner. *Die Polizeigesetzgebung zur Wirtschafts- und Arbeitsordnung der Mark Brandenburg in der frühen Neuzeit*. Aalen: Scienta Verlag, 1978.

Schwartz, Dieter. "Die Staatsangehörigkeit der Deutschen." Dissertation, Marburg, 1975.

Sidgwick, Henry. *The Elements of Politics*. 4th ed. (first ed. 1891). London: Macmillan, 1919.

Sievering, Ulrich O., ed. *Integration ohne Partizipation?: Ausländerwahlrecht in der Bundesrepublik Deutschland zwischen (verfassungs-) rechtlicher Möglichkeit und politischer Notwendigkeit*. Frankfurt, 1981.

Sieyès, Emmanuel Joseph. *Qu'est-ce que le Tiers Etat?* Geneva: Droz, 1970.

———— *What is the Third Estate?* Translated by M. Blondel, edited by S. E. Finer. New York: Praeger, 1963.

Simmel, Georg. *The Sociology of Georg Simmel*. Translated, edited, and with an introduction by Kurt H. Wolff. New York: Free Press, 1950.

Situation der ausländischen Arbeitnehmer und ihrer Familienangehörigen in der Bundesrepublik Deutschland. Representative Survey conducted by the Forschungsinstitut der Friedrich-Ebert-Stiftung, Arbeitsgruppe Ausländerforschung und Ausländerpolitik. Bonn: Bundesminister für Arbeit und Sozialordnung, 1986.

Skocpol, Theda. "Cultural Idioms and Political Ideologies in the Revolutionary Reconstruction of State Power: A Rejoinder to Sewell." *Journal of Modern History* 57 (1985): 86–96.

———— *States and Social Revolutions*. Cambridge: Cambridge University Press, 1979.

Smith, Anthony. *The Ethnic Origins of Nations*. Oxford: Blackwell, 1986.

Soboul, Albert. "Anacharsis Cloots: L'orateur du genre humain." *Annales historiques de la Révolution française* 239 (January–March 1980): 29–56.

————— "De l'Ancien régime à l'Empire: problème national et réalités sociales." *L'Information historique* (1960): 58–64, 96–104.

Sous-Direction des Naturalisations. See Primary Sources, French Government Reports.

Soysal, Yasemin. "Limits of Citizenship: Guestworkers in the Contemporary Nation-State System." Ph.D. dissertation, Stanford University, 1991.

Stedman Jones, Gareth. *Languages of Class: Studies in English Working Class History 1832–1982.* Cambridge: Cambridge University Press, 1983.

Sternhell, Zeev. *La droite révolutionnaire 1885–1914: les origines française du fascisme.* Paris: Seuil, 1978.

Stöcker, Hans A. "Nationales Selbstbestimmungsrehct und Ausländerwahlrecht: Über Versuche, die Bundesrepublik Deutschland in einen Vielvölkerstaat umzuwandeln." *Der Staat* 28 (1989): 71–90.

Stolleis, Michael. "Untertan—Bürger—Staatsbürger: Bemerkungen zur juristischen Terminologie im späten 18. Jahrhundert." Pp. 65–99 in Vieraus, ed., *Bürger und Bürgerlichkeit im Zeitalter der Aufklärung.*

Szücs, Jenö. *Nation und Geschichte.* Budapest: Corvina Kiadó, 1981.

Taguieff, Pierre-André. "Les métamorphoses idéologiques du racisme et la crise de l'antiracisme." Pp. 13–63 in Taguieff, ed., *Face au racisme,* vol. 2. Paris: La Découverte, 1991.

Taguieff, Pierre-André, and Patrick Weil. "'Immigration,' fait national et 'citoyenneté.'" *Esprit* (May 1990): 87–102.

Talmon, J. L. *The Origins of Totalitarian Democracy.* New York: Praeger, 1960,

Terré, François. "Réflexions sur la notion de nationalité." *Revue critique de droit international privé* (1975): 197–214.

Thadden, Rudolf von. "Umgang mit Minderheiten." Unpublished paper, 1987.

Thränhardt, Dietrich. "'Ausländer' als Objekte deutscher Interessen und Ideologien." Pp. 115–132 in Griese, ed., *Der gläserne Fremde.*

Tilly, Charles, ed. *The Formation of National States in Western Europe.* Princeton: Princeton University Press, 1975.

Tims, Richard Wonser. *Germanizing Prussian Poland: The H-K-T Society and the Struggle for the Eastern Marches in the German Empire, 1894–1919.* New York: Columbia University Press, 1941.

Tivey, Leonard, ed. *The Nation-State: The Formation of Modern Politics.* Oxford: M. Robertson, 1981.

Turner, Bryan S. *Citizenship and Capitalism: The Debate over Reformism.* London: Allen and Unwin, 1986.

Uhlitz, Otto. "Deutsches Volk oder 'Multikulturelle Gesellschaft'? Von den verfassungsrechtlichen Grenzen der Ausländer- und Einbürgerungspolitik." *Recht und Politik* 3/1986.

Vagts, Alfred. *A History of Militarism.* New York: Meridian, 1959.

Vanel, Marguerite. *Histoire de nationalité française d'origine.* Paris: Ancienne Imprimerie de la Cour d'Appel, 1945.

Vichniak, Judith. "French Socialists and *Droit à la Différence:* A Changing Dynamic." *French Politics and Society* 9 (Winter 1991): 40–56.

Vieraus, Rudolf, ed. *Bürger und Bürgerlichkeit im Zeitalter der Aufklärung,*. Heidelberg: Verlag Lambert Schneider, 1981.

Villers, Robert. "La condition des étrangers en France dans les trois derniers siècles de la monarchie." Pp. 139–150 in *Recueils de la Société Jean Bodin*, vol. X, *L'Etranger* (part two). Brussels: Editions de la Librairie Encyclopedique, 1958.

Voisard, Jacques, and Christiane Ducastelle. "La question immigrée en France en 1986." Note de la Fondation Saint-Simon, 15, December 1986.

Walker, Mack. *German Home Towns: Community, State, and General Estate, 1648–1871*. Ithaca, N.Y.: Cornell University Press, 1971.

Walzer, Michael. "The Obligation to Die for the State." Pp. 77–98 in *Obligations: Essays on Disobedience, War, and Citizenship*. Cambridge, Mass.: Harvard University Press, 1970.

―――― *Spheres of Justice*. New York: Basic Books, 1983.

Weber, Eugen. *Peasants into Frenchmen: The Modernization of Rural France, 1870–1914*. Stanford: Stanford University Press, 1976.

Weber, Max. *Economy and Society*. Edited by Guenther Roth and Claus Wittich. Berkeley: University of California Press, 1978.

―――― *Gesammelte Aufsätze zur Religionssoziologie*, vol. I. 2nd ed. Tübingen: Mohr-Siebeck, 1922.

―――― "Die ländliche Arbeitsverfassung." Pp. 444–469 in *Gesammelte Aufsätze zur Sozial- und Wirtschaftsgeschichte*. Tübingen, 1924.

―――― "The Social Psychology of the World Religions." Pp. 267–301 in *From Max Weber: Essays in Sociology*. Translated, edited, and with an introduction by H. H. Gerth and C. Wright Mills. New York: Oxford University Press, 1946.

Wehler, Hans-Ulrich. *Das Deutsche Kaiserreich 1871–1918*. 5th ed. Göttingen: Vandenhoeck & Ruprecht, 1983.

―――― *Krisenherde des Kaiserreichs 1871–1918*. 2nd ed. Göttingen: Vandenhoeck & Ruprecht, 1979.

―――― "Polenpolitik im Deutschen Kaiserreich." Pp. 184–202 in Wehler, *Krisenherde des Kaiserreichs*.

―――― "Das 'Reichsland' Elsass-Lothringen von 1870 bis 1918." Pp. 23–69 in Wehler, *Krisenherde des Kaiserreichs*.

―――― *Sozialdemokratie und Nationalstaat: Nationalitätenfragen in Deutschland 1840–1914*. 2nd ed. Göttingen: Vandenhoeck & Ruprecht, 1971.

Weil, Patrick. *La France et ses étrangers: L'aventure d'une politique de l'immigration 1938–1991*. Paris: Calmann-Lévy, 1991.

―――― "La politique française d'immigration (entre 1974 et 1986) et la citoyenneté." Pp. 191–200 in Wenden, ed., *La Citoyenneté*.

Weill, Georges. *L'Europe du XIXe siècle et l'idée de nationalité*. Paris: Albin Michel, 1938.

Weinacht, Paul-Ludwig. "'Staatsbürger': Zur Geschichte und Kritik eines politischen Begriffs." *Der Staat* 8 (1969): 41–63.

Weiss, Bernhard. "Erwerb und Verlust der Staatsangehörigkeit." *Annalen des deutschen Reichs* (1908): 836–849, 902–916 and (1909): 383–396, 472–494.

Wenden, Catherine Wihtol de, ed. *La Citoyenneté*. Paris: Edilig/Fondation Diderot, 1988.

Wertheimer, Jack. *Unwelcome Strangers: East European Jews in Imperial Germany*. New York: Oxford University Press, 1987.

Wertheimer, Mildred S. *The Pan-German League 1890–1914*. New York: Columbia University Press, 1924.

Wieacker, Franz. *Privatrechtsgeschicte der Neuzeit*. 2nd ed. Göttingen: Vandenhoeck & Ruprecht, 1967.

Young, M. Crawford. "Cultural Pluralism in the Third World." Pp. 113–135 in Olzak and Nagel, eds., *Competitive Ethnic Relations*.

Zimmerman, Heinrich. "Staatsangehörigkeit und Reichsbürgerschaft unter besonderer Berücksichtung des Judenproblems." Dissertation, Ruprecht-Karl-Universität in Heidelberg, 1940.

Zolberg, Aristide, R. "Contemporary Transnational Migrations in Historical Perspective." Pp. 15–51 in Kritz, ed., *U.S. Immigration and Refugee Policy*.

—— "International Migrations in Political Perspective." Pp. 3–27 in Kritz et al., eds., *Global Trends in Migration*.

Index